Black Music

AMERICAN POPULAR MUSIC ON ELPEE:

Black Music

Other volumes:

- *Jazz*
- *Grass Roots Music*
- *Contemporary Popular Music*

Black Music

Dean Tudor

Chairman
Library Arts Department
Ryerson Polytechnical Institute
Toronto, Canada

Nancy Tudor

Assistant Head
Cataloguing Department
Metropolitan Toronto Public Library Board
Toronto, Canada

Libraries Unlimited, Inc. - Littleton, Colo. - 1979

LIBRARIES UNLIMITED, INC.
P.O. Box 263
Littleton, Colorado 80160

Library of Congress Cataloging in Publication Data

Tudor, Dean.
    Black music.

    (American popular music on Elpee)
    Includes index.
    1. Afro-American music--Discography. 2. Music,
Popular (Songs, etc.)--United States--Discography.
I. Tudor, Nancy, joint author. II. Title.
III. Series.
ML156.4.P6T8   016.789912   78-15563
ISBN 0-87287-147-9

PREFACE

This book is a survey of and buying guide to one aspect of American commercial popular music on discs: black music. The other three modes—contemporary popular music, folk music, and jazz—are detailed through three companion books, all published by Libraries Unlimited. Coverage of the four volumes of "American Popular Music on Elpee" extends to all worthwhile discs since the advent of recorded sound that are presently available on long-playing records or tapes. Recently deleted items are included when they are still available from specialist stores, and the labels are international in scope, for many reissued records of American music are currently available in France, Scandinavia, West Germany, Japan, and in other countries.

For this book, approximately 1,300 recordings have been pre-selected and annotated, representing relatively current thought expressed through thousands of reviews and articles, plus hundreds of books, that we have read. This is fully explained in the section "What This Book Is All About. . . ." Thus, the recordings selection librarian can base his or her choice upon informed evaluation rather than random choice. In some respects, then, *Black Music* is to recordings what the H. W. Wilson *Standard Catalog* series are to books, or what Bill Katz's *Magazines for Libraries* is to periodicals. Our criteria have been noted through discographic essays and comments, mainly emphasizing musical development, "popularity," repertoire indexes, artistic merits of discs, and extra-musical developments.

Arrangement includes a division by anthologies, different stylings, different time periods, diverse instrumentation and vocal techniques, etc., along with explanatory narrative essays that present short musicological descriptions, definitions, brief histories, roots of development and progressions, and a discussion on the written literature (reviews, articles, books). Each album is numbered, and sometimes a few are grouped together for ease of discussion. All relevant order information is included: name of artist, title, label, last known serial number, and country of origin. A directory of specialty stores and label addresses appears at the rear of the book, also. Each annotation averages 300 words and specifically states why that record and/or material is significant. In each grouping, anthologies have been presented together, "innovators" have been carefully separated into their own section, and important discs have been starred to indicate a "first purchase."

This book can be used by both libraries and individuals to build a comprehensive record collection reflective of black music, within the constraints noted in each section. Other uses include tracing the background of musical interactions in the explanatory notes and annotations, gaining an overview of the black music field in general, and establishing criteria on which to base *future* purchases. Obviously, this aid is only as current as are clearly defined musical developments; thus, while the physical discs are, for the most part, "in-print," the actual performed music is lagging behind this book's printing date, because no one knows what "fresh" music of 1977 or 1978 will be the leader in the years to come. Other limitations include the placement of discs within the four books.

Our intent has been to select recordings indicative of a style, regardless of convenient popular (and often simplistic) classifications of an artist or group. The over-riding condition for each selection has been its manner of presentation—whether a pop or a jazz item, a country or a rock item—with serious consideration given to its ultimate placement. (But all classification schemes seem to have their exceptions.) However, we are confident that in our four books, viewed as a whole, no important available material has been overlooked.

For *Black Music*, classification meant making some obvious decisions such as excluding white blues and white soul (these may be found in the *Contemporary Popular Music* book), or excluding much jazz (especially modern jazz, which is in the *Jazz* book). However, there are equal problems of inclusion. Folk or rural blues in this book could just as easily be placed in the *Grass Roots* book, and indeed both books share popular religious music—with gospel music in *Black Music*, and sacred music in *Grass Roots*. Style really knows no color, and while a white blues group is in *Contemporary Popular Music*, so is Jimi Hendrix, an exceptionally gifted black musician who played rock music. The marketing patterns of cross-overs and fragmentation in the music world are, as indicated in the introduction, further examples of regional breakdowns in musical styles, and only further complicate hard and fast classification.

ACKNOWLEDGMENT AND THANKS

While this book is basically a summation and synthesis of existing thought about black music (as revealed through books, periodical articles, record reviews, and the music itself), we sought guidance from collectors in the field through letters and conversations. All are knowledgeable critics; some are even librarians. In no way did they comment on the text itself; that was our responsibility alone. Our thanks, then, go to (among others): Ed Brake (urban blues, rhythm 'n' blues), Dick Flohil (blues), Eric LeBlanc (blues, gospel, rhythm 'n' blues), and Roger Misiewicz (country blues, gospel). Our gracious thanks also to Nan Ward, who typed a good part of the manuscript.

Dean Tudor
Nancy Tudor

1978

"Popular music in America never was taken seriously by anyone
other than the people who produced it or bought it."
—Mike Jahn, *Rock* (1973)

TABLE OF CONTENTS

Preface 5

What This Book Is All About and How to Use It 9

Introduction to Popular Music 17

**The Best of the Best: Anthologies of Popular Music
     on Records** 25

BLUES 29

   Introduction 31
      Techniques 32
      Stylings 33
      Literature 35
   Anthologies 36
      Roots Anthologies 36
      General Anthologies 38
      Field Recordings 42
      Ribald Blues 45
      Instrumental Character 46
      Topical Blues 49
   Rural, Acoustic Blues 50
      Regional Anthologies 50
      Innovators 56
      Standards 63
   Urban, Electric Blues 84
      "Chicago" Anthologies 85
      Innovators 87
      Standards 93
   Female Singers and "Classic" Blues 103
      Anthologies 103
      Innovators 105
      Standards 108
   Jug Bands 111
   Vocal Jazz Blues and Jump Blues 113

RHYTHM 'N' BLUES 117

   Introduction 119
      Techniques 121
      Literature 122
   Roots Anthologies 123
   General Anthologies 125

RHYTHM 'N' BLUES (cont'd)
   Groups 131
      Innovators 131
      Standards 132
   Individuals 135
      Innovators 135
      Male Standards 138
      Female Standards 143

GOSPEL 145

   Introduction 147
      Literature 148
   Anthologies 148
   Groups and Individuals 153

SOUL 159

   Introduction 161
      Literature 163
   Anthologies 163
   Groups 166
      Innovators 166
      Standards 167
   Individual Males 169
      Innovators 169
      Standards 173
   Individual Females 178
      Innovators 178
      Standards 180

REGGAE 183

   Introduction 185
      Literature 186
   Anthologies 186
   Groups 188

CITATIONS, DIRECTORIES, INDEX 189
   Book Citations 191
   Periodical Citations 203
   Directory of Labels and Starred Records 206
   Directory of Specialist Record Stores 255
   Artists' Index 257

WHAT THIS BOOK IS ALL ABOUT
AND HOW TO USE IT

"Of all the arts, music has always been nearest
to the hearts of Americans and the most expressive of their
essential needs, fears, and motivations."
—William O. Talvitie

"Music is music and that's it. If it sounds good,
it's good music and it depends on who's listening
how good it sounds."
—Duke Ellington

"It's all music, no more, no less."
—Bob Dylan (1965)

This reference tool offers a complete pre-selected evaluative guide to the best
and most enduring of recorded black music (largely American) available on
long-playing discs and tapes. It can be used by both libraries and individuals to
build up a comprehensive collection reflective of every area of black music (except
jazz, which has a separate volume in this set of four). About 1,300 discs are
annotated within a space of 300 (average) words each indicating musical influences,
impact, and importance. This represents about a $7,500 investment. However,
about 220 key albums are identified and suggested as a "first purchase" (about
$1,000). These are seminal recordings. The interested individual can use the
selection guide to buy first, for instance, the key urban blues albums followed by
the balance. Then this person could start purchasing all other discs by favorite
urban blues performers, or perhaps move on to a related field such as rhythm 'n'
blues or gospel music. The approach is by ever-widening circles.

This book also is concerned with the preservation of recorded popular music
through the long-playing disc. The commercial disc, even though it does not
adequately reflect the total characteristics of musical genres, is a very convenient
way to scrutinize popular music and audience reactions in an historical perspective.
A disc preserves exactly the manner of a performance, with absolutely no chance of
change through future progression—except for the most recent materials that have
been altered by remixing or tape dubbing (e.g., Hank Williams with strings or Simon
and Garfunkel's "Sounds of Silence" with a soft rock background). Records are
constantly available around the country; some may be difficult to acquire, but the

waiting is worth the aggravation. By the 1970s, audiences for all types of music have been fully catered to in some form or another. However, at some point in the development of a genre, musical minorities can become cult fanatics who insist on having every single note a particular artist performed. At this point, the cult audience must seek out bootleg records, taped concerts, airshots, and so forth, most of which are outside the mainstream of the recording industry.

The discographic essays in this book provide information on the basic elements of musical genres, criticisms, and analysis, as well as literature surveys for book and magazine purchases. The introductory essay presents an overview of popular music generally; the bibliography lists core books and magazines dealing with popular music that were especially chosen to show broad historical trends of importance and influence. The narrative discographic essays head each category, beginning with musicological descriptions, definitions, and continuing with brief histories and roots of development, reasons why it succeeded, musical hybrids, recording company policies, leading proponents in the field, criteria for inclusion of records, a discussion on record critics, and the tendencies of specialist review magazines. A useful by-product of this mechanism is that significant data and criticism are presented on which the record librarian can base popular music phonodisc selection for future recorded issues and reissues. The *Annual Index to Popular Music Record Reviews* can serve to update this book for record purchasing.

ARRANGEMENT AND FORMAT

All records in this volume are arranged under such categories as anthologies, stylings, time periods, instrumentation, vocal techniques, and so forth, as laid out in the table of contents. Narrative essays not only introduce the world of black music (see page 31), but also head each category within. These essays include short musicological descriptions, definitions, brief histories, roots of development and progressions, the leading proponents in the field, general criteria for inclusion of the specific records that follow, and a discussion of relevant books and existing periodicals (plus some detail on record reviewing and critics).

Each album discussed is entered in abbreviated discographic style: an internal numbering scheme to pinpoint its location within the book; entry by group, individual or title (if anthology) with commonalities collected for comparison purposes; album title, the number of discs in the package, label and serial number; country of origin if *not* American. Prices have been omitted because of rapid changes, discounts, and foreign currencies. Annotations, which average 300 words, specifically state why the record and/or material is significant, with references to personnel and individual titles.

There are three clear special indications: one, the "innovators" have been carefully separated into their own section; two, important discs have been starred (*); and three, the anthologies have been collected (see the short essay on the anthology, page 25). In terms of budgets, the suggested order of purchasing is: 1) within each genre desired, the starred anthologies (approximately $250 total for each genre); 2) within each genre desired, the other anthologies (approximately $750); 3) within each genre desired, the starred recordings of the innovators (approximately $500); 4) within each genre desired, the rest of the innovators (approximately $500); 5) within each genre desired, the balance of the starred items (approximately $750); 6) within each genre desired, the rest of the recordings (approximately $4,750).

The repackaged anthology represents the best choice for even the smallest of libraries. This maximizes the dollar so that libraries can get a reasonable "flavoring" of the widest repertoires or themes in an attempt to manage on the smallest of budgets. Larger libraries which, for whatever reason, prefer not to collect in a particular genre could still supplement their collection by purchasing the worthwhile anthologies in those genres for about $250 a grouping. These books will not include "classical" music, spoken word and humor, children's, marching bands, foreign language, religious (except for gospel and sacred music, both exceptionally popular religious music), and non-commercial items such as instructional recordings, educational records if the commercial form co-exists on album, and field trips (except for significant folk music).

Additional information is provided after the text: a directory of latest known addresses for record companies, plus an indication of their albums that we have starred in label numerical order; a short list of specialist record stores; a bibliography of pertinent books and periodicals; and an artist index with entries for both musical performances in diverse genres and musical influences.

METHOD OF RATING

Written materials about important popular music phonodiscs exist in a variety of forms: scattered discographic essays; scattered citations as footnotes; short biographic essays of leading performers; books with lists of records; discographic "polls"; annual "best of the year" awards; "tops of the pops" lists and chart actions; and passing references in ordinary reviews. Written material about popular music genres in general—at an introductory level—exists mainly in books, but such books were not written with the intention of assembling a representative historical core collection of phonodiscs.

The basic method we have used is a manual version of citation analysis by consensus. Through the 1965-1976 period, we studied about 60 popular music periodicals, which contained over 50,000 relevant reviews and over 10,000 articles. We also read more than 2,000 books on popular music, some dating from the 1920s, and we actually listened to 14,000-plus long-playing albums. Although we didn't know it at the time, work began on this book in 1967—a decade ago. We started out by identifying, for personal use, *all* the important performers in popular music, and we then read widely and bought all of that person's material *before* going on to anyone else. The rationale here was that, since these performers are acknowledged as the *best*, even their "off" material might be considerably better than a second-generation or derivative imitator. By moving in ever-widening circles (somewhat akin to a Venn diagram), we then began to investigate influences, impacts, and importance—for whatever reasons. At the same time we began to categorize performers so that we could make some sense out of the profusion of records by time, place, and influence. Generally, the slotting of performers by genre does not really affect one's appreciation of them at all but rather produces common groupings for the novice listener. What has developed is the categorization of available records rather than of the performers. Thus, this book is about significant recordings rather than significant artists (although the two do coincide fairly often). By *not* first choosing artists and then seeking out important discs (which is what we started to do) but instead seeking important recordings first, we have neatly avoided the "star" approach, which has two main disadvantages: first, that individual reputations may rise and fall without reference to artistic merit; and second, that styles of performance rapidly change from fashionable to unfashionable.

Reading and listening widely, we developed several criteria for evaluation:

1. Musical development
   a) musical quality of the recording
   b) importance in relation to music history
   c) musical standards of musicians (soloists, sidemen, session artists)
   d) musical creativeness, inventiveness, devotion, drive
   e) each musical genre is considered on its own terms as being equally important

2. "Popularity"
   a) airplay listings since 1920s
   b) reviews of records
   c) purchases
   d) critics' notes
   e) amount of material available
   f) longevity of the artist
   g) music itself (words and/or melodies)
   h) indication of "influence on" and "influenced by"—the links in a chain

3. Index to repertoires
   a) the favorite tunes of the performers
   b) the tunes most recorded and performed constantly
   c) what was re-recorded and why
   d) what was best remembered by fans and friends
   e) sheet music and songbook availability
   f) the tunes still being performed by others

4. Artistic merit of a record
   a) the way the song or tune is structured
   b) the relation between its structure and meaning
   c) the manipulation of the medium
   d) the implications of its content
   e) art criticism

5. Extra-musical developments
   a) the record industry and media manipulation
   b) the concept album or one with a thematic or framing device (both original, long-playing recordings and reissued collections of singles)
   c) the impact of radio and regional breakdowns

5.   Extra-musical developments (cont'd)
   d)   the folklore process of oral transmission
   e)   consideration of differences in listening appreciation between singles (78 and 45 rpm) and albums (33-1/3 rpm)

Citation analysis revealed that certain artists and tunes keep appearing, and hence any important record is important by virtue of its historical worth, influence, best-selling nature, trend setting, and so forth. We have deliberately restricted ourselves to long-playing discs, believing that most of the major records of the past (available only as single plays before 1948) are now available in this format.

We would not be honest, though, if we stated that we personally enjoyed every single album. Each individual's cultural upbringing places limits on what he can enjoy completely, and these restrictions can be overcome only by an extensive immersion into the society that created the genre of music. Attempting to understand what the artist is saying will help build a vocabulary of listening. For example, modern soul has less impact on the rhythm 'n' blues fan, and rhythm 'n' blues music has little impact on the soul fan. Thus, we must treat each musical genre as being equally important in terms of what it attempts to do, with an eye to cross-fertilization among different horizontal structures. It must be recognized that we are *not* rating a gospel recording against a rhythm 'n' blues recording. Rather, we are comparing similar genre recordings against each other, such as a country blues against another country blues recording.

One difficulty we faced was that there is no historical perspective for the recordings of the past decade; this is particularly noticeable for soul and reggae. We have no idea how this music will be accepted ten years from now, but we certainly know that these recordings should have a prominent place because of their current importance. It was a different world fifty, forty, thirty years ago; of course, the artists of a prior generation seem funny-strange today. Let us hope that the future will still remain kind.

PROBLEMS IN SELECTING FOR A COLLECTION

The selection of better pop recordings poses a problem because of the profusion of unannotated "best listings," the current trend toward reissuing and repackaging, and the unavailability of some records due to sudden deletions. Record librarians, most of whom lack a subject knowledge of popular music, usually select the most popular recordings without turning to evaluations. With the impact of the music and its general availability at low prices, the record librarians may end up with a current collection without an historical core. Where can record librarians turn for the back-up record evaluations of older discs? The same problems of continuity and historical perspective exist with respect to best-selling books. A disc that received rave reviews a decade ago might be consigned to the wastebasket today.

There is another reason that libraries end up with purely contemporary collections of popular music. Records do wear out and get lost or stolen; replacements may be sought. However, the original record could be deleted and the librarian lacks a source for locating an appropriate and perhaps better record by the same artists. For lack of a better alternative, the selector usually chooses an artist's latest recording, if that artist is still to be represented in the collection. This means a continually contemporary collection with no historical perspective.

The problem of choosing older records (or new reissues of older records) becomes one of selecting blindly from the *Schwann—1* or *Schwann—2* catalogs, or else hunting for the occasional discographic essay or lists in whatever periodicals are at hand. Fortunately, the librarian can also turn to *Popular Music Periodicals Index, 1973-* (Scarecrow, 1974-) or *Annual Index to Popular Music Record Reviews, 1972-* (Scarecrow, 1973-), but these are indexes only to the substance. Our book is a selection tool of that substance, enabling selectors to base their choices on informed evaluation rather than on random choice.

The balance of material in these books is not always in proportion to the importance of a genre or an artist, and this is mainly because there are so many examples of *good* music—"a good song is a good song." A greater proportion of materials is included for the minority offerings in blues, bluegrass, rockabilly, etc.—the same forms of music that laid the foundations for more commercial offerings in soul, country, rock music, respectively.

THE MARKET PLACE—IN BRIEF

The year 1977 is a very significant anniversary year for records. In 1877, Edison invented the phonograph by embossing sound on a piece of tinfoil wrapped around a *cylinder* and reproduced that sound through an acoustic horn. (Marie Campbell, the girl who recited "Mary Had a Little Lamb," died in 1974 at the age of 103.) Ten years after Edison's success, in 1887, Emile Berliner invented the gramophone for *flat* discs. In 1897 the first shellac pressings were created, and in 1907, the first double-sided record was created by Odeon, the record company. In 1917, the first jazz disc was recorded by Victor (original Dixieland Jazz Band, January 30), and ten years later, in 1927, the first modern country music was recorded (Jimmie Rodgers and the Carter Family, August 2). That same year saw two inventions: the first sequential recording device (magnetic paper tape, by J. A. O'Neill) and Edison's development of the long-playing record. Also in 1927 came the first record changer, the first transmission of television, and the first feature-length talking picture. This book, then, is about some of those events and the impact on modern popular music of today, and it appears at a time in which more discs from the past are currently available than in any other previous year.

Records have always been popular purchases, despite their original high costs. And the market has always been flooded with as many discs as it could hold. For instance, in 1929, about 1,250 old-time music 78 rpm discs were released; by 1976, this number was about 850 for 45 rpm discs (the modern equivalent of country and bluegrass music). In terms of 1929 dollars, though, this music now costs less than a dime. At that time, there were 10 million phonographs; now, there are about 70 million phonographs. In 1929, there were about 100 record companies, but by 1976, the industry numbered over 1,500.

During those years, four types of companies have developed. First, there are the *majors* (CBS, MCA, RCA, UA, Capitol, Mercury, etc.), who have shared the bulk of the market. The *independents* (King, Imperial, Arhoolie, Savoy, etc.) arose as an alternative source of music, catering to musical minorities; these companies were interested not in getting rich but in promoting good music. A third category is the quasi-legal *bootleg* outfits. Some of these are sincere companies interested in reissuing treasures of the past by performers long since dead or missing (e.g., Biograph, Yazoo, Old Timey), while some are dubious operations that issue taped concerts and other unpublished items they feel should not be withheld from fans (e.g., Bob Dylan's *White Wonder* set, Rolling Stones' concerts, jazz and dance music airshots). The fourth grouping consists of *pirates*, who reproduce in-print records and tapes in the lucrative rock and country fields, and who, by false and misleading claims, make a high profit since they pay no royalties and no studio costs are collected. The records included in this book were produced by an uncommonly high percentage of independent and bootleg labels. This is because the roots of each musical genre lie in the beginning steps taken by independent companies and by the innovative performers themselves, who first recorded for these labels early in their careers.

It should certainly be noted that the historical worth of disc recordings will increase even more in the years to come. One reason that older recordings have not been popular is that modern higher fidelity equipment amplifies the poorer reproduction of bygone years. An early compensation from the late 1950s was the "electronically processed stereo" disc, in which the highs went to one channel and the lows to the other. This suited stereo consoles but not the hi-fi components market. By 1976, though, RCA had developed its "sound stream" process, in which a computer reduces not only surface scratch from older discs but also faulty resonance and reverberation. This computer "justification" works on the same principles as NASA's clarification of the 1976 pictures of the surface of Mars. RCA's first such disc was of Caruso recordings; within the next few years, certain forms of popular music may be added.

POST-1974 RECORDINGS: POTENTIAL CLASSICS

Although the discographic information and availability of albums are current with this book's imprint, *most* of the music described here had been recorded before 1974. This lead time of five years allows for settling/detecting trends rather than fads and letting the jury, as it were, have sufficient time to arrive at decisions. Recognizing, however, that certain modern discs just *might* be significant in the long run, we list those recent innovative records that have drawn exceptionally fine current reviews.

Blues

Luther Allison. Luther's Blues. Gordy G 967VI
Clifton Chenier. Out West. Arhoolie 1072
B. B. King and Bobby Bland. Together for the First Time. two discs. ABC DSY 50190/2
Fenton Robinson. Somebody Loan Me a Dime. Alligator 4705
Viola Wells. Miss Rhapsody. Saydisc Matchbox SDM 227 (British issue)

Soul

Joan Armatrading. A & M SP 4588
Ashford and Simpson. Gimme Something Real. Warner Brothers BS 2735
Bobby Bland. Dreamer. ABC 50169
Ray Charles. Message from the People. ABC 755
Manu Dibango. Soul Makossa. Atlantic SD 7267
Earth, Wind and Fire. Spirit. Columbia PC 34241
Isley Brothers. Live It Up. T-Neck PZ 33070
Millie Jackson. Caught Up. Spring 6703
Millie Jackson. Free and In Love. Spring 6709
Eddie Kendricks. People, Hold On. Tamla T 327L
Kool and the Gang. Light of the World. DeLite 2014
Main Ingredient. Euphrates River. RCA APL1-0335
Curtis Mayfield. Back to the World. Curtom CRS 8015
Harold Melvin and the Blue Notes. Black and Blue. Philadelphia International KZ
    31648
Meters. Rejuvenation. Reprise MS 2200
New Orleans Jazz & Heritage Festival, 1976. two discs. Island ISLD 9424
Ohio Players. Honey. Mercury SRM1-1038
Nina Simone. It Is Finished. RCA APL1-0241
Stevie Wonder. Songs in the Key of Life. two discs. Tamla T13-340C2

REFERENCES AND INDEX

   In the introductory comments to each section, reference will be made to the
literature on the topic of black music. When a name appears followed by a number
in parentheses—e.g., Evans (29)—the reader should consult "Book Citations" for a
full entry and a description of the book. When a title is followed by a number—e.g.,
Blues Unlimited (3)—the "Periodical Citations" should be consulted. (Items such as
"62a" represent updates or new entries and are filed in proper numerical sequence.)
   The alphanumeric code preceding each entry first locates that item in the
overall classification used for the four volumes (B here denotes *Black Music*; J will
be used for *Jazz*, etc.). The number immediately following the letter code then
indicates the major section of this book in which an item/artist can be found.
Additionally, the Artists' Index references all of the recordings listed in this book
by that code number.

INTRODUCTION TO POPULAR MUSIC

"Time has a way of making the style stick out,
rather than the music, unless
that music is exceptional."
—Joe Goldberg

Popular music is a twentieth century art form made available to the masses through records, radio and, to a lesser extent, nightclubs, concerts, festivals, and television. As an art form, it is in a state of constant evolution in which each generation redefines its own music. One's perception of popular music is based only on what is heard or what is available to be heard. "Access," then, becomes a key word that was not found before either the breakdown of regional barriers or the advent of mass media. Previous to bulk production of commercial recordings (about 1920), different styles had arisen to meet the moods of geographic areas and of the times. All that these diverse styles had in common were the elements of rhythm, melody, harmony, and form; each style went its separate way in emphasizing one of these elements over the other. Sorting out the musical strains and streams is confusing, then, because of the vast number of musical and extra-musical influences shaping the styles. Some of these will be explored in the introductions to the various volumes on specific musical genres, but it should be noted that there are five general statements that appear to be incontrovertible when discussing styles of popular music:

1) Styles persist past their prime, and often they are revived by a new musical generation, perhaps in a series of permutations.

2) One development in a style leads to another development through constant evolution.

3) Each style and stream of music influences the other styles and streams through the artists' awareness of trends in all areas, this caused by the exposure that the mass media give to such a variety of artists.

4) Styles are as much shaped by extra-musical influences (such as the recording industry and radio) as by other styles themselves.

5) To the novice, all music performed in one particular style may sound the same, but each stream is a language or form of communication, and to become familiar with it, the listener must consciously learn this new language.

Each of these statements will be further explored in this section and with the appropriate genres of popular music.

Schoenberg once wrote (in a different context): "If it is art it is not for all; if it is for all it is not art." Popular music relates to the existing mores of an era, and it falls in step with a current culture by reflecting popular tastes. In this sense, popular music is relevant to its audience's interests. But listeners evolve with time, for society never stands still. Popular music changes in response to audience manipulation or demand; consequently, *all* popular music styles of the past may make little sense to a modern audience. There appears to be little need *today* for the sentimental ballads of the late nineteenth century, the New Orleans jazz sound, the Tin Pan Alley pop music of the 1920-1950 period, and so forth, in terms of what that music meant to *past* generations. However, it is important to note the older styles of popular music because these styles have revivals that show an interest in the past (for stability or nostalgia) and also show the evolution of modern streams of music. In recordings, for each genre there exist at least three types of similar music: the original recordings of by-gone days; a revival of the style reinterpreted in modern terms; and the modern equivalent that evolved from that early style. An example would be the slick group singing of the 1930s and 1940s, as exemplified by the Andrews Sisters (in the original form), the Pointer Sisters (in the revival), and the Manhattan Transfer (in the modern equivalent). Through the phonograph record, all three co-exist, and future singers in this genre could borrow a different emphasis from each of the three closely-related styles to project a fourth synthesis of, to continue the example, the vocal group singing slick, catchy lyrics.

Over a period of years, each style of popular music loses much of the original drive, mood, and inventiveness that came from its roots in tradition. As a minority music style catches on with wider audiences, and as this style becomes influenced by both other genres and urban cultures, the original excitement of the innovation becomes diminished considerably. This is inevitable as styles evolve and as performers add something "a little different" to distinguish themselves from the increasing number of other similar musicians interpreting the same genre. This creates permutations and sub-genres, resulting in the creation of yet other musical streams. As these styles become commercially successful, performers self-consciously appraise their music as found in shows, concerts, or on record, and they become concerned over their image and saleability. They are frightened that they might fall into a rut (or, more appropriately, a groove). However, seeking reappraisal by becoming observers defeats both the spontaneity and the emotional impact of the music, and no emerging musical sub-genre would long survive if it stayed with a narrow conception of its style. This is what happened to the Beatles, and, to their credit, they split up when they recognized that they could no longer develop musically as a group. An emerging style at its beginnings can offer real excitement, emotion, and exuberance, all of which tend to fade (or be jaded or tired) in its mature years. This, then, is a prime rationale for the preservation and retention of early and historical recordings that helped to produce fanatical enthusiasm among both the performers and the audiences who knew and recognized new, emerging popular music styles.

It was David Reisman who identified two groups of performers and listeners as early as 1950 ("Listening to Popular Music," *American Quarterly* 2:359-71). There was the majority audience, which accepted the range of choices offered by the music industry and made its selections from this range without considering anything outside of it. And there were also the "cults," or minority audiences, more active and less interested in words and tunes than in the arrangement, technical virtuosity, and elaborate standards for listening and analysis. This audience (now scattered among the forms of early country music, jazz, blues, musical shows, rockabilly, etc.) preferred "personal discovery" of the music, and usually arrived at such listening pleasures by painstakingly searching for the roots of modern popular music. Their outlook was international, and they had a sympathetic attitude to black musicians, whom they considered to be the prime source of material. It was the cults that promoted "early music," wrote the books and magazines, and produced reissues of original recordings and issues of rediscovered early performers. The latter were past their prime but still active and often better in the musical style than current interpreters. The recordings cited in this book are based on both the cult image and the emerging musical stylings.

On a personal basis, as members of the cult, we have found that one of the most maddening things about loving minority musical styles is the frustration we feel when we try to share that love with others who are both ignorant of the form and apathetic towards it ("I don't know and I don't care"). In addition, there is an equally disheartening feeling—when that favorite minority musical style either changes into another form of expression which becomes more popular than the original while still being imitative, or when it gets raped by enterprising producers and performers who then try to pass it off as theirs alone. The circle becomes complete and the frustrations compounded when we try to convince others that this more "popular" music is but a pale imitation of the originals. We admit, therefore, that there is a proselytizing tone to the construction of this book.

The most dramatic influence upon the popular music of the twentieth century has been black African music. Its characteristics have pervaded all forms (except perhaps most musical comedies). Jazz, blues, and soul, of course, have direct roots. But the important innovators in other fields have had direct contact with black musicians and had assimilated black sounds, such as Bill Monroe (bluegrass music), Woody Guthrie (folk and protest music), Bob Wills (western swing), Jimmie Rodgers and the Carter Family (country music), Benny Goodman (big bands), Elvis Presley (rockabilly), the Yardbirds and the Beatles (blues rock), and Led Zeppelin (heavy metal music). Without this assimilation, there would have been no popular music as we know it today.

All of this relates to the essential differences between European (Western) and African (black) music. Black music, in its components, prefers an uneven rhythm but in strict time, and with a loose melody that follows the *tone* of the words. This tone is explained by the fact that the same syllable of a word can connote different things depending on whether it is sung in a high, medium, or low pitch of voice. For the African singer or instrument, beauty resides in the *expression* of music (the *how* of performance). Western music, on the other hand, prefers an even rhythm (which explains why rhythm is the weakest element here) in loose time, with a strict melody that follows the *stress* of the words. For the Western performer, the music stands or falls on its own merits (the *what* of performance), and, ideally, the performance could be perfectly duplicated by others in another place and time.

Much has been written about the differences between Western and black music (see the bibliography section), but little about why white audiences did not accept black music. Three assumptions, however, have arisen. One involves social barriers denying white access to black music; that access was a phenomenon brought about by mass media. Another relates to the musical traditions of black music that were foreign to white audiences (e.g., sexuality, ghetto life). A third assumption is that basic differences in musical cultural upbringing produce preconceptions of what is music and what is not (for example, the white listener defines a tune by its melody, whereas a black listener thinks of it in terms of its chord progressions; white song lyrics are either sentimental or sophisticated, while black song lyrics are experiential and improvised).

As an incidental note, it appears that the state of Texas is actually the well-spring of much of today's popular music. Most of the significant innovators were born and raised in Texas, where they perfectly assimilated the diverse musical stylings of the blues, ethnic materials (Chicano, Caribbean, Cajun), jazz, and so forth, to create and fashion swing jazz, western swing, urban blues, country music, troubador songs, rhythm 'n' blues, rock and roll, and country rock music. No appropriate written materials have yet emerged to explain this complex cross-fertilization of musical ideas, but it is important to remember that the vertical separation of white and black music did not exist in Texas (i.e., both groups shared a common heritage) and that literally all kinds of musical influences were at work virtually simultaneously—a true melting pot.

It is not our intention to present a history of the recording industry or of radio (elementary surveys can be found in Schicke's *Revolution in Sound* [99] for records, and in Passman's *The Dee Jays* [83] for radio), but we view these industries as being equally important as the music itself towards the shaping of popular music. Both recordings and radio had the power to encourage and to deny by their manipulation of public tastes. A brief overview of the highlights follows:

1917-1925—limited retention of sound through the acoustic recording method. Many companies formed.

1925-1931—electric recordings begin, capturing the sounds of a piano and larger groups. 1929 was a peak year, with different markets for different recording styles of regional characteristics (largely ignored outside the geographic areas of marketing; no cross-fertilizations except by musicians who borrowed from other records).

1931-1934—The Depression meant fewer sales (in 1933, these were 7 percent of the 1929 peak), fewer recordings, and the rise of recorded sound on radio. This was the beginning of regional breakdowns.

1934-1941—This period saw cheaper records ($0.25 to $0.35), more recording activities, and the beginning of *professional* musicians who aided in the shifting of the geographic centers of recording activities (pop moved to Hollywood, swing jazz to the West and Midwest, western swing to the Midwest, folk to New York, etc.).

1942-1945—Musicians were drafted, shortage of shellac appeared, there was the ASCAP ban, and the musicians' union went on strikes. Very little new music recorded here, but this was also the beginning of independent companies.

1946-1950—The post-War era saw the establishment of hit parades, the popularity of juke boxes, records becoming full-time radio programming, a complete break in regional stylings, and expenses rising for touring groups.

1950-1959—This period brought a resurgence of *different* forms of music existing simultaneously for diversified but separate markets (blues, jump music, rhythm 'n' blues; jazz, swing, bop, cool; rock and roll; folk, country, bluegrass, etc.), this because of many competing independent companies. The situation is similar to the 1920s.

1959-1963—An age of imitation and derivative music, this was highlighted by a watered-down folk revival, the beginnings of soul music, and the decline of specialized markets in bluegrass, jazz, and rock 'n' roll.

1964-1970—An age of cross-overs, this period sees country music go pop and rock music emerge as a symbiotic co-existent through country-rock, blues-rock, jazz-rock, theatre-rock, soul-rock, folk-rock, etc.

1970- —Now there is the simultaneous co-existence not only of separate musical styles, but also of merging styles and "roots" music. All three are widely known to a mass audience for the first time *ever*.

Recordings have had a troubled history, and it is a wonder at all that historically important recordings still remain. Many basic conflicts shaped audience appeal. First, it was the cylinder versus the disc, and then the conflict about early playing speeds that ranged from 60 to 85 revolutions per minute. Then, there were different types of materials used for the physical product (metal, shellac, paper, etc.). The method of reproduction varied from the "hill and dale" of the vertical groove cutting to the horizontal cutting, being compounded by the outward playing groove as against the inward playing groove. After World War II, further technological conflicts had to be resolved: tape versus disc; 45 rpm versus 33-1/3 rpm; ten-inch disc versus seven-inch disc; ten-inch disc versus twelve-inch disc; stereophonic sound versus monophonic sound; quadrophonic sound versus stereophonic sound; different configurations of quadrophonic sound (discrete, matrixed, compatible) and tapes (reel-to-reel, cartridge, cassette), and so forth. If an audience was expected to hear everything available and make judgments, then it would have to purchase a wide variety of equipment far too expensive for all but radio stations. Thus, unless recordings were issued and reissued in a variety of configurations, there would be music that people would simply never hear because they lacked the necessary play-back equipment.

Beyond the shape of the prime listening document, there were other conflicts. Various musician unions' strikes against the industry precluded hearing first-hand evidence of aural changes in music at crucial times. The various licensing bans called by ASCAP in the 1940s precluded listening to new records on radio and on the juke box. The rise of the disc jockey on radio led to an influence over what records the public could hear, which in turn resulted in scandals of "payola" and "drugola" for bribes that ensured that certain records were played (and others thus denied air time). And from time to time, there were various shortages of materials for reproducing the record, such as the wartime shellac crisis (to buy a new record, the customer had to turn in an old one for recycling) and the vinyl crisis of the 1970s. All of these slowed down the rate at which new music became acceptable.

The practices of the recording industry are also illuminating when trying to understand the popular music performer. The big schism in the industry occurred during World War II. Previous to this time, the type of singer the industry looked for was one who coupled low cost with better-than-average returns. Later, when the industry learned that it took money to make money, the shift would be to turn a fairly high investment into an astronomical return. Thus, the pre-war performers were largely middle-aged people who had already established for themselves a loyal fandom. These people were self-accompanied, and wrote or modified their own materials. Indeed, their major employment was not in records, or even in music. They were *not* "professional musicians," but simply better than adequate performers who were paid a flat recording fee and given no promotional tours for emphasizing any regional characteristics of their music. At this time, radio was viewed as a competitor, and each record was usually about 50 percent sold out within a year (and left in the catalog for up to 10 years or more). Post-war developments, taking into account the young returning servicemen and the later "war baby boom," concentrated on the under-30 performer, who then broke new ground with a solid financial investment behind him.

These singers and musicians usually performed other people's materials (except for the 1970s rock movement) and relied on great accompaniment from major studio session men. Their prime occupation was in music, especially records; they were "professionals" with a high profile from tours and promotions. They were paid royalties instead of a flat rate, no doubt as a result of collecting funds from radio stations that were now heavily dependent on records as a source of programming. As national markets were aimed for (there was obviously more money to be made here than in just one geographic or minority audience), the music's consistency became blander and more stylized. Tours and national exposure meant that record sales would peak in the first three months, and many records were generally withdrawn after a year. Economically, this meant that, of all elpees released in 1977, 85 percent *lost* money, with the remaining 15 percent being monster sellers that created the corporate profits.

Record companies are always quick to discover new audiences. The fast pace of the industry, plus the high failure rate, indicate which records sell and which do not. Whether they are *good* records or not is largely immaterial. Playlists of radio stations, and best-selling lists of trade magazines, provide an *index* to popular music rather than a *criterion*. This is in much the same way as lists of best-selling books, in that both reflect the interests of the time. Whether they are enduring or not is up to "history" to decide, and by tracing the development of musical styles, any record's impact and influence can be ascertained. As Robert Shelton (*Country Music Story*) has said: "Few popular music styles remain pure for long. Nothing can spread quite so quickly as a musical style that is selling." On this basis, each and every modern record must be regarded as a one-shot attempt. No matter what its popularity, just three months after its release few people appear to buy it. And if the record is successful, then it will generate hybrids and derivative imitations (in addition to making its originators duplicate their success with an exact follow-up copy). This is the determining factor in the preservation and continuation of music, despite the poor side effects caused by records.

There is a distinction that can be made between a *record*, a *broadside*, and the *oral tradition*. The latter is very limited, being based on one-to-one contact in a community, and changes in the music are prone to develop. The broadside, on the other hand, presents words only (it might have been sung at the time of sale), and the later "sheet music" added piano versions of the music. With a broadside, one had to find a tune. With sheet music, one had to find an accompanying instrument. Both, though, stabilized the texts. A record, on the other hand, has not only the words and melody but also the performance style: the text, tune, and style are together in one package, from one particular moment in time. It can be replayed and memorized, and the listener can learn from it—perhaps indicating variants in later performances—and also, of course, duplicate any of its success.

Not everybody could possibly buy all records. Originally, it was up to radio to provide a "free" service, which meant random selection until the days of "Top 40" playlists. Radio was the medium that not only transmitted older songs but also created the regional breakdown in styles, as one geographic area began to hear the songs of other adjoining areas. Radio used a lot of material, and because of its random nature, it created a demand for more and newer material. This was furnished by both new records and live performances. The latter were very important, for many programs were recorded off the air at home, and are now available via small reissue labels. Disc recordings have certainly never reflected any artist's entire repertoire, and it is questionable as to how many discs were actually favorites of the performer. It was up to the a. and r. men and producers to select the tunes for marketing, yet this interfered with the artist's natural choice of songs. This was the case with Uncle Dave Macon, who also never felt at home in the studio. With radio work, the performer could program what he or she liked to sing and usually (in the early days) performed in front of an audience. "Airshots," as they are called, could determine more about a performer's repertoire than discs, and they also plugged the gaps that existed when there were recording bans. This was absolutely crucial during the development of bop jazz because few people outside of New York were aware of the music (in its early period, it was not recorded because of the recording bans).

A graphic conceptual display of diverse major Western musical influences in the twentieth century is shown on page 24. There are, of course, many, many minor variations. (Relative size of boxes is not indicative of influence or importance.)

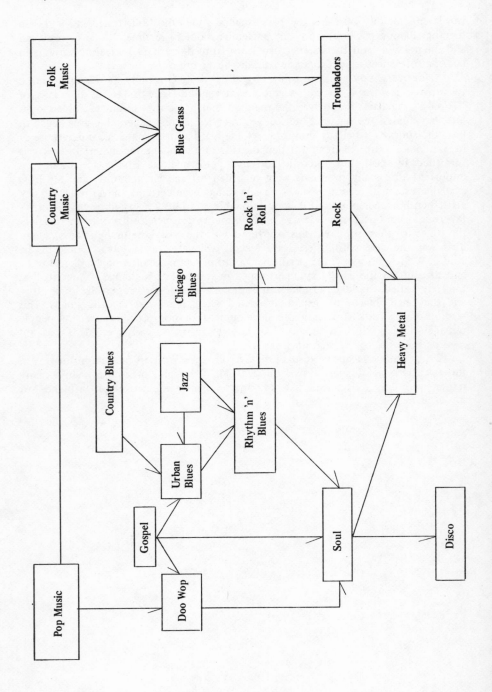

THE BEST OF THE BEST:
Anthologies of Popular Music on Records

"Anthology" is derived from Greek words meaning "flower gathering." Presumably, this means either the best that is available or a mixed bag, with some parts showing off the rest by means of contrast. Certainly the display should be stunning, for why else anthologize? In the music world, anthologies serve either as samplers or as introductions to a company's products. These collections of the works of popular performers sell to a captured audience that is used to having pre-selected convenience items before their eyes. At the same time, anthologies are invaluable for rapidly building up a music record library, or for fleshing out an area of music not already covered in the library. There will also be little duplication among the items in collections if the library does not already have the originals.

Within the past three years, aided by the soaring costs of studio time and performers' fees plus the recognized nostalgia fad, more anthologies and collections than ever before have been released. From a manufacturer's point of view, they are cheap to produce: the material has virtually paid for itself already; the liner notes are few (if any) or standardized; there is uniform packaging and design; a ready market exists, which the rackers and jobbers love, so little advertising is necessary; and anthologies act as samplers of the performer or to the catalog, hence promoting future sales. However, selection of the program depends on the cooperation of music publishers in granting reduced rates.

Personally, we are quite partial to anthologized performances. For a pure musical experience, there has been nothing quite like, say, on a hot and humid night, throwing on a pile of 45 rpm singles and sitting back guzzling beer while tapping to the rhythms. At this point, our attention span is about three minutes; thus a new record with a new voice comes on just as minds start to wander. With older records, the effect is one of familiarity, evoking fond, past memories. For the sake of convenience and better musical reproduction, though, a stack of anthologized long-play records makes this easier. Most new records today can be quite boring between the highlights, and it is not uncommon for a group to have an album with one hit single, fleshed out with nine duds. You really wouldn't want to hear it all again. Too, while most people might all like or remember one or two particular numbers, they also like other tracks individually. An anthology or "best" album attempts to take those most popular selections that we all enjoy and market them so that the most people might like the whole reissue album. One man's meat is not another man's poison in the case of the anthology.

Many reservations exist about compilations, especially with regard to trickery, motives, and shoddy packaging. Some of these are discussed here, but a few general comments are also necessary. In many instances, anthologies have only 10 tracks to a disc. This may be fewer tracks than the original albums had, and certainly it makes each number more expensive at a per selection cost. Yet, there are distinct advantages for a certain market that has low-fidelity equipment: the wider grooves give a full range of sound and increase the bass proportionately, thus making this particular type of disc virtually ideal for home stereo consoles and for older, heavier needle cartridges. Since these wider grooves don't wear out as quickly as compressed ones, the records may be played over and over again with less wear than on an "original" disc. In other instances, some "best" collections (especially multi-volume sets) almost equal the catalog material from which they are drawn and, hence, cost more in the long run.

Trickery involves a number of gimmicks, such as "electronic enhancement" for stereo, with its vast echoing sound being reminiscent of a train station lobby. These types are dying out, as it costs money to re-channel, some of the public are demanding original monophonic sound, and—the biggest marketing blow of all—these discs have been relegated to the semi-annual *Schwann–2* catalog with the mono discs. Sometimes the informative print is very small, or was printed say, yellow on orange, and the consumer virtually couldn't read the notice "enhanced for stereo." Some tricks are not solely for deception, though. Cute tricks include the title "The Worst of the Jefferson Airplane"—an obvious collection of best material. But what about an original first record by an unknown group that is titled "The Best of . . ." just to attract sales?

Another problem with the vinyl product is that anthologies are mostly regional pressings. Duplicate masters are used in factories not as careful as the home plant and are shipped directly to the regional distributor. Of course, a careless pressing sounds worse than a skillfully crafted product. And the polyvinyl chloride content can drop to below 85 percent. This is important, for the extender in a disc can be exposed to the stylus riding on the otherwise soft plastic and great harm can occur. Classical records are generally 95-99 percent vinyl, with pop recordings being around 90 percent. Anything lower than 90 percent can be detrimental to sound reproduction.

The material included in anthologies is another concern. It is usually selected by the producer or company, so that it may have no relation to what the performers themselves think is their best material. Many groups are anthologized *after* they leave one company for greener pastures, and the original manufacturer can keep churning out the reissues year after year, relying on the groups' future success to advertise the old reissued product. Some anthologies are shoddily passed off as memorials after a performer's death; others are issued if performers cannot produce an album in any one particular year, whether through accident (as in Bob Dylan's case), personal problems, laziness, or personnel changes. This keeps the name in front of the record-buying public, but too often the album is at full list price and the cover only mentions in passing that it is a reissue.

With the new packaging gatefold, is it likely that *all* notes on anthologies (as well as many others) will be inside the shrink-wrapped cellophane parcel. Thus, the consumer will not know what he is supposed to buy until he reads a review, ad, or opens the package (thus forfeiting a "return" if he already has the item). As these records rarely get reviewed or advertised, there is no certain way of knowing what is on them; Schwann does not often give track listings for them.

Anthologies are also notable for what they do not contain. The biggest performers are rarely anthologized while they are still under contract, and if they are, then the discs are sold at full price. There is no inexpensive introduction to the best material of Hank Snow, Charlie Pride, Elvis Presley, or the Rolling Stones.

When the latter group left Decca/London, the company released two anthologies at a full price of $10.98. Presley is available on a set of four discs, if you want virtually *all* of his better product. England is the best place to go for inexpensive reissues in all fields, particularly so if the reissue is not available on the North American market.

Mail order houses are a direct development from the recording companies, and some of the latter have gone into the business themselves. Being leased only for such a one-shot appearance, the selected items are pure gravy for the companies. Thus, with groove compression, 18 to 24 titles (2½ minutes long) can appear on some of these albums. Usually these discs are promoted only by television commercials or direct mail. Other reissue companies (prevalent in England) lease material from the original companies and repackage it as they see fit. Pickwick International is most successful at this, drawing on the large Capitol and Mercury catalogs (which is one reason why these two companies do not reissue many discs).

The anthologies listed in the musical genres herein consist of reissued material, either in the form of anthologies, "best" collections, or "live" versions of studio tracks that enjoy reasonably good sound. They are set apart as subsections entitled "anthologies." These records are offered as a pre-selected guide to really good performances, or as material that may lie outside of a library's main interest or collecting policy. For instance, a recorded sound library may want to capture a flavoring of the blues without exceptional expense and without culling lists of basic records, discographic essays, or even Schwann (which splits blues among "current popular" and "jazz"). Determining what records may be basic, essential, or important is not always an enjoyable listening experience; it is certainly expensive. What is being stressed here is quantity *with* quality: to get the best and most available at the cheapest price possible. In many instances, a well-rounded collection will result from buying anthologies, but not necessarily an in-depth collection.

Basic recordings are something else again—interesting for the derivative performers that will follow in the style, but mainly useful in a historical context. Such a collection is one to build on—to use the "basic" in its literal sense. These selections are listed to capture the whole field at once. The demise of the record shop's listening room has meant that the informed consumer can no longer hear an album before purchase; others might not have any real knowledge of music other than somewhat vague personal interests. How can they hear the "best" in another field? The same reasons for anthology production that are advanced by recording companies can be applied when libraries acquire such records: to introduce people to new listening pleasures (despite all the gimmicks of hard sell). Also, nearly all these records are also available on tape (except for most of the mono reissues).

Blues

Blues

BLUES

"You have to play who you are."
—Joe Willie Wilkins,
bluesman

INTRODUCTION

This section comprises material generally classified by blues record collectors as pre-World War II and post-World War II vocal blues; it is based on the two major discographies of Godrich and Dixon (40) and Leadbitter and Slaven (58).
Blues music is often of two types—country, rural, solo, and acoustic; or electric, amplified, and urban with ensemble playing. The former has been around since the turn of the century. The latter is a more recent development, often called "Chicago blues" and generally attributed to Muddy Waters, but also having roots in the string bands and the Mississippi Delta. Heavy white blues bands are in the ROCK genre, for they have used the technical aspects of blues as a format, not as a life style. Instrumental blues is more properly JAZZ, although the odd instrumental does turn up on an album of blue vocals (and vice versa). Scholars and collectors have tried to break blues into manageable forms with partial success. Regional styles, time periods, format of presentation, type of instrumentation, individuals— the blues get worked over as much as the grieving performer. This accounts for the vast number of anthologized offerings and the responses of the so-called "bootleggers" in reissuing recorded product.

Anyone can *play* the blues, for it is a simple technical form of music. Thus, all interest in the blues is dependent on the performer. But not everyone can *feel* the blues, since the message conveyed is essentially emotional. Real blues singers used the blues therapeutically to escape from their situations. They stood outside, looking in while singing about their problems. It always felt good to a blues singer to finish a song, for he had "talked it out," as many people in therapy do. Most typical white blues singers cannot feel the blues because they have not experienced it; they *see* injustices and become disturbed. The typical black blues singer is the actual recipient of those injustices; he not only sees them, he *lives* them. Thus, for all purposes, the typical white singer cannot get *into* the blues.

The blues appear to come from many sources, but the first blues performances on records undoubtedly came from three distinct roots: African percussive traditions, gospel music, work songs, and hollers ("Arhoolie," the name of a prolific blues recording company, means a cornfield holler). Any changes after the early 1920s were created by borrowing from other musical themes made widely known through the phonograph and radio. Indeed, after just a cursory listen to several anthologies, it is apparent that 90 percent of the techniques, ideas, and approaches to the blues had already been crystalized by 1930, and, despite the addition of electricity and ensemble work, little new has been added since that time.

How did the blues develop and peak in just a short time? Several explanations have been offered, the most common being development in the lives of blacks themselves—the shift from slavery to freedom. Blues was a distinct post-Civil War development; it did not exist as such before that time. The black was made *mobile* but not free. After removal from the communal life of the plantation, there was a distinct shift in emphasis from "we" and "us" to "I" and "me," an expression of the self-dependence of the itinerant who needed food and shelter. Blues is migratory music, developing as the singer searches not only for food and shelter but also for work, money, sex, love, and self-respect. Blacks moved up the Mississippi Delta to Memphis, then to Chicago; they moved westward to Texas and then to California. Each time, the blues went along, too, changing a little here and there. Of course, blacks stayed home as well, in Arkansas, Louisiana, Mississippi, the Piedmont area, etc., so regional stylings developed in isolation.

Prior to 1920, the phonograph industry issued few recordings made by blacks. What did appear reinforced the white perception of black life and early black music: the spiritual, the plantation air, the novelty comic song. None of this took into account the true conditions of misery, poverty, and lack of identity.

Techniques

Technically, the blues are almost always 12-bar in form (the lines fit more or less into a 12-bar measure). The bars are divided into three equal parts, with a different chord for each (1st, 4th and 5th notes of the scale). The time to sing the words in each line is a little more than one half of each of the three equal parts, which leaves considerable room for an instrumental response pattern. This made the blues attractive to sing while one was alone, filling in spaces with a guitar run or a harmonica wail. The first line of each verse is repeated, while the third line is stated once. Stearns called this a "capsule communication": the first two lines set the stage by repetition, while the third delivered the punch. This was a very common statement and comment pattern.

Melodic inflections were based on the "blues notes." Players flatted the third and seventh notes of the scale, and occasionally flatted the fifth. In this case, the flatted third is actually used simultaneously with the major third, even while a blues progression is played in the major key. Blues, in common with African music, is *not* modal in harmony. While European music is V-chord-dominant oriented, blues is subdominant-oriented (IV chord). Blues were originally sung to the accompaniment of whatever instruments were available, and rather than have silences with solo singing because of a lack of instrumentation, the singers also improvised on common items, such as wash boards, spoons, jugs, shoes, combs, and so forth.

The blues are thus a very individual creation. All the playing, singing, lyrics, and views of life are up to the individual. Each blues song tells a story—of love lost, love gained, or topical issues, of sex, drink, and usually about unhappy occurrences in the performer's life. Most of the pieces, as with those of Lightnin' Hopkins, are improvised on the spot. All that is needed is an idea or a refrain, for blues are among the easiest verses to create.

The audience is an indispensable part of any blues listening experience. Yet listening does require a sympathetic ear—a feeling of compassion or understanding, a sensitivity to changes in life. Once inside the music, a listener has a multiplicity of sounds, approaches, and lyric ideas to appreciate. Without the modal harmony, much has to be supplied by the singer himself, and some devices included nasal moans, spoken delivery, and on-the-beat phrasing. More sophisticated devices emerged in rhythm 'n' blues and soul music by borrowing melismatic techniques from gospel music.

It took a long time for white audiences to get inside black blues. Superstition, prejudice, and censorship prevented all but a few from appreciating an essentially Negro folk music. Blues needed popularization by "acceptable" black singers such as Leadbelly, Josh White, Lonnie Johnson, Big Bill Broonzy, Brownie McGhee, and Sonny Terry. All these singers sang the blues in their early days, but when they switched to the more lyrical soft ballads of folk music, they became better known to white audiences and helped to foster the folk music revival (starting with the Weavers in 1949, who popularized Leadbelly's folk music). This turned serious students to an examination of the roots, resulting in a rediscovery of black blues and performances by those same "acceptable" black singers, of more gut-level material.

The idea of racial distinctions also prohibited much understanding toward the black jazz bands. It was the Original Dixieland Jazz Band, a collection of white lads who played bland arrangements of hot numbers, that popularized jazz for the white market by recording in 1917, and ever since then, white bands have been more successful than black ensembles in terms of both appeal and money. This was a pity, for few appreciated the blues shouters Jimmy Rushing and Joe Turner at the time. It is also interesting to note that it was Charlie Christian and Muddy Waters who introduced the slick, professional stylings of the electric guitar.

Stylings

There are many different ways of performing the blues, and Charles Keil (53) has produced an interesting taxonomy of blues stylings, but more to fit various people into categories rather than to set up a system and let people find their places. Based on his outline, it is relatively easy to define styles. First, there are the country blues, characterized by unstandardized forms, acoustic guitar, and spoken words. These are divided into subgroups. Delta blues feature moans, bottle-neck guitar styling, and a heavy sound, as exemplified by Son House, Robert Johnson, and early Muddy Waters. Then there are the Texas blues, emphasizing single-string guitar work, loose vocals, and a light sound, as exemplified by Blind Lemon Jefferson and Lightnin' Hopkins. The Southern blues assume characteristics common of white folk music, as produced by Brownie McGhee and Blind Boy Fuller. Groups in this category include string bands, jug bands, and wandering minstrel shows.

Second, there are the city blues, characterized by a standardized form, regular beginnings and endings, and a variety of instruments. These, too, have separate forms—the piano blues (which include the "classic" female singers with jazz instrumental accompaniment, and the boogie-woogie raunchy male singers such as Leroy Carr and Speckled Red, with a rolling-bass effect); contemporary blues (electric guitar, harmonica, and drums, such as played by Muddy Waters); and "citified country" (a mixed bag, wtih electrified country characteristics, as played by Hopkins or John Lee Hooker).

Third, there are the urban blues, characterized by saxophones, free phrasing, arrangements, and usually no harmonicas. A breakdown of Urban blues shows four subforms: the jazz oriented sound of Kansas City, with Jimmy Rushing and Joe Turner shouting the vocals in front of a big riffing band; the post-war Texas ensemble of small bands, including piano and electric guitar, with relaxed vocals by T-Bone Walker and Lowell Fulson; the Memphis style with the three Kings (B.B., Freddy, and Albert); and cross-country industrial sound with everything amplified (saxophones, guitars, etc.) for Otis Rush and Earl Hooker.

The fourth category is soul music, rhythm 'n' blues, blues-jazz-gospel, call it what you will—perhaps "modern" would be better. These include the Motown sound, slick arrangements, "crying" instead of singing, and so forth. Paul Oliver (80) has worked out an alternative classification scheme. While Keil characterizes blues styles, Oliver categorizes record output. He lists the following: African and Anglo-American Background; Work Song and Negro Folk Song; Regional Collections—Mississippi, Texas, Louisiana, South, Alabama, Georgia, Missouri, etc.; Collections—Cities: Atlanta, Memphis, St. Louis, Detroit, Chicago, Oakland, etc.; String, Jug, and Washboard Band Collections; Piano Blues Collections; Classic Blues; and Individual Artists, either separately or with the subject categories above.

The first modern reissue on long-playing microgroove was the 12-side set from Folkways, the *Anthology of American Folk Music* compiled by Harry Smith in the early 1950s. Over the years, collectors had assimilated copies of rare 78s, and by 1961 there was sufficient backing for the Origin Jazz Library to commence production. Its first album was a collection of Charley Patton numbers, and it was exceptionally well received by collectors and novices. Folkways, meanwhile, had been busy transferring field trip results onto its new RBF (Record, Book and Film Sales) subsidiary label and later came out with significant reissues. Early transfers involved a noise reduction filter that also took out some of the music. This was usually just a treble cut, and the performances were left with a "muddy" low sound. As remastering techniques have since vastly improved, it is now possible to filter out a lot of noise and still retain the music. The height of perfection has presumably been reached with Columbia's ten-album series on Bessie Smith. Indeed, so many performances have been transferred that the novice now has an overwhelming choice from which to choose.

Reissues of regional music often take the form of anthologies, ostensibly because many blues people did not record enough material for the present day long-playing album, or because masters and/or issues had been lost (or presumed lost) at the time. Other reasons, though, include lack of author credit and capital, avoidance of repetitious sounds by one person, ease of packaging, and historical relevance. Some companies, like Blues Classics, Yazoo, Origin, Roots, and RBF, have the majority of their issues in this manner. Unfortunately, this leads to some duplication, but usually not within each label's series. Also, the sound quality is variable, probably because tapings were from the original issues (not in mint condition) and not from the masters. Also, most of these companies, not necessarily the ones mentioned above, cannot afford equalization equipment. Reissue of significant material is available as well on limited editions produced by small companies or individuals in lots of 500. These are exceedingly difficult to acquire as they go out of print within a few months. Their main market, despite poor to fair sound, is the collectors. Some of these labels (including some from England), which crop up from time to time in record stores, are: Down with the Game, Advent, Bounty, Special Delivery, Rebel, Sunflower, Jazz Collector, Kokomo, Red Lightnin', Flyright, Black and Blue, Southern Preservation Records, and so forth.

Thus it is difficult to find a number of bluesmen on solo albums—they have, instead, been widely anthologized. These include such important persons as: Texas

Alexander, Barbecue Bob, John Brim, Bumble Bee Slim, Butterbeans and Susie, Homesick James, Robert Nighthawk, Arthur Spires, and Robert Wilkins. To find recordings by these people, please consult the artists' index for an album reference.

Literature

Almost all aspects of the blues have been explored through numerous books and articles. Folk music survey books mention blues music at some point in their discussions (see the bibliography in the "grass roots" music volume). General blues surveys include Cook (19), Hughes (51), Jones (52), Leadbitter (56, anthology), Oliver (80, illustrated history), Stearns's (101a) jazz book, and Keil (53).

Materials concerning "roots" of black music in Africa can be found through Delerma's (22) edited proceedings, Jones's (52) tracings, Oliver's (79) thesis about Savannah origins in West Africa, Roberts's (90) detailed survey of black music in Africa and America, and Warren's (108) study of the music of Africa. Sociological works about black life are detailed in Dundes's (26) study of black folklore, and Courlander's (20) tracing of themes.

Other specialized descriptive materials on particular themes or specific regional variations are located at citations 2, 41, 54, 55, 57, 60, and 84. Many rock and soul books will cover urban blues, particularly Broven (20), Escott (28), Garland (36), Gillett (38), Groom (42), Guralnick (43), Hoare (47), Lydon (62, 62a), McCutcheon (63), and Shaw (99a, 100). Specific books about regions include Bastin (3) on East Coast blues, Broven (10) on the New Orleans jump blues, Ferris (32, 33) on the blues tradition in the Mississippi Delta, Olsson (81) on the Memphis area, Rowe (94) on the Chicago blues, Shaw (99a) on the jump blues.

Much biographical information that also contains musical analysis can be found in Charters's works (12, 13, 14), Evans's (29) biography of Tommy Johnson, Fahey's (31) discussion on Charley Patton, Garon's (37) story of Peetie Wheatstraw, Guralnick's (43) interviews, Jones's (52) historical tracings, Lydon's (62, 62a), interviews, Mitchell's (69) excursions through the Mississippi Delta, Oliver's (77) massive documentation of 68 singers, Ramsey's (87) rambling conversations, Rooney's (92) extensive work on Muddy Waters, Stewart-Baxter's (102) comments on Ma Rainey and the "classic" blues singers, Zur Heide's (113) study of Little Brother Montgomery and the piano tradition in the blues, and a few biographical entries of current country blues men in Stambler's (101) work.

Works of interpretation on the study of blues as a literary tradition include Bluestein's (6) comparative book, Charters's (14) explanation of words and poetry, Oliver's (76, 68) investigation of sexual imagery and life, Oster's (82) notes on poetry, and Pleasant's (85) study of vocal performing styles. A very good book on the blues harmonica has been written by Glover (39); other books on blues instruments and songbooks can be located through Sandberg (98). The interrelationships between black and white singers has been explored by Russell (96) for pre-World War II performers, while Groom (42) looks at the renewed interest in the "blues revival" of the early 1960s. Gillett's (38) study of Atlantic Records and Escott's (28) work on Sun Records do admirable jobs in detailing "behind the scenes" stories, while Dixon's (25) monograph traces recording the blues from the beginning in 1902 to 1945.

The basic books for discographic data about blues records are Godrich and Dixon (40) for the 1902-1942 period, and Leadbitter and Slaven (58) for the

1943-1966 period. While neither is absolutely complete or accurate, errors and omissions are noted in continuing columns in *Storyville* and *Blues Unlimited* magazines respectively. Some jump blues can be found listed under artist in the various volumes of Jepsen (51a). Two of the best "race records" series in the 1920s and early 1930s were Columbia and Paramount; Mahoney (64) provides a listing in numerical matrix order for the former while Vreede (107) lists the latter. Merriam's (67) classic work gives an annotated discography of African music on albums. Sandberg (98) presents his choices for country blues. Nearly every book has a list or reference to "recommended recordings."

There are only two international magazines in English that are concerned exclusively with blues music and records. *Blues Unlimited* (3), about 15 years old now, is the leading one from England, concerned with documenting all aspects of the blues, even the minor obscure personages. *Living Blues* (14), from Chicago, prefers to concentrate on "living" bluesmen in America today. Peripheral material can be found in black music publications such as *Black Music* (1) or *Blues and Soul* (2), both concerned with all interests of blacks (soul, reggae, jazz, blues, gospel, ethnic, etc.). There are occasional articles on the blues in jazz magazines, particularly record reviews. *Cadence* (4) will also have an interview or two; reviews are in *Coda* (6), *Downbeat* (9), and *Jazz Journal* (12). From a folk music point of view, *Sing Out!* (19) gives coverage of song texts plus the occasional article; the *Journal of American Folklore* (13) will give texts and comments (plus record reviews) from a folklorist point of view; the *Quarterly* of the John Edwards Memorial Foundation used to deal extensively with country blues until other magazines began coverage (an occasional article will still be found here). Of the general magazines, *Guitar Player* (10) is noted for its instructional columns and diagrams, and *Melody Maker* (15) always devotes a full page to stories, record reviews and photographs. Articles in all of the above magazines are indexed in *Popular Music Periodicals Index* (86).

ANTHOLOGIES

Roots Anthologies

This short section is, of course, not exhaustive. Many more records and variations could have been cited; but, because this is an annotated listing of *popular* music, only a few examples have been chosen from commercial companies. Many, many more field recordings can be found on several European labels that deal with ethnomusicology: Bärenreiter, Vogue, the Unesco series, plus others on Folkways. The prime purpose here is merely to show some of the antecedents of blues music, and by extension, all of black music and jazz. The best single disc that explores most aspects in a superficial way (along with comparisons generated by commercial blues records) is *Savannah Syncopators* (B1.4).

B1.1   **African and Afro-American Drums.** two discs. Ethnic Folkways FE 4502.

B1.2   **Negro Folk Music of Africa and América.** two discs. Ethnic Folkways FE 4500.

These two very sound compilations were collated by noted scholar Harold Courlander, who also furnished the essays. However, in both collections, Africa is represented only by West Africa's Yoruba and Ibo areas (mostly Nigeria). The North American items on the first set include some examples of jazz drumming by Baby Dodds and a children's street band that was recorded in New York City. The second set has 24 tracks, but covers a wider area in the Americas. In addition to unaccompanied songs from the United States, there are also examples of a Juba dance from Haiti and a Shango cult song from Trinidad.

B1.3   **Roots of Black Music in America.** two discs. Folkways FA 2694.

Subtitled "some correspondences between the music of the slave areas of West Africa and the music of the United States and the Caribbean," this admirable collection of 41 items was compiled and edited by the astute Sam Charters. What is unusual is that Charters had once stated that he didn't feel competent in this area, as he was a white man. The first three sides concentrate on instruments (such as drums, banjo, harp, xylophone) and the human voice, collated from sources including Nigeria, Bahamas, Ghana, Liberia, Jamaica, Senegal, Mexico, New Orleans, and New York. Side Four is mainly American, with gospel, blues, New Orleans brass bands, and Bahamaian dances. The listener is asked to judge for himself, and this is as it should be, for Charters has attempted a great deal in such a short stretch. The emphasis is definitely more on blues and dixie than on jazz (following the feelings of the late Richard Waterman). A different point of view is expressed by Paul Oliver, a better scholar than Charters, in his book and record *Savannah Syncopators* (CBS 52799, U.K. Import) which, while concerned with blues only, shifts the roots from coastal West Africa to the inland plains.

B1.4   **Savannah Syncopators: African Retentions in the Blues.** CBS 52799. (British import).

In the controversy over African roots for the blues, two distinct sides appear. The late Richard Waterman advocated that the blues were shaped by the coastal plains of West Africa. Paul Oliver makes an equally valid point for the roots coming from the interior savannahs or rain forests. He produced a book by the same title in 1970 to substantiate his claim, and this disc is the accompanying record. The book was released in America, but the record was not. The sixteen tracks here are almost equally divided between African and American styles. The two alternate so that field recordings by Oliver can be heard next to commercial productions from the twenties and thirties. Blues are represented by Peetie Wheatstraw, Blind Darby, Robert Johnson, Bongo Joe on steel drums in San Antonio, Texas, Lonnie Coleman's banjo (right after an example of the halam five-string chordophone from Senegal), plus others. African instrumentation included drum and bell orchestra, flutes, rattles, two string lutes such as garaya, various gourds, iron clappers and xylophones. This is a very interesting documentary production, and it should be ranked with the various sets by Oster and Charters in the educational collection. Paul Oliver provides summary notes from his book (but leaves the outright comparisons to that effort for want of space), and the sound is clear. Full discographical data is provided even for the field recordings.

General Anthologies

The general anthology serves many purposes, not the least of which is to introduce the subject to a non-specialist. Several types are listed here, not all of which need be purchased by libraries. One is the *festival*, as exemplified by both the (fixed-location) Newport festival and the American Blues Festival that annually tours Europe. Here there is excellent rapport with the audience and unusually good sound. The festival also served the purpose of introducing many blues rediscoveries of the 1960s. Another general anthology is the material prepared by a recording company from its own vaults. This can allow the specialist to trace the development of that company's history, showing the types of blues recorded and perhaps why. The MCA and CBS catalogs are especially rich in this matter, although the CBS sets have been put together with more intelligence. RCA, the other leading major company, has not yet put together a retrospective, beyond two albums, preferring to release integral sets on its Bluebird series.

B1.5   **Blues at Newport, 1963.** Vanguard VSD 79145.

B1.6   **Blues at Newport, 1964.** v.1/2. two discs. Vanguard VSD 79180/1.

B1.7   **Newport Blues, 1965.** Vanguard VSD 79219.
The blues *concert* is perhaps the best of all possible milieu for the blues musician. He is allowed to interact with the audience and give them what they want in a more spontaneous fashion than on a recording. These Vanguard releases all came from a three-year period at the Newport Folk Festival, 1963-1965, and clearly show a wide variety of influences and styles. Appearing in 1963 were Mississippi John Hurt, the Rev. Gary Davis, John Lee Hooker, and Sonny Terry and Brownie McGhee. The peak of the folk blues revival was surely in 1964, as this is a two disc offering. On one record, there are representative performances from Fred McDowell, Sleepy John Estes, and Robert Pete Williams. On the other, Hurt reappears, as well as Skip James, the Rev. Robert Wilkins, Elizabeth Cotton, and Willie Doss. The 1965 recording finds Son House, Hurt again, Skip James, Ed Young, Mance Lipscomb, and Lightnin' Hopkins. Many of these performers were rediscoveries, and the Newport appearances were their first major public concerts. Vanguard also has available the two-record set *Great Bluesmen: Newport* (Vanguard VSD 77/8), which has all of its tracks lifted from the above albums plus others from 1959.

B1.8   **Blues Box 1, 1934-1940.** four discs. MCA Coral PCOX 7526/1-4.
(German issue).

B1.9   **Blues Box 2, 1938-1934.** four discs. MCA Coral PCOX 7758/1-4.
(German issue).
For PCOX 7526, collator Robert Hertwig has assembled 64 of the priceless pre-war blues put out by American Decca and Champion. Many are completely new to albums, and a few have never been issued before. All tracks have been taken from the original masters, with excellent transferring, which leads to three hours of superb sound. Most blues reissues have concentrated on the 1920s (or 1950s). But since Decca didn't come into existence until 1934, and since

they recorded blues material, it has seemed logical that someday the blues of the 1930s would be explored. That moment is at hand, since this set came out at the beginning of 1976. The emphasis in the previous decade had been on traditional lyrics and a powerful driving guitar style. In the middle thirties, these elements were making way for more composed lyrics and more emphasis placed on vocal than on instrumental prowess. This accurately models the development of country and folk music—using up the traditional items first before moving on to unique compositions. More than half of the performers here come from St. Louis, and the dominant instrumental accompaniment (definitely subservient to vocals) is that of the guitar/piano duet. Highlights are too numerous to mention, but excellent performances come from Blind Boy Fuller, Blind Willie McTell, Black Ace, Oscar Woods, Walter Davis, Lonnie Johnson, Cow Cow Davenport, and such outstanding women as Alice Moore and Mary Johnson. The second set, released in 1977, has 64 tracks.

B1.10   **Blues Rediscoveries.** RBF 11 (distr. by Folkways).
     This record adequately documents the blues phenomena of the 1960s: rediscovery of country blues singers who last performed in the early thirties (a thirty year time gap here). These are not fresh recordings, but reissues of the better blues that were once performed by those rediscovered singers. If an influential singer like Charlie Patton or Peetie Wheatstraw had died in the meanwhile, well, too bad: they are not on this disc because they were not alive to be rediscovered, obviously. Heard among the 14 tracks are Mississippi John Hurt's "Avalon Blues," Bukka White's "Aberdeen, Mississippi Blues," Sleepy John Estes's "Liquor Stores Blues," the Rev. Gary Davis's "Oh Lord, Search My Heart," Furry Lewis's "Jelly Roll," and Joe Williams's "Highway 49." Since being rediscovered, half of the eight bluesmen had died, proving that Folkways was just in time. There are no discographic sources, but there are good notes by Sam Charters, and the lyrics are reproduced. This is an excellent sampler for the beginner interested in blues.

B1.11*   **The Country Blues.** v.1/2. two discs. RBF RF and 9.

B1.12   **Country Blues Encores, 1927-1935.** Origin Jazz Library OJL 8.

B1.13   **Really: The Country Blues, 1927-1933.** Origin Jazz Library OJL 2.
     The 28 selections of the RBF anthologies (all with superb notes, texts and illustrations furnished by Samuel Charters) are probably the most comprehensive and important of all the anthologies dealing with rural bluesmen. Significant tracks include "Matchbox Blues" (Blind Lemon Jefferson), "Stealin', Stealin' " (Memphis Jug Band), "Careless Love" (Lonnie Johnson), "Walk Right In" (Cannon's Jug Stompers), "Statesboro Blues" (Blind Willie McTell), and "Key to the Highway" (Big Bill Broonzy). Other singers represented here include Peg Leg Howell, Charlie Pickett, Sleepy John Estes, Robert Johnson, and so forth. The Origin Jazz Library series is probably just as good (no duplications here), with "Cool Drink of Water Blues" (Tommy Johnson), "I'm So Glad" (Skip James), and "My Black Mama" (Son House). The 28 selections feature a few performers who are not well-known but are representative of the country styles around the nation. No notes are on the Origin records, but all the lyrics are given.

B1.14*   **Country Blues Classics.** v.1/4. four discs. Blues Classics. BC 5, 6, 7, 14.

Of all the anthologies of country blues, this set can be used the most. It is constantly quoted as a source for illustrative matter dealing with regional styles. Some of the 62 tracks were the first of a series of imitations, or radical departures, such as Elmore James's first recording (and first success) of "Dust My Broom," based on the Robert Johnson epic. Other selections include Joe Williams's "I'm Getting Wild about Her," Bobo Jenkins's "Democrat Blues," Scrapper Blackwell's "Ramblin' Blues," Blind Boy Fuller's "Rag Mama Rag" (which had a tremendous upsurge in the 1960s folk revival period), an early Johnny Shines' recording of "Ramblin'," Casey Bill's "WPA Blues," Harmonica Frank's "Tom Cat Blues," Memphis Minnie's "Bumble Bee Blues," and James McCain's "Good Mr. Roosevelt."

B1.15*   **The Great Bluesmen.** two discs. Vanguard VSD 25/26.

This is a very good sampler from the Vanguard catalog, which includes a wealth of material. First, it owns the rights to the *Spirituals to Swing*, Carnegie Hall concerts from the late thirties, and from there are Sonny Terry, Ida Cox, Bill Broonzy, Joe Turner, and Pete Johnson on those occasions. Second, Vanguard recorded many Newport Festivals and thus there are John Lee Hooker, Sleepy John Estes, Jesse Fuller, Rev. Gary Davis, Robert Pete Williams, and Brownie McGhee. Third, Vanguard recorded rediscoveries of country bluesmen, such as Skip James and Mississippi John Hurt. Fourth, with Sam Charters, Vanguard recorded much in the way of Chicago blues, with Junior Wells, Buddy Guy, Homesick James, Otis Spann, James Cotton, and Otis Rush. And fifth, Vanguard made three excellent recordings (1954-1957) with Jimmy Rushing. Representative tracks from all of them are on these discs in some form.

B1.16   **Nothing but the Blues.** two discs. CBS 66278 (British issue).

B1.17*   **The Story of the Blues.** v.1/2. four discs. Columbia G 30008 and CBS 66232 (v.2 is a British issue).

All six discs were issued as records accompanying books. *Nothing but the Blues* (Hanover Books) was a series of reprinted articles plus new material from *Blues Unlimited*, the leading British blues periodical. Issued under the auspices of the now defunct Blue Horizon record company, the discs were meant to illustrate the book. There are also rare photographs on the jacket covers. This is mainly a post-war collection, from 1954 through 1969. The 24 tracks include field recordings (such as by J. B. Lenoir) and rare efforts by Otis Spann, Elmore James, John Brim, and so forth. Sources included Chicago, Los Angeles, and the Louisiana area (the latter through Excello records). The *Story of the Blues* illustrates the Paul Oliver book of the same title (Allen Lane). There are 64 tracks, covering 1924 through 1968. Oliver also wrote new liner notes for these sets.

The arrangement of the two sets varies, although there are no duplications. One way—on volume one—is arrangement by area. There is a side for the origin of the blues, with Mississippi John Hurt's "Stack O'Lee Blues," Blind Willie McTell's "Travellin' Blues," and Texas Alexander's "Broken Yo-Yo." The second side is for blues as entertainment (Bertha Hill's "Pratt City Blues"). The third side covers the 1930s (both country and urban blues), with Peetie Wheatstraw's "Good Whiskey Blues," and side four is all post-war material, such as Johnny Shines's "I Don't

Know." Volume two places emphasis on the little-known, obscure figures of the blues, and its four-part division is guitar pickers (Curley Weaver, J. B. Lenoir), piano players (Alex Moore, Bumble Bee Slim), blues girls (Big Maybelle, Martha Copeland), and blues groups (Otis Rush, John Littlejohn). These six discs are some of the better anthologies in the blues.

B1.18   **Out Came the Blues.** v.1/2. two discs. MCA Decca DL 4434 and Ace of
          Hearts AH 158 (the latter, a British issue).

B1.19   **"The Blues" and All That Jazz.** v.1: 1937-1947. MCA Decca DL 9230.
          (v.2 never released).
     These three discs present a cross-section of the Decca blues recording output. As the company was not founded until 1934, it had no blues items from before this period. While it was late in moving into this market, Decca existed at a time when there was very little other recording of blues. Many companies were simply shutting down or shifting emphasis; thus, Decca was virtually alone. The 44 titles here are simply a hodge-podge, with no real theme linking them. Thus, there is the jazz-influenced Cousin Joe with the Sammy Price trio in "Beggin' Woman" from 1947, Kokomo Arnold's "Wild Water Blues" (1937), Memphis Minnie's "Chickasaw Train Blues" (1934), Big Joe Turner, Rosetta Howard, Lonnie Johnson, Trixie Smith, et al.—reflecting the country blues, the folk blues, the urban blues, the "classic" singers, the jazz singers, etc. The third album listed is a bit more coherent, with the background accompaniment being small jazz groups. This had the unusual effect of placing all the female singers on side one and the males on side two, simply because male blues singers used solo accompaniment until the studios decided on a larger backing. This resulted in the ludicrous Peetie Wheatstraw cuts "Jaybird Blues" and "Pocket Knife Blues," with 1940 accompaniment by Jonah Jones's trumpet, piano, and drums. But the overall importance of these sets is to demonstrate that the blues did not die in the 1930s as many writers have conjectured.

B1.20*   **Recording the Blues.** CBS 52797 (British issue).
     This album illustrates the book *Recording the Blues* (London, Studio Vista), and presents key recordings that determined the future of blues records. Established stars and their first recordings include Blind Lemon Jefferson's "Rabbit Foot Blues," Alex Moore's "Blue Boomer Blues," the Mississippi Sheiks' "Loose Like That," and so forth. The sixteen tracks show a wide geographic area of recording, from New York, Chicago, Dallas, Atlanta, San Antonio, New Orleans, and Jackson, Mississippi. Of note, too, is one of the first gospel records, from 1926: Rev. J. M. Gates in Atlanta. Previous to this, many sermons had been recorded, but not singing. So successful was this particular record that soon every race series sprouted gospel items. The Tampa Red item began a whole series of hokum, ribald music, while still others introduced an urbane style that led to the city blues. This is an important historical document of some of the best recorded blues in particular styles.

B1.21   **Rural Blues. v.1: Goin' up the Country; v.2: Saturday Night Function;
          v.3: Down Home Stomp.** three discs. Imperial LM 94000, 94001, 94006.
     These forty-two tracks come mainly from the Aladdin and Imperial catalog, and were mostly recorded from 1946 through 1953, some a little later. Most of the singers had shown up on the West Coast, or were residents there; thus, these

are migration pieces that focus on the shift from a rural to an urban environment after World War II. Most of the recordings on volume two were cut in Louisiana and reflect the party atmosphere of Saturday night dances. As time progresses, the amplification becomes heavier and the music more diverse to catch a declining market. Among the performers are Snooks Eaglin, Lightnin' Hopkins, Clifton Chenier, Slim Harpo, Papa Lightfoot, Roosevelt Sykes, Lowell Fulsom, and Little Son Jackson. With tunes such as "Take It Easy," "Disgusted," "West Coast Blues," "Paper in My Shoes," and "Sad Letter Blues," this three-disc set shows the panorama of blues influences in the immediate post-war period as they cut a swath through Mississippi, Louisiana, Texas, and on to the West Coast.

B1.22*   The Rural Blues: A Study of the Vocal and Instrumental Resources.
          two discs. Folkways RBF 202.
     The beginning blues collector could not wish for anything better than this set. The forty-three selections were compiled and edited by Sam Charters, with the usual erudite notes, discographies, and texts. There is mostly one bluesman per tune, so everybody of some importance gets a chance to sing. Included are representative tracks by Robert Johnson, Furry Lewis, Sleepy John Estes, Blind Boy Fuller, Arthur Crudup, Kokomo Arnold, Blind Willie McTell, Bukka White, John Hurt, Skip James, et al. Surprisingly, there is no Charlie Patton—a major defect in the set. These seminal recordings have variable sound for the most part, but they are excellent examples of regional performance characteristics—from the days before radio and then television broke down stylistic regionalism.

Field Recordings

     Field trip reports can be illuminating, although they tend to be documentary and historical. In the 1930s, the Library of Congress (through its Archive of Folk Song) sponsored a series of trips to Southern states and to certain urban ghettos to record black and white folk musicians, both amateur and semi-professional. John A. Lomax was in charge, and later his son Alan took over. The LC field trips ceased in the 1940s. While a few of the thousands of recordings have been published, most are accessible only by personal visit to the Library of Congress. The quality of the discs are rather poor, as they were cut "on location."
     In the 1950s, the tape recorder took over and produced reasonably good sound quality. Frederick Ramsey, Jr., made five trips for Folkways Records between 1951 and 1957, covering Alabama, Louisiana, and Mississippi. At the same time, Harold Courlander made a number of excursions. Sam Charters has traveled extensively for the past 20 years collecting New Orleans Jazz and rural blues, some of which are on the RBF label. Harry Oster discovered Robert Pete Williams at the Angola Farm, the same place Lomax found Leadbelly. Alan Lomax found Fred McDowell in 1959, and by the start of the 1960s, collectors and researchers from France and England were well on their way to setting songs on tapes. Paul Oliver has made numerous visits, not just to the United States but also to West Africa. In 1960, he found Alex Moore in Texas. Interest had now grown with the reissues of early race records, and subsequent field trips now usually took one of two forms: the purpose of rediscovery for white exposure or the purpose of research and documentation. Sometimes the motive was a mixture of the two.

Field trips produce relaxed sessions with no commercial overtones. The sound is, of course, not usually up to studio standards, but many personal recollections have been recorded and transcribed. It has been difficult for an interviewer to break down suspicions on the part of the "discovered" person, but once this is accomplished, the words flow freely. Too often, bluesmen who had recorded in the past were ripped off by record producers, so they didn't want to repeat the nasty experience. Fortunately, their reminiscences sometimes also would lead to the rediscovery of other singers. At the same time, however, a lot of old bluesmen's personal accounts would be exaggerated through the hazy clouds of time, or would be slanted to put themselves into a better light, especially if they were bitter about something. Both exaggerations and mention of names would work at cross-purposes sometimes.

B1.23   **Afro-American Blues and Game Songs.** Library of Congress AAFS L4.

B1.24   **Afro-American Spirituals, Work Songs, and Ballads.** Library of Congress AAFS L3.

B1.25   **Negro Blues and Hollers.** Library of Congress AAFS L59.

B1.26   **Negro Work Songs and Calls.** Library of Congress AAFS L8.
These four discs from the Library of Congress barely tap the enormous resources of the entire collection, some 16,000 plus recordings. Saydisc in England has been reissuing a few of the selections, while librarian-researcher Richard Spottswood works his way through the American Archive of Folk Songs to put it in shape for the post-Bicentennial years. As field recordings go, the wide range generously covers all types of blues music. Unfortunately, even by the late 1930s and early 1940s (when the bulk of such recording was done by Alan and John Lomax), the disc cutting units were exceptionally primitive, and there is much "low-fi" sound. The only excuse is lack of government funding, for Victor and Okeh (two commercial firms) were using better field recording equipment a decade before!

L4 was put together and edited by Alan Lomax, who also wrote the descriptive booklet. The 25 tracks cover hollers from Parchman Penitentiary, diverse blues from Alabama ("Boll Weevil Blues") and Texas ("Two White Horses"), a guitar rag, and harmonica solos (the latter by Sonny Terry). Twelve songs of children's music, games, lullabies, and ring games complete the set. L3 takes its material (17 tracks) from various state farms, and it includes "Handwriting on the Walls," "Long John," and "Look Down that Long, Lonesome Road." It too was edited by Alan Lomax, who wrote the notes. L59 (edited with notes by Marshall Stearns)comes from 1941-1942, and it is probably one of the most famous of the LC records. All of it is from Mississippi and Arkansas, with Son House, David Edwards, and William Brown (plus two hollers and two gospel items among its 12 tracks). L8 is composed of 18 rhythmic tracks collated by B. A. Botkin (who also wrote the notes). Some are hollers; others are lining track songs for working on the railroad. Although euphemistically titled "work" songs, a more realistic name would be "prison" or "chain gang." Here is where Leadbelly found inspiration for his song materials.

B1.27 **Boot That Thing.** Flyright Matchbox SDM 258 (British issue).

B1.28 **Fort Valley Blues.** Flyright Matchbox SDM 250 (British issue).

B1.29 **Mississippi River Blues.** Flyright Matchbox SDM 230 (British issue).

B1.30 **Out in the Cold Again.** Flyright Matchbox SDM 257 (British issue).
 The Library of Congress collection of blues field recordings contains a great
deal more material than are available on long-playing records through the Library
itself (see the above annotation). It has taken the initiative and resources of a
British blues reissue record company, associated with *Blues Unlimited*, to put
out a series of LC recordings. This series is still in progress, but by 1977, the above
four discs had been released. The same notes as above hold true for these discs,
although the sound for these is better than the LC albums. All four discs exhibit
a wide range of styles, generally with 18 or so tracks apiece, utilizing all sorts of
instruments found in the blues spectrum (guitar, harmonica, a cappella vocals,
etc.) in different configurations of trios or duos. There are extensive photographs
and notes. SDM 257 and 258, released together, are interesting. Both come from
Florida in June of 1935. Blues scholars of the Piedmont style and Louisiana
variances (John Cowley and Bruce Bastin) collated and annotated the set. SDM
257 features guitar duets and solos, with vocals, from Rochelle French and Gabriel
Brown, among others. Titles include "John Henry," "Casey Jones," "Sail On,"
and the topical "Education Blues." SDM 258 is more limited, with two harmonicas
and a guitar from Booker T. Sappa, Roger Mathews, and Willy Flowers. Titles
include "The Weeping Worry Blues" and "Levee Camp Holler." This series is in
progress.

B1.31 **Conversations with the Blues.** Decca LK 4664.
 Paul Oliver made these 1960 field recordings in conjunction with writing
his book of the same name. But unlike other such recordings, there are many
extracts here of personal reminiscences that consist of just talking—no music.
And many of the performers are well-known, and even operate in the urban blues
mode: John Lee Hooker, J. B. Lenoir, Otis Spann, Lightnin' Hopkins, Roosevelt
Sykes, Little Brother Montgomery, and others. This, then, is not a "typical" field
recording session with simple guitar and rural people. The entire texts are reproduced, of both the songs and the narratives. In the main, all of the material is autobiographical, showing how these particular bluesmen were influenced and how they
became involved with the blues and blues recording.

B1.32 **Murderers' Home/Blues in the Mississippi Night.** two discs. Vogue
   VJD 515 (French issue).
 This is a classic reissue of two of the most famous blues documentary albums
of all time, recorded by Alan Lomax in the 1930s. The "Murderers' Home" was the
Mississippi State Penitentiary at Parchman, and all of the recordings on this first
album were by black prisoners. They sing with passionate "soul" in the truest sense,
but they also sing with great accomplishment, and it's hard to believe they were all
amateurs in the singing business. The second album here comprises talk and discussion between Lomax and three blues performers, identified as "Leroy" who
plays piano (in reality, Memphis Slim); "Natchez" who plays guitar (in reality,

Big Bill Broonzy), and "Sib" who plays harmonica (in reality, Sonny Boy Williamson, No. 1). Some of the album notes are the originals from over a decade ago, and while they are comprehensive, no clues were given at that time as to the identity of these three singers.

Ribald Blues

Sexual imagery abounds in the blues, and many reissue companies have seen fit to distribute albums around that theme. The seven albums noted below do an excellent job of introducing the subject to the specialist.

B1-33*   **Copulatin' Blues.** Stash 101.

B1.34*   **Party Blues.** Melodeon MLP 7324.

B1.35   **Risky Blues.** King 1133.

B1.36*   **Screening the Blues.** CBS 63288 (British issue).
Blues music, of course, abounds with the "dirty dozens"—allusions and images with such sexual innuendos as "buns" and "wieners," "cream," "thing," and so forth. These four anthologies do a marvelous job of briefly surveying the scene, although the King set is not as good as the CBS. From the King roster of bluesmen (Champion Jack Dupree, Roy Brown, Wynonie Harris, etc.) come modern, uptempo versions of post-war material entitled (are you ready?): "Big Ten Inch Record," "It Ain't the Meat," "Sixty Minute Man," and "Something's Wrong with My Loving Machine." The CBS set includes Bumble Bee Slim, Memphis Minnie, Robert Johnson and Clara Smith. Its 16 tracks explore religion and sex, and also introduce the concept of white covers or emasculated music. As an example, there are two versions of Lucille Bogan (Bessie Jackson) singing "Shave 'Em Dry"—one very tame and the other very raunchy. Butterbeans and Susie were most effective at this type of music, and here is a track "Papa Ain't No Santa Claus (Mama Ain't No Christmas Tree)." This record accompanies and illustrates Paul Oliver's book *Aspects of the Blues Traditions* (the British title was *Screening the Blues*). The Melodeon set draws on a number of catalogues and includes such raunchy items as Blind Lemon Jefferson's "Bed Spring Blues," Tampa Red's "It's Tight Like That," Red Nelson's "Mother Fuyer," and Blind Blake's "Diddie Wa Diddie." The liner notes come complete with full lyrics—you cannot mistake anything. The Stash disc presents 16 jazz and blues efforts from 1931-1940, and includes Sidney Bechet ("Preachin' Blues"), Lil Johnson ("Stavin' Chain," "Press My Button," and "You Stole My Cherry") and Jelly Roll Morton's pornographic "Winin' Boy."

B1.37   **Hokum Boys. Can't Get Enough of That Stuff.** Yazoo. L 1051.

B1.38   **Let's Go Riding.** Origin Jazz Library OJL 18.

B1.39*   **Please Warm My Weiner.** Yazoo L 1043.
Ribald blues, when mixed with good time music, becomes what is known as "hokum"—a strange area of dance songs, sexual innuendoes, blues music, and good

fun. The best exponents were undoubtedly Georgia Tom Dorsey (see item B1.162) and Tampa Red (see item B1.242-244), and together they were known as the Hokum Boys. Here they perform 14 selections, out of the many they recorded, including the title track, "I Was Afraid of That [Parts 1 and 2]," "Gambler's Blues," and "Pat-a-Foot Blues." The "Weiner" anthology exploits hokum to the full, with Dorsey on several cuts, Butterbeans and Susie (the most risqué of all the blues singers, with "Elevator Papa, Switchboard Mama"), Memphis Minnie, Bo Carter, Papa Charlie Jackson ("You Put It In, I'll Take It Out"). This is a good judicious selection of the lighter side of the blues, but perhaps only fully appreciated by those who already love and understand the blues mainstream. A clearer indication of the roots can be found in the Origin set. The humorous variety of hokum actually predated "city" blues, yet it *was* urban based, and related directly to vaudeville and the "dirty dozens." Ragtime roots are indicated here with rag guitar, and jazz similarities crop up, for early jazz men exploited the good time elements in their dancing traditions. The emphasis on this recording appears to be one of cultural terms and folk history. David Evans provides very good notes, distinguishing among the different forms, and there are lyrics presented for such songs as Pink Anderson's "Gonna Tip Out Tonight," or Sylvester Weaver's "I'm Busy and You Can't Come In."

Instrumental Character

Blues music is, of course, more than just a vocal expression. Some bluesmen have become dextrous enough to be virtuosi of their instruments. The anthologies noted below show off many good forms of bottleneck or slide guitar, the ragtime guitar of the Piedmont, and the single noting of the Texas and West Coast area. The piano was influential as well, deriving its character from the saloon environment as pianos were not found in every home and were hardly portable. Thumping barrelhouse styles of the 1920s led to the slick urbane styles of Leroy Carr in the 1930s, which is demonstrated on the following discs. Other instruments not commonly employed in country, pre-World War II blues are also included here. The violin was not used much outside of jug bands, but it had a flavor all of its own and varied tremendously from the character of white "old time" music. The harmonica was also a weak instrument until Sonny Boy Williamson, No. 1, showed how to use it properly to derive all the blues notes from blowing in and out. But he appeared rather late on the country scene, and is often judged a transitional figure in the late 1930s move toward modern, urban blues. The harmonica would later assume greater magnitude with Sonny Boy Williamson, No. 2, and Little Walter, both playing in the "Chicago" mold.

B1.40*   **Country Blues Bottleneck Guitar Classics, 1926-1937.** Yazoo L 1026.

B1.41*   **Guitar Wizards, 1926-1935.** Yazoo L 1016.

B1.42   **The Voice of the Blues: Bottleneck Guitar Masterpieces.** Yazoo L 1046.

Since most of the blues are performed on guitar, it seems a little ridiculous to have guitar anthologies. Yet these three discs succeed in presenting both bottleneck stylings and guitar picking. The former occurs largely in the Delta, and appears to be derived from various Hawaiian guitarists who toured the area around 1900—twenty-five years before recordings began on an extensive basis. While the originators played the guitar flat on their laps with a steel bar, the expediency of the situation meant that the bluesman would supplement holding the guitar in his arms with a knife, or "bottleneck," broken from a bottle. This would be played in the same sliding motion. The 28 tracks here illustrate "nifty" styles of playing, not all from the Delta area. The "Wizards" set is largely from the East Coast, where finger picking predominated. Most players were fluent, rapid, versatile, and accurate. Some improvised; others played fixed rags. There is a tremendous contrast here between the slide and the picking, and Yazoo has succeeded in presenting good examples.

B1.43*   **Barrelhouse Blues, 1927-1936.** Yazoo 1028.

B1.44   **Blues Piano: Chicago Plus.** Atlantic SD 7227.

B1.45   **Blues Piano Orgy.** Delmark 626.

B1.46   **Piano Blues.** RF RBF 12.

B1.47   **Piano Blues.** v.1/2. two discs. Storyville 671.168 and 671.187 (Danish issue).

B1.48   **Rugged Piano Classics, 1927-1939.** Origin Jazz Library OJL 15.
    Blues piano works have fallen into a number of categories: if solo with no vocals, they tend to be lumped in jazz; if fast with a boogie woogie tempo, then they fall into that category. So successful were pianists in the blues idom that they succeeded in making great recordings; hence, most of the piano blues are found under individual names. Indeed, only three discs satisfactorily compile documentary information on the stylings of blues piano: the Origin, the Yazoo, and the RF set. They clearly show that the piano blues were harmonically more sophisticated than guitar blues. Pianists made use of many techniques, such as tone clusters, two (or more) simultaneous harmonies, and other devices to "bend" notes. Chording was virtually unknown without *some* runs. Many influences stemmed from ragtime and the jazz piano and, of course, not all pianists owned their own instrument. Rather, they had to rely on what could be found in the various bars and recording studios. The liner notes on all three discs go rather deeply into explaining piano blues, with musical examples. Selections include works by Montana Taylor, Little Brother Montgomery, Cow Cow Davenport, Will Ezell, Walter Roland, Walter Davis, Roosevelt Sykes, and Cripple Clarence Lofton, as well as many obscure performers. Some of these pianists were better known as guitarists, while some others could play guitar adequately. The Delmark selection is eclectic, and it includes some material that they own but never issued before (as is the case with the Storyville items). The oldest works are from 1947, and feature Little Brother Montgomery in a jazz session. Speckled Red, Curtis Jones, Sunnyland Slim, Roosevelt Sykes and Otis Spann complete the personnel. The Atlantic effort is mainly 1951-1954, largely unissued, and featuring Little Johnny Jones (with Elmore James on guitar), Floyd Dixon in sophisticated

interpretations, some jazz solos from Little Brother Montgomery, and a Meade
Lux Lewis 1951 "Riff Boogie." The Storyville collection is from the early 1960s,
and it features Champion Jack Dupree (in Leroy Carr's "Sunrise Serenade"),
Speckled Red, Henry Brown, Roosevelt Sykes, Memphis Slim, Otis Spann, and
Sunnyland Slim.

B1.49   **Favorite Country Blues Guitar-Piano Duets, 1929-1937.** Yazoo
         L 1015.

B1.50   **Uptown Blues: A Decade of Guitar-Piano Duets, 1927-1937.** Yazoo
         L 1042.
         Guitar-piano duets were widespread throughout the nation, and they often
demanded discipline in following and in leading, as well as singing. Such a person
as Scrapper Blackwell was well-known for his guitar accompaniment to Leroy Carr.
Naturally, the piano figured large with the advent of urban blues, providing a foil
to the amplified guitar. Guitar accompaniment had to be fluid and finger-picked,
rather than strummed, so that the notes could be heard. Involvement included
complicated musical dialogues between pianist and guitarist at the levels of both
instruments and vocalizing. Quite often, the pianist would chord behind the
guitarist. As recording techniques improved, it was possible to have the sound
from both instruments recorded equally well. Pianists here include Charlie Spand,
Leroy Carr, Roosevelt Sykes, Springback James, Joe Evans, Walter Davis, and
Cripple Clarence Lofton. Guitarists include Willie Harris, Clifford Gibson, Blind
Blake, Big Bill Broonzy, Scrapper Blackwell, and Bo Carter.

B1.51   **The Country Fiddlers.** Roots RL 316 (Austrian issue).

B1.52   **The Great Harmonica Players.** v.1/2. two discs. Roots RL 320/1
         (Austrian issue).
         Surprisingly, neither the harmonica nor the violin were used much in pre-war
recordings of blues music. The violin is still not used, while the harp has become
the pre-eminent instrument solely because of Sonny Boy Williamson, No. 1, and
his influence. Who were the fiddlers? They were mostly men from jug and string
bands performing their brand of hokum and good time music, such as the
Mississippi Sheiks, the Mobile Strugglers, the State Street Boys, or Jack Kelly's
Jug Band. There was little differentiation in style since the violin was taken intact
from white sources. Harmonicas are a different thing, though. They were imported
into the United States by the hundreds of thousands; yet, few appeared on record
because it was felt that the harmonica was a cheap instrument, and who would pay
75 cents for a recording of that instrument? It proliferated on street corners, and
surprisingly, many performers never really bothered to explore its worth (tonguing,
bent notes, amplification, etc.). The 32 tracks here are for historical purposes,
since the material and performers are merely average workers in the blues idiom.
The first volume goes from 1925 through 1929, the second from 1929-1940. It is
at this time, near the start of World War II, that harp playing got better, and there
are a few tracks here by Sonny Terry ("Harmonica and Washboard Breakdown") and
Sonny Boy Williamson, No. 1 ("Tough Luck").

Topical Blues

Topical works are exceptionally rare in the blues genre because the bluesman has enough to worry about without considering the problems of others. However, he does get affected enough, when prodded, to comment on many events and tragedies. These are quite rightly "topical" songs rather than protest, for the black bluesman very rarely protests except in an oblique way. To protest would lead to much more trouble.

B1.53   **Can't Keep From Crying.** Testament S 01.

B1.54   **Hard Times.** Rounder 4007.
Topical blues are rare in this genre for the simple reason that the blues have long been an introspective music. Thus, protest music simply does not exist as such; and sometimes when it did, it was crushed (J. B. Lenoir's critical "Eisenhower Blues" was withdrawn at the last minute at the request of White House; Big Bill Broonzy often got into trouble for singing "Black, Brown and White"). The music on these two sterling collections are more in the topical variety, and if they appear to be of the protesting type, then that is one of "resignation blues." The Rounder anthology is a reissue of mostly pre-war material about the Depression and the lot of the working man. It is one of the few thematic anthologies in blues reissue programs, and its success may elicit more such compilations. Bluesmen include Barbecue Bob, Lonnie Johnson, Texas Alexander, Pinetop Smith, and Smokey Hogg. Testament's theme is the subtitle: "topical blues on the death of President Kennedy." These 11 songs are noted for their depth of feeling, especially Big Joe Williams's "A Man Amongst Men" and Otis Spann's "A Sad Day in Texas." Other titles are indicative: "I Want to Know Why," "A Man for the Nation," "Why Did He Have To Go?," and "He Was Loved by All the People." While topical music and event songs have always been a small part of the blues (e.g., Bessie Smith's "Backwater Blues" and other blues reflecting the tragedies of the 1927 Mississippi floods), they simply have not been collated onto long-playing records for thematic or conceptual purposes.

B1.55*   **Prison Work Songs.** Arhoolie 1021.
This is an absolutely indispensable record for the blues, folk, or social commentary collection. Previously available as Folklyric A-S and recorded by noted folklorist Dr. Harry Oster, these songs are absolutely revealing of prison life up to about 1959. As the notes point out, "today most of the time the prisoners toil in sullen silence." The work-cum-prison song has, then, probably been irretrievably lost. The scene is Angola Prison (Louisiana), where Leadbelly and Robert Pete Williams served time and developed their rich mastery of blues interpretation. The songs accompany such various activities as wood cutting, clothes scrubbing, cane cutting, track lining, plowing, gravel shovelling, and so forth—all in time to the motion. Very, very important.

RURAL, ACOUSTIC BLUES

Regional Anthologies

There are two types of anthologies here: those recordings indicative of a style, and those recordings produced in one region but not necessarily part of the style. Styles covered herein are Detroit, East Coast, Memphis, Mississippi, St. Louis, Texas (pre-War and post-War), and West Coast. Many books and articles have been written on the different regional variations of the blues, particularly before the advent of radio and phonographs, which tended to break down those regional patterns. For a generalization, though, it is safe to say that bottleneck slide predominated in the Delta, ragtime syncopation was played in the Piedmont, and single note phrasing developed in Texas.

B1.56   **Blues Sounds of the Hastings Street Era.** Fortune 3012.

B1.57   **Detroit Blues.** Kent KST 9006.

B1.58*   **Detroit Blues: The Early 1950s.** Blues Classics BC 12.
     Although blues went largely unrecorded in the 1930s and 1940s, Detroit exhibits many characteristics of Chicago: on Lake Michigan, a pull from the rural farms, good employment, clubs, and so forth. Yet the form of the blues diverged from the Chicago quartet or quintet to the soloist in Detroit, and often to an acoustic one! No real explanation has emerged unless it is somehow related to the ups and downs of the automotive industry, or the lack of funds available to producers in Detroit. These three albums, all post-war, are very satisfying but rich in content. Maybe it is just as well that recordings *were* limited; thus, the cream becomes easily available. The Fortune label recorded quite a few singers, such as Dr. Ross, Big Maceo (later in his life), John Lee Hooker, Grace Brim, Bobo Jenkins, and Eddie Kirkland (who often played second guitar to Hooker). All here are from the early fifties (and this includes both the Kent and the Blues Classics as well). Kent (from the Modern/RPM/Flair catalogs) has Hooker, Kirkland, Eddie Burns, and Sylvester Cotton. The Blues Classics (with strong notes by Paul Oliver), is the only anthology not drawing on just one label. Thus, all of the Detroit classics are here: Dr. Ross's "Thirty Two Twenty," Bobo Jenkins's "Ten Below Zero," the Detroit Count's marvelous story on "Hastings Street Opera [parts one and two]," the emotional "I Need $100" from One String Sam, and Hooker's "House Rent Boogie." Most of the stylings were rural, and the greatest Detroit player (Hooker) himself came from Mississippi.

B1.59   **Alabama Blues, 1927-1931.** Yazoo L 1006.

B1.60   **Alabama Country, 1927-1931.** Origin Jazz Library OJL 14.

B1.61   **Alabama Country Blues, 1924-1933.** Roots RL 325 (Austrian issue).
     Very few recordings were issued in the Alabama area, and when they were, they came from the 1920s for the most part. This state exhibited typical "East Coast" sound, but there were few guitarists. Instead, pianists and gospel groups abounded. Of note from the area were Clifford Gibson, Edward Thompson, and

Marshall Owens, and the mysterious "Barefoot Bill." The 44 tracks here also include some material by the Birmingham Jug Band.

B1.62   **Blues from Georgia, 1926-1931.** Roots RL 309 (Austrian issue).

B1.63*   **Blues Roots: The Atlanta Blues.** RBF RF 15.

B1.64   **The Georgia Blues, 1927-1933.** Yazoo L 1012.
     The Georgia blues are fairly well-documented, and probably form the bulk of "East Coast" reissue programs. Much field recording activity occurred in Georgia, notably in Atlanta, where it seems that almost every singer was armed with a twelve-string guitar. Performers on the RBF include Barbecue Bob, Blind Willie McTell, Peg Leg Howell, Buddy Moss, and Lonnie Coleman, among others. All types of expression abounded; however, the attitude was definitely more light-hearted than in Mississippi. Some of the same performers show up on the Yazoo compilation, and others are used to illustrate the idiosyncratic nature of the music and the dexterity of the left hand. The Roots series concentrates on just four performers: Barbecue Bob, Charlie Lincoln, Blind Willie McTell, and Peg Leg Howell—all as leading proponents of Georgia stylings.

B1.65*   **East Coast Blues, 1926-1935.** Yazoo L 1013.

B1.66   **East Coast States, 1924-1940.** v.1/2. two discs. Roots RL 318/326 (Austrian issue).

B1.67   **Mama Let Me Lay It on You, 1926-1930.** Yazoo L 1040.

B1.68   **Piedmont Blues.** Flyright LP 104 (British issue).
     The East Coast takes in the Carolinas, Georgia, and Virginia. Some people might extend it to all of the Piedmont (Florida) and even Alabama. Most of the efforts are light-hearted, almost like a medicine show, and they incorporate many aspects of ragtime. The smooth and fluid flow here is absent from the Delta area. The Yazoo 1013 features eight different singers, including Blind Blake and Carl Martin. The Roots double set includes Buddy Moss, Blind Boy Fuller ("Crooked Woman Blues"), Kokomo Arnold, Luke Jordan, and Sylvester Weaver. Yazoo 1040 continues with Josh White, Smith and Harper, Walter Coleman, plus others. The Flyright disc is more from the Carolinas, with Josh White, Curley Weaver, and Brownie McGhee.

B1.69   **The Blues in Memphis, 1927-1939.** Origin Jazz Library OJL 21.

B1.70   **Frank Stokes' Dream: The Memphis Blues, 1927-1931.** Yazoo L 1008.

B1.71   **Kings of Memphis Town, 1927-1930.** Roots RL 333 (Austrian issue).

B1.72   **Low Down Memphis Barrelhouse Blues, 1928-1935.** Mamlish 3803.

B1.73   **The Memphis Area, 1927-1932.** Roots RL 307 (Austrian issue).

B1.74   **Memphis Blues, 1927-1939.** v.1/2. two discs. Roots RL 323 and 329 (Austrian issue).

B1.75   **Memphis Jamboree, 1927-1936.** Yazoo L 1021.

B1.76*   **Ten Years in Memphis, 1927-1937.** Yazoo L 1002.
     Memphis was a distinct centre for bluesmen. It was at the top of the Delta; it was a gateway to the north; it developed several recording studios for northern recording companies; it was a wide open town for vices and sinning. The surrounding area of Arkansas, Tennessee, and the Delta contributed many singers who migrated. In fact, most of Memphis's bluesmen were not novices (as was the situation with the West Coast blues). Most of the music was excellent, and the variety of styles leads one to the conclusion that there was no such thing as a "Memphis sound" or style. It simply existed as a place where performers were cheaply recorded. Scattered throughout these nine albums are good representative stylings, from the fun and raunchy character of the Mamlish (Memphis Minnie, Will Shade, Jim Jackson) through the standard blues on Yazoo 1002 (Furry Lewis, Frank Stokes, Tom Dickson, Robert Wilkins). Along the way, there are Gus Cannon's Jug Stompers, Sleepy John Estes, Yank Rachel, Casey Bill Weldon, and diverse jug bands. Memphis was first the scene of jug bands, weird instruments (early harmonicas, spoons, etc.), jazz, r'n'b, and country through Sun Records and Stax, and then of soul, with Stax and Hi.

B1.77*   **Memphis and the Deltas: 1950s.** Blues Classics BC 15.

B1.78   **Memphis Blues.** Kent KST 9002.

B1.79   **River Town Blues.** Hi SHL 32063.
     Post-war Memphis was unsettled as the town was cleaned of sex and sin, migrants passed through to Detroit and Chicago, and (after 1954) rock and roll and then soul music predominated. The Arhoolie (Blues Classics) collection contributes some insights into the activities of the Mississippi Delta during the early 1950s, with selections by Harmonica Frank, Willie Love, Roosevelt Sykes, Forest City Joe and others. Several artists appear on both the Arhoolie and the Kent: Joe Hill Louis and his one man band, for instance. More modern sounds emanate from the early beginnings of blues "stars" who moved elsewhere after finding success: Bobby Bland, Elmore James, James Cotton, Sunnyland Slim, Walter Horton, Howlin' Wolf, and Junior Parker. The Hi collection features three minor performers who stuck it out through the 1960s: Big Lucky, Big Amos, and Don Hines. They might have made more money had they gone into r'n'b, but they decided to stick with the blues.

B1.80   **Memphis Swamp Jam.** two discs. Blue Thumb BTS 6000X.
     Recorded in 1969 by Chris Strachwitz of Arhoolie (but released on the Blue Thumb label), this twofer shows the continuance of the rural tradition in the Memphis area blues. Emphasis continues to be on the Delta, with Booker White's "Columbus, Miss. Blues" and "Christmas Eve Blues," or the fife and drum of Napoleon Strickland and Other Turner, or the rag guitars of R. L. Watson and Josiah Jones, or the piano stylings of Piano Red's "Mobile Blues" and "Abel

Street Stomp." Different styles and diverse instrumentation predominate. Additional material is supplied by Sleepy John Estes, Furry Lewis, Nathan Beauregard, and a surprisingly transposed Fred McDowell.

B1.81*   **Blues Roots: Mississippi.** RBF RF 14.

B1.82   **Jackson Blues, 1928-1938.** Yazoo L 1007.

B1.83*   **Lonesome Road Blues: 15 Years in the Mississippi Delta.** Yazoo L 1038.

B1.84*   **Mississippi Blues, 1927-1941.** Yazoo L 1001.

B1.85   **Mississippi Blues, 1926-1937.** v.1/3. three discs. Origin Jazz Library OJL 5, 11, 17.

B1.86   **Mississippi Blues, 1927-1941.** v.1/3. three discs. Roots RL 302, 303, 314. (Austrian issue).

B1.87   **Mississippi Blues, 1952.** Kent KST 9009.

B1.88   **Mississippi Delta Blues.** v.1/2. two discs. Arhoolie 1041/2.

B1.89*   **Mississippi Moaners, 1927-1942.** Yazoo L 1009.

These 14 records adequately describe the tremendous impact of the Mississippi Delta style on the blues. Coverage is wide, both in time and in individual performances. For instance, there is Charlie Patton, once that state's most popular singer, with crude and rough versions of "Hang It on the Wall" or "Mean Black Moan." On the other hand, there is the suave Robert Johnson with such as "Dead Shrimp Blues" or "Drunken Hearted Man." In between are such renowned performers as Cryin' Sam Collins ("Signifying Blues"), Robert Wilkins ("Rolling Stone [parts one and two]"), Skip James ("Cypress Grove Blues"), Son House ("Jinx Blues"), and others—Bukka White, Ishman Bracey, Mississippi John Hurt, Bo Carter and the Mississippi Sheiks, and Tommy McClennan. The Yazoo 1038 provides a good survey of Depression blues (12 of the 14 tracks here are from post-1930) with Big Joe Williams and Robert Lockwood, among others. This disc clearly shows the breaking up of the intense Delta style as the years passed, revealing varied techniques, lyrics, and topics. The bottleneck—or slide—wail, coupled with intense moans and gut feelings, was being dragged into a more sophisticated sound, aided by infiltration from other regions. Yet, the Delta area was the last to achieve some homogenization because there were few radios and visits by other singers. During the 1940s and 1950s, "jook joints" (drinking bars with a juke box) developed. To provide a continuous stream of music, recordings were needed, and these were often furnished from Memphis, at the head of the Delta.

Occasionally, field trips would still be made, and one of these resulted in the Kent disc above. All those selections are from 1952, and feature an amplified, updated style. Particularly geared to the emerging rhythm 'n' blues and jook markets. They are all from Clarksdale, and feature Ike Turner (then a Modern Records talent scout) on piano in a quartet format. Lead performances are from Boyd Gilmore, Houston Boines, and Charlie Booker—four tracks apiece. This is an interesting slice of modern Mississippi; unfortunately, it was not to last because of the emergence of Sun records in Memphis within a year and the subsequent lack of local recording activity.

With the advent of the long-playing record, with the emergence of the folk blues scholar and the folk revival, and with some collectors and fans demanding more records, it was relatively easy to venture into Mississippi and do field recordings that became issued exclusively on albums. This helped to establish whatever remnants were left of the original, country style. Some of the results can be heard on the double Arhoolie set, which was meant to supplement George Mitchell's book *Blow My Blues Away* (Louisiana State University Pr., 1971). Mitchell did the recordings in the late 1960s, and there are some very interesting interpretations by R. L. Burnside, Joe Calicott, Furry Lewis, Fred McDowell, Houston Stackhouse, and the wonderful Rosa Lee Hill ("Pork and Beans"). Good notes on the styles and on individual selections by Mitchell.

The Yazoo 1007 collection turns further southward than the Delta—to the central and southern areas, notably around Jackson, Mississippi. This was the home base of Tommy Johnson, and all of the selections here show his influence: Ishman Bracey's "Trouble Hearted Blues" and "Pay Me No Mind Blues," Willie Harris's "Never Drive a Stranger from Your Door," Walter Vincent's "Overtime Blues," and others (including Johnson). Blues activity peaked in Mississippi with the advent of the Great Depression, but the styles continued into the thirties and forties, being carried by Lofton, Skip James, Little Brother Montgomery, Tommy McClellan, and Arthur "Big Boy" Crudup—showing a line from the raw primitivism of country blues to the raw primitivism of rock 'n' roll.

B1.90   **The Blues in St. Louis, 1929-1937.** Origin Jazz Library OJL 20.

B1.91   **Good Time Blues: St. Louis, 1926-1932.** Mamlish S 3805.

B1.92   **Hard Time Blues, St. Louis, 1933-1940.** Mamlish S 3805.

B1.93   **St. Louis Blues, 1929-1935: The Depression.** Yazoo L 1030.

B1.94*   **St. Louis Town, 1927-1932.** Yazoo L 1003.
  The country blues developed some of its most slick brilliance and innovation in St. Louis, perhaps because of its influence as a jazz centre. Despite the laid back style, accompaniment is ingenious: timing and phrasing are important, sometimes wandering beyond the 12 bar format. The Mississippi rhythms are augmented by the exposure to jazz, and the immediate result of this is some dexterity with the left-hand previously neglected. Many artists living and performing around St. Louis were equally proficient on both guitar and piano, so duos sometimes emerged. The Origin set of 14 tracks is subtitled "All the Great Guitar and Piano Styles of the City where the Blues Changed Stride," with examples from Kokomo Arnold, Peetie Wheatstraw, Henry Townsend, and Walter Davis. The Mamlish sets supplement these with Lonnie Johnson's "Love Story Blues," "Hi" Henry Brown, Lee Green (who influenced Roosevelt Sykes) and J. D. Short. The effects of the Depression are clearly shown on S 3806. The Yazoo introduces Charlie Jordan, Teddy Darby, and others.

B1.95   **Buddy Boy Hawkins and His Buddies.** Yazoo L 1010.

B1.96   **Tex-Arkana-Louisiana Country.** Yazoo L 1004.

B1.97*   **Texas Blues.** Paltram PL 102 (Austrian issue).

B1.98   **Texas Country Music.** v.1/3. three discs. Roots RL 312, 315, 327
            (Austrian issue).

    The Texas area produced more singers and influences on blues than any other
region than the Mississippi Delta. There are more styles, such as a higher pitch of
singing and less rhythm, than the Delta, a quicker tempo, more idiosyncratic pacing,
and heavier jazz influence as the years passed. Progression was greater as Texas
bluesmen travelled, assimilated, returned home, and taught others. Radio made an
impact, which it did not in Mississippi. The two Yazoos are essentially country
blues featuring Hawkins, Will Day, "Funny Paper" Smith, Little Hat Jones, and
Six Cylinder Smith through the years 1927-1934. The Paltram is more extensive
(1928 through 1952) and includes the makers of the Texas style: Henry Thomas,
Blind Lemon Jefferson, Black Ace, Texas Alexander (accompanied by Lonnie
Johnson or Eddie Lang), Oscar Woods, and Smokey Hogg. The most comprehensive survey, covering the same years as the Yazoo, is on the Roots triple set. In
addition to performances by artists already named, there are Ramblin' Thomas,
Blind Willie Johnson, the Dallas String Band (for jug music), Leadbelly, Alex
Moore, and Jesse "Babyface" Thomas—in all, 48 tracks with full discographic
information.

B1.99   **Texas Blues.** v.1/2. two discs. Arhoolie R2006 and 1017.

B1.100   **Texas Blues.** Kent KST 9005.

B1.101*   **Texas Blues—The Early '50s.** Blues Classics BC 16.

    Documentation on Texas Blues is difficult, primarily because so much of
what is there came out on lots of small labels that proliferated when the bigger
companies ignored that state. Only the big names of Blind Lemon Jefferson,
Texas Alexander, and Lightnin' Hopkins have been recorded in their home
regions. Texas country blues even migrated to the West Coast and formed part of
the scene at Oakland and Los Angeles, developing into rhythm 'n' blues. The Kent
reissue covers 1948-1953. Smokey Hogg is here, along with piano blues by Charlie
Bradix and Alex Moore. The record is made worthwhile by the three Jesse Thomas
selections. He had last recorded in Dallas in 1929 for Victor (on Roots RL 327
or Yazoo L 1038), and his style comes very close to that of Mississippi John Hurt—
deep tone, sentimental, good folk background. Li'l Son Jackson and Lowell Fulson
complete the set.

    The Blues Classics disc has 8 performers, including Texas Alexander's last
record, "Crossroads." Smokey Hogg's best record ("Penitentiary Blues") is here,
and he strings out this prison work song by adding new lyrics. Other selections
include Mercy Dee, Lightnin' Hopkins, and Buddy Chiles. Exemplary notes by
Paul Oliver.

    The first volume of the Arhoolie set documents 14 tracks from the Gold
Star label, located in Houston, from 1948-1951. In addition to performers

mentioned above, there are also Thunder Smith (half of the Thunder 'n' Lightnin' team, the other being Hopkins) and L. C. Williams. The second Arhoolie is a collection of new material from various singers on the Arhoolie label: Mance Lipscomb, Mercy Dee Walton, Alex Moore, Black Ace, and Robert Shaw (including some mentioned above).

B1.102   **Blues from the Western States, 1927-1949.** Yazoo L 1032.

B1.103   **California Blues.** Kent KST 9003.

B1.104*   **Oakland Blues.** Arhoolie 2008.

B1.105   **Oakland Blues.** World Pacific WPS 21893.

B1.106   **West Coast Blues.** Kent KST 9012.
     The strongest influence on the blues of the West Coast comes from Texas. These blues are a post-war, urban phenomenon that was created by the thousands of migrants that moved west during the industrial heyday of post-war California. With electric amplification and the ills of city living, there was a drastic shift in performing styles, also augmented by the slick r'n'b styles of the West Coast (notably in Los Angeles). For these reasons, the "truest" of the blues are still to be found in the Oakland region, as exemplified by the two discs of that name; also, blues are still recorded in the Oakland area. The Arhoolie set reissues several from the late forties and early fifties, including Johnny Fuller, Jimmy Wilson, Juke Boy Bonner, K. C. Douglas and L. C. Robinson. The latter reappears on the World Pacific issue with an entire side. The Yazoo anthology is largely Texas and Oklahoma, but it shows the directions that West Coast blues was assuming. The two Kents come from the Modern/RPM/Flair collection of labels, based in Los Angeles and run by the Bihari brothers. They recorded extensively, particularly in the Memphis area, under various leasing arrangements. But the material here is strictly their own efforts. The most "California" of the lot is Pee Wee Crayton. His "Blues After Hours" became a monster hit. Roy Hawkins's "The Thrill Is Gone" was the original version of that title, and this piano player still lives in Los Angeles. The bulk of the remaining material features Johnny "Guitar" Watson, James Reed, Johnny Fuller, and Saunders King; and they were mostly recorded by Bob Geddins in Oakland (who also recorded the material on the Arhoolie set).

Innovators

    These 10 bluesmen were the key performers who shaped, influenced, and extended the blues genre. It is back to them that all of blues music must flow. Leroy Carr virtually created the slick, urban blues stylings for a sophisticated audience—and he did it from the Midwest (Indianapolis). Robert Johnson brought stinging slide guitar rhythms and a poetry of feeling to the blues. Blind Lemon Jefferson fused the Texas patterns with powerful guitar picking in the single note style. Tommy Johnson's progressions and timings on guitar extended the classic Delta guitar form of playing. Leadbelly, not usually thought of as being a blues-man, projected the thundering 12 string guitar in Texas fashion; additionally, he

created a strong corpus of material for white singers to lead the way through Josh
White, Bill Broonzy, Sonny Terry, and Brownie McGhee to the typical bluesman.
Fred McDowell developed a very strong bottleneck style and strongly influenced
the emerging white blues performers. Blind Willie McTell had a vibrant, powerful
voice and a strong 12 string guitar that helped to shape the Piedmont blues.
Charley Patton is the epitome of the Mississippi Delta blues singer, influencing
Bukka White, Son House, Robert Johnson, and Muddy Waters. Robert Pete
Williams is the modern improviser of the country blues, seeking personal themes
and minor keys—he is totally original. Sonny Boy Williamson, No. 1, was an
important transitional figure in the development of the "Chicago blues" and was
the most influential of all harmonica players. All of the records annotated in
this section are "first buys" for the definitive blues collection.

B1.107*   **Leroy Carr. Blues before Sunrise.** Columbia C 30496.

B1.108*   **Leroy Carr. Naptown Blues, 1929-1934.** Yazoo L 1036.

B1.109   **Leroy Carr. Singin' the Blues, 1934.** Biograph C 9.
    Carr was probably one of the most important bluesmen in history. Both he
and Blackwell helped to create the urban blues of the philosophical vocal, pointed
against a rolling piano and an astringent guitar. Every blues piano player has been
influenced by Carr. In sequence, then, the Yazoo disc comes first. The popularity
of some of these titles, such as the title selection or "How about Me?" probably
opened the doors to other city pianists, such as Roosevelt Sykes and Charlie
Spand. Initially, Carr's material was autobiographical, as in "Carried Water for
the Elephant"; however, as time passed, he tended to concentrate on songs of
strong lyrical qualities, within the realm of poetry, such as "How Long Blues,"
"Midnight Hour Blues," "Blues before Sunrise," and especially about women. The
12 selections on the Biograph come from his last Vocalion session (December 14
and 17, 1934). Half had never been issued before, but all of it was first-rate; so,
we must assume that the economics of the Depression did not allow pressing
everything, rather than assume that the material was not considered good.

B1.110*   **Robert Johnson. Complete.** three discs. Columbia [not yet released
           April 1978].
    Johnson was *the* major blues guitarist and composer. Apparently, he succeeded
in influencing just about everybody in the blues today (Muddy Waters, Elmore
James, Johnny Shines, Otis Spann, and various white British performers such as
Eric Clapton, John Mayall, and the Rolling Stones). He, in turn, was influenced
by several wide sources, such as Son House, Kokomo Arnold, and Leroy Carr. Thus,
he must be seen as a distiller of blues music, the one locus or focal point where all
blues music comes to a head: everything passed through Robert Johnson. An aura
of mystery has developed, for he was quite young when murdered, roamed around
the country (and even into Canada) while many of his contemporaries stayed at
home, and, according to dubious accounts, met and performed with every bluesman
of the 1930s. He is noted for his musical sombreness and anguish, plus deep
emotional intensity. His walking bass and bottleneck style has been copied widely.
This set includes all thirty titles from five sessions in 1936-1937 (recorded at San
Antonio, Texas), plus a variety of alternate tracks (which clearly show his deliberate

style, as most of these outtakes are different from the master eventually released). His most important selections include: "Crossroads," "Ramblin' on My Mind," "I Believe I'll Dust My Broom" (later made electric by Elmore James), "Love in Vain" (covered by the Rolling Stones), "Phonograph Blues," the weird vocal on "Hellhound on My Trail," and the tremendous anthem "Sweet Home Chicago." The set is arranged chronologically, including the alternates, with superb annotations by Steve LeVere. There is a lyric sheet, a guide to song tunings, and a musical analysis and biography by LeVere, along with a previously unknown photograph (the only one known).

B1.111   **Blind Lemon Jefferson. v.1/2. 1926/29.** two discs. Biograph BLP 12000/15.

B1.112*   **Blind Lemon Jefferson, Volumes 1-3.** Roots RL 301, RL 306, RL 331.
    Blind Lemon Jefferson was among the greatest singers of the blues. His 100 sides were *very* influential with blues singers of the thirties and forties. In fact, one could say this about virtually all Texas bluesmen, including Texas Alexander, Huddie Ledbetter, and Lightnin' Hopkins. Jefferson was an excellent lyricist. His personal involvement, coupled with a sharp edge to his high singing voice, made him the prototype of the street singer tinged with sadness. Most modern interest, though, seems to lie with his guitar work. His melodic guitar runs and arpeggios were never decorative; they augmented his voice, and this is found quite often among blind bluesmen (like Blind Willie McTell). The guitar—or harmonica, in the case of Sonny Terry—was the friend of the blind man, something that he could talk with that could also answer. This also explains why most blind bluesmen either started out, continued, or finished their careers with gospel music (as Rev. Gary Davis did) for some form of companionship. In fact, Jefferson's first two records were as a religious singer under the name of Deacon L. J. Bates (these can be found on the Roots records).
    Jefferson retained several elements of religious singing, most notably in his prison moans and in his breakdowns. A wandering minstrel, Jefferson embraced all forms and absorbed all localisms into his music. Somewhere in his travels, he developed the rapid-picking style that was featured on his later recordings. But this reputation was established early in 1926 by "Got the Blues" and "Long Lonesome Blues." Of course, everybody knows about "One Kind Favor" (or its original title: "See That My Grave is Kept Clean") with that marvelous guitar break simulating the tolling of a church bell. This religious motif is a carry-over from his "religious" days. "'Lectric Chair Blues," part of his prison blues repertoire, is very morbid, and the symbolism in "Matchbox Blues" is one of his best. Every blues collection should have as much Jefferson as it can afford. Even allowing for duplications, here are 64 titles, two-thirds of his total output.

B1.113*   **Tommy Johnson/Ishman Bracey. Famous 1928 Session.** Roots RL 330 (Austrian issue).

B1.114   **The Legacy of Tommy Johnson.** Matchbox SDM 224 (British issue).
    Although Johnson recorded only a handful of tunes (eight tracks are on one side of the Roots reissue), he has been judged by some critics as being one of the most influential bluesmen from the Delta area. Paul Oliver claimed that Johnson's

progressions and timings were very important, and that they helped to shape the development of blues music for the next fifty years. This is quite evident from examining his first record, "Cool Drink of Water Blues," which reveals him as a deliberate singer, complete with hollering and falsettos. The important "Big Road Blues" employed one of the first examples of a walking bass pattern. The expressive "Canned Heat Blues" (one of Johnson's most memorable recordings) revealed the pains of Sterno drinking (and this was the reason for the rock-boogie group naming itself Canned Heat). The eight Bracey tracks are slightly less interesting, but Bracey was Johnson's number one disciple. His nasal whine appears on "Saturday Blues," "Leaving Town Blues," and "Four Day Blues." The *Legacy* anthology quite properly belongs here rather than distributed with the other compilations, for it is a thematic collection (rare in the blues long playing record field) of Johnson songs that he sang but never recorded. On this set, they are sung by his friends and relatives, such as Isaac Youngblood, Majer Johnson, Arzo Youngblood, Boogie Bill Webb, Houston Stackhouse, Babe Stovall, and Roosevelt Holts.

B1.115*   **Leadbelly. Last Sessions.** v.1/2. four discs. (2 boxes). Folkways FA 2941/42.

B1.116   **Leadbelly. Shout On.** Folkways FTS 31030.

B1.117   **Leadbelly. Take This Hammer.** Folkways FTS 31019.
    Huddie Ledbetter had an incredibly rich recording life, making items for ARC, RCA, and Capitol (among commercial outfits) and various taped sessions or concerts found on Folkways, Fantasy, Playboy and Elektra. The two boxed sets are from 1948, originally released in 1953, and represent four hours of music. They were edited by Frederic Ramsey, Jr. who also supplied the notes. Collectively, the 94 songs represent the bulk of Leadbelly's repertoire in gospel, children's music, reels and hollers, dance tunes, and breakdowns. It was unfortunate that his commercial recordings stressed a "folksy" singalong attitude, for, at heart, Leadbelly was a bluesman. The vitality lacking on the major labels is certainly to be found here, interspersed with bits of chatter, and it is known that he was satisfied with the recording results. Selections 1-34 were sung without instrumentation, but with his wife Martha joining on some choruses. There is a preponderance of shouts and hollers here, these being largely unaccompanied songs anyway. Many of the titles in these boxes he had never recorded before, and they were derived mostly from his early days. Could there be a foreshadowing of death, especially with the last number being "Leaving Blues"? In any event, this set rates right up there with the acclaimed LC recordings on Elektra 301/2.
    In the boxed set, Leadbelly refers to his radio work. The *Shout On* disc comes from this very work, a series of six broadcasts from WNYC-FM in New York (Sept.-Oct, 1948). Ramsey was only able to record 4 of these 15 minute programs, presenting 18 tracks divided into "Dance Tunes and Breakdowns," "Reels and Hollers," "Jail," and "Children"—all in the order presented on the air minus spoken commentaries. *Take This Hammer* is a repackaging of Folkways 2004 and 2014, one edited by Alan Lomax, the other by Ramsey. It is a long set, with 20 items, but it also has the clearest sound of all the records discussed here. The others are all subject to some form of hiss or fading. But their intrinsic worth is very

high, and while there are duplications in material listed here, Leadbelly never sang the same song in the same manner.

B1.118*   **Fred McDowell.** Everest Archive of Folk and Jazz FS 253.

B1.119*   **Fred McDowell.** v.2. Arhoolie F 1027.

B1.120*   **Fred McDowell. Delta Blues.** Arhoolie F1021.

B1.121   **Fred McDowell. "I Don't Play No Rock 'n' Roll."** Capitol T 409.

B1.122   **Fred McDowell. In London.** v.1. Transatlantic TRA 194 (British issue).

B1.123   **Fred McDowell. Long Way from Home.** Milestone 93003.
     McDowell, first discovered by Alan Lomax on a 1959 field trip, appeared on the Atlantic Heritage set. His strong bottleneck slide and bass notes set up a self-contained rhythm; his experiences are told to his guitar, which often substitutes for the vocal part (in total opposition to B. B. King, for example). Broken lines and individual expressions are hallmarks of his work. Through the Arhoolie records he reached a wide audience, which cumulated with "You Got to Move," later covered by the Rolling Stones. Surprisingly, his strongest influence has been on Bonnie Raitt, but almost all newer bottleneck performers of the sixties have fallen under his spell. The Arhoolie material is a little derivative, with his later recordings being more original. His "commercial" recording on Capitol serves as a good introduction to his music, and contains some spirituals (as do almost all his albums). The Milestone complements a similar effort with Big Joe Williams—that of producing influences in the Delta blues—and here, McDowell tackles traditional items such as "Milk Cow Blues" and "John Henry." The Everest is a live recording (actually released in England as v.2 of the Transatlantic concert), and both sets show the affinity for audiences that McDowell had.

B1.124*   **Blind Willie McTell, 1927-1935.** Yazoo L 1037.

B1.125*   **Blind Willie McTell. Atlanta Twelve String.** Atlantic SD 7224.

B1.126*   **Blind Willie McTell. The Early Years, 1927-1933.** Yazoo L 1005.

B1.127*   **Blind Willie McTell. The Legendary Library of Congress Session, 1940.** Melodeon MLP 7323.

B1.128   **Blind Willie McTell/Memphis Minnie. Love Changin' Blues, 1949.** Biograph 12035.
     McTell was essentially a street singer in Atlanta; he was recorded extensively over a thirty year period, with much emphasis on his twelve string guitar. This instrument was exceptionally powerful, and his voice was vibrant and forceful. His repertoire included spirituals such as "I Got to Cross the River Jordan," "Amazing Grace," "Old Time Religion"; instrumentals such as rags; "classic" items that have influenced many singers, such as "Statesboro Blues" or "Dark Night Blues" (most of these were of the dark character, such as "Death Cell Blues"

or "Broke Down Engine"); and sexual images, such as "Southern Can Is Mine" and "It's a Good Little Thing." The LC session shows the variety of his material, and there is also some talking and autobiographical recounting on this set. The Biograph material is derived from 1949, as is the largely unissued Atlantic set. This latter is mostly a gospel session, but together, both records capture McTell at his finest. Later recordings were generally poor because of his deteriorating health. Over his lifetime, McTell employed many pseudonyms in recording, such as Pig and Whistle Red, Barrelhouse Sammy, Georgia Bill, and Blind Willie.

B1.129*   **Charley Patton. Founder of the Delta Blues.** two discs. Yazoo L 1020.
   Patton is the epitome of the Mississippi Delta blues singer. His influence extended over Bukka White, Son House, and others. With a predominantly rough voice full of multi-textured emotional patterns that seem to give no quarter, his vocals set the pattern for many years to come. His varied guitar work was exceptionally simple, but he employed the common devices of strumming, rhythm, and bottleneck as well. Material included personal experiences, such as "High Water Everywhere [parts 1 & 2]" and "High Sheriff Blues" (both heard on this 28 track compilation), dance tunes, ballads, and, of course, the sexual imagery in the blues. Spirituals were in his repertoire (he was the son of a preacher), and these may be heard on the Origin OJL 12 gospel set (*In the Spirit*) described at B3.13. Although recognition came late to Patton (he died in 1934), his life and spirit lived on in the continuation of the Mississippi Delta blues pattern. The accompanying notes clearly show his deep personal involvement in that music. These notes, compiled by the "Yazoo" team of collectors, are virtually unmatched for their musicological analysis of Patton's style, comments on the individual selections, and full lyrics. Other Patton items are found on Yazoo 1001, 1009, and 1020.

B1.129a*   **Robert Wilkins. Before the Reverence, 1928-1935.** Magpie PY 18000
         (British issue).
   Mississippian Wilkins spent most of his life in Memphis, which accounts for his easy relaxed style, based as it was on the prevalent musical mood of Memphis bluesmen. His finger-picking was exceptionally fluid, being influenced by Frank Stokes. His deceptively light voice followed the stylings of Memphis Minnie. The imaginative melodic blues tunes are complemented by the richly original lyrics that made him a master craftsman (e.g., "That's No Way to Get Along," "Nashville Stonewall Blues," or "Jim Canaan"). In 1935, he joined the church and turned his musical activities to gospel singing (see that section for an annotation of his music). This present disc collates 14 tracks, most of his pre-war secular output. All of these songs were already available scattered over a dozen anthologies, but, of course, any perspective of his career was lacking. Wilkins, although limited in his quantity of records, was one of the finest country bluesmen ever to record: "Rolling Stone," "Long Train Blues," "Falling Down Blues," "Police Sergeant Blues," etc.

B1.130   **Robert Pete Williams. Ahura Mazda** AMS 2002.

B1.131*   **Robert Pete Williams. Angola Prisoner's Blues.** Arhoolie 2011.

B1.132   **Robert Pete Williams. Louisiana Blues.** Takoma B 1011.

B1.133   **Robert Pete Williams. Sugar Farm.** Blues Beacon Roots SL 512
         (Austrian issue).

B1.134*   **Robert Pete Williams. Those Prison Blues.** Arhoolie 2015.

B1.135   **Robert Pete Williams/Snooks Eaglin. Rural Blues.** two discs. Fantasy
         24716.

Williams is probably the blues find of the 1960s. He is a totally original
creator of the blues, employing considerable use of minor keys and a modal
approach. He was discovered by Harry Oster at Angola, and the two Arhoolies
are reissues of the original Folk Lyric sets. On these records, one can hear much
improvisation, such as in "Prisoner's Talking Blues" or "Levee Camp Blues." His
life in prison is clearly told in "Pardon Denied Again." Both records have good
notes and lyrics. The Fantasy is a reissue of Williams's first commercial recordings
since leaving prison, again recorded by Harry Oster (in New Orleans) and originally
Bluesville 1026 (*Free Again*). The other three discs are more modern recordings
that show that Williams has managed to maintain the same intensity of personal
blues.

B1.136*   **Sonny Boy Williamson, No. 1.** v.1/3. three discs. Blues Classics BC
         3, 20, 24.

B1.137   **Sonny Boy Williamson, No. 1. Bluebird Blues.** RCA International
         INT 1088. (British issue).

B1.138   **Big Joe Williams and Sonny Boy Williamson.** Blues Classics 21.

B1.139   **Sonny Boy and His Pals.** Saydisc Matchbox SDR 169. (British issue).

John Lee Williamson ("Sonny Boy," No. 1) actually formulated modern
harmonica stylings. He was the most influential of all harp players, although
contemporary modernists have made the most impact in terms of audience appreciation. One of his techniques was alternating the harmonica with the vocal to
create one long melody. Also, he was often an accompanist, along with Bill
Broonzy, Big Joe Williams, and Washboard Sam. These men all created the
"Bluebird sound" of blues when they were virtually the house band for a decade
at RCA's Chicago studios. Williamson's role can be heard in the Saydisc anthology
reissue, where he plays with Walter Davis, Yank Rachel, Elijah Jones, and Joe
Williams. The 14 tracks on the Williams Blues Classics release show Williamson in
a very great supportive role. His speech impediment led to a very gutteral vocal
sound, which was very much imitated by later singers. The RCA reissue highlights
this, as the 16 tracks come from two 1938 sessions, one year after he began
recording. The Blues Classics skirts this period in its survey of 1937-1947, and
shows his development. His material had many themes and always something to
say, as in "Insurance Man Blues," "Win the War Blues," "Welfare Store Blues,"
or "My Black Name."

Standards

B1.140   **Kokomo Arnold.** Saydisc Matchbox SDR 163 (British issue).

B1.141   **Kokomo Arnold.** Blues Classics BC 4.

B1.142   **Kokomo Arnold. Bottleneck Trendsetters.** Yazoo L 1049.
     Kokomo Arnold has been scattered over several dozen anthologies and
compilations. Most of his work, as a cohesive whole, can be viewed from these
three discs, even though on the American labels he is present on only one side
of each disc (for a total of 15 tracks). Arnold went against regional stylings, for,
although he was born in Georgia, he utilized the Delta manner of a knife blade
for slide guitar and a harsh voice. At the same time, he was an excellent finger-
picker. His biggest successes were "Original Kokomo Blues" and "Milk Cow Blues"
(both for Decca and both after 1935). But unfortunately, quite a few of his other
records were spinoffs of these two themes. His other tough songs included "The
Twelves" and "Back on the Job." In 1938, after less than three years, he packed
it in and never recorded again.

B1.143   **Black Ace.** Arhoolie F 1003.
     Very few bluesmen played the flat Hawaiian guitar blues style. Oscar Woods
can be found on Decca DL 4344, and Kokomo Arnold (B1.140-142) is perhaps the
greatest exponent in the pre-war blues period. This Texas recording from 1960 is
important, then, for being the work of a singer that may never recur again. One
important aspect of B. K. Turner's (to give him his real name) songs is that he has
been totally uninfluenced by the musical changes that have occurred since the
1930s, when he began performing for station KFJZ in Fort Worth. His vocals can
be characterized as "haunting"; others may say weird, mystical, or just simply
"moaning." Material here includes titles that bear this out: "Bad Times Stomp,"
"Evil Woman," "Fore Day Creep," and "I Am the Black Ace."

B1.144   **Scrapper Blackwell. Virtuoso Guitar.** Yazoo L 1019.
     Blackwell has not done too well with the reissue companies, for he has been
overshadowed by his partner Leroy Carr (items B1.107-109). Besides this partnership, Blackwell made a few recordings in his own right, but most of these are
scattered on diverse anthologies. The exception listed above proves Blackwell's
work to be crisp and sensitive, following in the urban patterns laid down by
Johnson and Broonzy but without the hokum. His soft, melodic voice contrasted
with his stinging guitar (it was precisely this feeling that counter balanced Leroy
Carr's sweet voice), but after Carr died in 1935, Blackwell did not make many
recordings. Some of his earliest (1928) efforts are here such as "Penal Farm Blues"
and "Trouble Blues, [parts 1 & 2]." Good scholarly notes and instrumentation
analysis.

B1.145*   **Blind Blake.** v.1/5. five discs. Biograph BLP 12003, 12023, 12031,
     12037, and 12050.
     These discs present the most significant work of this prolific East Coast blues
singer. Although not all of the seventy plus songs here were recorded under his name,
at least he is on all of them in some capacity. Blake was born in Florida but worked

his way up through Georgia, arriving in Chicago in 1926 and recording for the Paramount company until 1932. He sold well for them, third only to Ma Rainey and Blind Lemon Jefferson. His style was diverse, embracing ragtime blues, hokum, country dance, vaudeville—anything he felt that he could perform, and not always on the guitar, as he also employed xylophone and rattlebones. He worked with clarinetist Johnny Dodds, and he often accompanied Leola Wilson and Bertha Henderson. His significant songs and contributions include "Rope Stretchin' Blues," "Fightin' the Jug," and "Too Tight Blues." His hokum "Diddie Wa Diddie," based on sexual imagery, was recently covered by Ry Cooder and Earl Hines.

B1.146*   **Juke Boy Bonner. I'm Going Back to the Country Where They Don't Burn the Buildings Down.** Arhoolie F 1036.

B1.147   **Juke Boy Bonner. The Struggle.** Arhoolie 1045.
    Bonner is one of the most poetic and grim figures in blues history. Coming up through the Depression and running around in most of Texas, he had developed a bitter style that was augmented by his failed marriage. During the late fifties, he recorded for Irma records (heard on *Oakland Blues*, Arhoolie 2008), but then returned to Texas. He was in a hospital in Houston for removal of 45 percent of his stomach when he heard the depressing news of Kennedy's assassination. During recovery, he wrote and had published most of his over-400 poems. Subsequently, he turned them into song lyrics. While his instrumentation is derivative (harp from Jimmy Reed, guitar from Lightnin' Hopkins), the accompaniment for his poems is basically all that is needed. Powerful music includes the title selection of Arhoolie 1036, "Life Is a Nightmare," "Stay Off Lyons Avenue" (subtitled "Blood Alley"), "Struggle Here in Houston," "Being Black and I'm Proud," and "I Got My Passport." These two discs are very good combinations of black music, the blues, and social commentaries.

B1.148   **Big Bill Broonzy.** Folkways FG 3586.

B1.149   **Big Bill Broonzy. Sings Folk Songs.** Folkways FA 2328.

B1.150   **Big Bill Broonzy. Sings Country Blues.** Folkways FTS 31005.

B1.151   **Big Bill Broonzy. Blues, with Sonny Terry and Brownie McGhee.** Folkways FS 3817.
    One of the masters of the folk blues was Big Bill Broonzy, although in his early career, he was deep into the urban blues. The folk side (the only way he could earn a living until blues were revived in the sixties) are on these Folkways and some Storyvilles, a Danish label. During his lifetime, Broonzy wrote over 360 songs and adapted hundreds of others. FG 3586 comes from his last session, where he poured out all that he knew about the blues. This was a marathon effort, much like Jimmy Rodgers's last session. Here are definitive, summarizing renditions of "Key to Highway," "Black, Brown and White," and finally, the last thing he did, the very sensitive "Joe Turner No One (Blues of 1890)," which expresses the tragedy of slavery. FA 2328 continues the feeling, but the items here are mostly adapted from a jazz context, such as Bessie Smith's "Backwater Blues," "Bill Bailey," and

"Alberta." The side one songs are from not long before his death; on side two, he is joined by Pete Seeger's banjo at a concert. The third album has remained the most popular of all Folkway's Broonzy records. Formerly FA 2326, and again from his last sessions, it presents the country sounds of "Louise, Louise," "Frankie and Johnny," "Trouble in Mind" and the bitter "I Wonder When I'll Be Called a Man!" Broonzy also suggested an idea to Studs Terkel (who has provided the notes and running commentaries for these Folkways): a program for blues on Chicago's WFMT. This last collection is from that show, built on improvisations and round robin singing of individual but common lines. Half of it is talking, and there are quite a few spirituals. It seems that the program was centered around women and religion, if the titles are any indication: "Willie Mae," "Daisy," "Crow Jane Blues," and so forth.

B1.152*   **Big Bill Broonzy. Big Bill's Blues.** CBS 52648 (British issue).

B1.153   **Big Bill Broonzy. Do That Guitar Rag.** Yazoo L 1035.

B1.154   **Big Bill Broonzy. 1930s Blues.** Biograph C 15.

B1.155*   **Big Bill Broonzy. Young Big Bill Broonzy.** Yazoo L 1011.
Big Bill reached his highest acclaim as a folk-blues artist in the 1950s, mostly through concerts and Folkways records (see above). As a blues artist, he had been recording since 1927, and he produced about 200 records during the 1930s, more in the forties, and sat in as a session man primarily responsible for the "Bluebird Beat." He brought with him an essentially urban style, with smooth flowing arpeggio work along the same lines as Lonnie Johnson. Yet, he was from Mississippi but not of the Delta style. Everything he did was exceptionally rhythmic and professional, with the high-caliber lyrics that led naturally into a Chicago style of playing (he accompanied mainly Chicago bluesmen). The 58 selections here reflect all of this. The Yazoo sets tell the story up through 1935, with a number of selections in the hokum vein, all tunes ending with the words "shuffle," "strut," or "stomp," and containing the important 1932 "Big Bill Blues" and "Mr. Conductor Man." The Biograph and CBS sets contain ARC and OKeh material, with a semi-jazz setting of trumpet, piano, drums, and occasional sax. Accompanists include Punch Miller, Joshua Altheimer, Blind John Davis, Memphis Slim, Washboard Sam, etc. Typical tunes included "I'm Gonna Move to the Outskirts of Town," "Southern Flood Blues," and "Night Time Is the Right Time." Other material can be heard on Sonny Boy Williamson, No. 1, Jazz Gillum, and Washboard Sam discs.

B1.156   **Bo Carter.** Yazoo L 1034.

B1.157   **Bo Carter. Greatest Hits.** Yazoo L 1014.
Bo Carter achieved success with the Mississippi Sheiks and also pursued a solo career. He was firmly in the hokum vein, and was heavily influenced by the white music of his time. The 28 tracks on these two records cover the 1930s up through 1940. Using a National steel body guitar to produce a heavier, greater volume sound, Carter sold many records at a time in the Depression when blues recording had dropped off very seriously. He sang the "party blues" that incorporated many double-entendres, and his original humor served him well in such tunes as "The Law

Gonna Step on You," "Howling Tom Cat Blues," "Twist It Baby," "Pussy Cat Blues," "The Ins and Outs of My Girl," and "Your Biscuits Are Big Enough for Me." Yet he could be bitter, as on "Sales Tax" or "Policy Blues."

B1.158   **Arthur "Big Boy" Crudup. The Father of Rock and Roll.** RCA LPV 573.

B1.159   **Arthur "Big Boy" Crudup. Mean Ole Frisco.** Trip BSP 7501.
Recording between 1941 and 1956 for RCA, Crudup was already middle-aged when he began, and his style was pretty well fixed by his first date. His high pitched voice, reminiscent of a field holler, did not exactly fit the Bluebird beat, but his recordings were consistent and highly stylized in a conventional format. As a routine bluesman, his sole claim to fame lay in the homage given him by one Elvis Presley, who appeared to be influenced by the riffing beat and lyrics, mostly uptempo, that Crudup produced—most notably on "Rock Me Mama" and "That's All Right" (the latter covered by Presley for Sun records). With the Sun policy of merging blues and country music into the so-called "rockabilly" mould, Crudup's music survived in that it fashioned the future of rock music. His renditions were a milepost in the history of popular music today. The sixteen tracks on the RCA compilation are representative of the more than 80 songs he recorded for that company. He had a brief resurgence in 1959 for Fire Records, and this disc has been reissued by Trip records. The 12 selections here include the title track, "Look on Yonder Wall," "Too Much Competition," and "Greyhound Bus."

B1.160   **Walter Davis.** Yazoo L 1025.

B1.161   **Walter Davis. Think You Need a Shot.** RCA International INT 1085 (British issue).
Davis arrived in St. Louis from Mississippi and formed the nucleus of the St. Louis blues style of piano playing. He made around 180 sides for Victor, almost all of them slow moving numbers with sparse piano accompaniment. His lyrics were his strong point. The seven selections on the Yazoo (which he shares with Cripple Clarence Lofton) range from 1935 to 1940. They show a heavy note-by-note progression with a bass line syncopation, as in "Can't See Your Face" and "Call Your Name." The sixteen tracks on the RCA extend from 1930 (the historic "M & O Blues" with Roosevelt Sykes) through 1941 ("Just Want to Talk Awhile"). Double-entendre music prevailed, with the title selection, "Let Me in Your Saddle" and "The Stuff You Sell Ain't No Good." He has been widely anthologized in St. Louis collections and piano anthologies (Yazoo 1015, Mamlish 3800, and Origin OJL 20).

B1.162*   **Georgia Tom Dorsey. Come On Mama, Do That Dance, 1928-1932.** Yazoo L 1041.
Another innovator of city blues, Dorsey had a wide background before moving to Chicago. He had played with Ma Rainey and other singers. In partnership with Tampa Red (see items B1.242-44), he led the way with hokum music and dance tunes (e.g., "Tight Like That," "Hip Shakin' Strut," and "Beedle Um Bum"). Much of his work was an accompanist to other singers in this same genre, but he was a prolific composer and lyricist as well. With the Hokum Boys (first, Tampa Red,

than Big Bill Broonzy), he created much good time music. Most of this material is scattered on many anthologies, including *Rare Blues, v. 1* (Historical 1) and *Please Warm My Weiner* (Yazoo L 1043). Later in life, he turned to gospel music, and was known as Thomas A. Dorsey (see item B3.19), the most prolific of all gospel composers.

B1.163   Snooks Eaglin. New Orleans Street Singer. Folkways FA 2476.
   Eaglin is in the blind street minstrel tradition of such blues artists as Johnson, McTell, Jefferson, Blake, Taggert, et al. But almost all of his extensive repertoire was learned from listening to the radio and to recordings. The material on these sixteen tracks come from the originators, Champion Jack Dupree, Amos Milburn, Sister Rosetta Tharpe, Hot Lips Page, Lil Green, Jimmy Rodgers, Jimmy McCracklin—truly a representative sample of the hot material from both blacks and whites. Traditional tunes include "Careless Love," "High Society," and "See, See, Rider," reflecting his New Orleans environment. Snooks had recorded r'n'b for Imperial (a New Orleans label) in the 1950s, and this is available on United Artist reissues. Beyond Harry Oster's Folklyric recording (now available on Arhoolie) of similar but more blues-based material, there is nothing more from Snooks. This present disc is a good record to begin study of the effects of commercial and standardized media upon tradition.

B1.164*   Sleepy John Estes. v.1/2. two discs. Swaggie S 1219/1220 (Australian issue).

B1.165   Sleepy John Estes. Brownsville Blues. Delmark DS 613.

B1.166   Sleepy John Estes. Legend. Delmark DS 603.
   Estes presents the most authentic rural blues (as opposed to country blues). The Swaggie set covers 1934-1940 (originally recorded for the Decca company) and clearly reveals his style: one of anguish, pleading, and exhaustion plus innumerable time and tempo changes. On these recordings, as on the Delmarks, his accompanist was harpist Hammie Nixon, who had to be constantly on his toes to insert his lines at the right moment, weaving around the broken vocals and the guitar patterns. Most of Estes's work was autobiographical, such as "Drop Down Mama," "Vernita Blues," and "Airplane Blues." Unfortunately, he was not always easy to understand. Yet, the action of listening actually enhanced his worth, for he simply could not be passed off. Then the aura of mystery prevailed, for he dropped out of sight and an extensive search was made, resulting in his discovery in, of all places, his home town—Brownsville, Tennessee. Shortly, there appeared about a half dozen albums on Delmark, the better of them listed above. Many of his older blues were reconstructed, but new items were added; a lot had happened in 20 years, and this came out in his autobiographical songs (e.g., "Rats in My Kitchen" and "I'd Been Well-Warned"). The Brownsville album is interesting, for it contains all kinds of stories and gossip about the local inhabitants ("Pat Mann," "Young Lawyer," "Al Rawls," "City Hall Blues," "Government Money," etc.).

B1.167   Blind Boy Fuller. Death Valley Days. Oldie Blue OL 2809. (Dutch issue).

B1.168   **Blind Boy Fuller. On Down, v.1.** Flyright 110 (British issue).

B1.168a   **Blind Boy Fuller. With Sonny Terry and Bull City Red.** Blues
Classics 11.

Fulton Allen was the prime example and leader of the East Coast vocal and
instrumental style: relaxed and ragged. North Carolina was the one area in which
rags caught on, and this is revealed in the stylings of Blind Blake and the Rev. Gary
Davis. Unfortunately, with Fuller's death in 1940, rags petered out, and the style
is not available today (for instance, Sonny Terry and Brownie McGhee won't
play rags). Being influenced by banjo tunes from the 19th century, and embracing
the steel guitar, Fuller produced a "sound" that was instantly recognizable. Some
of these items are here, such as "Piccolo Rag," "Step It Up and Go," and "She's
a Truckin' Little Baby." His classic "Rag Mama Rag" is available on Blues Classics
BC 6. The "true" blues style of Fuller revealed a deep, penetrating voice and a
sombre repertoire that included "Little Woman You're So Sweet" and "Lost
Lover Blues." In general, he fostered other singers' careers, most notably those
of Sonny Terry and Brownie McGhee. Because he was blind, he needed a "lead
boy" to guide him and collect the street singing money, and most often this boy
would be an accompanist. The British Flyright label presents "What's That
Smells Like Fish," "Worn Out Engine Blues," "Get Your Ya Yas Out" (a recurring
blues theme, with extensions through the Rolling Stones rock group), and "Baby
Quit Your Low Down Ways." The Dutch Oldie Blues contains 18 tracks from
1935-1940, including "Evil Hearted Woman," "Keep Away from My Woman,"
"Hungry Calf Blues," and "Screamin' and Cryin' Blues."

B1.169   **Jesse Fuller. Frisco Bound.** Arhoolie R 2009.

Fuller was one of the more successful "one man bands" (others include
Dr. Ross and Joe Hill Louis), embracing much instrumentation and many songs
in his repertoire. He called himself the "Lone Cat" and stayed a loner all of his
life. While recording prolifically since the late fifties, he never had any great
amount of recognition beyond the epic "San Francisco Bay Blues." The Arhoolie
reissue captures Fuller at the beginning of his career, in 1955, when much of his
material was "homemade" or homespun. From this time on, he was living in
Oakland. To the "footdella" (his own invention)—a foot-operated bass—he added
harmonica, kazoo, and twelve-string guitar. Typical blues include the travel song
("Leavin' Memphis, Frisco Bound"), the city song ("Cincinnati Blues"), and the
sexual innuendo of "Flavor in My Cream." Five of the selections here are
spirituals, two of which are "Just a Closer Walk with Thee" and "Motherless
Children."

B1.170   **Clifford Gibson. Beat You Doing It.** Yazoo L 1027.

Gibson was one of the better blues guitarists and singers in the St. Louis
scene. His technique, based on Lonnie Johnson's influences, was largely geared
to long treble runs and accenting patterns. The 14 tracks here all come from 1929,
and include "Hard Headed Blues," "Levee Camp Moan," "Bad Luck Dice," and
"Society Blues." True to bluesmen's form, the lyrics and substance dealt mainly
with grief and grieving. What made Gibson's work unique was the application of
picking the strings rather than just strumming. The liner notes include an analysis
of his style, some lyrics, and biographical material.

B1.171   **Jazz Gillum. You Got to Reap What You Sow.** RCA International
          INT 1177 (British issue).

The workmanlike, unspectacular blues of Gillum are important for his role in
creating the "Bluebird sound" for RCA and in developing the Chicago blues (or
more correctly, the blues in Chicago) into its present electric, loud format. The
16 selections here are from 1938 through 1942, with such accompanying musicians
as Big Bill Broonzy, Washboard Sam, and Blind John Davis. His perfunctory
harmonica is played in a straightforward style with none of the devices used by
Sonny Boy Williamson, No. 1. The 1936-1937 recordings reveal a country dance
atmosphere; the 1944-1950 period is transitional, a sort of "country swing" not
unlike a smaller scale Bob Wills. Certainly, there was a lilt to such tunes as "You're
Laughing Now" and "I'm Gonna Get It," almost a lightheartedness that customers
wanted to buy in order to escape the "blues," the Depression, and the coming war.
Most of the recordings here are quite frankly of the commercial, almost stereo-
typed variety, but in all, they form a welcome body of blues entirely suitable for
the novice listener.

B1.172   **Guitar Slim and Jelly Belly. Carolina Blues.** Arhoolie R 2005.

Alex Seward and Louis Hayes, their original names, respectively, presented
relaxed and rocking blues from the East Coast and the Coastal Plains. Although
Sonny Terry and Blind Boy Fuller are more well-known, these two singers are
more than representative of the genre. Their easy-going style is most evident on
the traditional or folk-blues of such items as "Betty and Dupree" or "Working
Man Blues." These 15 tracks illustrate many of their personal encounters and
smooth flowing guitar lines. As a regional style, the East Coast blues were none
too popular outside of that region; and with the advent of radio and mass
recordings, it began to falter. By 1940, there were few adherents left. These
selections are later than that period and consequently must stand as interpretive.

B1.173   **Smokey Hogg. Original Folk Blues.** Kent KST 524.

B1.173a   **Smokey Hogg. U Better Watch That Jive.** Specialty SNTF 1058
          (British issue).

Here is an interesting brace of records for the cataloger. The Kent reissue
represents Andrew Hogg; the Specialty reissue is John Hogg. Both claim to be
one legendary "Smokey" Hogg, operating out of Texas. At any rate, both records
are superb performances by a modern Texas bluesman, employing the slow mode
and slide or bottleneck guitar, with some dances and novelties. Both singers
became exceptionally popular, with Kent's version having the edge on "Little
School Girl" and "I Bleed through My Soul."

B1.174   **John Lee Hooker. Alone.** Specialty SPS 2125.

B1.175*   **John Lee Hooker. Detroit, 1948-1952.** three discs. United Artists
          UA LA 127-J3.

B1.176   **John Lee Hooker. Goin' Down Highway 51.** Specialty SPS 2127.

B1.177   **John Lee Hooker. Mad Man Blues.** two discs. Chess 60011.

B1.178   **John Lee Hooker. Original Folk Blues.** Kent KST 525.

B1.179   **John Lee Hooker. Slim's Stomp.** Polydor 2310 256 (British issue).
The above records cover mainly one period in Hooker's recording career.
Since he was a prolific artist, there are many discs about; unfortunately, most
are trite and routine. His best efforts have always been as a solo artist. He has been
a highly individual performer, with a rich, vibrato voice and a primitive guitar style.
Some aspects of his personal music include riffing his guitar against strong foot-
tapping (and occasionally an echo chamber for dramatic effects; often, though,
this "chamber" was simply a microphone placed in a toilet bowl), while others
included singing with, against, or augmented by his guitar. He used the choke
quite a lot, and rarely followed time sequences and tempo changes. This played
hell with his accompanists; hence, most of the selections above are solo, or with
second guitar (usually Eddie Kirkland) and/or bass. By the mid-fifties, Hooker was
popular enough to continue in r'n'b. Most of the material here comes from 1948-
1955, with the 1948-1952 period produced by Bernie Bessman being the best
("Boogie Chillen," "Hobo Blues," "Catfish Blues," "It Hurts Me So," "Late Last
Night," etc.). The Polydor material came from the King and JVB catalog; the Kent
from RPM/Modern/Crown; and the United Artists from the Bessman sessions.

B1.180   **Lightnin' Hopkins.** Arhoolie F 1011.

B1.181*   **Lightnin' Hopkins. The Blues.** Mainstream MRL 311.

B1.182*   **Lightnin' Hopkins. Early Recordings, v.1/2.** two discs. Arhoolie
          R 1007 and 2010.

B1.183*   **Lightnin' Hopkins. In New York.** Barnaby Candid Z 30247.

B1.184   **Lightnin' Hopkins. A Legend in His Own Time.** Kent KST 9008.

B1.185   **Lightnin' Hopkins. Lightnin' Blues.** Upfront UPF 158.

B1.186   **Lightnin' Hopkins. Original Folk Blues.** Kent KST 523.

B1.187   **Lightnin' Hopkins. Texas Blues Man.** Arhoolie F 1034.
Hopkins has been the most prolific recorder of the blues. The above 9 albums
cover his best periods, and it would be difficult to choose one over another, except
to mention my own personal favorites: the Arhoolie 2007, 2010, and the Barnaby.
As a personal singer, Hopkins's autobiographical songs are the best. He has inherited
the Texas country blues tradition, through Jefferson and Leadbelly, and most of
his material is spontaneous, which is why he was able to record so much. He simply
showed up with an electric guitar and recorded for three hours. Much of his work
is brilliant, being pure genius; and if it was any less, then it is still good or better
than that of imitators. Thus, from 1947, some of his earliest work is on Kent KST
523, from Los Angeles sessions; Arhoolie 2007 and 2010 have the 1947-49 Gold
Star singles from Houston; the Mainstream item is from 1948 and 1951, when he
produced for Bobby Shad his first real big hits in terms of sales: "Hello Central"

and "Coffee Blues"; Kent KST 9008 returns to Hollywood around 1950-51, and includes more unissued tracks. With some of these hits, though, Hopkins began to be promoted in a commercial sense. This, of course, failed, and Hopkins drifted off into Houston street playing. Rediscovered by Sam Charters and Mack McCormick in 1959, Hopkins played the East Coast in 1960, producing two of his finest efforts: the Candid sessions on Barnaby (all autobiographical material), and the Fire sessions reissued on Upfront. Commercialism struck again, and Hopkins played along with it. Companies tended to issue whatever he did, and the market became glutted again. With Arhoolie, first in 1961 and then in 1967, Hopkins found a sympathetic company that he did not jive, and all the records on Arhoolie are of uniformly high quality.

B1.188   **Son House.** Biograph BLP 12040.

B1.189*   **Son House. The Legendary 1941/42 Recordings.** Folklyric 9001.
     Son House is a Delta blues singer of a fierce, hollered blues reminiscent of the work fields. As with most Delta singers, he plays a bottleneck on the treble strings and uses the bass to push along the beat. He made six well-known sides in 1930 that betray the influence of Charley Patton (three others were never released). Then, with the Depression cut-back, he didn't record commercially again until the 1960s (for Columbia). In 1941 and 1942, he made 17 songs for Alan Lomax and the Library of Congress. The Biograph contains the 1930 selections, plus one ("Delta Blues") from 1941 (also on Yazoo 1001 and the Folk Lyric disc). Some of these earlier ones can be found on Origin OJL 2, 5 and 11. Folklyric has 3 of 5 from the 1941 tracks and 11 of 12 from the 1942 tracks. Of interest is the 1942 "American Defense"—not really a blues, but more a patriotic song about the war. The Biograph reissue's liner notes contain all the lyrics to the 1930 session, as well as lyrics to Jefferson's "Wartime Blues" and "Big Night Blues." The sound of the Folklyric is marginally better than that of the Biograph. Paramount (the original label) had terrible sound and cheap shellac when these recordings were initially released, and, of course, that sound has further deteriorated today.

B1.190*   **Mississippi John Hurt. 1928: His First Recordings.** Biograph BLP
          C 4.

B1.191*   **Mississippi John Hurt. Folk Songs and Blues.** v.1/2. two discs. Piedmont
          PLP 13157 and 13161.

B1.192   **Mississippi John Hurt. Best.** two discs. Vanguard VSD 19/20.
     Essentially a folk singer in the blues tradition, Hurt made the 13 recordings for OKeh in 1928 and then promptly disappeared. He carried forth the songster idiom by performing "Frankie," "Stack O'Lee Blues," "Nobody's Dirty Business," "Spike Driver Blues," etc. His immediate appeal was a result of the intricate finger-picking now known as "Hurt style": rapid treble against an existing rhythm on the bass. His re-discovery is an incredible story, much along the same lines as that of Estes: after much searching, he was found right back in his home town of Avalon ("Avalon Blues"). Thirty-five years later, his voice and guitar were found to be exactly the same, with no noticeable changes. The incredibly rich voice, the folk tradition, the finger picking—all contributed to make Hurt a minor star in the

1960s folk revival. Dick Spottswood was the first to get him on disc, and the two Piedmonts resulted, with "Salty Dog," "Spanish Fandang," "Casey Jones," "Candy Man Blues," and "My Creole Belle," in addition to newer performances of his earlier works. Moving over to Vanguard through the Newport Festivals, Hurt had better sales through better distribution, although the Piedmonts were undoubtedly his best work ever. Rather than choose any of the Vanguard studio sessions, one should acquire the "twofer"; it's a concert at Oberlin College (April 15, 1965) and presents Hurt in an easy-going mood with an audience, singing all the old blues in a more intimate style than in the studio.

B1.193   **John Jackson. Blues and Country Dance Tunes from Virginia.** Arhoolie F 1025.

B1.194   **John Jackson. More Blues and Country Dance Tunes from Virginia, v.2.** Arhoolie F 1035.

Frankly, John Jackson will sing anything so long as it's melodic and tells a story. The 26 tracks on these two records illustrate that point while concentrating on folk-blues in the Mance Lipscomb style. The music here knows no geographical or color boundaries, and musical influences are borrowed at will: tunes, texts, and techniques—anything that would be appropriate for the moment. Hence, he performs Blind Blake ("Police Dog Blues"), spirituals ("Near the Cross"), traditional ("Cindy," "John Henry," "Reuben," etc.), Jimmie Rodger ("Muleskinner Blues,"), and other white country influences in "Going Down the Road Feeling Bad," "Don't Let Your Deal Go Down," "Poor Boy," or "Lay Down My Old Guitar." These discs, plus the Mance Lipscomb records, are interesting ones to try out in popular music classes (especially for purposes of identification and stylings, probably all being exceptions to the rules).

B1.195   **Papa Charlie Jackson. 1925-1928.** Biograph BLP 12042.

B1.196   **Papa Charlie Jackson. Fatmouth, 1924-1929.** Yazoo L 1029.

Jackson was unique in the blues for sticking with the banjo, although he did record with a guitar from time to time. His repertoire included many vaudeville songs (he was a minstrel and medicine showman), which were created before the blues, as we know them, were made. His "Airy Man Blues" (August 1924) was the first important, wide-selling country blues*man* recording, and it opened the door for other male singers to come through. Much of his music could have crossed over to jazz, folk, or even ragtime, for he played in all of these genres. The limiting nature of the banjo does not lend itself to blues performances. A large amount of his material was humor, in the "hokum" field, such as "Skoodle Un Skoo," "Cat's Got the Measles," and "No Need of Knockin' on the Blind." These 28 tunes represent about half of Jackson's Paramount output, and contain his first significant material such as "Spoonful," "Salty Dog," and "Shake That Thing"—all from 1924 or 1925, before others re-recorded them in the late twenties.

B1.197   **Skip James. Devil Got My Woman.** Vanguard VSD 79273.

B1.198*   **Skip James. Early Recordings.** Biograph BLP 12029.

B1.199*   **Skip James. Greatest of the Delta Blues Singers.** Melodeon MLP 7321.
James was the exception that tests the rule about Mississippi Delta singers.
Although he was from the area, he exhibited none of the characteristics of its
players. He sang with a falsetto vocal and a guitar style that was characterized by
Paul Oliver as "organ." In addition, he played suitable piano. His fingerpicking
was extra-ordinarily fast, but most of his material was disturbing in a dark character
(e.g., "Hard Time Killing Floor Blues"). He was rediscovered in 1964, and he made
the above Melodeon disc before moving on to Vanguard (where he recreated his
biggest, earlier successes). More autobiographical material came from this Melodeon
session, such as "Sick Bed Blues" and "Washington D.C. Hospital Center Blues,"
both derived from his recent bout with illness. Most of his earlier material is
scattered throughout various anthologies, such as on *They Sang the Blues*
(Historical 22), *Mississippi Moaners* (Yazoo 1009), *Mississippi Blues* (Yazoo 1001),
Lonesome Road Blues (Yazoo 1038), and various Origins, especially OJL 2, 15,
17. The Biograph makes available his most significant recordings, such as "Throw
Me Down," "Devil Got My Woman," "Cypress Grove," and "Cherry Ball Blues."
These are from 1931, along with 2 from 1964 (remaining from the Melodeon
sessions) and a very interesting 1929 test pressing.

B1.200   **Herman E. Johnson Louisiana Country Blues.** Arhoolie 1060.
Recorded by Harry Oster in Baton Rouge, Louisiana, in 1961, Johnson
revealed a rich life and conveyed his experiences in his travels. Good critical notes
by Oster show the diversity of styles and influences. Much of the material here
is in the folk idiom, such as "You Don't Know My Mind," "Motherless Children,"
and "Po' Boy." Throughout, Johnson employs a knife for the bottleneck style,
one of the few performers still using that implement. Problems discussed include
"I Just Keeps On Wantin' You" (about women) and "Depression Blues." Some
songs particularly show off his ability to keep a running dialogue between his
singing and guitar playing, such as "She's A-Looking for Me." His religious work
is more in the vein of spirituals, as with "Where the Mansion's Prepared for Me."

B1.201   **Lonnie Johnson.** Collector's Classics CC 30 (Danish issue).

B1.202   **Lonnie Johnson.** Jazum 2.

B1.203*   **Lonnie Johnson.** Storyville 671.162 (Danish issue).

B1.204*   **Lonnie Johnson.** Swaggie S 1225 (Australian issue).

B1.205   **Lonnie Johnson. Losing Game.** Prestige 7724.

B1.206   **Lonnie Johnson. Tomorrow Night.** King KS 1082.

B1.207*   **Lonnie Johnson and Eddie Lang. Blue Guitars, v.1/2.** two discs.
Parlophone PMC 7019 and 7106 (British issue).

B1.208*   **Lonnie Johnson and Victoria Spivey. Idle Hours.** Bluesville BV 1044.
Johnson was one of the most eclectic blues singers. He accompanied rural
singers such as Texas Alexander (heard on the *Blue Guitars* set), played with

Louis Armstrong and Duke Ellington and several female singers, and, because of his fluent, sophisticated style (along with his high voice), he helped to shape the urban blues. The Parlophone set documents his jazz collaboration with guitarist Eddie Lang in a successful series of guitar duets; half of the Jazum presents some tough OKeh issues from 1927 ("Mean Old Bed Bug Blues," "Sweet Potato Blues"); the Collector's Classics ranges from 1925 through 1932, with 14 sides of fluidity; the Swaggie takes the Decca "urban" sound from 1937 and 1938; the King set shows him being developed into a r'n'b singer and is most notable for "Tomorrow Night," a monster hit for Johnson (300,000 copies); and the Storyville record, probably his best of the modern recordings, pits him with Otis Spann on accompanying piano (Johnson returns the favor on Spann's own Storyville album). This latter has an interesting remake of "Tomorrow Night," in a softer vein, as well as many originals. Of the half dozen Bluesvilles, the above two (one revised on Prestige) are the best, including a sterling duet album with Victoria Spivey on the title track, "Long Time Blues" and "I Got the Blues So Bad."

B1.209*   **Leadbelly. The Library of Congress Recordings.** three discs. Elektra EKL 301/2.

B1.210   **Leadbelly.** Columbia C 30035.
   The recordings in the Elektra box were done by the Lomaxes between 1933 and 1942. Sound quality is not too good since portable disc-cutting equipment was used. In any case, the material was of Leadbelly's own choosing and he was completely relaxed. The time span of the recordings is significant, as a whole decade is covered, but, at times, changes can be found in what one would expect Leadbelly to do, based on prior knowledge or evidence. The accompanying booklet provides the text of both the conversation and the songs. The scope is exceptionally wide, from folk to blues, topical and universal, children's songs and songs of murders, barrelhouse and social, etc.—the whole gamut. The Columbia set comes from ARC recordings of 1935, and, surprisingly, all are blues except for one item. Most of these titles had never been released before, so that it is difficult to state how influential they might have been. But, at least they show a powerful 12 string guitar in the same vein as Blind Lemon Jefferson's in the Texas blues tradition. And, after all is said and done, Leadbelly was ultimately a blues singer first, as was Big Bill Broonzy.

B1.211   **Furry Lewis. In His Prime, 1927-1929.** Yazoo L 1050.

B1.212   **Furry Lewis. Shake 'Em On Down.** two discs. Fantasy 24703.
   Walter Lewis grew up through the traveling medicine shows and his nickname came naturally from his vocal style of slurred enunciation. An intricate guitar player, he was responsible for the epic classic "Casey Jones [parts 1 & 2]." Other early songs are on the Yazoo, such as "Rock Island Blues," "Falling Down Blues," and "I Will Turn Your Money Green." Some 30-odd years later in his career, Lewis recorded for Bluesville (1961), turning out two albums (now on the Fantasy twofer) of remakes, bottleneck classics, some previously unrecorded traditional material (such as "Frankie and Johnny"), and a great many original songs that reveal life in Memphis and in the old medicine shows.

B1.213*   **Mance Lipscomb. Texas Sharecropper and Songster.** Arhoolie F 1001.

B1.214   **Mance Lipscomb. Texas Songster, v.2.** Arhoolie F 1023.
     Lipscomb was one of the eclectic virtuosos of the 1960s. Previously unknown and thus unrecorded, he was the last of his kind. His music embraced every known form of blues playing: instrumentals, dances, spirituals, folk-blues, ballads, reels, etc. He claimed to have never heard certain performers, yet sings some of their repertoire, such as Leadbelly's music, giving rise to the idea of common material being spread throughout Texas. A comparable, though younger singer, is John Jackson from Virginia, who appears to be carrying on the tradition of cross-influences and reinterpretations. These first two long playing records (out of 6 available on Arhoolie) come from 1960 and 1964 respectively. The earlier effort concentrates on such as "Rock Me All Night Long," "Ella Speed," and "Mama Don't Allow." The second set is both more primitive (with "Spanish Flang Dang") and more original (with "Cocaine Done Killed My Baby," "Charlie James," and "If I Miss the Train").

B1.215*   **Cripple Clarence Lofton/Walter Davis.** Yazoo L 1025.

B1.216*   **Cripple Clarence Lofton/Jimmy Yancey.** Swaggie S1235 (Australian issue).
     Lofton has not been served too well by reissue companies, and much of his work has been scattered in bits and pieces on anthologies and compilations, from all time periods. He played in the rent party style of fast blues and boogie, and he accompanied both female and male singers. His vocals appear on about half his recordings under his own name. His eclecticism is clearly revealed on the Yazoo set from 1935, with such tunes as "South Side Mess Around" and "Change My Mind Blues." The Swaggie material comes from a private party in 1939, and reveals much more of Lofton's temperament, as well as his feeling for audience reactions.

B1.217   **Tommy McClennan. Cross Cut Saws Blues.** Roots RL 305 (Austrian issue).
     McClennan's records were cut between 1939 and 1942, some forty titles in all. The 16 tracks on this set represent the best of a bluesman who has been acknowledged as the most primitive and least sophisticated of the Mississippi singers. He was fierce in his shouting, chuckling, vocal comments, and growls. He treated his guitar savagely, pounding on the treble strings to produce eerie effects. Sexual images predominate on this collection, such as "She's Just Good Huggin'-Size," "My Little Girl," and "She's a Good-Looking Mama."

B1.218*   **Martin, Bogan and Armstrong. Barnyard Dance.** Rounder 2003.

B1.219   **The New Mississippi Sheiks.** Rounder 2004.
     Black and blues string bands in the 1920s and 1930s were a parallel development to the white, old time mountain music groups. While much of the latter's qualities were solemn, the former's were happy and infectious, and later, with jazz elements, they formed the basis for western swing. The music on both of these albums is very similar, with perhaps the *Barnyard Dance* being a little more

sophisticated and with more vocal duets. Both discs were recorded in Chicago in 1972. The Sheiks had Walter Vinson (National guitar) from the original group, with Mississippi Sam Chatmon (Bo Carter's brother) on Gibson. Carl Martin and Ted Bogan (of *Barnyard Dance*) provide backup support. Martin is to be well-noted for his searing violin, occasional mandolin, and vocals. "Stop and Listen" is a recreation of their former hit; "I'll Be Glad When You're Dead" is from the jazz idiom ("You Rascal You"); "What Is It Tastes Like Gravy?" is the original riff and melody of "Walk Right In," a Sheiks hit that was later covered by the Roof Top Singers; and "Railroad Blues" is an old item from Martin's Four Key String Band days. *Barnyard Dance*'s title tune is a vegetable song, featured on the artful cover, where the vegetables are doing a cute dance. Howard Armstrong was responsible for the painting, and he can also speak seven languages, including Mandarin Chinese. With Armstrong on violin and mandolin, there is Carl Martin, mandolin and violin, Ted Bogan, guitar and violin, and L. C. Armstrong, bass— truly a diversified string group. From 1931 on, they were the Four Keys String Band, and played at square dances, parties, church socials, taverns, and on the radio until they disbanded. Material, then, as now, was comprised of blues, fiddle tunes, and pop. Either the fiddles or the mandolin would play around the melody, being supported by rhythm guitar and a bowed bass. "Cacklin' Hen" is the fiddle tune; tradition is represented by "Corinna," "Sweet Georgia Brown," and "Mean Mistreatin' Mama." There is a very interesting "Lady Be Good," where guitarist Bogan makes extensive use of minor ninths to elaborate the chord structures. Really, these are two *astonishing* albums, full of gleeful vocals and dazzling instrumental work.

B1.220*   **Mississippi Sheiks. Stop and Listen Blues.** Mamlish s3804.
    They were one of the most popular recording teams of the time in the 1930s. This album is a superb collection of 14 tracks illustrating the violin-guitar blues of Walter Vinson and Lonnie Chatmon. Vinson's simple guitar and rasping voice were nicely complemented by the swing violin of Chatmon. Their three biggest numbers are here: "Sitting on Top of the World," the title selection, and "Unhappy Blues." Good sound and excellent notes. Other material can be found on Biograph 12041, Yazoo 1034, and various anthologies.

B1.221   **Little Brother Montgomery.** Collector's Classics CC 35 (Danish issue).

B1.222*   **Little Brother Montgomery. 1930-1969.** Matchbox SDR 213 (British issue).

B1.223*   **Little Brother Montgomery. Blues.** Folkways FG 3527.

B1.224   **Little Brother Montgomery. Chicago Blues Session.** "77" Records LA 12/21 (British issue).

B1.225   **Little Brother Montgomery. Farro Street Jive.** Xtra 1115 (British issue).

B1.226   **Little Brother Montgomery. No Special Rider.** Adelphi AS 1003S.

B1.227   **Little Brother Montgomery. Tasty Blues.** Prestige PR 7807.
     Montgomery's career has been continuous since his first recording in 1930, as the above records attest. Through the years, he has simply grown older, but his style has not wavered one bit. Master of the lyric and melodic content of the blues, he quickly produced two themes: "Vicksburg Blues" and "No Special Rider," which he has recorded often in later life. These themes—classic ones in the blues tradition—have since been recorded by others, most notably Roosevelt Sykes. Both of these titles are on the Matchbox set. In 1936, Montgomery produced 18 titles at one session, all of them usable and top-notch, a feat rarely achieved in blues recording history. These are on the Collector's Classics (originally from Victor) and Matchbox ("Crescent City Blues," "Shreveport Blues," etc.). His smooth piano playing enabled him to sit in on many jazz sessions as an accompanist; his voice was high and grating, in perfect contrast to the fluent piano. His next best period was around 1960, when he created the remarkable Folkways and Xtra albums (from the same sessions), the "77" effort, and the Prestige (originally on Bluesville 1021)—over 50 titles of great interest ("Pallet on the Floor," "Trembling Blues," "Bob Martin Blues").

B1.228*   **Alex Moore.** Arhoolie F 1008.

B1.229   **Alex Moore. In Europe.** Arhoolie 1048.
     Only a few of Moore's CBS records from the twenties have made their way onto reissues (CBS 52797, 66232, and Historical 32 come immediately to mind). He never recorded extensively again until these two Arhoolie discs from the 1960s. In the meantime, his voice had deepened with age and his piano assimilated intervening techniques, such as a smooth boogie roll. A completely original Texan improviser, Moore can just sit down and play endlessly with little or no repetition. At times he whistles, not too unpleasantly, such as on "Whistling Alex Moore's Blues." Originals include "Pretty Woman with a Sack Dress On" and "Going Back to Froggy Bottom." There is a nine years' difference between the two albums, and if anything, Moore had become more languid and drawn out, allowing more time for reminiscences, as in the 9:20 timing of "Rolling Around Dallas," in which he talks about almost everyone he once knew there. Equally inventive is "Alex Thinking." Other Moore material can be found on a wide variety of Arhoolie anthologies (such as 1006 and 1017).

B1.230   **Buddy Moss. Rediscovery.** Biograph BLP 12019.
     Moss is another giant of the East Coast blues scene, recording quite a few songs for CBS in the 1930s before dropping out of sight. His revival comes from the Gas Light in Washington, DC, in 1966, and the resulting disc immediately found a good response from the blues world. Heavily influenced by the Texan Blind Lemon Jefferson and Blind Blake, his flowing, progressive style is carefully attained on such extended (over five minutes) numbers as "Everyday Seems Like Sunday" or "I Got A Woman, Don't Mean Me No Good." With occasional harp added to his guitar, this solo album contains quite a few gems in the folk-blues tradition.

B1.231   **Jimmy Reed. At Carnegie Hall.** two discs. Vee Jay 2SR 1035.

B1.232*   **Jimmy Reed. Roots of the Blues.** two discs. Kent KST 537.

Reed's forte lies in being influential over certain rock performers, and even certain bluesmen. Other than that, most of his material shows no new development, being a twelve-bar blues sung against a walking bass and shrill harmonica. His main pattern is to establish a compelling boogie rhythm and repetition. Including a slurred vocal (sometimes difficult to understand), his total impact is based on simplicity, and perhaps this is what attracted the white musicians. Rock music is easily susceptible to riffs, and that's what Reed does best. The pattern was established early, with items on the Kent reissue: "Big Boss Man," "The Moon Is Rising," "Baby What You Want Me To Do," "Hush Hush," "Bright Lights, Big City," "Take Out Some Insurance," and "Honest I Do." The Carnegie Hall set has an interesting set of circumstances. His appearance was such a success that he was asked to "recreate" the same songs in the studio. Thus, this is not a live recording but merely a time in Reed's life when he was "up" for the occasion: "Found Joy," "Hold Me Close," "You Got Me Dizzy," etc. Another set here was the recreation of his big hits, and since the style never changed, an upgrade of sound helps the recording quality.

B1.233   **Robert Shaw. Texas Barrelhouse Piano.** Arhoolie 1010.

Robert Shaw inherited the traditional Texas blues piano. Overtones of rags and barrelhouse music are in evidence, and this disc is a significant example of the genre. Local items include the famous "Hattie Green" and "Groceries on My Shelf," but his style is exceptionally important on such as "Here I Come with My Dirty, Dirty Duckings On" or the distillations of piano history, "The Clinto" and "The Cows."

B1.234   **Johnny Shines. Sittin' on the Top of the World.** Biograph BLP 12044.

B1.235   **Johnny Shines. Standing at the Crossroads.** Testament T 2221.

Shines is one of the few bluesmen who had direct contact with the legendary Robert Johnson over a period of time. They used to bum around together over most parts of America and even into Canada. Thus, the Mississippi influence on Shines is enormous. His high, impatient voice is pure Delta, and throughout these solo albums, he plays fine slide with a National steel guitar. Many tunes are derived from Johnson: "Ramblin' Blues," "Dynaflow Blues," "Tell Me Mama," "Milk Cow Blues." On the last, the understated guitar is very effective, emphasized by the incessant beat on the bass. Other material comes from Memphis Minnie and the gospel tradition. The title tune from the Biograph album is from the Mississippi Sheiks (later recorded by Howlin' Wolf and the Cream). A few originals complete the albums, with "Glad Rags" being a contemporary item about drugs.

B1.236   **Funny Papa Smith. The Original Howling Wolf, 1930-1931.** Yazoo L 1031.

J. T. Smith is an acknowledged pioneer of the Texas blues style, far more so than Blind Lemon Jefferson. But recognition came too late, for this was the period of the Depression. Although he had the distinction of releasing more than 20 sides during this period (more than any other Texas bluesman), he had been pushed aside. His main forte was the thumb: thumb-picking, thumb-rolls, rapid thumb-runs, thumb-bass, and thumb double-timing. These can all be heard to great advantage on important efforts such as "Howling Wolf Blues [parts 1 and 2]," "Tell It to the Judge [parts 1 and 2]," and "Mama's Quittin' and Leavin' [parts 1 and 2]." The voodoo motif appears in "Seven Sisters Blues [parts 1 and 2]." The importance of extended versions of songs, indicated by [parts 1 and 2], cannot be underrated, for this allowed time for extended runs and exposition of the story.

B1.237   **Roosevelt Sykes. Blues.** Folkways FS 3827.

B1.238*   **Roosevelt Sykes. The Country Blues Piano Ace.** Yazoo L 1033.
     Known as "Honeydripper," Sykes has had a vast career of ups and downs throughout his almost 50 years of recording. He was instrumental in creating the St. Louis piano flavor of a sophisticated rural and urban mixture. The Yazoo disc covers his first three years as a solo artist, and includes works that introduced the ominous bass figures, most particularly in "Kelly's 44 Blues." He achieved this merely by playing unsyncopated, single-note bass (a forerunner of the heavy black soul music) and a facile technique on the complex treble runs. He accompanied many singers in his journeys (St. Louis, Chicago, Memphis, New Orleans, Mississippi, the West Coast, and even Europe), and, indeed, will sit in with anyone at the drop of a hat. His extroverted sound helped to shape the Chicago blues. When he began touring in the late thirties, it was mostly for one night audiences. He played all kinds of music—whatever was in vogue—which left him open to the criticism that his music was very superficial and commercial. Certainly he has been an enormous crowd pleaser, playing what the audience wished to hear. Indeed, on a number of occasions, he has actually dismissed the pick-up accompaniment because the audience wanted solo blues. His band or group recordings have generally not been successful because of this attitude, and many trite songs got recorded (as happened with Fats Waller, except that Waller was able to overcome this by means of parody). He is also a master of the raunchy sexual innuendo, as exemplified by "Dirty Mother Fuyer" or "Ice Cream Freezer Blues." He has also been widely anthologized, with various reissue companies picking up his better recordings.

B1.239   **Taj Mahal.** Columbia CS 9579.

B1.240   **Taj Mahal. The Natch'l Blues.** Columbia CS 9698

B1.241   **Taj Mahal. De Ole Folks at Home.** two discs. Columbia GP 18.
     Taj Mahal is an enigma. He has willingly foregone a career in agricultural science to reinterpret the roots of black music and to expand upon them. He started (on CS 9579) to transpose traditional country blues into the tight, closed sound of Chicago blues. He had an integrated band with Jesse Davis on lead guitar and Ry Cooder on rhythm and mandolin, while he himself played slide, harmonica, and the vocal line. Material included three from Sleepy John Estes ("Everybody's Got to Change Sometime," "Leaving Trunk," and "Diving Duck Blues"), two traditional items ("EZ Rider" and "The Celebrated Walking Blues"), plus one each from the best repertoire of Blind Willie McTell, Robert Johnson, and Sonny Boy Williamson, No. 2. ("Statesboro Blues," "Dust My Broom," and "Checkin' Up On My Baby"). His importance as a creative artist is that, with him and for the

first time, country blues were updated in the style currently available on a major label and performed by a black man. The road has not been easy, and several changes were in order. Mahal had a painfully weak harp, and most of the recorded proceedings were overshadowed by a strong bass.

The Natch'l Blues, his next album, was a better disc than the first. More traditional music was featured ("The Cuckoo," "Corinna," "I Ain't Gonna Let Nobody Steal My Jelly Roll," among others), and some originals were included. His re-workings appeared to be more serious—more into the consciousness of the music. While his first disc was almost in fun, on this album, his voice is more full of emotional tension. To complement his raw singing, Mahal had his now-recognized National steel body guitar, a device designed to create a more metallic, hence more brittle sound. Here, though, the beginning of rock heaviness intrudes.

De Ole Folks at Home is the real winner. This is mostly traditional material that Mahal has culled over the years, and he solos on each track. These are tasteful, really rural outings, more in the folk vein than in the blues tradition. Leadbelly's "Linin' Track" is sung a cappella and "Candy Man" is the Rev. Gary Davis tune; but while "Stagger Lee" is credited to Lloyd Price, it is actually the John Hurt version. "Cajun Tune" has a solo harmonica, and "Country Blues #1" has a solo guitar. "Annie's Lover" is pure comedy, while "Coloured Aristocracy" is deadly serious. "Fishin' Blues" is probably the best known Mahal number. The only complaint about this record is the poor mixing, with instrument on the left channel and voice on the right. Mahal often tours alone, playing at out-of-the-way clubs and folk festivals. He leads workshops, recreating much material, as on the *Old Folks* album, and demands audience involvement, sometimes in conflict to his abrasive personality. This is what he likes best, and he uses the proceeds from the rock albums and such performances to carry on his solo efforts.

B1.242*   **Tampa Red.** two discs. RCA AXM2-5501.

B1.243   **Tampa Red. Bottleneck Guitar, 1928-1937.** Yazoo L 1039.

B1.244   **Tampa Red. The Guitar Wizard, 1935-1953.** Blues Classics 25.
    Red was even more of a "hokum" player than Georgia Tom, and it was because of this that he has largely been ignored in reissued recordings. Perhaps it is significant that Frank Driggs picked Tampa Red for the beginning of RCA's blues reissue series. Essentially, Red was best at accompanying others, such as Ma Rainey or Georgia Tom. His fluent bottleneck style fitted in neatly with their melodies. He later became part of the "Bluebird sound," recording with Big Maceo on occasion. Although there is some duplication (inevitable) between the smaller reissue companies and the 32 track RCA compilation, the Yazoo does bring in additional tracks from his early period, while half of the Arhoolie covers 1936 through 1953. On the latter album, the initial sides were released under his own name. Included, then, are some of his bigger efforts: "It's Tight Like That," "Black Angel Blues" (the definitive bottleneck re-working of Lucille Bogan's version, and 20 years later to be known as "Sweet Little Angel," covered by both Robert Nighthawk and B. B. King in that same bottleneck style), "Love with a Feeling," "It Hurts Me Too," and the epic "You're Gonna Miss Me When I'm Gone." Various accompanying musicians include Black Bob, Big Maceo, and Walter Horton.

B1.245   **Sonny Terry. On the Road.** Folkways FA 2369.

B1.246   **Sonny Terry. The Jaw Harp in Blues and Folk Music.** Folkways FS3821.

B1.247   **Sonny Terry and Brownie McGhee.** Folkways FW 2327.

Sonny Terry is a harp virtuoso whose tense and emotional vocals alternate with harmonica runs, whoops, and hollers. He makes excellent use of his fingers and cupped hands. He comes from the Carolinas, once worked with and was influenced by Blind Boy Fuller, and formed a team with Brownie McGhee. McGhee is not as good by himself as Terry can be when alone, but together, they are dynamite. The thirteen selections on 2327 are solid in the folk blues tradition, with "Preachin' the Blues," "Heart in Sorrow," and "Better Day" being the outstanding cuts of especially wide appeal. On 2369, Terry appears with "Sticks" McGhee (Brownie's brother) and J. C. Burris (Terry's nephew). Sticks repeats his 1949 hit, the great r'n'b "Drink of Wine Spoo-Dee-Oh-Dee." Bones are prevalent throughout the disc, and the sharpness of the 14 selections here makes it the best of the three. The marvelous picture of Terry by David Gahr (with the road reflected in his glasses) is alone worth the price. Birmingham, England, once supplied over 100,000 jaw harps a year to the U.S., and they are now solidly rooted in the folk tradition. This novelty item is billed as "Sonny Terry's New Sound" and the accompanists are Brownie McGhee and J. C. Burris. Not surprisingly, by bending or pushing blue notes through the harp, it can sound like a harmonica. The thirteen numbers are complemented by strong historical notes.

B1.248*   **Sonny Terry and Brownie McGhee. Back Country Blues.** Savoy MG 14019.

Harp virtuoso Terry and guitarist McGhee (a successor to the East Coast's Blind Boy Fuller) have formed one of the longest lasting partnerships in musical history—over 35 years. Most of the time it was McGhee's vocals, but often Terry would sing and McGhee would accompany on guitar. This Savoy recording, from the late forties, shows the duo at their performing peak, with such interrelating songs as "Diamond Ring" and "Bottom Blues." Four of the tracks were supported by Mickey Baker's quartet, which produced a tough, harsher sound, and even resulted in a hit record—"My Fault." Although they tried to duplicate this feeling again (most notably with Bobby Shad's Sitting In With label, now reissued on Mainstream MRL 308), they were never successful until they got caught up in the folk revival.

B1.249   **Henry Thomas. "Ragtime Texas"; Complete Recorded Works, 1927-1929 in Chronological Order.** two discs. Herwin 209.

Thomas was known as "Ragtime Texas." He was an older performer of blues music, and indeed forms a very positive link between what went on previously in folk roots and what we now call "country blues." The origin of much Texas music is thereby traced on this album, as displayed in Mack McCormick's notes to this set. Many of Thomas's songs are the only known examples of texts reproduced by collectors, such as "Honey Won't You Allow Me One More Chance?" (from 1927). However, not all his singing was blues music. While "Don't Ease Me In," "Texas

Easy Street Blues," and "Cottonfield Blues" are self-explanatory from their titles, other songs were regular ballads, such as "Bob McKinney" or "Run, Mollie, Run." The "Fishing Blues" is common to both white and black repertoires, and "Old Country Stomp" is actually a dance tune with country square dance calls. On both of these latter tunes, Thomas accompanies himself with the pipes of Pan. His importance is twofold: first, as a transition in early blues history (with some material from the past); and second, as an influence on the younger Texan performers who tried to emulate his styles. Thomas was one of many influential singers who contributed to the regional Texas music style that has manifested itself in all forms (rock and roll, rock, folk, blues, jazz, and gospel). Bernie Klatzko has taken some fine Vocalion recordings in good shape (as indicated on the covers) and has applied excellent remastering. Most of the 23 tracks can also be found on assorted anthologies in a hodge-podge fashion (Origin, Yazoo, and Folkways).

B1.250   **Ramblin' Thomas. Chicago Blues, 1928.** Biograph BLP 12004.
Thomas was a Texas bluesman who happened to record these 12 tracks in Chicago; hence the title. They are indicative of Texas blues guitar music in that he employed bottleneck and an equally plaintive, whining vocal style. Some typical tunes include the stunning "No Job Blues," and work songs such as "Sawmill Moan," "Hard Dallas Blues," and "Ramblin' Man." Basically, his is the story of an unsettled man moving from city to city. Other of his material can be found on Yazoo anthologies 1026, 1032, and 1046.

B1.251   **Washboard Sam.** Blues Classics BC 10.

B1.252   **Washboard Sam. Feeling Lowdown.** RCA LPV 577.
Robert Brown (his real name) was one of the few "washboard" players that could also manage to do a good job singing, although, in the main, his lyrical creations were far better. As early as 1935, he recorded for Vocalion (and these are heard on the Blues Classics set) such items as "Mama Don't Allow." With Big Bill Broonzy, he then began recording for RCA's Bluebird label, a contract that lasted until 1949. He recorded over 150 songs under his own name up to 1942, and sat in on countless others. His records were often retained in the RCA catalog, never going out of print. The 32 selections here are broadly representative of his style, and include such seminal sellers as "I'm Going to St. Louis," "I Been Treated Wrong," and the lyrically important "Levee Camp Blues." Although commercially successful, neither Sam nor any of the "Bluebird beat" bluesmen could ever be thought of as slick, cloying, or profiteering.

B1.253*   **Peetie Wheatstraw.** Blues Classics BC 4.

B1.254*   **Peetie Wheatstraw. v.1/2.** two discs. Matchbox SDR 191/2 (British issue).
Styled "The Devil's Son-in-Law" after one of his songs, Wheatstraw was an extremely popular blues performer in the 1930s. Complete with falsetto swoops, asides, hummings, cries, and so forth, his records appealed to a wide group of people. His piano was heavily influenced by Leroy Carr. The eight tracks on BC 4 complement the 32 on Matchbox, ranging from 1930 through 1938. His guitar

accompaniment was often Charley Jordan, Lonnie Johnson, or Kokomo Arnold. Original lyrics predominate, especially on "Mama's Advice" or "Ice and Snow Blues." Many topical items surfaced, such as "Road Tramp Blues" and "Working on the Project" (both Depression songs). Mid-tempo music was the norm, but sometimes he would let go with a stomp. A lot of the rest of his material has been scattered over two dozen anthologies and compilations.

B1.255   **Bukka White. Big Daddy.** Biograph BLP 12049.

B1.256*   **Bukka White. Mississippi Blues.** Takoma B 1001.

B1.257*   **Bukka White. Parchman Farm.** Columbia C 30036.
Washington "Bukka" White is an overpowering performer in the Delta style. His ferocious attack on the strings, aided by a brass slide, produces a cacaphony of noise and drive, but all with purpose, for he is usually angry. And he is one of the few bluesmen whose style has not changed since his first recording. Most of his early work is on the Columbia set (March 7 and 8, 1940; after his release from prison). These are all autobiographical, with titles such as "Strange Place Blues," "Where Can I Change My Clothes?," and "District Attorney Blues." His rediscovery album, from 1963, is on Takoma, with some re-recordings of the Parchman era, as well as "Army Blues" and "The Atlanta Special." Most of his work in the sixties was at coffee houses and folk festivals, making just enough to get by. It was with delight that he resurfaced for the 1973 Biograph record. Here he plays National steel-bodied guitar throughout, with a wide sampling of personal material ("Black Cat Bone Blues"), dances ("1936 Trigger Toe"), gospel ("Cryin' Holy Unto the Lord"), sexual imagery ("Workin' Man's Jelly Roll Blues"), and good-time ("Mama Don' 'Low").

B1.258   **Big Joe Williams. Classic Delta Blues.** CBS 63813 (British issue).

B1.259*   **Big Joe Williams. Crawlin' King Snake.** RCA FXMI 7323 (French issue).

B1.260   **Big Joe Williams. Nine String Guitar Blues.** Delmark 627.

B1.261   **Big Joe Williams. Thinking of What They Did to Me.** Arhoolie 1053.

B1.262   **Big Joe Williams. Tough Times.** Arhoolie F 1002.
Williams, once known as "Poor Joe," is the classic example of what a bluesman should be. He has wandered all over the continent, playing on many people's labels and with many others as sideman (particularly Sonny Boy Williamson, No. 1) and pointing the way for blues rediscoveries in the 1960s by virtue of his knowledge of where people were still living. He has assisted many people through his kindness. No one style typifies his playing. Born in Mississippi, he exhibited an intensity of his playing (as found on the RCA set). The fifteen tracks from 1935-1941, some with Williamson, clearly show a fascination with travelling songs ("Highway 49") and primitivism. Percussive notes on the bass and ringing trebles come through clear with his "nine" string guitar ("Stack of Dollars," "My Baby Keeps Hanging Around"). The Arhoolies are some of his better, later works from

the sixties, such as "Greystone Blues," "Vitamin A Blues," the topical "President Roosevelt," and "The Death of Dr. Martin Luther King." The CBS reissue of a Milestone recording concentrates on Delta blues made famous by others (e.g., Patton's "Pony Blues" and Robert Johnson's "Hellhound on My Trail" and "Terraplane Blues").

B1.263   **Bill Williams. Blues, Rags and Ballads.** Blue Goose 2013.

B1.264   **Bill Williams. Low and Lonesome.** Blue Goose 2004.

Williams was a partner to Blind Blake, yet he himself never recorded before the age of 73. These new recordings, his only ones, reveal heavy influences from the East Coast blues school. He was equally proficient with blues, rags, and ballads (as the record title indicates). His departure from solid blues form can also be found in the work of such bluesmen as Mance Lipscomb and John Jackson (both on Arhoolie). Like them, he has assimilated many stylings, such as "Najo Rag," "St. Louis Blues," "Railroad Bill," "Frankie and Johnny," the pop "Up a Lazy River," "Listen to the Mockingbird," and "Darktown Strutter's Ball." Although he is a little slow because of age, Williams's technical prowess is superb, and he can handle any styles tossed his way. Good notes on both discs illustrate the interaction of white and black music.

B1.265   Omitted.

URBAN, ELECTRIC BLUES

Muddy Waters must be given some credit for the great current interest in the blues. Waters (or McKinley Morganfield) is from the Mississippi Delta area, where he hung out with blues performers and heard Robert Johnson, master of the blues. Working his way to Chicago, Waters developed his style and added electric instruments to make himself heard over the noise in the saloons. He discovered that he had more scope with the amplified guitar and changed his style accordingly. When Muddy first recorded, a post-war hit blues record normally sold 60,000 copies, mostly around Chicago, Gary, St. Louis, Memphis, and in the South. There was no distribution on the East or West coasts, no radio play, and no real money. Blues recorded outside Chicago were on regional labels and were lucky if they sold 1,000 copies. Muddy had more of these hits than any other blues singer, and, as a consequence, he attracted or sought out first-rate sidemen. Most modern Chicago-styled blues musicians have played with Muddy Waters (for example, Earl Hooker, Junior Wells, Walter Horton, Jimmy Rogers, James Cotton, Willie Smith, Buddy Guy, and so forth), and in this regard, he is truly a "bossman" in the blues (as Miles Davis is in jazz and Bill Monroe in bluegrass). It was Muddy Waters's recording of "Rollin' Stone" that influenced the Rolling Stones rock group and gave them their name; it also became the title of a rock magazine.

"Chicago blues," then, is simply an electrified ensemble playing Mississippi Delta blues music. The other variants (most importantly, B. B. King's single noting because of his inability to play with a slide) came from Memphis, Los Angeles, Texas, the jump blues of jazz, and so forth. It should be emphasized that many "Chicago blues" songs were major r'n'b successes in the 1950s, and many bluesmen subsequently began to play in that more lucrative field. Hence, many of the blues records here might fit equally in the r'n'b section of black music.

"Chicago" Anthologies

As with other anthologies, the same purposes are stressed here. Several records collate different and similar styles from smaller labels in the "Chicago" pattern. Others, such as the *Genesis* boxes, show the various developments emerging from the late 1950s, as Chess began to record widely in both Memphis and Chicago. This is a good example of the recording company compiling an anthology from its catalog. The Vanguard sets, along with Testament and Delmark, were recorded around 1965 and show the electric blues at that period in stereo, in the studio and with top-notch performers.

B1.266*   **Chicago/The Blues/Today: v.1/3.** three discs. Vanguard VSD 79216/8.

B1.267   **Goin' to Chicago.** Testament T 2218.

B1.268   **Sweet Home Chicago.** Delmark DS 618.
Contemporary Chicago blues is a distinct phenomenon that rarely needs an anthology, for there are so many good records around. However, these recordings were done expressly for their respective companies as illustrative material (in addition to just being *good* music). Sam Charters put together the Vanguard set, and some of that material led to recording contracts for Junior Wells, Buddy Guy, and others. The emphasis is on music available in pubs, and although the set is about a decade old, not that many changes have taken place in Chicago blues. Bands include J. B. Hutto (slashing slide guitar), Homesick James (in the same musical bag), harpists James Cotton and Big Walter Horton, guitarists Otis Rush, Johnny Shines, and Johnny Young, and pianist Otis Spann. The four groups on the Pete Welding-produced Testament offering include Sam Lay, Billy Boy Arnold, J. B. Hutto again, and the Floyd Jones-Eddie Taylor band. The Delmark set (from 1966-1968) features Magic Sam, Luther Allison, and Louis Myers.

B1.269   **Chicago Ain't Nothin' But a Blues Band.** Delmark 624.

B1.270*   **Chicago Blues: The Beginning.** Testament T 2207.

B1.271   **Chicago Boogie.** Barrelhouse BH 04.

B1.272   **Electric Blues "Chicago Style."** Buddah BDS 7511.

B1.273   **On the Road Again.** Muskadine 100.

B1.274*   **When Girls Do It.** two discs. Red Lightnin' RL 006 (British issue).
The majority of post-war blues came from Chicago recording studios; these discs, along with the Genesis sets, provide ample documentation of the various formats and influences. The tight constricted sound, the amplified Mississippi

feeling brought north by Muddy Waters, and the jangling piano confined to produce a distinct electric style. The Testament set contains 12 previously unissued 1946 recordings made by Muddy Waters, Johnny Shines, Homer Harris, and James Clark. These were made for Columbia, but never released. Hard tunes such as "I'm Gonna Cut Your Head" or "Evil-Hearted Woman Blues" reflect the performing scene at the time, for Chicago has always been a performing city, not just a place to go to cut a few records and then split.

The Delmark material, with Sunnyland Slim, Eddie Clearwater, J. T. Brown, etc., comes from the Rev. Harrington's Atomic-H label, just one of many based in Chicago. They, too, show all kinds of derivation and imitation. The Barrelhouse record is from 1947, with Jimmy Rogers, Little Walter, and Johnny Young (among others); the Muskadine goes from 1947 through 1954, with Johnny Shines, Floyd Jones, Little Walter, J. B. Hutto, and John Brim. The Buddah has more commercial material (from 1955 through 1960, as originally released on Vee Jay records), with Junior Wells, Snooky Pryor, and many of the above named persons. The Red Lightnin' set embraces mostly Chicago, from 1960 to 1970. Thus, all these discs give some coverage, in a chronological sense.

B1.275*   **Genesis. v.1: The Beginnings of Rock.** four discs. Phonogram 6641 047 (British issue).

B1.276*   **Genesis. v.2: Memphis to Chicago.** four discs. Phonogram 6641 125 (British issue).

B1.277*   **Genesis. v.3: Sweet Home Chicago.** four discs. Phonogram 6641 174 (British issue).

This series is in progress, with an open completion date dependent on the time available to the compilers. The idea was to collate the more important Chess blues recordings in an attempt to portray the Chess story, blues in Chicago, certain bluesmen, and indeed the whole story of the blues. Of all the record labels in the post-war blues mode, Chess figured most prominently and was the most important. From this label sprang ideas for British blues groups and subsequent blues influences in rock music today.

Briefly, each set follows a theme, with either 7 or 8 tracks to a side. Each set has a large booklet, with illustrative matter (photographs, posters, etc.) and some large commentary. The first set covers 1947 through 1955 and tries to show "roots" of rock music through blues and the r'n'b stylings of Sunnyland Slim, Muddy Waters, Leroy Foster, Robert Nighthawk, Memphis Minnie, and Big Bill Broonzy. The second set covers the period when the recording masters were made in Memphis, then leased to Chess in Chicago. Eventually, the singers themselves migrated to Chicago, including Sonny Boy Williamson, No. 2, as well as Elmore James, Howlin' Wolf, Dr. Ross, Arthur Crudup, and Joe Hill Louis. This set stresses amplified country blues. The third album finds Chess ensconced in the Chicago mold, with Otis Spann, Big Boy Spires, Floyd Jones, Muddy Waters, John Brim, Little Walter, etc. Occasional tracks have been out on an elpee before, but most are either unissued or were previously available only on singles. These are exciting compilations, and should be in every blues library for both their historical worth and entertainment value.

B1.278   **Take a Little Walk with Me: The Blues in Chicago, 1948-1957.** two discs. Boogie Disease 101/2.

A handful of post-war Chicago blues anthologies (Muskadine 101, Blues Classics 8, Chess 411, and Testament 2207) have been joined by this superb monster reissue. Of all the companies recording this musical genre, Chess was perhaps the strongest, and has already released much of its material under the names of individual artists (in fact, the complete Chess catalogue is currently being massively reissued by Phonogram in England). However, a lot of the records from Chicago have been lost through careless handling, bankruptcies, and misplaced information. Here, though, through the golden and formative years of 1948-1957, are 32 superb tracks from such diverse firms as Chance, JOB, Cobra, Aristocrat, Planet, Tempo-Tone, Regal, State, and Vee-Jay. Luminaries include Floyd Jones, Eddie Taylor, Robert Nighthawk, some excellent Johnny Shines, and a handful of lesser-known lights, but including two women—Grace Brim (wife of John) and Memphis Minnie (from her last session in 1954). Inevitably, there are some duplications such as Jimmy Rogers's "Ludella" (also on Biograph 12035), but the whole anthology is strong with good sound, a competent selection, and some excellent notes.

Innovators

For the electric blues pattern, many solid innovations were made. However, they were not as great as the extensions fashioned by the country bluesmen. Earl Hooker preceded Jimi Hendrix in creating weird sounds from his single-noting style (wah-wah pedals and fingering). Howlin' Wolf contributed great material and interpretations. Elmore James was the master of the slide riff on electric guitar, a device picked up from Robert Johnson's "Dust My Broom." B. B. King had a high sound to his voice and guitar, and he was very effective in his long, single note phrases. He also opened up the blues to white British rock performers. Little Walter was a master harmonica virtuoso. Muddy Waters is the most important bluesman after Robert Johnson in bringing the Delta style home to a wider audience. He was the bluesman primarily responsible for "electrifying" the blues. Otis Spann was an all-round bluesman (composer, performer, accompanist) who was very sensitive when playing solo piano. T-Bone Walker employed electric guitar at an early age and extended the Texas mode of playing (and thereby influenced B. B. King). Sonny Boy Williamson, No. 2 was very individualistic in his broken lines as performed on the mouth harp, but he also created a considerable body of original compositions.

B1.279*   **Earl Hooker. His First and Last Recordings.** Arhoolie 1066.

B1.280   **Earl Hooker. Hooker 'n' Steve.** Arhoolie 1051.

B1.281*   **Earl Hooker. There's a Fungus Amung Us.** Red Lightnin' RL 009 (British issue).

B1.282   **Earl Hooker. Two Bugs and a Roach.** Arhoolie 1044.

Earl Hooker was a cousin of John Lee Hooker, but the family ties do not matter. Possessed of a strong will on the guitar, Hooker was able to craft strange and weird sounds using wah-wah pedals and other devices. Always rhythmically sound, he was able to fuse a great many influences into the mainstream of his work, namely country music (such as "Guitar Rag," based on Remington-McAullife riffs from western swing), solid blues (such as Robert Nighthawk's "The Moon Is Rising"), and funky instrumentals (such as "Two Bugs in a Rug," based on his bout with tuberculosis. Never a flashy showman, Earl Hooker always tried to stay behind the scenes and work proficiently on his guitars. He hated to sing, and, consequently, less than half of the work under his name has his vocal. Yet he had a very pleasant, dry, gutsy voice. His accompanying work was exceptionally masterful, especially with Junior Wells, Muddy Waters, and his cousin John Lee. He recorded many singles for small Chicago labels, beginning in 1953, always with the band's current vocalist on one side and an earthy instrumental on the other. Some of these include "Sweet Black Angel" and "Earl's Boogie Woogie" on Arhoolie 1066. The Red Lightnin' record comes from the American Cuca recordings in the mid-sixties, and are all instrumentals. Listening to this album, one can clearly detect the assimilation of B. B. King and Jimi Hendrix, although it predates Hendrix! His last recordings are from Pepper's Lounge in 1969 and feature a jam with Eddie Taylor on "Dust My Broom" and "Frosty."

B1.283*   **Big Maceo. Chicago Breakdown.** two discs. RCA AXM 2-5506.

The 32 tracks here are virtually the entire output of this tragic blues figure. From 1941-1945, Maceo had three good recording years for 28 tracks. A stroke finished his piano hands, and four tracks here from 1947 present just his vocals with a quartet led by Eddie Boyd. A resident of Chicago, he was instrumental in the "creation" of a Chicago blues style. His thundering, rolling piano style is most evident in the epic "Chicago Breakdown," and, on most other tracks, his style is neatly contrasted by Tampa Red's guitar. His vocals—plaintive and sincere—were influential on Ray Charles and other "soul" singers. Rollicking boogies were also in his bag.

B1.284*   **Howlin' Wolf. A. K. A. Chester Burnett.** two discs. All Platinum 2ACMB 20.

B1.285   **Howlin' Wolf. Original Folk Blues.** Kent KST 526.

A harsh and compelling voice emanates from the Wolf, truly a howl. Raised in Mississippi, he was one of the last and the oldest to make the transition to Memphis and Chicago. Thus, his style is heavily infused with the influence of old time bluesmen such as Charley Patton and Tommy Johnson. His work is in the medium and slow modes, thus allowing him time to stretch out and gather his thoughts. His harp playing was simple but loud. Hubert Sumlin has played guitar for Wolf since 1952, submerging his own ideas always to the Wolf's. Aggression, as in "Spoonful" or "Smokestack Lightnin'," is really Wolf's forte, and he was a masterful interpreter of the blues. His material and output has been varied for the past 15 years. The Kent reissue of Crown and Modern material comes from the early fifties, when Wolf recorded for Sam Phillips of Sun records. The All Platinum reissues are largely from the 1950s and early 1960s, and feature "The Red Rooster," "How Many More Years," "Sitting on Top of the World," "Killing

Floor," and "Built for Comfort." Other material can be found on various Chess anthologies, especially the *Genesis* series (items B1.266-268).

B1.286*   **Elmore James. Legend, v.1/2.** two discs. Kent KST 9001 and 9010.

B1.287   **Elmore James. Original Folk Blues.** Kent KST 522.

B1.288   **Elmore James. To Know a Man.** two discs. Blue Horizon 7-66230 (British issue).

B1.289   **Elmore James/Eddie Taylor. Street Talkin'.** Muse MR 5087.

B1.290   **Elmore James/John Brim. Whose Muddy Shoes.** Chess 1537.
James took a song and a riff from Robert Johnson ("Dust My Broom"), and, following his early death, a very strong cult of blues fans developed. Distortion was his forte: guitar riffs based on a walking bass, and a bottleneck slide on the treble; a tortured, agonizing voice; and a lean emaciated appearance. Over the years, James recorded a number of Johnson tunes, such as "Standing at the Crossroads." His appeal was an exhilarating, powerful sound that immediately turns on the listener. The Kent material comes from the Modern/Flair/RPM singles (and includes some unissued material) of the early 1950s, and this is some of his best material; the Muse items (7 tracks) are from 1957, just after he moved to Chicago permanently. The Chess material comes from a variety of sessions in the 1950s (and it too includes unissued material), and the Blue Horizon set is the complete tape of his last session for Fire records (1961), including all the false starts and outtakes. This latter is a very interesting documentary, and presents James at his varied best. His very first record was a 1949 trumpet single of "Dust My Broom," and it is strictly in the country blues mold, with Sonny Boy Williamson, No. 2, on harp (this is found on Blues Classics 5). Thereafter, James joined a r'n'b band, and changed his playing methods.

B1.291   **B. B. King. 1949-1950.** Kent KST 9011.

B1.292   **B. B. King. Boss of the Blues.** Kent KST 529.

B1.293   **B. B. King. Back in the Alley.** ABC 878.

B1.294*   **B. B. King. From the Beginning.** two discs. Kent KST 533.

B1.295   **B. B. King. Let Me Love You.** Kent KST 513.

B1.296*   **B. B. King. Live at the Regal.** ABC 724.
King's vocal influences have been Joe Turner and Jimmy Rushing, and his guitar stylings are a logical extension of T-Bone Walker. For years (1949 through 1962), he had been a favorite with the black r'n'b-blues audience, recording for the Modern/Flair/RPM company (and reissued on the above Kent discs). His impact after that period was one of "discovery" by the white audience, most notably through the music of Eric Clapton and other British musicians. His guitar playing was extremely dexterous, emphasizing long, lean lines and fluent arpeggio

picking. An extension of this style can be found in Buddy Guy's performances. Vocally, King's high, strained shouts and screams were very emotional, but he was one of the few bluesmen who never sang while playing guitar, and vice versa. Assorted r'n'b and jazz accompaniment appear on all his records, but many blues fans wait for the day when he may perform with just a trio backing. The discs in the Kent series are the ones with the least duplications from their reissue program, and contain important hits such as his theme "Everyday I Have the Blues," "Sweet Little Angel," "Five Long Years," "Rock Me Baby," "Three O'Clock Blues," etc. His first recordings were in 1949 (as above). Generally, the ABC period is uneven, and largely poor for blues or r'n'b fans. The producers had taken over, but the better of the efforts are on *Back in the Alley*, which significantly covers only to 1967. B. B. is usually at his best before a live audience, and the 1964 Regal is the best disc to show his relationships with screaming fans.

B1.297*   **Little Walter. Boss Blues Harmonica.** two discs. All Platinum 2 ACMB 202.

B1.298   **Little Walter. Confessin' the Blues.** Chess 416.

B1.299   **Little Walter. Hate to See You Go.** Chess·1535.
        Walter never possessed a strong or distinctive voice. His main strength lay in being a harp virtuoso: long, wailing tones, with a number of techniques to make his harmonica actually talk or sing, such as underblowing, overblowing, flutter-tonguing, and so forth. He accompanied Muddy Waters and contributed much to the distinctive sound of the Chicago blues in general (and to Muddy's blues band in particular) before striking out on his own with the Myers brothers (known as the Aces) with the monster hit "Juke." Little Walter's recordings with others will be found in the Genesis boxes or under the names of other Chess performers such as Muddy Waters. The five discs above present almost all of the tracks under his own name for Chess; the more important ones include "My Babe," "Blues with a Feeling," "Off the Wall," "Thunderbird," "Quarter to Twelve," "Lights Out," "Roller Coaster," "Key to the Highway," and, of course, "Juke."

B1.300*   **Muddy Waters. At Newport.** Checker 6467 306 (British issue).

B1.301*   **Muddy Waters. Down on Stovall's Plantation.** Testament T-2210.

B1.302*   **Muddy Waters. Folk Singer.** Chess 1483.

B1.303*   **Muddy Waters. McKinley Morganfield A. K. A. Muddy Waters.** two discs. All Platinum 2ACMB 203.

B1.304*   **Muddy Waters. They Call Me Muddy Waters.** Chess 1553.
        Muddy Waters is the king of the Chicago blues, and probably the most important bluesman after Robert Johnson. Yet, this reinforces Johnson's position since Waters was heavily influenced by him. The Testament set is derived from the Library of Congress 1941-1942 recordings and clearly shows Waters's debt to Johnson. A decade later, Waters is playing in the same style—vibrato

guitar, bottleneck slide, dusky voice, punching lyrics—but with amplification and sidemen, particularly with second guitarist Jimmy Rogers, pianist Otis Spann, and harmonica player Little Walter. Yet, it is interesting to compare Chess 1483 with the Testament. This 1963 Chess effort spotlights Waters with a trio, playing such Mississippi blues as "My Home Is in the Delta," "Big Leg Woman," and "Country Boy." There is really not much difference once the harp and piano are removed. The twofer collates some of his biggest successes (originally in the r'n'b market), such as "Louisiana Blues," "I Just Want to Make Love to You," "Hoochie Coochie Man," "Long Distance Call," "Rollin' Stone," "Got My Mojo Working," and so forth. The Newport set includes re-recordings plus "I Wanna Put a Tiger in Your Tank," but it is mainly important because it was Waters's first exposure to a predominantly white crowd (1960). This got him campus bookings, and the long extended "Mojo" was the version endlessly copied by many British rock bands.

B1.305*   **Otis Spann. Everest Archive of Folk Music FS 216.**

B1.306   **Otis Spann. The Blues Never Die!** Prestige PR 7719.

B1.307*   **Otis Spann. Chicago Blues.** Testament T-2211.

B1.308   **Otis Spann. Cryin' Time.** Vanguard VSD 6514.

B1.309   **Otis Spann. Heart Loaded with Trouble.** Bluesway BLS 6063.

B1.310*   **Otis Spann. Otis Spann Is the Blues.** Barnaby Candid Z 30246.

B1.311*   **Otis Spann. Walking the Blues.** Barnaby Candid KZ 31290.
        Otis Spann was simply the best all-around bluesman that musical history has produced. He was a superb composer, performer, and accompanist. There are three main aspects to his career. He began as pianist for the Muddy Waters band, contributing the well-known piano bass style with occasional solos. Then he performed as a solo artist, most notably for the Everest (from the Danish Storyville label in 1963), the Candid, and the Testament labels. His third side was as band leader in a number of collaborations with the Muddy Waters band (Bluesway, Prestige, Vanguard, and Testament). With Spann leading, the material was strong and the groups mostly tight. With the added vocals of his wife Lucille on a few tracks scattered throughout the above albums, he came very close to assimilating the real gist of the blues. Heavily influenced by Big Maceo, Spann was, though, at his best in a solo context. The two Candids clearly show the inheritance of the blues tradition, with such as "Great Northern Stomp" or "Worried Life Blues." His bass playing of great depth was accompanied by a broken voice of a hushed introspective nature, and his piano solos were the epitome of ceaseless questioning in the blues. Complex rolls, cascading trebles, introverted singing— all earmarks of pain and anguish (particularly on "Otis in the Dark").

B1.312   **T-Bone Walker. Capitol ECR 8185 (Japanese issue).**

B1.313*   **T-Bone Walker. Classics of Modern Blues.** two discs. Blue Note BNLA 533-H2.

B1.314   **T-Bone Walker. I Want a Little Girl.** Delmark DS 633.

B1.315*   **T-Bone Walker. T-Bone Blues.** Atlantic SD 8020.
Walker began recording with Columbia at the age of 16 in 1919, breaking in later on electric guitar with many swing and jazz bands of the Southwest. Emerging as a solo artist after World War II, he recorded the Capitol set around 1947, and it remains his best work, with such items as "Hypin' Woman Blues," "Lonesome Woman Blues" (with a Bumps Myers tenor sax), and "Vacation Blues" (with trumpeter Teddy Buckner). Walker was heavily involved with jazz, and he has been one of the few blues performers accepted by jazz collectors. His solo notes on guitar were very important in influencing B. B. King, and he did his best work with a small jazz backing (reflecting this during twenty years of playing). Hailing from Texas, and influenced by Blind Lemon Jefferson, Leroy Carr, Scrapper Blackwell, and Lonnie Johnson, Walker came up the hard way via Ma Rainey and the classic "Stormy Monday Blues (Call It Stormy Monday)."
In the early 1950s, Walker recorded some 56 sides for Imperial, and 28 of these have been reissued on the Blue Note twofer. Of all his records, these were the most accessible to the r'n'b market, and the ones that featured a large horn and reed backing. It was these records that certain "rock" stars paid attention to, such as Eric Clapton, Jimi Hendrix, Duane Allman, Jimmy Page, Doug Sahm, Johnny Winter, Jeff Beck, and Mike Bloomfield. His single note phrasing was very influential, as in "Strollin' with Bones." The backing is particularly effective during this time because it was arranged in a call-and-response pattern, with Walker's guitar upfront. The latter also had a scraping quality about it, a sort of pre-distortion period dirty sound that could only be achieved by the manner of picking, not by electric devices (then unknown). Typical tracks here include "Street Walking Woman," "Railroad Station Blues," "Evil Hearted Woman," "Party Girl," and "Get These Blues Off Me." The Atlantic offering highlights his next good period in the mid-fifties, and features a number of instrumentals, such as "Two Bones and a Pick" and "T-Bone Shuffle," with guitarist Barney Kessel and saxist Plas Johnson. The Delmark record, recorded in France in 1968, presents a variety of Walker styles, such as the "jump blues" of McShann, Jordan, and Turner. With him are Hal Singer on reeds, who completes the Southwest influence, along with blues drummer S. P. Leary. Rocking numbers include the tough "Someone's Going to Mistreat You," and two instrumentals, "Late Hour Blues" and "Feeling the Blues." One typical Walker ballad, featuring his hard edged voice, is "Baby Ain't I Good to You," written by Don Redman and once recorded by the McKinney's Cotton Pickers in 1929.

B1.316   **Sonny Boy Williamson, No. 2. Bummer Road.** Chess 1536.

B1.317   **Sonny Boy Williamson, No. 2.** two discs. All Platinum 2 ACMB 206.

B1.318*   **Sonny Boy Williamson, No. 2. The Original.** Blues Classics BC 9.

B1.319*   **Sonny Boy Williamson, No. 2. This is My Story.** two discs. Chess
2CH 50027.
Born Rice Miller, this Sonny Boy is relatively easy to distinguish from No. 1 by the simple chronological fact that he never recorded commercially until after

No. 1 died. His 1951 Trumpet recordings (on the Blues Classics disc) were instant
classics, featuring an individual style with many broken lines. Rhythm was his
business, and he played his harmonica with a flourish of bent notes, sometimes
using his whole mouth. His early experience was on radio with the King Biscuit
Time of Helena, Arkansas. Important tunes from these early recordings include
"Mighty Long Time," "Mr. Downchild," "Pontiac Blues," and "Nine Below Zero."
Moving to Chess, he figured prominently in the tight Chicago sound—a situation
that forced him into some small restraints, probably producing better records
because of it. The *Bummer Road* album is notable for the "Little Village" series
of takes, a complete 12 minute runthrough with the tape left running all the time.
Many false starts were made, and it is interesting to hear the disagreements. The
double set contains all of his big Chess successes, accompaniment being given
by the roster of Chess stars: Muddy Waters, Otis Spann, Jimmy Rogers, Buddy
Guy, Willie Dixon, etc. This ten year period led to such epics as "Fattening Frogs
for Snakes," "Your Funeral and My Trial," "Got to Move," "Help Me," and
Willie Dixon's "Bring It On Home."

Standards

B1.320*   **Luther Allison. Love Me Mama.** Delmark DS 625.
     Allison is the prototype of the second-generation bluesman in the Chicago
style. His sources are varied (B. B. King, Buddy Guy, and others in the melodic
guitar vein), and his lyrics are reinterpretations of some blues classics, such as
"Little Red Rooster," "Five Long Years," "Dust My Broom," "The Skies Are
Crying," and "Love Me Mama." Yet he manages to breathe new life into these
pieces. This is due no doubt to a very sincere playing style, proper accompaniment,
and an incredibly rich, lustrous screaming voice that has no equal. Allison works
hard at the blues, and could easily make more money with soul music. Some
attempts to bridge soul and blues have resulted in two fairly good Motown albums
under Allison's name. Meanwhile, he continues to tour the country, bringing
with him his brand of no-nonsense, hassle-free blues, playing at the drop of a hat
the music he knows and loves best.

B1.321   **Charles Brown/Jimmy McCracklin. Best of the Blues, v.1.** Imperial
     9257.
     The twelve items on this set are simply some of the best blues tracks owned
by the UA Imperial catalog. Previously available in the Aladdin series, the six
songs by Charles Brown include the seminal "Drifting Blues," "Seven Long Days,"
and "Get Yourself Another Fool." He was a soft singer who moulded several
attempts at West Coast blues singing styles. Similarly, McCracklin, on "Bitter Pill"
and "Sooner or Later," both original compositions, projected a laid-back feeling
together with a plush exciting background. The tension was enormous.

B1.322*   **Clarence "Gatemouth" Brown. San Antonio Ballbuster.** Red Lightnin'
     RL 0010 (British issue).
     "Gatemouth" was one of the influential blues performers working in the
jump blues idiom. He recorded often in Texas for the Peacock label (from whence
these 16 singles were taken). He could play guitar, harmonica, and even violin.

Though he now performs as a soul singer (because that's where the money is),
the performances here are acknowledged as classics. The violin on the instrumental
"Just before Dawn" is incredible, filled with many swoops and frills. The riffing
horns on the 1949 "Didn't Reach My Goal" are phenomenal. This is certainly
one record to play at loud volume.

B1.323   **Clifton Chenier. Louisiana Blues and Zydeco.** Arhoolie 1024.

B1.324*   **Clifton Chenier. Black Snake Blues.** Arhoolie 1038.
    "Zydeco" is a miraculous blend of blues and black music with Louisiana
Cajun music. Thus, Chenier appears to be the only blues performer who plays
the accordion. All of the music is mainly for dancing, and assorted accompanying
instrumentation includes fiddles, piano, and either drums or washboard. Some of
the more Cajun pieces include "Eh, 'tite Fille," "Zydeco et Pas Salé," and
"Monifique." In his blues outings, Chenier has been compared to Count Basie,
for he sets up similar riffs on his bass notes while playing solo line in the treble.
This comes up again in the jazz item "Things Ain't What They Used to Be,"
although this is written by Duke Ellington. Blues items include "Banana Man,"
"Black Snake Blues," and the traditional "I Got a Little Girl." In the past,
Chenier had recorded a number of singles only, and the top-selling, most attractive
of these can be found on Imperial LM 94001 and the *Rock Bottom* anthology
(Chess 9033-60003).

B1.325   **James Cotton. Pure Cotton.** Verve Forecast FTS 3038.
    Cotton is best known as a harmonica accompanist for Muddy Waters and
others. Striking out on his own, though, he is noted for the high quality of his
own accompanists in the 1960s. Of all his records, this one stands heads and
shoulders above the rest. Luther Tucker on guitars and Francis Clay on drums
are the most able performers. Memorable selections include the novelty-story
"Who's Afraid of Little Red Riding Hood?," the long harp solo on "The Creeper"
(from Little Walter influences) and the slow "Fallin' Rain" and "Heart Attack."

B1.326   **Champion Jack Dupree.** Vogue CLVLX 271 (French issue).

B1.327*   **Champion Jack Dupree.** Archive of Folk Music FS 217.

B1.328   **Champion Jack Dupree. Blues for Everybody.** King KS 1084.

B1.329*   **Champion Jack Dupree. Blues from the Gutter.** Atlantic SD 8255.

B1.330   **Champion Jack Dupree. The Woman Blues.** Folkways FS 3825.
    Dupree was first recorded in 1940; he has not changed anything since. He
remains a barrelhouse pianist in the Texas-New Orleans vein. The Folkways set
is from that early period, and he here began his affair with "woman songs" that
still goes on. Rough voice, rolling piano, tempo changes—they are all here. Dupree
is difficult to accompany because he does not believe in 12 bar blues and will
shift gears at will. At times, though, he does become repetitive, utilizing certain
lyrics and melodies over and over again. Perhaps his best overall work was the
half dozen or so albums created for Storyville in Denmark around 1960-1962.

The Archive of Folk Music issue is the American release of Storyville 161, as good a representative sampling as any. Some of the lyrics are reproduced, and they show high originality and autobiographical detail. Some of the songs are half-sung, half-spoken, in a pitiful, sorrowful voice. Often, though, he can be tasteless, as in "Harelip Blues," where he affects that speech impediment (on the King disc) or on "Everybody's Blues." Accompanist then as now was guitarist Mickey Baker, who was able to keep up with Dupree's time tables after knowing him for over 20 years. He is also heard on the Vogue set, which has the topical blues "Death of Luther King," rather unusual for Dupree. The Atlantic set was his best record from the fifties, and with titles such as "T. B. Blues," "Can't Kick the Habit," and "Junker's Blues," it may very well have been the best of any blues record. For once, with a group here, Dupree kept his changes to a minimum.

B1.331   **Johnny Fuller. Fullers Blues.** Bluesmaker BM 3801 (Australian issue).

Fuller has been one of the most active mainstays of the West Coast blues scene for over a quarter of a century. His previous material can be found on several West Coast anthologies (see items B1.102-106) that emphasized Oakland blues, particularly his recording for Bob Geddins. Most of Fuller's influences have been either blues shouters or Texas bluesmen (although Fuller himself was born in Mississippi). Although this disc was recorded in the Los Angeles area, it was released only by an Australian company and re-imported into the United States. With a wide range of supporting musicians, including Phillip Walker on guitar and Big John Jambezian on harp, Fuller works his way through 12 items, mostly original, but including the Memphis Slim "Miss You So."

B1.332*   **Lowell Fulson.** Arhoolie R 2003.

B1.333   **Lowell Fulson. In a Heavy Bag.** Polydor 2384 038 (British issue).

B1.334   **Lowell Fulson. Let's Go Get Stoned.** Kent KST 558.

B1.335   **Lowell Fulson. Soul.** Kent KLP 5016.

Fulson picked up most of his Texas blues experience (he's part Indian, from Oklahoma) by working as a guitarist for Texas Alexander. He used the arpeggio style and was extremely popular in southern California clubs. The Arhoolie set of 14 tracks is derived from the Los Angeles Swing Time label in a post-war setting. In addition to blues music, he had assimilated the styles of western swing that were so prominent at the time. When accompanied by brother Martin on rhythm guitar, Fulson was able to improvise around the melody, but as the solo guitarist with a piano trio (or larger group), he turned in only perfunctory guitar runs. In this time period, he experimented with jump blues and country blues, always keeping one step ahead of the trends. In the 1950s, it was rock and roll and r'n'b that he tried to get into with Chess. In the 1960s, it was funky-soul, and these turned out quite successfully, the Kent discs illustrating such as "My Aching Back," "Shattered Dreams," "The Letter," and "Funky Broadway." At this time, he also returned to updated blues—again, ahead of the rock stars—with the perennial "Feel So Bad," "Everyday I Have the Blues," "Going to Chicago," and "Confessin' the Blues" (from his McShann days). After a dismal attempt (for Muscle Shoals) at pure "rock," Fulson moved to Jewel in 1968, and the result was incorporated into a Polydor reissue: a mixture of r'n'b and rock.

B1.336   **Buddy Guy. I Was Walking through the Woods. Chess 409.**

B1.337*   **Buddy Guy. In the Beginning.** Red Lightnin' RL 001 (British issue).
    Guy was a logical extension of the B. B. King mold. The material on these two discs dates from 1958 through 1964, Guy's best and most productive blues period. Since moving to Vanguard, he has become more florid and decorative, to the extent that he now has a fifty-foot lead on his amplifier so that he can travel at will amongst the audience. His best work, apart from these two discs, has always been with Junior Wells, his co-partner off and on for the past decade. It just seems that when Guy has a record under his own name, he performs poorly; or, he just performs better (excels himself?) with others. The Chess material includes Otis Rush, Otis Spann, Lafayette Leake, and Sonny Boy Williamson, No. 2, in different group lineups. The extensive tunes (for which he was prepared by being the house guitarist at Chess for many years) include "Stone Crazy" and "I Found a True Love." Outstanding performances from 1960 include "First Time I Met the Blues" and "Ten Years Ago." For his other records, check under Junior Wells (B1.370-372).

B1.338*   **Curtis Jones. Lonesome Bedroom Blues. Delmark 605.**

B1.339   **Curtis Jones. Trouble Blues.** Vogue LDM 30202 (French issue).
    Being over thirty by the time he first recorded (near the end of the Depression), Jones had already assimilated his influences and was fashioning his style, which featured a high pitched voice about to give out and fairly fluent piano playing (Texas influence). He was rediscovered in 1959 and 1962, and recorded for Delmark and Prestige's Bluesville series (the latter now deleted and only available as French Vogue). The most sensational material here was his remake of "Lonesome Bedroom Blues," a sterling classic, "Stackolee" (more a ballad), and an instrumental version of "Rolling the Blues." The Delmark is a solo effort, while the Vogue features a tight little group.

B1.340   **Freddy King. Hideaway.** King 1059.
    These 12 tracks are recordings from the Federal catalog, by way of King records. In 1961, King was a leader in the blues r'n'b field with such hits as "I'm Tore Down" and "Hide Away." Texas-born and Chicago-influenced, King paid tribute to his mentors—T-Bone Walker and B. B. King, on guitar; Otis Rush and Magic Sam, for vocal lines—in more than just a technical sense. It was, rather, a distillation of the state of the blues in 1960. Freddy King was superb on the instrumental tracks alone (such as "Hide Away"). Although he has since recorded prolifically, he has never attained the initial success of these tracks, which was no doubt due to the back-up musicians on rollicking piano and solid bass and drumming. Instrumentals include "Low Tide," "Driving Sideways," "The Stumble," "Washout," and "Side Tracked." On the love songs, King's vocals excel with, for instance, "Have You Ever Loved a Woman" and "I Love the Woman."

B1.341   **J. B. Lenoir. Natural Man.** Chess 410.

Lenoir was unusual in that he appeared to have two distinctive styles. One was for fast tunes, with a clear, whining voice over a rolling guitar, often with saxophone accompaniment, as in the funny "Mama, What about Your Daughter." Another was serious, slow blues, usually with a small group. In this latter style, he concentrated on socially relevant "messages," and he was one of the few bluesmen to embrace topical songs. One of these was "Eisenhower Blues," initially withdrawn from circulation when the White House clamped down. Others were "Korea Blues" and "I'm in Korea"—treatment of blacks in the services during that war was the message.

B1.342   **Lightnin' Slim. Rooster Blues.** Excello Ex 8000.

Recorded in 1959-1960 by Excello in Crowley, Louisiana, these 12 selections represent a laid-back country blues artist at his best. The tunes are so relaxed that one might be inclined to fall asleep. But then, that was the style of Jay Miller's recording company. Lazy Lester assists with his harmonica for "Hoodoo Blues," "Long Leanie Mama," "Red Bug Blues," "It's Mighty Crazy," "I'm Learning You, Baby," and so on.

B1.343   **Lonesome Sundown.** Excello EX 8012.

From various sessions (1958 through 1965), these twelve selections again present the "lazy" character of the Louisiana blues through the Excello record company—with an interesting variation. The music was heavily amplified and the droning quality of the tunes seemed the voice of doom. Woman troubles predominate, as well as voodoo influences. Although saxophones were rarely used, occasionally a harp would blow over the "tinkly" piano, another characteristic of the "Crowley" sound. Mellow selections include "Love Me Now," "I'm Glad She's Mine," "Please Be on that 519," and "Lonesome Lonely Blues."

B1.344   **Joe Hill Louis. The One Man Band.** Muskadine 101.

The sixteen tracks here range from 1949 through 1956, and reflect the phenomenon of a self-taught musician who played harmonica, guitar, and high-hat to accompany traditional songs. All the tunes were recorded in Memphis, some for the Sun label (most of his Sun material was unissued). Sam Phillips, the label's owner, leased certain masters to Chess in Chicago and to RPM on the West Coast. Thus, Louis got what was then "national" exposure in that he appeared in several markets at the same time. Yet, he continued to perform on street corners for loose change. Good material here includes the unusual "Hydramatic Blues," "Chocolate Blonde," and "Cold Chills." Other material can be found on *Memphis Blues* (Kent 9002), *Memphis and the Delta* (Blues Classics BC 15), *Genesis, v.2* (Phonogram 6641 125), *Blue in the Morning* (Polydor 2383 214), and *The Sun Story* (Phonogram 6641 180).

B1.345   **Louisiana Red. Sings the Blues.** Atco SD 33-389.

Iverson Minter (a. k. a. Louisiana Red) plays guitar and harp, and once worked as Elmore James, Jr., for awhile in Mississippi. He's still young (36) as far as bluesmen go. His screaming guitar notes are modelled after B. B. King, and so is his slightly rough voice. Only the track "Louisiana Blues" features his coarse harp, but the other five harp lines are played by Bill Dicey, who blows every chance he gets. Red's tragic early life was reflected in the four sides he cut for Chess in the 1950s, which culminated in a Roulette album now available only in the United Kingdom as Carnival 2941 002, and worth acquiring. Most of the twelve tunes here on Atco are hits by others (Muddy Waters's "Rolling Stone" and those of Reed, Crudup, and Dixon), with organ by Dave "Baby" Cortez!!! The rest are autobiographical: "I Am Louisiana Red," "The Story of Louisiana Red," "Red's New Dream," etc. His "Freight Train to Ride" is an Elmore James "Broom" variation.

B1.346*   **Magic Sam. 1937-1969.** Blue Horizon 7-63223 (British issue).

B1.347   **Magic Sam. Black Magic.** Delmark DS 620.

B1.348   **Magic Sam. West Side Soul.** Delmark DS 615.
    Sam Maghett died in 1969 from a heart attack at the age of 32. During his short 12-year career, his first and last records were among some of the finest in Chicago blues. The Blue Horizon contains 12 tracks made for Cobra in Chicago between 1957 and 1958. The tight staccato style of guitar playing was all accomplished by his fingers without picks, no mean feat at the time. Included here are the very important recordings of "All Your Love" (redone by Otis Rush, John Mayall's Bluesbreakers, and Magic Sam again on DS 615). The funky eerie guitar riff was in Sam's innovative repertoire, and it stands as a milestone of 1950s blues guitar riffs, predating all of the British rockers' efforts. His most intense records were probably "Everything Gonna Be Alright" and "Easy Baby." The two Delmark records present some updated versions, but still retain the tight, disciplined style that made Sam such a favorite on the West Side.

B1.349   **Memphis Slim.** RCA 730 581 (French issue).

B1.350   **Memphis Slim. Old Times, New Times.** two discs. Barclay 90013/14 (French issue).
    Memphis Slim (Peter Chatman) packed it in a while back, to move to France to live and perform. Unfortunately, the welter of records under this pianist's name are routine, unexciting, and even full of errors of performance. Occasionally, though, there are flashes of brilliance. The RCA material represents perhaps the best efforts of his chequered career. These sixteen tracks, with bass accompaniment, come from 1940-1941, and include his first song—and first, big hit—"Beer Drinking Woman." On balance, he was a better composer than performer, having written the B. B. King theme "Everyday I Have the Blues." Then, of all things, he surfaced again in 1970 with a great double album. The first disc features just Slim and Roosevelt Sykes trading stories and singing some of their best efforts in a series of piano duets (with one guitar effort from Sykes). The second disc is one of the better group efforts (Slim's most notable failures have been in these kinds of records), featuring the Buddy Guy-Junior Wells Blues Band, and occasional vocals by Guy to supplement Slim's lead vocals. All the material was by Slim, except for Muddy Waters's "Rolling and Tumbling" and Leroy Carr's "How Long Blues." Of the two discs in the set, the Sykes encounter is the best, yet WEA in America chose to release only the Guy-Wells collaboration.

B1.351*   **Johnny Otis. Cold Shot.** Kent KST 534.

This is one of the finest urban blues records to appear in the 1970s—just at a time when critics were claiming that it was dying because nothing new appeared. True, much music was reinterpreted in the same manner, but the Johnny Otis show was always reinvigorating, reverting back and forth between rhythm 'n' blues and uptempo (or uptown) blues. This is a roots type of album, emphasizing the urban blues and was one of a series of discs·Otis made to help launch his son Shuggie's career. Shuggie Otis plays guitars and drums; Johnny Otis plays piano, drums, and vocals. Various other people join in, but the prime singer is Mighty Mouth Evans, displaying a rich, contemporary voice. The album takes off from "The Signifyin' Monkey" (a song about teasing, with the "dirty dozens," etc.), through a thoroughly modern "I Believe I'll Go Back Home," a takeoff on the tune right back through Robert Johnson; a marvelously funky "High Heel Sneakers," and the final instrumental—the title selection, with Sugarcane Harris on electric violin. Truly, an amazing and surprising record, this is complemented by the other Kent recording, *Snatch and the Poontangs*, rated "X."

B1.352*   **Junior Parker. Best.** Duke DLP 83.

B1.353   **Junior Parker. Sometime Tomorrow My Broken Heart Will Die.** Bluesway BLS 6066.

B1.354   **Junior Parker. You Don't Have to Be Black to Love the Blues.** Groove Merchant GM 502.

B1.355   **Junior Parker. With Jimmy McGriff.** United Artists UAS 5597.

These four records pretty well capture the essence and the ups and downs of Herman Parker, noted harpist from the Memphis area. The Duke collation presents his more bluesy efforts, such as "Mother-in-Law Blues," "Peaches," "Driving Wheel," "Things I Used to Do," and "Annie Get Your Yo-Yo." The Bluesway item (from ABC, which bought the Duke/Peacock catalog) uses later Duke material to present a more slick, modern-sounding Parker (complete with big band and strings) in some soft soul ballads, such as "My Love Is Real," "If You Can't Take It," and "Today I Sing the Blues." The Groove Merchant set updates the early Duke material, with "Five Long Years" and such originals as "Blue Shadows Falling," "Man or Mouse," and "That's Alright." The set with Jimmy McGriff is particularly illuminating. Heavily electrified with various saxophones, electric piano, and organ, it was recorded at the Gold Slipper in Newark, New Jersey. It was one of the last things that Parker did, for he died shortly after. The material is firmly in the r'n'b area, with some blues overtones: Percy Mayfield's "I Need Love So Bad," "Don't Let the Sun Catch You Cryin'," and even a sterling "Baby Please Don't Go," credited to Muddy Waters. Parker's long career has shown brilliance in interpretation of songs, and he has been strongly influential in the r'n'b field.

B1.356   **L. C. "Good Rockin' " Robinson. Ups and Down.** Arhoolie 1062.

This is one of the better fresh blues albums of the 1970s. Playing around the Oakland area, Robinson had made a few earlier records stretching back to the late forties. But this was his first album, and it clearly shows the influence of western swing music on the blues. Robinson plays guitar, violin, and steel guitar (being instructed in the latter by the great Leon McAuliffe). The first side here has the Muddy Waters blues band (with Waters sitting out) performing a wide variety of material, such as "Across the Bay Blues" or "Pinetop's Boogie Woogie." The second side features a quartet, with the piano trio of David Alexander, another eclectic bluesman from the Oakland area. They start off with a perfect remake of Robinson's 1945 single on Black and White, "I've Got to Go," and then move on into social commentary such as "Things So Bad in California." Firm blues bowing on the fiddle establishes Robinson as a leader in the field.

B1.357*   **Otis Rush. This One's a Good 'Un.** Blue Horizon 7-63222 (British issue).

B1.358   **Otis Rush/Albert King. Door to Door.** Chess 1538.
     Otis Rush is a pathetic performer in the history of the blues. He has been exceptionally well-recognized as being an important influence, as much as B. B. King, but he has, unfortunately, recorded little. Basically, he extended the flowery guitary style of B. B. King (a style that reaches its most commercial application in the music of Buddy Guy), and he sings in a tremulous but intense vocal. By far his best material was on the Cobra recordings of 1956-1958, which included "All Your Love," "Checking on My Baby," and "Violent Love." These are on the Blues Horizon set. The Chess material includes the sterling "So Many Roads."

B1.359*   **Johnny Shines.** Advent 2803.

B1.360   **Johnny Shines. Masters of Modern Blues, v. 1.** Testament T 2212.

B1.361*   **Johnny Shines. With Big Walter Horton.** Testament T-2217.
     Johnny Shines is that rare blues performer—equally at home with acoustic, solo, or country blues, and with electric, band, or Chicago blues. Much of the material that he learned with Robert Johnson in the thirties has been transformed into urban blues by such stylists as Muddy Waters. Thus, it seems logical that someone who actually sang with Johnson should re-interpret the work of the master in the urban format. This is most evident on "Walkin' Blues," "Mr. Tom Green's Farm," or "Two Trains Runnin'." All of it is consummate bottleneck style. The urban support given by (in the case of the Testaments) Walter Horton (harp), Otis Spann (piano), and Fred Below (drums) is superb. The Advent release presents Shines along with a younger, funkier group of accompanists, but the results are virtually the same as on his earlier 1966 work. If anything, his voice had become more emotional, as on "My Love Can't Hide," which is most expressive of his falsetto and vibrato. Throughout his guitar playing, there is a feeling of toughness and persistence.

B1.362   **Slim Harpo. Best.** Excello EX 8010.
     Beyond any doubt, Harpo (born James Moore) was the most successful of the Louisiana singers that Miller nourished on his small Excello label. In 1961, Harpo's first record ("I've Got Love If You Want It,") was released and it was (along with "I'm a King Bee," on the reverse side of the single) immediately added to the repertoire of many British rock bands. "Raining in My Heart" was the disc that put him on top of the r'n'b polls in America, and that was later followed by

"Baby, Scratch My Back," "Shake Your Hips," and "Tip On In." As a harp player, his style was vigorous but ordinary compared to Sonny Boy Williamson, No. 2, or Little Walter; however, it was his material that really shone.

B1.363   **Sunnyland Slim.** Storyville 671.169 (Danish issue).

B1.364   **Sunnyland Slim. Chicago Blues Session.** "77" Records LA 12/21 (British issue).

B1.365   **Sunnyland Slim. Doctor Clayton and His Buddy (Pearl Harbor Blues).** RCA International INT 1176 (British issue).
        Albert Laundrew is a powerful and direct bluesman who recorded after World War II, and was another person instrumental in shaping the Chicago blues. Most notable as a featured sideman on hundreds of recordings, especially for Muddy Waters, he also produced a few of his own efforts. Recording as Doctor Clayton's Buddy, he made 8 tracks for RCA in 1947, along with Blind John Davis and Big Bill Broonzy. In 1960, he recorded the "77" set, which includes a theme, "The Devil Is a Busy Man," and a superb re-interpretation of "One Room Country Shack," the Mercy Dee Walton epic. For Storyville, he fashioned 12 very good tracks of solo piano plus vocal blues. Of all his works, this is the only album to reflect his own thoughts and compositions, including "Tin Pan Alley," "Anna Lou Blues," and "Johnson Machine Gun." Much of his musical strength lies in his superb reworkings of other blues themes.

B1.366   **Eddie Taylor. I Feel So Bad.** Advent 2802.

B1.367   **Eddie Taylor. Masters of Modern Blues, v.3.** Testament T 2214.

B1.368*   **Eddie Taylor. Southside Blues.** Muse MR 5087.
        Better known as a rock solid "second" guitar, Taylor has accompanied most of the classic blues laid down by Jimmy Reed, Elmore James, John Lee Hooker, John Brim, etc. The Advent is a new production, under his own name, with Phillip Walker and George Smith as the main back-up personnel. The biographical notes illuminate the selections, which are mostly country blues transposed into the modern Chicago idiom, e.g., the title selection, "Jackson Town Blues," "Highway 13," and "Blues in the Rain." He shares the Testament set with Floyd Jones, each using the same band, but with each reversing their roles as leader-accompanist. The vintage recordings on Muse, which he shares with Elmore James on one side, come from 1955-1956. The surprising note here is that Reed accompanies Taylor for a change, on both guitar and harmonica. Taylor has long been considered a master of rhythmic playing, and his recordings are the most satisfying examples of the blues' ability to make strong statements with simple means. There is nothing flashy here—just a fine demonstration of the tightly disciplined nature of Chicago blues.

B1.369*   **Mercy Dee Walton. Mercy Dee.** Arhoolie F 1007.
        Texas piano man Walton was one of the more significant figures in the genre during the early 1960s. At a time when older practitioners were coasting or repeating their past successes, Walton was doing the opposite: short bass, rolling

right hand, and perfect interplay with his voice. His hit recording for Specialty was "One Room Country Shack," which got covered by many other blues and jazz performers. Many traditional tunes reappear in his lyrically strong, Southwestern make-up and musical characteristics. Work songs or local-interest material predominate on this Arhoolie album, such as "Walked Down So Many Turnrows" or "Betty Jean." His material from the fifties can be found on an assortment of compilations, such as Kent 9012, Imperial LM 94002, and Blues Classics BC 16.

B1.370*   **Junior Wells. Hoodoo Man Blues.** Delmark DS 9612.

B1.371*   **Junior Wells. In My Younger Days.** Red Lightnin' RL 007 (British issue).

B1.372   **Junior Wells. Southside Blues Jam.** Delmark DS 628.
Wells was heavily influenced by Sonny Boy Williamson, No. 2 and Little Walter. His early recordings, on the Red Lightnin' record, are mainly from the Chief label, 1957 through 1960. They feature raw, gutsy singing and open harp playing. "Junior's Wail" is perhaps most indicative of this. Some of the tracks here feature Earl Hooker on blazing, slashing guitar, and they must be ranked as the best recordings that Wells ever made, such as "Messin' with Kid" (the original version), and "Universal Rock." He later made his mark with Muddy Waters as the latter's harp player before striking out on his own with Buddy Guy in 1965. These have been fruitful collaborations, each performer responding to the other in a way that was better together than each alone. Their Delmark recordings have been the best of a long series (others are on Vanguard, Atlantic and Blue Thumb) under Wells's name, with such titles as the title track, "Yonder Wall," "Early in the Morning," and "Snatch It Back and Hold It." The second Delmark also features Otis Spann on piano in what must be a reunion of the Muddy Waters Band of the late fifties, and highlights "Stop Breaking Down," "Trouble Don't Last Always," and the topical "Blues for Mayor Daley."

B1.373   **Johnny Young. Fat Mandolin.** Blue Horizon 7-63852 (British issue).
The late Johnny Young had the distinction of being the only active mandolinist in the blues. (The premier mandolin performer in the country or rural mode had long been Yank Rachell, with his memorable Sleepy John Estes accompaniments.) On guitar, though, Young was perfunctory and average. Recording occasionally since 1947, for such companies as Chess and Arhoolie, he made his biggest impact only in 1969, with this present record. The lineup is all of the Muddy Waters Band: pianist Spann, harpist Oscher, guitarist Lawhorn, and drummer Leary. The set is primarily a study of the influences of the present-day Chicago blues. Thus, there appear "Mean Black Snake" and "Prison Bound," as well as "Lula Mae" and "Deal the Cards." The mandolin is a particularly good bluesy instrument, and that is how it is used sometimes in the bluegrass genre, as manifested by the great Bill Monroe.

FEMALE SINGERS AND "CLASSIC" BLUES

The woman who sings the blues has usually been treated very unkindly by both recording companies and critics. The "classic" blues means simply blues with a jazz-like accompaniment (piano, cornet, ensemble). Country blues were limited to just a handful of singers.

Anthologies

B1.374*   **Blues Singers: Jazz Sounds of the 20's.** Swaggie S-1240. (Australian issue).

B1.375*   **Ma Rainey and the Classic Blues Singers.** CBS 52798 (British issue).

B1.376   **Pot Hound Blues, 1923-1930.** Historical HLP 15.

B1.377   **Rare and Hot, 1923-1926.** Historical HLP 14.

B1.378   **Rare Blues, 1927-1935.** Historical HLP 4.

B1.379   **Rare Blues of the Twenties, 1924-1929. v.1/2.** two discs. Historical HLP 1/2.

B1.380*   **Women of the Blues.** RCA LPV 534.
      "Classic blues" are derived from vaudeville and medicine shows. They usually feature a *female* blues singer, with so-called "hot" accompaniment, such as a cornet blowing obbligatos behind the singer, plus a piano and maybe some reeds (clarinet, saxophone, etc.). Often, there might be a full New Orleans group with both the front and back lines. The definitive collection exemplifying this style is the CBS set, compiled by leading authority Derrick Stewart-Baxter as a supplement to his book of the same title (London, Studio Vista, 1970). Ma Rainey was probably the most "classic" of the group since virtually all of her work (with such groups as the Georgia Jazz Hounds) was within the context of vaudeville and traveling groups. Not everything here is blues, and the wide range of stylings features Lucille Hegamin, Edith Wilson, Ida Cox, Ma Rainey, and Bessie Smith. Show business was the name of the game, and if the performance or singing was not always "polished," the intent and sophistication, the timing, and the accompaniment were. Blues singers who did not have much experience with this showmanship were mostly rural-based, and they came to prominence during the late twenties as recording companies strove to cash in on early successes. Thus, they began with their roots; but as they became assimilated into the touring shows, they soon developed their "experience." By that time, though, the Depression had arrived and recording activities were cut back drastically. On this CBS disc is the first so-called blues recording, Mamie Smith's "Crazy Blues" (1920) with a full accompaniment. Of all these singers, only Victoria Spivey and Sippi Wallace were still active through the 1960s. The set concludes with a 1939 Ida Cox version of "Hard Hard Times Blues," accompanied by Charlie Christian on guitar, Hot

Lips Page, Ed Hall, Fletcher Henderson, and Lionel Hampton (on drums). She was active longer than many of the other singers, and she was still performing very well here.

Historical HLP 14 contributes such singers as Monette Moore (1924), Hazel Meyers, Rosa Henderson, and Lillian Goodner—all some of the more popular minor figures. The Swaggie set is notable for its strong jazz accompaniment by such various instrumentalists as Louis Armstrong, King Oliver, Eddie Lang, the Hot Five of Armstrong, and the Blue Five of Clarence Williams, these behind Bertha Hill, Margaret Johnson, Sara Martin, Sippi Wallace, Mamie Smith, and others. There is the ribald team of Butterbeans and Susie, with "He Likes It Slow" accompanied by the Hot Five. The Swaggie and CBS come from OKeh and other Columbia labels; the RCA is derived from its own catalog, and features Alberta Hunter, Lizzie Miles, and Sweet Peas Spivey (sister to Victoria) in addition to some of the above. Again, the context is fairly sophisticated jazz, with New Orleans accompaniment or piano-cornet duos. Important songs here include Victoria Spivey's "Moaning the Blues," Sweet Peas's "Cold in Hand," Lizzie Miles's "My Man of War," Sippi Wallace's "I'm a Mighty Tight Woman," and Margaret Johnson's "Dead Drunk Blues." The other Historical anthologies contain more "classic" singers, mixed in with a few country male bluesmen.

B1.381*   **Rare Recordings of the Twenties, v.1/4.** four discs. CBS 64218, 65379, 65380, and 65421. (French imports).

During the period that Louis Armstrong was recording with his Hot Five and Seven, he was also providing the trumpet-cornet obbligato behind "classic" blues singers in small group instrumentation configurations. Until recently, his work with them was not that well-known, but, on balance, it certainly was creative and impressive, establishing a brand-new style of blues accompaniment. These discs, while geared and marketed to Armstrong fans, also provide a stunning commentary on the "classic" blues recordings for OKeh and Columbia during the 1920s. The sixty-four tracks cover largely the 1924-1926 period with a few extending as far as 1929. The Bessie Smith sessions are not here, as they are on her epic Columbia sets.

Featured performers include such well-known female blues singers as Clara Smith, Sippi Wallace, Eva Taylor, Bertha "Chippie" Hill, and Victoria Spivey. Accompaniment was usually limited to a cornet-piano duo, but often clarinet, guitar, drums, and sax were added. The most frequent pianist on these records is the renowned Richard M. Jones, but Earl Hines is along, as well as Clarence Williams. Reeds included Bechet, Redman, Hawkins, Dodds, and Noone. Some titles: Maggie Jones's "Poor House Blues" and "Thunderstorm Blues"; Clara Smith's "Shipwrecked Blues" and "Court House Blues"; Sippi Wallace's "Special Delivery Blues" and "Flood Blues"; Eva Taylor's "Santa Claus Blues"; and Chippie Hill's "Pratt's City Blues" and "Lonesome All Alone and Blue." For the most part, the sound is reasonably good, and there are full discographic details.

B1.382   **The Country Girls, 1927-1935.** Origin Jazz Library OJL 6.

B1.383*   **When Women Sang the Blues.** Blues Classics BC 26.

There were very few female country blues singers performing solo or duo with simply guitar and/or piano accompaniment. Memphis Minnie and Lucille Bogan come to mind, but the others were few and far between. Most went into the "classic" mode, and when interest in that form died, the recording companies didn't bother to continue with solo efforts. This was stereotyping of the worst sort—thinking that women had to have full accompaniment—but when economics precluded the continued recording of this genre, all activities ceased. Women have still not made the transition to "urban" or Chicago blues. Only Koko Taylor and Big Mama Thornton are apparent names, and their recordings are few and far between. The Origin set comes with notes and lyrics, plus full discographical information. The sixteen selections include Lottie Kimbrough's "Rolling Log Blues," Geesie Wiley's "Pick Poor Robin Clean," Lulu Jackson's "Careless Love Blues," Lillian Miller's "Dead Drunk Blues," Pearl Dickson's "Little Rock Blues," and Mae Glover's "Shake It Daddy." The Blues Classics set covers the 1920s and 1930s with standout performances by Chippie Hill accompanied by the spine-chilling guitar of Tampa Red. The three tracks of Bessie Tucker's mournful crying reminds the listener of Texas Alexander ("Bogey Man Blues," "Key to the Bushes"). Other unique renditions are given by Lillian Glinn, Bobby Cadillac ("Carbolic Acid Blues"), Emma Wright, Georgia White, and others.

B1.384   **A Basket of Blues.** Spivey LP 1001.

B1.385   **Songs We Taught Your Mother.** Prestige Bluesville BV 1052.
　　　Both of these discs feature beautiful recreations of the bygone "Classic" blues period. The obvious leader of both sessions was Victoria Spivey. The Bluesville record comes from 1961, and features Alberta Hunter, Lucille Hegamin, and Spivey, with accompaniment by Buster Bailey, J. C. Higginbotham, Cliff Jackson, Zutty Singleton, and Willie "The Lion" Smith, among others. Some of these tunes were big hits back in the 1920s, from the sophisticated Hegamin's "You'll Want My Love" to the rural-based Spivey's "Black Snake Blues" to the in-between (and, significantly, Memphis-born) Hunter's "I Got a Mind to Ramble." All of these singers had stopped performing by the late thirties, but all are in excellent form. The Spivey collection features the band of Buddy Tate, with Eddie Barefield. Hegamin and Spivey are back, and they introduce Hannah Sylvester of Philadelphia, who last recorded in 1923 with Fletcher Henderson. She sings the title selection and four others. Most of the material here was expressly written by Spivey, so that these are modern songs but in a recreated setting.

Innovators

　　　Lucille Bogan (Bessie Jackson) and Memphis Minnie were the two leading country blues singers. They both sang mean and nasty, with raw sexual images. Several of Bogan's recordings were never released because of this. Memphis Minnie was also an excellent patterned guitar player. Ma Rainey is "the mother of the blues," for it was through her vaudeville and touring shows that the blues got to be thought of as entertainment. Her voicings and group ensemble work strongly influenced the emerging Bessie Smith. Smith was acceptable to both jazz and blues; her powerful voice and timing made her a success with other people's materials.

B1.386*   **Lucille Bogan and Walter Roland. Alabama Blues, 1930-1935.** Roots
           RL 317 (Austrian issue).

B1.387*   **Bessie Jackson and Walter Roland. 1927-1935.** Yazoo L 1071.
           Nobody really knows which name is the pseudonym; Lucille Bogan recorded
first, and then it was Bessie Jackson after 1933. But the person was one and the
same. She was one of the major women blues singers of the period, favoring the
slow, mean and nasty blues (her voice had a good hard edge to it). Her songs were
more sexually ribald than any other single person's during the blues recording
period: "Sloppy Drunk Blues," "My Man is Boogan Me," "Sweet Man, Sweet Man,"
"Shave 'Em Dry," "Man Stealer Blues," "Stew Meat Blues," etc. The tune "Tricks
Ain't Walking No More" was about unemployed prostitutes during the Depression.
Other songs dealt with lesbianism. This raises the interesting point that many white
producers did not know what the black lingo was all about; phrases like "hot dog,"
"buns," "grinding," "ice cream freezer," "weiner," and so forth were totally foreign,
and perhaps accepted in a humorous sense (did anyone really believe a song about
ice cream *freezers*?) Her major accompanist after 1933 was Walter Roland, who is
also heard solo on a few tracks in the Yazoo set.
           Other good material can be found on the anthologies *Screening the Blues*
(CBS 63288), *Pot Hound Blues* (Historical 15), four tracks on *Rare Blues*, v.4
(Historical 4), and on *The Country Girls* (Origin OJL 6).

B1.388*   **Memphis Minnie. v.1/2.** two discs. Blues Classics BC 1 and 13.

B1.389*   **Memphis Minnie. 1934-1949.** two discs. Flyright LP 108/9 (British
           issue).

B1.390   **Memphis Minnie. Early Recordings of Memphis Minnie and Kansas
           Joe.** Paltram PL 101 (Austrian issue).

B1.391   **Memphis Minnie/Blind Willie McTell. Love Changin' Blues, 1949.**
           Biograph 12035.
           Minnie McCoy was the best female vocalist in the country blues tradition. She
was entirely apart from the "classic" singers, and probably equal to the best of the
country bluesmen guitar pickers. Her tough, hard, brittle voice was nicely accompanied by both her guitar and that of her first husband, Kansas Joe McCoy. Their
relationship ended in 1934, after producing such gems as "Frankie Jean," "Picking
the Blues," "New Dirty Dozen," "Goin' Back to Texas," and "I'm Wild about My
Staff." The Paltram reissue concentrates on Kansas Joe's vocals with Minnie's
accompaniment. After this period, Minnie was accompanied by Black Bob on piano
and other diverse instruments. All of her work was of exceptional quality, and there
is not a clinker in any of her over 200 sides. The 80 tracks on all of the above sets
represent the *crème de la crème*, if one can take such a large number. The sets with
her second husband, Lil Son Joe (1939-1949) were largely on the Flyright set, and
show her employment of Big Bill Broonzy-type modifications into the Chicago
blues. By 1949 (on the Biograph album, minus Joe), she seems firmly in the Chicago
mold with Sunnyland Slim on piano, bass, and drums accompanying. Shortly
thereafter, she had a stroke and never recorded again.

B1.392*   **Ma Rainey.** two discs. Milestone M 47021.

Accurately billed as "The Mother of the Blues," Ma Rainey was the first and one of the very best in the great tradition of women who sing the blues. Her 1920s recordings still display a vocal and emotional power unequalled by anyone except her protégée Bessie Smith. This generous selection of 32 tracks are arranged in chronological order, and cover her Paramount material from 1924 to 1928. Her accompaniment was in three distinct typings. First was a small band grouping (the term "classic" blues singer developed here, from the use of a "classic" jazz backing), where her support came from Louis Armstrong, Charlie Green, Buster Bailey, Coleman Hawkins, Fletcher Henderson, Claude Hopkins, Kid Ory, and Shirley Clay in various configurations. She also employed a jug band, rural style, utilizing piano, kazoo, jugs, banjos, and washboards (most often with her own touring band, or with Tom Dorsey and Tampa Red). And, of course, there were her vocals with sparse solo piano, such as those done with Jimmy Blythe and Lil Henderson. When recordings came in after Mamie Smith's break through in 1919, Ma Rainey was already "old" (about 35), and carried with her a rough and tough, rural style bordering on that of vaudeville or medicine shows. She toured the South extensively, but was unable to find much work in the North. Her voice was either heavy and tragic on the sad songs, or jubilant and vital on the humorous or farcical numbers. Her hokum music was superb, such as "Black Cat, Hoot Owl Blues," "Hear Me Talking to You," and other country-based songs. The good notes are by Dan Morgenstern.

B1.393*   **Bessie Smith. The World's Greatest Blues Singer.** two discs. Columbia GP 33.

B1.394*   **Bessie Smith. Any Woman's Blues.** two discs. Columbia G 30126.

B1.395*   **Bessie Smith. Empty Red Blues.** two discs. Columbia G 30450.

B1.396*   **Bessie Smith. The Empress.** two discs. Columbia G 30818.

B1.397*   **Bessie Smith. Nobody's Blues But Mine.** two discs. Columbia G 31093.

These 10 discs, arranged in automatic turntable sequence as well as chronologically, present about 160 titles (some with splices) of her Columbia output, her sole recording company. Missing only a few tracks (available as a bootleg set, along with the sound track from the short film *St. Louis Blues*), this has to be one of the most ambitious and comprehensive reissue programs ever. Bessie Smith was a jazzman's blues singer; as such, she was acceptable to both jazz and blues. The nature of her accompaniment—both solo piano and small groups—fell right into the "classic" singing tradition, while at the same time, she represented personal involvement and real tragedy enough to be acknowledged as a blues singer in her own right by blues collectors. Much has been written about Bessie Smith, and it is virtually impossible to recommend only a few recordings for that "basic" one-album distillation. The price of these five twofers is not much more than the 1950 four solo albums reissues (if one can still find them), and Bessie's material was usually superb. Columbia had a policy of withering the opposition by having Bessie re-record, as a cover version, songs made famous by other female blues singers, as with Ma Rainey's "Moonshine Blues" and "Bo Weavil Blues"; but of course she reinvigorated them so that they were better than the originals. Titles include: "Down Hearted Blues," "Jail House Blues," "Weeping Willow Blues," "Yellow Dog Blues," "St. Louis Blues," "Backwater Blues," and "Nobody Knows You When You Are Down and Out."

Standards

B1.398*   **Olive Brown and Her Blues Chasers.** Jim Taylor Presents JTP 103.

Olive Brown is virtually alone today in her continuance of the classic blues. While all the works on this disc are older, she infuses new life into them by virtue of her emotional singing. With a quintet led by Mike Montgomery, Teddy Buckner and J. C. Heard, she utilizes the repertoire of Bessie Smith and early Ethel Waters. Tunes include "Aggravatin' Papa," "Back Water Blues," "Sugar," "Gimme a Pigfoot and a Bottle of Beer," and "Empty Bed Blues." The mixture of earthy grittiness and round-toned smoothness makes her singing authentic and immediate, and the musicians play with a sympathetic feel.

B1.399   **Elizabeth Cotten.** Folkways FG 3526.

B1.400   **Elizabeth Cotten. v.2 (Shake Sugaree).** Folkways, FB 31003.

Elizabeth Cotten had sharp ears and early on could easily pick up tunes. Later, she turned to the church, and, later gained employment with Charles Seeger in Washington, D.C. She was "rediscovered" by this musical family and taped by Mike Seeger. In style, she approaches country ragtime music, picking the guitar upside down (she's left-handed) and using a two finger "banjo" strum on both guitar and banjo. She concentrates her very sad, scratchy voice on blues and spirituals, while instrumentally she relies on rags and tuning styles. On 3526 this is evident for "Vastopol," "Spanish Flang Dang," and various country rags such as "Wilson Rag." She sings such tunes as "Freight Train," her *own* composition subsequently lifted by Rusty Draper for a big commercial hit. As many singers did, she joined the coffee house circuit, and the results are a much cleaner voice, heard on *Shake Sugaree*. Six fresh compositions grace the 16 items here, and also included are many variations such as "I'm Going Away" and "Washington Blues" (actually a rag). Side two features four religious items—traditional hymns rather than the usual gospel or spirituals.

B1.401*   **Ida Cox. v.1, 2.** Fountain Vintage Blues Series FB 301, FB 304.
        (British issue). [in progress].

Ida Cox was one of the most perfect "classic" singers, one who bridged the gap between folk blues and vaudeville blues. It is Fountain's intention to reissue all her recordings from the twenties. This first set covers June to December, 1923, and features her sophisticated vocal stylings together with simple piano accompaniment by Lovie Austin throughout, or with a small group led by Tommy Ladnier (on cornet with the necessary obbligatos) and including Jimmy O'Bryant (on clarinet). Typical tunes included "Any Woman's Blues," "Lovin' Is the Thing I'm Wild About," and "I've Got the Blues for Rampart Street." The original Paramount recordings were in bad shape before they even left the factory, and combined with acoustical recording techniques, the resulting quality of sound is necessarily low-fidelity. However, the Fountain team have done a superlative job in bringing the sound transfers up to a reasonably good standard. Excellent liner notes and discography are by Derrick Stewart-Baxter.

B1.402   **Odetta. And the Blues.** Riverside RLP 9417.

B1.403   **Odetta. Sometimes I Feel Like Cryin'.** RCA LSP 2573.
      These two records, produced and recorded in 1962, show that Odetta is a pretty good blues singer in the Bessie Smith tradition, although her voice lacks the depth in carrying. Odetta is mainly a folk revival singer, although she does incorporate country blues into her repertoire. Sometimes she also sings the "classic" blues, such as "Special Delivery Blues," and gives them new life through superb guitar arrangements. On these two discs, she is accompanied by a jazz group. Each record has Buck Clayton (who once played with Billie Holiday) for the trumpet obbligatos, Vic Dickenson on trombone, pianist Dick Wellstood, and other rhythm playing as a tight ensemble. Clarinetist Buster Bailey is on the RCA album, while Herb Hall is on the Riverside. There is no duplication of material, which includes such sterling tracks as "House of the Rising Sun," "Empty Pocket Blues," "How Long Blues," "Make Me a Pallet on Your Floor," and the above mentioned "Special Delivery Blues."

B1.404   **Clara Smith. Volumes 1/3.** VJM Records VLP 15/17 [in progress] (British issue).
      Along with Bessie Smith (no relation), Clara Smith dominated the Columbia female "classic" blues output. Little is known about her life, and all that remains are her recordings. Her voice was clear, flexible, and often melodious, in contrast to the lower-toned imperial stylings of Bessie Smith. Clara could come on strong with all kinds of material, although she preferred the slow blues tempo. Unusual accompaniment sometimes included ukelele, which gave a vaudeville effect not unlike that of Ma Rainey. She shared a number of duets with Bessie Smith (she was the only singer to do so), and these are on v. 3: "Far Away Blues" and "I'm Going Back to My Used to Be" (both from 1923). She recorded for Columbia for a decade (1923-1932), and the 43 tracks arranged here in chronological order cover to the end of 1924, just before she approached her peak of greatness. Traditional small accompaniment included Fletcher Henderson, Charles A. Matson, or Porter Grainger on piano, Don Redman on clarinet or Coleman Hawkins on tenor, and very rarely a cornet. Other sets (described also in this book) with her material include *Jazz Odyssey: Harlem* (Columbia C3L 33) and various "classic blues" collections on CBS 52798, 66232, 63288, and 64218.

B1.405*   **Victoria Spivey. Recorded Legacy of the Blues.** Spivey 2001.

B1.406   **Victoria Spivey. Victoria and Her Blues.** Spivey 1002.
      A Texas blueswoman, Spivey fits into the mould of the Texas bluesmen. That she was treated and recorded as a "classic" singer is no one's fault, for she was only 16 at the time of "Black Snake Blues" in 1926. She was also unique in being a composer of highly original material, a ukelele player, and a Texas-style pianist. Her best material is ably documented on the various anthologies (see above), but, in the 1960s, she assumed a business-like attitude and formed her own company for

her own protection. Spivey 2001 comes from two distinct periods, 1927-1931 and 1936-1937, and features some un-issued tracks. One of her most popular accompanists was Lonnie Johnson (see under his name for duet recordings from the 1960s), with a fluid, melodic guitar that counter-pointed her harsh singing. Various other groups here include small bands with Lee Collins, Louis Armstrong, Zutty Singleton, Tampa Red, and Henry "Red" Allen. The 1962 Spivey (1002) continues in this vein, being merely updated. With Eddie Barefield on reeds and Pat Wilson on drums, Spivey approaches her material (all created by herself) with a vengeance, including some rather personal auto-biographical songs (e.g., "Grant Spivey"—about her father, "When I Was Seven," and "Buddy Tate"). Other tracks from around this time are found on virtually all Spivey anthologies, a series noted for its hodge-podge collections that drive collectors mad. But then, that's Victoria!

B1.407*   **Koko Taylor. I Got What It Takes. Alligator. Al 4706.**

After years of mismanagement at Chess as a soul singer, Taylor finally gets to perform the material that she adored all along: raw, earthy, gutsy blues in the Memphis Minnie fashion (not the "classic" blues). Her gravelly and energetic voice assisted her to become one of the finest and leading blueswomen singers. She has always been with the blues, singing with J. B. Lenoir and the Wells-Guy band after arriving in Chicago in 1953. In line with Alligator's programming policy, the 11 tracks here are arranged in order of diverse styles, all appropriate to Koko's style. "Trying to Make a Living" is a driving shuffle, with topical lyrics; "I Got What It Takes" is raw blues with a biting guitar solo furnished by Sammy Lawhorn; "Be What You Want To Be" is a slow blues from Taylor's own composition; and there is material from Ruth Brown, Jimmy Reed, Otis Spann, Elmore James, and Magic Sam.

B1.408*   **Big Mama Thornton. In Europe. Arhoolie F 1028.**

B1.409   **Big Mama Thornton. v.2. Arhoolie F 1032.**

Willie Mae Thornton was distinctly in the "classic" blues tradition when she recorded "Hound Dog" in 1952, albeit with a more socking tempo to produce an r'n'b hit. Later, of course, the tune would be covered by Elvis Presley. Her style closely approximated Big Maybelle's. In 1965, she surfaced with a touring blues act in Europe, a group that also included Buddy Guy, Eddie Boyd, Walter Horton, and Fred McDowell. These men accompany her, in diverse groups, on the first Arhoolie album. Big Mama tried many blues styles, all successfully, such as gut moans with "My Heavy Load" and a medium tempo "School Boy." She occasionally played harmonica, and duets with Horton on "Down Home Shakedown." Traditional items included "Sweet Little Angel," the comic "Little Red Rooster" (with a put-on guitar from Guy), and a remake of "Hound Dog." The second disc comes from after a Monterey Festival appearance, when the Muddy Waters Band accompanied her in the studio. More traditional material was introduced then, such as "Bumble Bee" and Memphis Minnie's "Looking the World Over." Of late, Big Mama has lost a lot of weight, and she isn't so big anymore (either physically or as an entertainer).

B1.410   Sippi Wallace. Sings the Blues. Storyville 671.198 (Danish issue).
Wallace was one of the stronger "classic" blues singers. Her material from
the 1920s can be found scattered on various anthologies (see the sectional
anthologies, above). The importance of the present disc, recorded in 1966, is
that she can still sing these blues, and she had masterful accompaniment from
none other than Roosevelt Sykes and Little Brother Montgomery (as well as
herself on piano for "Up the Country Blues"). Her wide range of material and
masterful reinterpretations are clearly shown in the efforts "I'm a Mighty Tight
Woman," "Shorty George Blues," and "Special Delivery Blues." Wallace has also
been an influence on Bonnie Raitt.

B1.411*   Ethel Waters. Jazzin' Babies' Blues, v.1/2. two discs. Biograph BLP
12022/26.
The mainstream listener probably does not remember—or even realize—that
Ethel Waters started out singing the blues. This set nicely illustrates and documents
the period leading up to her 1925 Columbia contract, and her subsequent diverse
popularity with show tunes and musical comedies (for this latter period, see Columbia
KG 31571). All of the tracks here, some 24 of them, are from such various early
labels as Cardinal (her first recorded outing), Black Swan, and Paramount (issues
of 1921-1924), with some ringers lifted from Columbia of 1927. She was firmly
in the "classic" mould, even if her voice was a little light for this genre (she never
had to appear with medicine shows as Ma Rainey did). Accompanists here varied,
but usually they included either Fletcher Henderson at the piano or Lovie Austin's
Blues Serenaders. All but five of her pre-Columbia discs are now available through
Biograph. The sound is reasonable in light of the early recording techniques involved
here (acoustic sound), and it was these very same tracks that sold like hotcakes
throughout the black market and led to the fat Columbia contract.
Waters's success was in no small measure attributed to the fact that, of all the
black blues female singers of the twenties, she was the most slim and attractive,
particularly to the white market that developed after 1925.

JUG BANDS

The jug bands—which played with real jugs—were a version of good-time,
happy-time music that involved blues patterns and instrumentation. Novelties,
risqué material, dancing, and social music were emphasized.

B1.412*   The Great Jug Bands, 1926-1934. Historical HLP 36.
This is a very useful compilation of musicians, showing the range and diversity
of what some may think is a limited musical form. These were working blues bands,
the direct predecessors of the Chicago bands (in fact, almost half of this disc was
recorded in Chicago). Such well-known groups as Cannon's Jug Stompers, the
Memphis Jug Band, and Jed Davenport and his Beale Street Jug Band are fleshed
out by other, not so well known names. They recorded also in Memphis (which
seems to be home of the jug band) and Atlanta. Instrumentation, taken from vaudeville roots, included any number of jugs filled to all levels, banjos, harmonicas,
guitars, violins, kazoo, violins—even piano and saxophone. These are street singers

and ramblers, who could (and did) stroll along at will. Yet few were recorded, and most original 78 rpm discs of this genre are rare. Good notes by Dick Spottswood, and the album nicely complements a similar effort on Origin OJL-4.

B1.413   **Harmonicas, Washboards, Fiddles, Jugs.** Roots RL 311 (Austrian issue).

B1.414*   **The Jug, Jook and Washboard Bands.** Blues Classics 2.

B1.415   **Jugs, Washboards and Kazoos.** RCA LPV 540.
    Sometimes called "spasm" bands, these street-roaming groups largely used the instrumentation noted in the anthologies listed above. Many were children who could not afford regular instruments; when they grew up, they began to record for the "race" records, once it was determined that this was a form of music that people would listen to in their homes. Some of the material was hokum, other of it was outright blues, and, even more, there were game songs and dances. The Roots set includes such colorful names as Kansas City Blues Strummers and the Whistler's Jug Band. The RCA set is derived from Victor recordings, and is necessarily more limited to just one catalog, but worthwhile are five tracks by the Dixieland Jug Blowers, which feature occasional Johnny Dodds's clarinet. More jazz elements are here with a number of selections by Tiny Parham. Everything is lively, with a strong rhythmic pulse, simple harmonics, high spirit, and much warmth.

B1.416   **The Jug Bands.** RBF FR 6.

B1.417.   **The Great Jug Bands.** Origin Jazz Library 4.

B1.418   **More of That Jug Band Sound.** Origin Jazz Library OJL 19.
    These three records concentrate more on the "jug" aspects of certain bands. The RBF issue presents one side by the Birmingham Jug Band, the other by the Old Southern Jug Band. There are informative notes and texts. Origin OJL 4 also presents a rare Memphis Minnie from 1930, probably performing with the Beale Street Jug Band, and an equally rare example of sanctified singing with guitar and jug (Elder Richard Bryant's Sanctified Singers performing "Come Over Here"). OJL 19 is an entertaining set, with Daddy Stovepipe and Mississippi Sarah doing the "Greenville Strut." It is more a country album than the other two.

B1.419*   **Cannon's Jug Stompers; The Complete Works in Chronological Order, 1927-1930, including Gus Cannon as Banjo Joe.** two discs. Herwin 208.
    Cannon and his jug band were masters of the idiom. All of these tracks were recorded in Chicago and Memphis, where Cannon's was performing as a street band. Instrumentation in these hokum outfits was largely home-made, such as jugs and kazoos. But he did make the very important contribution of a unique banjo style, employing a bottleneck in much the same manner as slide guitar was played. This additional "weird" sound undoubtedly helped him to produce many commercially acceptable records. The thirty-five tracks here (quite a lot of records) include such important songs and alternate takes as "Jonestown Blues," "Poor Boy, Long Ways from Home," "My Money Never Runs Out," "Cairo Rag," "Walk Right In," and the "Rooster Crowing Blues." Full texts to all the selections are included, as well

as exhaustive notes by Bengt Olsson, in very tiny print. Full discographical information is provided, including the condition of the 78 rpms that were used for transfers.

B1.420   **Jug Band.** Collector's Classics CC 2. (Danish issue).

B1.421*   **Jug Band. v.1/2.** two discs. Roots RL 322 and 337 (Austrian issue).
    The MJB was the most recorded of all jug bands (over 73 sides between 1927 and 1934, plus many others as accompaniment), and it was one of the most successful sellers as well. It recorded some of the first blues music for the Victor company. One reason for their success was that they actually rehearsed. Will Shade, the leader, was a first class arranger and composer. He made the front line a kazoo (usually the great Ben Ramey) and a harp, with guitars and jugs in the backline for bass response. Occasionally he would add washtub bass, violin, mandolin/banjo, or some other percussive grouping. "Stingy Woman Blues" illustrates the marvelous interplay between Shade's harp and Ramey's kazoo, as does "Memphis Jug Blues"—yet these were their first recordings, and they were in prime shape right from the beginning. Over the years, their material changed as the group evolved, but there was always room for the blues. Perhaps some of the best elements of what jug band music is all about could be found on their definitive recordings of "Stealin', Stealin'," "K.C. Moan," and "Mary Anna Cut Off." The pop and traditional elements are derivative in "I'll See You in the Spring When the Birds Begin to Sing." Good time music formed a large part of their repertoire, with such items as dance tunes (e.g., "Sugar Pudding"), waltzes, scat singing (some of the earliest examples of this genre), and risqué hokum fun. Some of the better aspects of life are covered here by means of talking and answering back on record. Other examples of their music can be found on the specific surveys of jug music, or on the general anthologies Columbia G 30008, RBF RF 1, and RCA International 1175.

VOCAL JAZZ BLUES AND JUMP BLUES

    These blues forms could just as easily go into the **Jazz** or **Rhythm 'n' Blues** sections, but they are here for the purpose of exploring a variant style. The blues is a strong part of jazz, and the singer treats the orchestra as if it were his guitar or a second person. Of course, the material has to be arranged so that all persons concerned know what they are doing; however, there is a chance for improvisation during solo work or through melismatic figures. From the jazz-blues vocals came the jump blues, so called because they were uptempo stylings meant strictly for dancing. They arrived at a time of frustration for blacks: the war, the bop period, the withdrawal within an instrument. Jump blues are loosely characterized as having a wailing saxophone section or a solo saxophone. It was, of course, but a mere step to the beginnings of r'n'b music.

B1.422   **Singin' the Blues.** two discs. MCA2-4084.
    The purpose behind this compilation is vague. Its subtitle is "a treasury of great jazz singers of the 30s, 40s, and 50s," all drawn from the Decca catalog. As a sampler, it's a good introduction to jazz versions of the real blues, and features Lil Armstrong, Louis Armstrong, Walter Brown, Ella Fitzgerald, Wynonie Harris, Billie Holiday, Helen Humes, Louis Jordan, Jay McShann, Sister Rosetta Tharpe,

Jack Teagarden, Lee Wiley, Dinah Washington, and Josh White in a variety of jazz settings. Singers are mainly black performers who may not be too well known for their interpretation of "blues," but it is instructive as a *singing* album with the intent of presenting some not-so-serious, introspective blues. Tunes include "Ella Hums the Blues," "I Gotta Right to Sing the Blues," "Rainy Day Blues," "Careless Love," "Confessin' the Blues," and "Jelly, Jelly," from among 27 selections.

B1.423*   **Wynonie Harris. Good Rockin' Blues.** King 1086.

B1.424*   **Wynonie Harris. Mister Blues Meets the Master Saxes.** Phoenix LP 7.
    In the Joe Turner tradition, but also heavily influenced by Louis Jordan, Harris presented his brand of the "jump" blues: simple arrangements, a solid backbeat, and meaningful lyrics. Of all such bluesmen, Harris was the greatest of the shouters. He could really do an effective "shout" (despite other limitations), with a voice that seemed to carry for miles. His usual material pre-dated Ray Charles's efforts to transform country music, for Harris took a good number of country and western swing items, such as "Good Morning Judge" and "Bloodshot Eyes," and moulded them into the jump blues. An exuberant dancer and comic, Harris recorded prolifically for a number of small independent companies in the forties. In 1945-1946, he recorded "Wynonie's Blues," "Straighten Him Out," and "Baby Look at You," all on the Phoenix album, along with such jazz musicians as Illinois Jacquet, Arnett Cobb, Bill Doggett (later to turn to r'n'b), and even Charles Mingus. The immediate post-war years needed happy music. Turning to the King label in 1947, Harris continued to promote the shouting blues with "I Want My Fanny Brown," and "Confessin' the Blues," plus covers of Roy Brown material. However, he only had one style, and he was one of the first to go when rock and roll arrived.

B1.425*   **Jimmy Rushing. Best.** two discs. Vanguard VSD 65/66.

B1.426*   **Jimmy Rushing. Blues I Love to Sing.** Ace of Hearts AH 119 (British issue).
    "Mr. Five by Five"—so called because he was as wide as he was tall—was the premier blues singer with big bands of the 1930s. Although he sang ballads and uptempo numbers, his high, light weighted vocals were admirably suited to the blues of the Count Basie band (more of Rushing's recordings can be found under the annotation for Count Basie). The Ace of Hearts disc draws from Decca material of the 1937-1938 period for 12 very laudable cuts of blues. For thirteen years (1936-1949), Rushing was a part of the Basie organization, and this period—just into the swing era and into that time when Basie's recordings really started to sell well—produced the best work he had ever done. Lester Young, Buck Clayton, and Count Basie give exceptional but occasional solos behind such items as "Good Morning Blues," "Sent for You Yesterday and Here You Come Today," and "Blues in the Dark." The 1950s saw a Rushing comeback, and under John Hammond's guidance, he recorded for Vanguard with a select group of ex-Basie performers (1954-1957). The Vanguard twofer draws from the original three discs released from this series. The 1954 session has the Buddy Tate band, along with Sammy Price on piano and the Page-Jones rhythm from Basie. Featured are "I Want a Little Girl," "Goin' to Chicago Blues," and "How Long, How Long Blues." On

the second disc, the Greene-Page-Jones rhythm combines with Pete Johnson (filling in for Basie on piano), and Tate, Rudy Powell, Emmett Berry, and Lawrence Brown. This allows for some good improvisation, plus the chance to record "Roll 'Em Pete" with Johnson, "Take Me Back, Baby," and the influential "Everyday I Have the Blues." The last of the three discs was heavily criticized for its use of organ and amplified guitar, but it is Rushing with the ex-Basieites nevertheless.

B1.427   Joe Turner. **"And the Blues'll Make You Happy Too."** Savoy MG 14012.

B1.428*   Joe Turner. The Boss of the Blues. Atlantic 1234.

B1.429   Joe Turner. Careless Love. Savoy MG 14016.

B1.430*   Joe Turner. His Greatest Recordings. Atco SD 33-376.

B1.431*   Joe Turner. Jumpin' the Blues. Arhoolie R 2004.

B1.432   Joe Turner. Texas Style. Black and Blue 33.028 (French issue).
    Joe Turner was the originator of the "shouting" blues that became "jump" blues and later formed the basis for r'n'b. In fact, when rock and roll developed, Turner was able to make a comeback. Coming from the Kansas City area, he made several recordings with Art Tatum and then with his greatest accompanist, Pete Johnson. The two Savoys are from National recordings of 1945-1947, with various solos contributed by Pete Johnson, Frankie Newton and Don Byas. The Arhoolie set reissues material from Swing Time, 1948-1949, and features Johnson again with a tight studio group. Throughout this time he was making "Careless Love," "Lucille, Lucille," and "Tell Me Pretty Baby." Atlantic suggested that Turner record again during the formative years of rock and roll, and uptempo items from this period include "Shake, Rattle and Roll" (the anthem of the fifties), "Flip, Flop and Fly," "Corrina, Corrina," and "TV Mama" (the latter with Elmore James on guitar). His success led to a more blues and jazz album with the Atlantic issue, simply the best thing he has done in terms of his limited voicings and accompaniments. The full line includes Joe Newman, Lawrence Brown, Pete Brown, Frank Wess, with Pete Johnson on piano and the Basie rhythm of Freddie Green and Walter Page: "Cherry Red," "Roll 'Em Pete," and "I Want a Little Girl." Johnson and Turner fitted together hand-in-glove. The French set comes from 1971 when Turner's voice was still reasonably good, and features Milt Buckner, Slam Stewart, and Jo Jones.

B1.433*   **Jimmy Witherspoon. Ain't Nobody's Business!** Black Lion BLP 30147 (British import).

B1.434   Jimmy Witherspoon. The 'Spoon Concerts. two discs. Fantasy 24701.
    Jimmy Witherspoon has been a prolific recording artist in the "blues shouter" genre. In fact, he is the leading exponent behind Joe Turner. His best work has always been with a jazz setting; consequently, his straight blues material has been lackluster and never a really good product. He broke into the scene through the Jay McShann band, and most of that material is on the Black Lion set,

originally recorded in 1947 and 1948. Coming from Arkansas, Witherspoon was fascinated by the Southwestern blues band jazz scene. He replaced Walter Brown in the McShann organization. Standouts here include "Skidrow Blues" and "Money's Getting Cheaper"—both contemporary topics for the forties, and both written by Witherspoon. Other songs are (by now) traditional items, such as Leroy Carr's "In the Evening" and "How Long Blues," Bessie Smith's "Backwater Blues," plus the title selection. The Fantasy material is probably the best overall set of Witherspoon available. It is a reissue of the former Hi Fi label material, and it includes Earl Hines and a group at a live festival, and a group co-led by Gerry Mulligan and Ben Webster from a Hollywood club. All of the selections are long, and they are all favorites of Witherspoon, including "How Long Blues," "See See Rider," "Going to Kansas City," and so forth. Although this is a "twofer" set, the playing times are ridiculously short, and the whole thing could have been reissued on just one disc.

Rhythm 'n' Blues

RHYTHM 'N' BLUES

INTRODUCTION

Rhythm and blues is the logical modern extension of the cramped blues style. By 1933, all the ideas, approaches, and techniques in performing the blues had been crystalized. There has been little new since, except the addition of electricity and a wider source of instruments to draw on, including saxophones and brass. Updating the blues had produced an "urban" sound in which the harshness of "rural" singing has been eliminated. Post-war blues made their statements by 1955, and for the past 20 years, the same matter has been reiterated in countless ways. The development of "r 'n' b" has been attributed to a happier way of singing the blues, as exemplified by Joe Turner, Wynonie Harris, and Lowell Fulson before 1950.

"Rhythm and blues," as a term, developed in the late 1950s. Previously, all blues and some vocal jazz were referred to as "race music" (beginning with Mamie Smith's first blues record in 1920). *Billboard* continued with the "race music" term in 1946, when it actually began to chart sales positions of black music—a tremendous influence, as the music would continue to be listed and given national prominence. Other companies and publications used "ebony" or "sepia." RCA used "r 'n' b," and, in January 1949, *Billboard* switched to using "rhythm 'n' blues."

Tracing the development of r 'n' b is very difficult, except through listening to music in chronological order. One should always remember that r 'n' b (like soul) was market-oriented. It was popular music for blacks; thus, it was not self-expressive but rather self-centred as uninhibited entertainment for the masses. It was full of fun and (quite often) self-caricature. Coupled with the nonsense lyrics that served only as rhythmic patterns, this music definitely mystified the white audience, which then naturally ignored it. Sources included the Harlem stride piano, which turned into boogie woogie, the improvised combos of New Orleans jazz, and the highly rhythmic, big black band blues of the Southwest (Kansas City, Texas, Oklahoma), St. Louis and Chicago. Migratory bluesmen also helped to break down what had been regional patterns of development. They moved north and created the electrical amplification approach in Chicago, Memphis, and Detroit. This amplification was needed so that singers could be heard without having to shout; similarly, big band singers had the same problems of screaming over riffing horns in the territory bands. With amplification came the exploitation of guitar tones and volumes, and the Fender bass.

While the black bands were training grounds for urban blues singers and shouters, the r 'n' b combo was a training ground for the 1960s black jazz of Albert Ayler, Ornette Coleman, and John Coltrane. Indeed, there was much musical activity and ferment during the post-war years that led to all new forms of popular music: electric blues, British blues, rock and roll, r 'n' b, rockabilly, rock music, soul, bop, modern jazz, etc. There were three main sociological reasons for this. First, there was the *urbanization* of the black during and after World War II. This was part of the migratory pattern, where T-Bone Walker and B. B. King moved to Los Angeles, Joe Turner and Louis Jordan moved to New York City, and Muddy Waters,

Howlin' Wolf, and Elmore James moved to Chicago—all places where the large audiences were.

Related to urbanization was the problem of *segregation*, the second reason. Black music, more than ever before, became closely entwined with urban life, where all problems were magnified. Not only did blacks have to contend with personal problems, but they also had to combat racial segregation, a vicious, impersonal demoralizing thing. Frustration, hostility and alienation were vented through crude emotional responses, such as honking or squealing contests with saxophones. The classic example of this was tenor saxist Big Jay McNeely lying on his back, repeatedly during his performances, howling out just one note over and over. Bop music was a creature of alienation, when black musicians, fed up with white dominance of jazz, took to expanding their own musical vocabulary and extending the horizons of jazz beyond the means of the ordinary white performer, who did not know what they were doing. Also, by the 1940s, *all* forms of music had exhausted the traditional songs and motifs, and the amateur musician ceased to record commercially. The era of professionalism had arrived, and if music was to advance or go into new areas, it had to be *composed* or created anew, the third factor. Thus, professionally trained instrumentalists and composers began to fashion materials based on their experiences (which was, of course, the source of traditional music at one time)—and these experiences were of bitter feelings and alienation.

Many different styles and regional variations exist in r 'n' b. For instance: the urban jump blues pattern of Joe Turner, Wynonie Harris, Louis Jordan, and Jimmy Witherspoon; the Chicago blues stylings of a rough Muddy Waters or of an urbane uptempo Chuck Berry; the Memphis blues of B. B. King, Junior Parker, Bobby Bland, and the use of riffing horns; the New Orleans school of Fats Domino, Professor Longhair, Smiley Lewis, et al., who employed Latin, French, and African rhythms together with lyric simplicity; the "doo wop" style, based on the Ink Spots, that was to affect so many black singing groups.

One of the keys to this development was the position of newly independent recording companies, which offered poor pay but were ready to take a chance with unknowns. The large bulk of independents came into existence during the numerous work stoppages in the 1940s caused by the American Federation of Musicians, as the three large firms (now known as RCA, CBS, and MCA) refused to sign contracts with the AFM for long periods of time. Similarly, ASCAP created work stoppages, and BMI developed as a major performance rights collection agency.

With the major companies not producing records, the "indies" (as they were known) signed with AFM and BMI, and had the record buying public all to themselves for a considerable time. They flourished in a weak jazz market and in large black population centers (with the advantage that a smaller distribution outlet served a lot of people at lower cost). The two most significant indies were King and Chess. King was Cincinnati-based from the early 1940s, and, in addition to its dramatic country and western catalog, it featured such r 'n' b greats (or started them off on their career) as: Bullmoose Jackson, Ivory Joe Hunter, the Dominoes, Clyde McPhatter, Jackie Wilson, Hank Ballard, Bill Doggett, the Platters, James Brown, Little Willie John, Joe Tex, Nina Simone, and Otis Redding through its King/Federal/Bethlehem labels. Chess, in Chicago from the late 1940s, presented Muddy Waters, Bo Diddley, Howlin' Wolf, Little Walter, Otis Spann, Chuck Berry, the Moonglows, Etta James, et al. through its Chess/Checker/Argo labels. In other parts of the country, a typical sound developed rather than a dominant independent label, this sound keyed to instruments and vocals rather than regional variations.

The "West Coast" took in all of Louisiana to California, with emphasis on Texas migrants. The style was mainly of wailing saxophones in unison, loud driving drums, and constant riffing of all kinds. Specialty had Little Richard as its star; Imperial concentrated on New Orleans material, with Fats Domino and others; Aladdin was mainly Texas with Lightnin' Hopkins and T-Bone Walker; the Modern/RPM/Flair Complex (later, Kent) promoted the Memphis music of B. B. King and West Coast singers; the Houston-based Duke/Peacock also went into Memphis with Junior Parker and Bobby Bland. The East Coast also had its sound: sophisticated blues and polished jazz. With the demise of big bands because of their uneconomic structure, many jazz vocalists took to the urban blues of New York. In the New Jersey-New York City area were Prestige, Apollo, National, Jubilee, Savoy, DeLuxe, Manor, Herald, and one later to become a giant—Atlantic. Women were especially favored in such settings (Big Maybelle, Esther Phillips, Ruth Brown, LaVern Baker, etc.).

Techniques

Rhythm 'n' blues is music for jive dancing. One of its main predecessors was Harlem stride piano, which in the 1930s revival was recast as *boogie woogie* through Albert Ammons, Meade Lux Lewis, and Pete Johnson. This eight-to-the-bar pattern became a syncopated form of 8/8 in r 'n' b. The shuffle rhythms and stomping style are easily found in Little Richard, Chuck Berry, Fats Domino, and even in white rockabilly music. By the early 1950s, though, with the electric "Chicago" blues and the jump blues patterns, there developed a new 12-to-the-bar phrasing—triplets of 12/4 that made for a hammering piano style. At the same time, the saxophone became a pre-eminent instrument by borrowing phrases liberated by the bop movement (honks, screeches) and from Kansas City Swing (riffing phrases). By the late 1950s, the bass guitar became dominant when the Fender bass was perfected. Previous to this time, the main purpose of the bass was to underline the down beats (one and three), or the after beats (two and four), or all the beats in the case of swing music. This was achieved by either plucking the first or fifth note of the scale, or by "walking" figures of successive notes. The electric bass removed all evidence of "plucking" figures, and instead emanated a powerful low tone that shook the body. This was to have great impact later in soul music with the development of straight eighth-note rhythms. Electric amplification was needed to cut through the party noise.

Vocally, there was little sophistication in r 'n' b, as it was mainly for dancing. Words were used for their own rhythmic properties and not for their meaning. Thus, the lyrics were often incomprehensible in performance, and this effect carried over to rock and roll music. In this light, it is relatively easy to see why such lyrics were used in white rock and roll, and also why they were criticized by an audience who, out of habit, actually tried to listen rather than dance. Thus developed two aspects: the use of sexual imagery and other (for the time) not so nice items (who was listening?) and use of jargon and slang to cut themselves off from white listeners and white imitators.

In essence, the character of r 'n' b was threefold: one, a dance rhythm; two, self-centered lyrics; and three, emotional vocal phrasing for communication. Rhythm 'n' blues was *the* black music from the late 1940s to 1956 or so. After that period, two things happened. First, many innovators disappeared through death, retirement, jail, religious callings, etc., and second, the 1955-1959 transitional period to soul was a time when r 'n' b tunes were covered by white artists, who turned them into rock and roll as watered down r 'n' b. Black music during this period almost lost its identity as recording companies smelled the money of rock and roll. Then, too, there was the problem of "payola."

A secondary stream in the rhythm 'n' blues pattern was the development of the "doo wop" groups, which can be traced back to the Ink Spots and the Mills Brothers. These were *group* performers and were also known as "bird groups" since they took their names from birds: the Crows, the Robins, the Ravens, the Orioles, etc. They were the soft crooning singers who had a widely appealing style (even to white listeners). The Ink Spots, under Bill Kenny, developed a vocal pattern that was almost a cappella (and can be found today in the singing of the Spinners) with a touch of gospel. There was a high tenor lead, pointed off by a bass singer who did a response pattern to the tenor's lead. Any instrumental accompaniment was spartan, and the other members of the group merely harmonized. Almost all their material was lushly romantic, and the more successful ones, such as the Platters, sold more to a white audience than to a black one. "Doo wop" was a more verbal form of the background harmonic chants, which was a direct ancestor of the modern soul ballads sung by the Stylistics, the Chi-Lites, and even some of the Motown groups. The sparse accompaniment had been replaced by lush strings and mixed horns, while the bottom heavy bass line was now carried by the drummer and the electric bass. The only vocals left were the high tenor lines; hence, these modern soul groups are often called "castrato groups."

Literature

Books on rhythm 'n' blues are very disorganized. Each author has his own interpretation of the start and finish, as r 'n' b is as essentially "dead" as rock 'n' roll is, and both are transitional musical forms. Soul survey books present elementary data on r 'n' b to show the roots—Cummings (21) on Philadelphia, Garland's (36) emotional account, Hoare's (47) scholarly version, Redd's (89) polemic, Haralambos's (44) acknowledgement of its transitory nature, and Shaw's (100) basic history. Peripheral details come from Passman's (83) work on disc jockeys; Rowe's (94) book on Chicago blues ceases coverage by the mid-fifties. "Urban Music" is looked at through Keil (53) in his work on urban blues, Shaw again in his *The Rockin' 50s* (Hawthorn, 1974), and Gillett (38a) in his search for the sound of the city. There are very few regional works, but Cummings (21) looks at Philadelphia, Shaw (99a) examines New York roots of the 1940s (and the jump blues) while Groia (41) concentrates on street singing groups in the New York of the 1950s—two works looking at the jump blues and "doo wop" respectively. Broven (10) considers the multi-ethnic musical scene of New Orleans. The only real survey of this 15-year period is McCutcheon's (63) closely written analysis. However, individual biographical details can be located through Nite (73a), Lydon (62, 62a), and Millar's (68) work on the Drifters—which also covers many other black vocal groups of the 1950s. Gillett (38) and Escott (28) look at Atlantic Records and Sun Records, respectively, to examine their impact. Biographical details of other artists and companies are scattered throughout all of the above-mentioned books.

Basic discographic information can only be found for the jump blues in Jepson (51a); specialist periodicals such as *Shout* extend the listings available for other r 'n' b stylings. Whitburn (111) has produced an alphabetically-arranged "top hits" chart from *Billboard*, covering 1949-1971. Some slight material about bluesmen who worked in the area of r 'n' b can be found in Leadbitter and Slaven (58). Leadbitter, until his death, was going to publish an r 'n' b discography to 1961, but the project is now in abeyance until Rowe can find spare time to re-edit the book. Propes (86a) presents a useful price guide to collecting black records from the 1950-1960 period.

Rhythm 'n' blues is apparently music for dancing; no one wants to write about it anymore. There are some fanzines such as *Record Exchanger* and *Who Put the Bomp* but no widely circulated magazines. Occasional articles on jump blues or jazz vocal blues can be found in *Blues Unlimited* (3), *Living Blues* (14), and *Jazz Journal* (12). The soul magazines *Black Music* (1) and *Blues and Soul* (2) might do a "nostalgia" retrospective. Rock magazines will also survey the field— *Creem* (8), *Rolling Stone* (18). Best to try *Popular Music Periodicals Index* (86) under the name of the artist or **Rhythm 'n' Blues** as a genre heading.

ROOTS ANTHOLOGIES

The following anthologies adequately summarize the roots of the classical rhythm 'n' blues tune of the 1946-1956 period. For more exhaustive documentation, please refer to the **Blues** section, the **Gospel** section and the **Jazz** section.

B2.1   **The Changing Face of Harlem.** two discs. Savoy SJL 2208.
This is an excellent program of swing and jump music, mostly from 1944, all of which is appearing on twelve-inch discs for the first time. Here are direct precursors to r 'n'. b and early soul music. Among the performers are Buck Ram's All Stars ("Ram Session"), altoist Pete Brown's Band ("Pete Brown's Boogie"), Herbie Fields, jazz guitarist Tiny Grimes ("Groovin' with Grimes"), tenorist Ben Webster, the legendary blues singer Viola Wells (Miss Rhapsody), and Clyde Hart's All Stars with Benny Harris, Budd Johnson, and bassist Oscar Pettiford. Ram would later go on to form the Platters, an influential group in the fifties. Typical titles from this period include, in that unique lingo of the times, "Ooh-Wee," "Bellevue for You," "Nuts to Notes," "Romance without Finance," "Blooey," and "Shoot the Arrow to Me Cupid." A delightful twofer album.

B2.2*   **The Original Boogie Woogie Piano Giants.** Columbia KC 32708.
This anthology covers 1938-1941, and features selections from the Columbia archives on boogie woogie music. It is not definitive, but it represents several styles that were emerging from this time (boogie woogie as a name was over ten years old; Pinetop Perkins first recorded a fast blues called "Pinetop's Boogie" in 1928). Included here are items from the boogie trio of Meade Lux Lewis, Pete Johnson, and Albert Ammons ("Boogie Woogie Prayer," "Cafe Society Rag"), solo piano from Lewis in "Bear Cat Crawl," early Champion Jack Dupree with "Dupree Shake

Dance," some solo work from Pete Johnson and Albert Ammons, and five selections with Joe Turner belting out tough vocals over the pulsating themes provided by Pete Johnson and His Boogie Woogie Boys (important early recordings of "Cherry Red" and "Roll 'Em Pete"). When one listens to Jimmy Yancey here, in context with the other performers, it is not hard to realize the direct trend from blues to fast blues (or barrelhouse) to boogie woogie, to dance crazes and jitterbug, through the development of r 'n' b and thence to soul music. It is all interrelated, being separated only by points in time.

B2.2a   **The Roots of Rock 'n' Roll.** two discs. Savoy SJL 2221.

Although the title of this anthology pertains to the development of white music in the rock and roll period, all of the 32 tracks are clearly in the rhythm and blues genre. Side one is mainly instrumental, with classic interpretations of the big blues ballads and the upbeat jump number prominent in the late 1940s. Both Hal Singer's "Cornbread" and Paul Williams's "The Hucklebuck" are here in definitive versions. Johnny Otis and Little Esther are represented by "Cupid's Boogie," "Head Hunter," and "Lost in a Dream." Side four contains the gems of the bird groups: the Ravens' masterly "Old Man River" and "Marie," and early Robins' selections: "If I Didn't Love You So" and "Our Romance is Gone." Savoy Records was, of course, one of the early leaders in the r 'n' b stream of musical discovery.

B2.3*   **Stars of the Apollo.** two discs. Columbia KG 30788.

This Columbia set can be likened to a short aural history of black blues and jazz roots and of early r 'n' b. The Apollo is a record that you really cannot pin down because its territory is so wide—jazz, blues, hokum, sex, r 'n' b, and vaudeville, 1927-1965; with 10 unissued tracks and one V-Disc out of 28 selections. Yet, this was the type of material that could be heard any night at the Apollo theatre on 125th Street in New York. Everybody knows about Ella Fitzgerald and that place. Here she is with Teddy Wilson in 1936 on "All My Life." Also, there in 1935 was Billie Holiday, heard here with Wilson from a 1942 "Wherever You Are." None of the present tracks were recorded at the Apollo itself. Indeed, some were cut in Chicago and Hollywood. But no matter—it is the spirit which counts. And *that* can certainly be found on Butterbeans and Susie's "I Wanna Hot Dog for My Roll"—so risqué (a long and lean dog for a roll that will take a hog) that it was never released when recorded in 1927. This is an excellent cross-section, with Bessie Smith, Mamie Smith, Claude Hopkins, the Mills Brothers, Cab Calloway, Bill "Bojangles" Robinson, Cottie Williams, "Hot Lips" Page, Ida Cox, Count Basie, Pearl Bailey, etc. You had to be good to be at the Apollo—good and naughty—or else you got booed off the stage. All in all, though, it was still a ladies' place, with people like Big Maybelle (on her greatest recording "Gabbin' Blues," heard here)—nice to hear her again. The only drawback to this set is that all the material comes from the vaults of only one company; thus, it barely qualifies as a representative sampling, but rather as a salute.

B2.4*   **This Is How It All Began.** v.1/2. two discs. Specialty S 2117/8.

This is the best introduction to the early era before rock and roll and rhythm and blues. The 14 selections on volume one have been divided into five sections.

"Gospel" presents examples from Alex Bradford, the Soul Stirrers, and the Swan Silvertones, each reflecting different approaches to gospel music (smooth satin sounds, call-and-response, a cappella). "Country Blues," with Frankie Lee Sims, Mercy Dee's incredible "One Room Country Shack" in the original version, and John Lee Hooker again reflect different approaches to the idiom. "City Blues " points off the smooth sophisticated Roy Milton against the rougher jump blues of Joe Liggins. "Ballads" features Percy Mayfield and the Four Flames, and "Jump and Boogie," includes Roy Milton ("The Hucklebuck") and Joe Liggins ("Shuffle-Shuck") again. The second volume (in 12 selections) presents people rather than styles, the outstanding tracks here being Guitar Slim's "The Things I Used to Do," Lloyd Price's "Lawdy Miss Clawdy," Jerry Byrne's "Lights Out," and Don and Dewey's "KoKo Joe." There is a comprehensive, big brochure written by Barret Hansen, who has been researching Specialty for his M.A. thesis. The superb notes include photographs, full discographic and composition details, and short blurbs about each performance.

GENERAL ANTHOLOGIES

B2.5*   **Carats 6. Oop Shoop.** Polydor 2383 251 (British import).
     This disc is one of eight released in England that is derived from a wide variety of labels. Most of the tunes on the other seven albums largely duplicate what is available in North America (and also in this book). However, *Carats 6* contains a goldmine of 18 rare tracks from the Kent archives. The Bihari brothers, who own Kent, put out a continual stream of discs in the fifties under the names Modern, RPM, Kent, Crown, and Flair. The Kent catalogue has been dormant since 1966, when Lowell Fulsom had his last hit "Tramp" (emphasizing body-shaking Fender bass). That item is on this set, but the other material covers 1952-1957. Included here are such seminal recordings as Young Jessie's ground-breaking "Mary Lou," successfully covered four years later by Ronnie Hawkins; the Teen Queens' evocative "Eddie My Love," with gritty lyrics concerning possible death after being scorned (again, a hit before the white cover version); Jesse Belvin's "Goodnight My Love," now an r 'n' b classic; Marvin and Johnny's "Cherry Pie," from 1954 but given an insipid cover by Skip & Flip in 1960; and Etta James's response to Hank Ballard in "Roll with Me Henry," which ultimately led to a second sequel entitled (naturally): "Annie Had a Baby." Another good party record, and well worth importing.

B2.6*   **Chess Golden Decade. v.1/5.** (The Early Fifties, to 1961). five discs.
            Checker 6445 150/2 and 6445 200/1 (British import).
     This Chess series has struck a balance between enjoyable items from the "goldie oldie" period and those items with a strong history but with little enjoyment value. The eighty tracks here show the diversification of the Chess/Checker catalogue, although there have been more black performers than white. The material ranges from the sublime doo wop of Harvey Fuqua and the Moonglows to ridiculous utterances in the Ideals' "Knee Socks." White performers include Bobby Charles and Dale "Susie-Q" Hawkins. The whole range of black singing is here: doo wop, blues, New Orleans, early soul, rough r 'n' b, jazz, gospel, etc. The wide spectrum gives this set historical credence, and it could easily be

recommended for educational purposes. Highlights are numerous, such as Rufus Thomas's "Ain't Gonna Be Your Dog," Jackie Brenston's "Juiced," Lowell Fulsom's "Reconsider Baby," Little Walter's "My Babe," Willie Mabon's "I'm Mad," Bobby Charles's "See You Later Alligator" and "Take It Easy Greasy," and contributions from Howlin' Wolf, Chuck Berry, Bo Diddley, Clarence "Frogman" Henry, Jimmy McCracklin, and Eddie Boyd. Chess was an active promoter of their music; at one time in the fifties, they had almost everyone performing blues in Chicago under contract to them. Their rich catalogue is nicely illustrated here with photographs and specially written notes by British critics Bill Millar and Clive Richardson. Like many of these projects, this British effort must be imported as it is not domestically available.

B2.7*   **Doo Wop.** Specialty S 2114.

"Doo wop" refers to a style of r 'n' b singing that was instrumental in the development of modern soul music and Motown. It was a direct descendent of Bill Kenny and the Ink Spots, with a little more motion in the rhythm accompaniment. The features—an outstanding high tenor (some might say "castrato"), a low bass for the response portions of the song, and distinctive voicings in the back-up performers as they mumbled nonsense lyrics or some other repetitive patterns. Doo wop itself was one of the sounds that was heard ("doo wop, doo wop, doo wop, sha bah," etc.). The groups were nearly all male quartets, and they didn't play any instruments. In fact, some of the better efforts could be done a cappella, but, then, of course, they would lack the necessary punch of the funky instrumental sound. The fourteen tracks here are very illustrative of the changing styles within the doo wop idiom. None of these tracks ever became great sellers, but they are indicative of the style's influence and the fact that imitation breeds imitation. The Four Flames' "Wheel of Fortune" was better known under the cover version by Kay Starr. Nonsense songs included Roddy Jackson's "Moose on the Loose," King Perry's "Animal Song," Joe Lutcher's "Traffic Song," and the Monitors' "Our School Days." Love ballads included such as Vernon Green's "Sweet Breeze," the Chimes' "Pretty Little Girl," and Jesse and Marvin's "Dream Girl." This is a nicely packaged set, and representative of an important style of singing.

B2.8   **14 Golden Recordings from the Historic Vaults of Duke/Peacock Records, v.1/2.** ABC 784/789.

These 28 tracks can be said to be representative of the vast treasure of early r 'n' b music contained on the Duke and Peacock labels. Singers appearing here, with rare items or moderate hits, include Bobby Bland, Johnny Ace, Junior Parker, the Lamp Sisters, Pauletta Parker, Clarence and Calvin, Jeanette Williams, the Rob Roys, Willie Mae Thornton ("Big Mama"), and early Clarence "Gatemouth" Brown.

B2.9   **14 Golden Recordings from the Historic Vaults of Vee Jay Records.** ABC 785.

Late in 1973, ABC Paramount Records began to cash in on the oldies market by buying up other record companies and their rights to older tunes. It has been estimated that ABC took over 50 companies, some of which were near bankruptcy. This comprehensive sampler from Vee Jay contains many unissued recordings, some of them quite good. Betty Everett sings "You're No Good," Jerry Butler performs "He Will Break Your Heart," and other groups include the Dells, early Gladys Knight and the Pips, and Dee Clarke's "Raindrops." There are even some blues here with Jimmy Reed and John Lee Hooker (including Hooker's seminal "Boom-Boom").

B2.10*   **The Golden Age of Rhythm 'n' Blues.** two discs. Chess CH 50030.
        Chess and its subsidiaries Checker, Argo, and Cadet, was a fairly successful r 'n' b label in the fifties. Many of its blues stars had their hits cross over to the r 'n' b or pop charts. Thus, the development of the singer-soloist in soul music had its greatest development with Chess. But Chess also had groups that were direct descendents of the Ink Spots (and Bill Kenny), and gospel music plus a little Louis Jordan music as well. While the better r 'n' b undoubtedly came from such small labels as Jubilee, Atlantic, Savoy, King, Modern, Specialty, Imperial, etc., Chess was firmly in the mainstream, having its fair share of the bird groups (named after birds, in imitation of the Ravens, the first successful r 'n' b doo-wop group; that group is heard here, but on a 1956—hence later—version of "Give Me a Simple Prayer"). Some groups: the Bluejays' "White Cliffs of Dover," the Coronets' "Nadine," and the Flamingos' "I'll Be Home" (the original, not the whitewashed Pat Boone version). Other important groups include the Moonglows, with their original "Sincerely" and "In My Diary." Lead singer Harvey Fuqua is still active, and is, in fact, a nephew of one of the Ink Spots.

B2.11   **The Great Groups.** Buddah BDS 7509.
        A few years back, Buddah acquired the rights to many items in the important Vee Jay catalogue when that company went under. The thirteen items here come from those vaults, and feature such black groups as Rosie and the Originals ("Angel Baby"), the Nutmegs ("Story Untold"), the El Dorados ("Crazy Little Mama"), the Spaniels ("Goodnight Sweetheart"), and the Moonglows ("Secret Love"). Not too much of it is inspired, but these groups are solidly in the line from r 'n' b through soul, softening many of the harsh accents of the earlier works. These are strictly urban groups, whose moderate success inspired the Motown and Philly scenes and helped ensure the later immense successes of those sounds.

B2.12*   **Great Hits of R & B.** two discs. Columbia G 30503.
        These 25 tracks all come from the seminal King label, one of the few important regional independents in the late forties and early fifties. Centered in Cincinnati, it extensively recorded up and coming rhythm and blues singers, passing them on to the major recording companies. It also recorded fading blues singers, such as Lonnie Johnson (a star in the 1920s with Eddie Lang) and his "Tomorrow Night") the only real hit he ever had. Every item on this set is important as a three minute (or less) miniature that either sold well or established someone in the field. Bill Doggett's "Honky Tonk," featuring brash brass, was constantly being played on the juke box as a national symbol for dancing instrumentals. "Work with Me Annie," by Hank Ballard and the Midnighters, was the first in a series of Annie songs that had suggestive lyrics (at least for the white audience). It was covered in a watered-down version by Georgia Gibbs ("Dance with Me Henry"). Ballard also started "The Twist," but it did not get off the ground until Chubby Checker recorded it; the version here is the important original. He produced as well the epic "Finger Poppin' Time" (hey now, hey now, hey now. . . .). Little Willie John's "Fever" and "Talk to Me, Talk to Me" are

outstanding examples of how this tragic singer's material was done before covering began. Other singers and groups here included the Platters' "Only You," Otis Williams and the Charms' "Hearts of Stone" (before the McGuire Sisters), the Five Royales' "Dedicated to the One I Love," Otis Redding's "Shout Bamalama," James Brown's "Please, Please, Please," and some instrumentals by Freddy King.

B2.13*   History of Rhythm & Blues. v.1/4. four discs. Atlantic SD 8161/4.

This set (see also item B4.3 for v.5-8) was among the first to be released by a record company as an integral series with good notes, designed to expound on the development of a particular form of music from a record company's files. While Atlantic only began in 1949, it has since acquired the rights to earlier material, most notably to the National label for the Ravens' definitive "Ol' Man River" from 1957. This tune alone was responsible for both the turning of groups to older material to revise it in a jump blues format and the naming of many similar groups after birds (leading to the phrase "bird groups" in the r 'n' b context). Thus, here also is the Orioles' "It's Too Soon to Know," the Cardinals' "Shouldn't I Know?;" and "Wheel of Fortune." Other performers include Leadbelly ("Goodnight Irene") and Big Joe Turner ("Chains of Love"). The 1953-1955 period extended the career of the Clovers, the Drifters, and presented definitive versions of songs later covered by white performers. These include the Drifter's "Money Honey," the Chords' "Sh-Boom," and Joe Turner's "Shake, Rattle and Roll." New singers here are the phenomenal Ray Charles in a jazz bag ("I've Got a Woman") and LaVern Baker. The 1956-1957 period for Atlantic yielded the Coasters, the late Ivory Joe Hunter ("Since I Met You, Baby"), Clyde McPhatter (as a single, away from the Drifters), and Chuck Willis. In 1958-1960, Atlantic introduced the young Bobby Darin with the monumental "Splish Splash," a white version of r 'n' b material. This "Big Beat" was where r 'n' b and rock and roll were fused.

B2.14   New Orleans R & B. v.1/2. two discs. Flyright LP 4708/9 (British import).

Flyright has done several good jobs in the past of compiling anthologies of American blues music. With this set, they move into rhythm and blues. All of the material here is from New Orleans, with three exceptions (Memphis, Nashville, and Natchez; these exceptions, though, are in the style of New Orleans). Coverage is from 1949 to 1967, with emphasis on the early years. The happy-go-lucky sound from New Orleans blossomed in the late forties, and its roots can be traced right back to the long musical heritage of the Crescent City. Many of the major artists are represented here, such as Huey "Piano" Smith (with "You Made Me Cry" and "You're Down with Me" from 1949), Earl King, Smiley Lewis, Roy Brown, Lloyd Price, Guitar Slim, Dave Bartholomew, Allen Toussaint, and Mac Rebennack (better known as Dr. John in the sixties). The emphasis on instrumentation shows in a strong reed section, with tough saxophone solos based on jazz figures. Bartholomew, who did many arrangements for Fats Domino, and Toussaint were particularly adept at this. Professor Longhair, with seven tracks here out of 28, is given prominence. His seminal piano treatment of boogies created such standards as "Bald Head," "She Ain't Got No Hair," and "No Buts, No Maybes." These discs, both superb compilations of a style no longer with New Orleans, accompany the book *Walking to New Orleans* (Bexhill-On-Sea, England, Blues Unlimited, 1974) by John Broven.

B2.15 **Original Gold Soul.** two discs. Mercury SRM2-600.
This set is a selection of tracks from the Mercury vaults, and it owes more to the jazz antecedents of r 'n' b rather than to the blues. Most of the tracks are from the 1950s, but there are a few from the early part of the 1960s, such as Ivory Joe Hunter's "I Almost Lost My Mind," Joe Liggins's "The Honeydripper," and several copies of earlier hits for Ruth Brown, Louis Jordan, and Clyde McPhatter. Entertainers here include Red Prysock, Dinah Washington, Jimmy McCracklin, Josh White, Billy Eckstine ("Jelly, Jelly"), Eddie Vinson, and Jay McShann.

B2.16 **Out of the Past. v.1.** Joy JS 5007 (British issue).
Here is more "doo wop" music from the groups of the fifties. The Flamingos take on "I Only Have Eyes for You," the Channels sing "The Closer You Are," and the Dells swing nicely on "Oh, What a Night." Two important songs from this period include the Spaniels' "Painted Pictures" and the Capris' "Moon Out Tonight." While this is not as comprehensive a collection as the Specialty *Doo Wop* (see item B2.7), it is a good introduction to the more commercial aspects of this musical genre.

B2.17 **Rhythm 'n' Blues; v. 1: End of an Era; v. 2: Sweet and Greasy.** two discs. Imperial 94003 and 94005.
Here are 14 rare Imperial and Aladdin tracks from 1952-1956. So rare are they that this must be seen as a compilation of regional hits (the Los Angeles area). Certainly, they were not given national exposure. The groups include the Sharp-tones, Kidds, Bees, Dukes, Pelicans, and Jivers. The second anthology covers a wider period, 1949-1957, and attempts to be a "roots" type album, drawing material from Imperial, Aladdin, and Score Records. Some of it is better known, such as "Dear Lori" by the Shades, "I Miss You" and "Love Me" by the Avalons, and "Is It Too Late" by that marvelously named group, the Fidelitones. Other groups represented here include the wild Sha-Weez, the Savoys, the Robins, the Jewels, and the Pelicans again. Both records have a superb set of notes.

B2.18 **Rhythm & Blues Explosion.** Ember SE 8003 (British issue).
Most of the twelve tracks here illustrate the 1959-1962 period of r 'n' b, when it was slowly gestating into soul music. The material on side one comes from the various labels owned by Bobby Robinson, one of the first black record company owners. Musically, this period in rock and roll was barren, and to some extent, rhythm and blues music stepped in to fill the vacuum. There are fine efforts here from best-selling works, such as Wilbert Harrison's "Kansas City," early Gladys Knight and the Pips in "Operator" (a monster hit), "Guess Who" and "Letter Full of Tears." Of course, these latter hits were from their pre-Motown days. Of note in this collection are two tracks from Ike and Tina Turner (1960-1961) entitled "It's Gonna Work Out Fine" and "A Fool In Love." These selections, on the Sue label from New York City, were their biggest selling works, save for the 1966 "River Deep, Mountain High." All of the music here is r 'n' b at its efficient best.

On the dance songs, the beat keeps going without becoming monotonous; on the emotional songs, the musical arrangements are simple and inconspicuous, letting the singer dominate.

B2.19*   **Sound of the City; New Orleans: Where Rock 'n' Roll Began.** United Artists UAS 29215 (British import).

This record was produced to illustrate the New Orleans portion of Charlie Gillett's *The Sound of the City*. The material chosen for it nicely presents a broad portrait of the existing musical structure in the Crescent City during the 1952-1962 decade. The first eight tracks contain items from the Imperial sessions, 1952-1957; the last eight tracks are from the Minit label, 1960-1962. The impact of New Orleans on both rock and roll and rhythm and blues music is not too well known for a number of reasons. First, only one studio in town would take coloured performers: Cosimo's. Second, the record companies that spread this music around were not based in New Orleans but, rather, were on the West Coast. And third, the two innovators and producers in the field (Dave Bartholomew, who did a and r work for Fats Domino, and Allen Toussaint) were and are modest men. The rich musical heritage of New Orleans comes from jazz, blues, and Creole influences, and also includes Spanish and West Indian rhythms. This amalgam really produced superior music, such as the efforts by Fats Domino ("Little School Girl"), Roy Brown ("Let the Four Winds Blow," with a slap-and-shuffle drum effect, and recorded four years before the Domino version), and Barbara George ("I Know," an exceptional r 'n' b shouter).

B2.20   **The Unavailable 16 Hits of Yesteryear.** Vee Jay 1051.

These rare tracks had never before been issued on an album, and, in fact, the amusing rendition of "Red Sails in the Sunset" by the Spaniels on this set was only released on this album. Certain elements of doo-wop singing dominate the release, containing material from 1955 and 1956. The Magnificents manage to inject some gospel on "Up on the Mountain," while the Dells chant on "Dreams of Contentment." Other items include the Delegates' "Mother's Son," the Quintones burbling on "Down the Aisle of Love," and the Orchids' "Newly Weds," backed with "You Said You Loved Me."

B2.21   **Urban Blues. v.1: Blues Uptown; v.2: New Orleans Bounce.** two discs. Imperial LM 94002 and 94004.

The titles here are deliberately misleading. While it is possible that two or three tracks from amongst the 28 could be called blues, the material is definitely all rhythm and blues, especially the second volume. Modern urban stylings are combined with jazz overtones, gospel music, and perhaps the effect of commercial pressures to create definitive r 'n' b records of the 1947-1954 period, produced from the West Coast and issued on either Imperial or Aladdin labels. The label had the final say on the product, despite its being recorded in such diverse places as Chicago, New Orleans, Houston, New York, and Los Angeles. Selections include a number of outtakes by Fats Domino, Smiley Lewis, Amos Milburn ("Chicken Shack Boogie"), Mercy Dee Walton, T-Bone Walker, Roosevelt Sykes, Joe Turner, and Wynonie Harris. Of interest is a Joe Turner version of "Lucille" played with Fats Domino, as well as such risqué numbers as "Shake Shake Baby,"

"Mother Fuyer," and "Too Many Drivers." Joe Turner reappears with a previously unissued selection that also includes Wynonie Harris in a "Battle of the Blues"— and each shouter goes hammer and tong at each other.

GROUPS

The groups in r 'n' b music usually worked in one of two formats: the doo wop specialty developed by the Ink Spots (see their place of prominence in the next entry); and the uptempo r 'n' b dance music pioneered by the instrumentalists.

Innovators

B2.22*   **The Ink Spots. Best.** two discs. MCA 2-4005.
This quartet was perhaps one of the most influential groups upon black urban music. Charles Fuqua was a tenor (his son Harvey became part of the Moonglows in the 1950s, and helped to develop soul music with a particular sound), and Bill Kenny was the high tenor, whose soaring voice on "If I Didn't Care" spawned a whole series of imitators. They formed in 1934, visited Jack Hylton in England, and returned for 20 years of success with Decca Records. In addition to the above tune, this group was responsible for "We Three," "My Prayer" (later done by the Platters), "Whispering Grass," "Street of Dreams," and "Do I Worry?" from amongst the 24 selections here. The high tenor of Kenny contrasted with the deep baritone voices of Ivory Watson and Orville Jones, producing many innovative vocal patterns that directly affected several groups in the forties. The Ravens in 1948 modelled themselves on this pattern, and the vogue of the "doo wop" groups was started: slow, emotional statements of life, with a high tenor or soft baritone intoning the pleas. When merged with heavier r 'n' b funky beats and instrumentation, soul resulted. There is a direct line from the Ink Spots to every contemporary soul group that uses a high tenor.

B2.22a*   **Lucky Millinder. Lucky Days, 1941-1945.** MCA 5L0.065 (French issue).
Millinder was the nominal leader of the Mills Blue Rhythm Band until it broke up in the late 1930s. While a good organizer, he apparently was not too successful as a leader. His band played the romping stomping boogie music of the 1940s, with strongly featured soloists and vocalists. Gospel singer Sister Rosetta Tharpe here tackles "Trouble in Mind" while pianist Bill Doggett (later to be a prime influence on the organ in 1950s r 'n' b music) and guitarist Trevor Bacon solo in the background. Other tracks with Tharpe include "Rock Daniel," "Shout, Sister, Shout!," "That's All," and "I Want a Tall Skinny Papa." Millinder occasionally took a humorous vocal outing as on "Ride, Red, Ride," but it was Wynonie Harris, in 1944, who helped to define the jump blues with "Hurry, Hurry" and "Who Threw the Whiskey in the Well?" Powerhouse performances were usually led by Panama Francis's drumming ("Little John Special," with excellent solo work by such second-line performers as Buster Bailey on clarinet), George Duvivier or Al McGibbon on bass, Tab Smith or George James on alto sax, Dizzy Gillespie on trumpet, Ellis Larkins on piano, Eddie Davis on tenor sax, and so forth. This excellent reissue features all the above tracks among its 14 cuts.

Standards

B2.23 **The Cadillacs. Fabulous.** Jubilee 1045.
The twelve items here come from the Josie record catalogue of 1955 and 1956. This group was well known for its one big smash hit "Speedo," also on this disc, but it is interesting to note how it developed from the traditional r 'n' b jump style into an uptown style. "Let Me Explain" is an out-and-out blues song, yet the group's producer employed a falsetto tenor and echo effect. "No Chance" is basically a Jesse Powell instrumental on a 12 bar boogie blues theme, with overlays of bass guitar for that heavy sound (in 1956 yet!). Other interesting tracks here include "You Are" and "Sympathy."

B2.24* **The Cats and the Fiddle. I Miss You So.** two discs. RCA Bluebird AXM2-5531.
While there is no fiddle here, there is plenty of smooth hokum as well as vocal harmonies and some hot solos (both instrumental and scatting) on these 32 tracks from 1939-1941, their most popular period. This is really modified Ink Spots and Mills Brothers, but with a more black quality to the performances, reminiscent of the finger popping music of Harlem nightclubs and cabarets. This punch is evident in both "Blue Skies" and "I Don't Want to Set the World on Fire," plus the title selection. They took pop songs and covered them for the black market, the reverse of the process of white singers of but a decade in the future. They had a strong influence on the r 'n' b bird and doo wop groups of the 1950s, particularly with Austin Powell's smooth tenor work on the vocal leads. The up-tempo songs—"Hep Cats' Holiday," "Public Jitterbug No. 1"—showcased the tipple (12 strings) of Ernie Price. In 1941, Tiny Grimes would join them with his idiosyncratic four string guitar performances. Typical tracks include "Stomp, Stomp," "Killin' Jive," "We Cats Will Swing for You," and "Gangbusters."

B2.25 **The Chantels.** End 301.
The Chantels, in the period 1955-1958, were the most widely acclaimed r 'n' b female group. The reason is clear: their singing style (peppy and bouncy) and their material (honest). Such numbers include "He's Gone," "Maybe," "I Love You So," "Whoever You Are," and "Every Night"—most of them hits.

B2.26* **The Clovers. Their Greatest Recordings.** Atco SD 33-374.
The Clovers were the best and most successful of the early r 'n' b groups, except perhaps for the Ravens, who barely made it into the fifties. The material on this disc covers 1951-1955, which was pre- rock and roll. To round out the album, Atlantic has also added "Love Potion No. 9," a belated 1959 hit. The Clovers turned in a youthful sound with hard-punching rhythmic backgrounds, in contrast to other groups that produced either high tenor sentimental ballads in the Ink Spot tradition or novelty and humorous ballads. The easiest way to express what the Clovers were doing is to state that they were a *group* version of *solo* artists who were also rhythmically successful, such as the early B. B. King. Their gospel punch is quite evident on "Fool, Fool, Fool," "Little Mama," or "Ting-A-Ling." The success of the Clovers resulted in gross imitation, as perfected by the Dominoes and the Midnighters. Other items here that were a success include "Down in the Alley," "Your Cash Ain't Nothing but Trash," and the

big effort "One Mint Julep." It is interesting to note that most people think of the 1959 Clovers, who, well past their prime, had a freak hit with "Love Potion No. 9." The tracks here are their early and even greater works. Good notes, including little tidbits on how to duplicate a 1952 record player sound and the information that the love potion song here includes an expurgated verse that was left out by United Artists.

B2.27* **The Coasters. Their Greatest Recordings; The Early Years.** Atco SD 33-371.

The Coasters were Atlantic's great comedians. Young people spent many years laughing to "Along Came Jones," "Yakety Yak," and "Charlie Brown." Their situation comedies preceded the Mothers of Invention by a decade; their material was universal, and each story was complete (as in a play) by itself. Whether the locale was the ghetto or suburbia, the songs came from Everyman. Their earlier efforts were more heavy, and reflected black areas more than their later efforts. Such items as "Riot in Cell Block Number Nine," "Down in Mexico," and "Smokey Joe's Cafe" are self-indicated titles. All the material on this disc (except "Shoppin' for Clothes") was written by that remarkable team of Leiber and Stoller (who also wrote "Hound Dog" for Big Mama Thornton, later covered by Elvis Presley). They were also a and r men, as well as producers and managers. Early in the fifties, they produced the Robins for a regional label, Spark Records. Quite often, they managed to sell 100,000 discs in California alone, but they lacked national exposure. Atlantic picked them up and changed the group's name to the Coasters (from the West Coast), and at the same time, Leiber and Stoller became the first truly independent producers, signing a contract with Atlantic for recorded works, not for salary. Their first effort that appealed to white America was the epic "Searchin'." This was in 1957, when many racial barriers had been dropped. Other permanent comedy items here include "Poison Ivy" and "Little Egypt." The Coasters' distinctive sound of rolling bass vocal and hysterical lead tenor was unique; it has never been successfully imitated.

B2.28 **The Crows/The Harptones. Echoes of a Rock Era: The Groups.** two discs. Roulette RE-114.

B2.29 **The Heartbeats/Shep and the Limelites. Echoes of a Rock Era: The Groups.** two discs. Roulette RE-115.

These two double discs represent a minor break-through in the production of r 'n' b past hit material. Most anthologies had utilized a common repertoire of records, say, from a pool of 150 songs, for a constant stream of re-issues of the same material. In addition, the field of r 'n' b fifties collecting is notoriously secretive; but it is no secret now that the mere presence of these great r 'n' b artists on record with their original material and original hits has already driven the price down for original pieces of their vinyl from the fifties. Certainly, this will benefit libraries, as it now allows them to buy superb social music of a kind that we may never see again. The Crows probably had the first rock and roll records with "Gee"; the Harptones had cornered the market on ballads. James Sheppard was the leader of both groups on RE-115, and for over almost a decade, he had a string of minor hits celebrating life with his baby. The superb notes were put together by three hard-core doo-wopers.

B2.30   **The Drifters. Golden Hits.** Atlantic SD 8153.

After 1959, when the first Drifters disbanded, George Treadwell, who still had a five-year contract with the group, plus two semi-annual shows a year at the Apollo Theater, pulled a group called The Five Crowns out of obscurity and made them the "new" Drifters. Thus it happened that one week they were the lowest group on the bill at the Apollo and returned the very next week as headliners—with the new name, of course. Ben E. King, who later went solo with "Spanish Harlem," was lead singer, and under Leiber and Stoller's production methods, hit after hit was ground out for five years. The result was "There Goes My Baby," a Billboard hit at number 2 (their biggest record in over six years). Others followed: "Save the Last Dance for Me," "Up on the Roof," "Under the Boardwalk," and "On Broadway." Quality material, even of a pop nature that strayed far from rhythm 'n' blues, plus a socking rhythm tempo was important in preceding the Motown sound, and eventually became characteristic of "soul" music for groups.

B2.31*   **The Drifters. Their Greatest Recordings; The Early Years.** Atco SD 33-375.

The Drifters have been a phenomenon since 1953. The name of the group still carries on, although two of their greatest lead singers have since died (Clyde McPhatter was perhaps the best-known lead to emerge from the group; Ben E. King, still alive, was the other). Johnny Moore, lead on "Ruby Baby" (which was effectively covered by Dion in 1963), is still with the present Drifters. Over the years, of course, the sound of the group has changed. But this disc carefully illustrates two major periods in their life. First, the period with Clyde McPhatter, and including such perennial numbers as "Money Honey" (their first hit), "Honey Love," and "Whatcha Gonna Do." For laughs, they also produced straight versions of "White Christmas" and "Bells of St. Mary's," both of which sold reasonably well among the black markets. The second period, which extends to 1959, was the Leiber-Stoller era, when these two white craftsmen took on the a and r job of creating hit material for the Drifters. Here were the above-mentioned "Ruby Baby," "Fools Fall in Love," and "Drip Drop." This was quality r 'n' b material, sung by a superior vocal group. Its members disbanded in 1959, but the owner of the name rounded up another group which promptly began to record hit bound material of a pop nature. But that's another record, and another story.

B2.32   **El Dorados.** Vee Jay 1001.

The El Dorados were the most respected group working in r 'n' b sounds. Listening to this disc, it is easy to hear why. Tight harmonies, good material, and sparse instrumentals made them almost the *crème de la crème* of the musical world. "There in the Night," the seminal "A Fallen Tear," "Now That You're Gone," and "At My Front Door" are important works in their history and in their influence on younger groups at the beginning of the 1960s.

B2.33   **The Flamingos. Meet the Moonglows.** Vee Jay 1052.

B2.33a   **The Flamingos. Serenade.** End 304.

The Vee Jay disc contains 16 golden items from 1953, when both the Flamingos and the Moonglows were under contract to that company. The title "Golden Teardrops" probably epitomizes their style at the time, with Sollie

McElvoy's vocal being pointed against the soaring tenor background, and complicated by an echo chamber. The Moonglows assist ably on "Lonely Christmas." The softer nature of their singing is documented on the End set, and comes from 1959-1961. Their pop material here, assisting in the transition from r 'n' b to soul, included vague phrasings and determined efforts in "Where or When," "I Only Have Eyes for You," and "Nobody Loves Me Like You."

B2.34*   The Isley Brothers. Twist and Shout. Wand 653.

The Isley Brothers had done a good job in combining gospel and blues elements into a unique sound, thereby paving the way for other dynamic, swinging groups. Their seminal "Twist and Shout" was neatly covered by the Beatles and turned into a monster hit. "It's Your Thing" and "Twistin' with Linda" were not far behind in assisting the dance craze.

B2.35   Little Anthony and the Imperials. We Are. . . . End 303.

From the golden year of 1958, at the beginning of the transition from r 'n' b to soul music, Little Anthony and his group began cashing in on the trends with hit material. The effort, of course, was tempered by whatever was available to be sung by high vocal lead with chanting group. Anthony's whine and wail seemed most appropriate on "Tears on My Pillow" or "When You Wish upon a Star," but slightly out of place on other successes (which must have had some different reason for being successful) such as "Go" and "Two People in the World."

INDIVIDUALS

Innovators

These innovators were leaders in their regional stylings. Other innovators may also be found in the **Urban Blues** section. Hank Ballard promoted many new kinds of dances, as well as providing a source for rock and roll versions of lewd songs. Chuck Berry fused r 'n' b with country music and added new rhythms that turned on the British. Roy Brown contributed a crying, pleading, gospel style. Ray Charles worked on the funky piano and gospel's call and response patterns. Sam Cooke, raised with a gospel singing group, took his melismatic singing style over to the pop crooning world with soft ballads. Fats Domino retained the jazz character of New Orleans plus stomping piano with saxist Dave Bartholomew. Louis Jordan contributed humor and legitimatized the jump blues of the 1940s into national success, in addition to influencing just about every major black saxophone player in later years. Little Richard added gospel screams and stage antics, plus superior material to which to dance, and influenced the Beatles.

B2.36*   Hank Ballard and the Midnighters. Greatest Jukebox Hits. King 541.

By 1960, Hank Ballard had fizzled out with hits and influences. But, during the 1950s, he was instrumental in creating a wave of new dances, such as the retread "Hucklebuck" (originally a jitterbug from the 1940s), "The Twist" (as the original writer), and "Finger Poppin' Time" ("Hey now, hey now, hey now . . . "). He developed the first series of songs that continued from record to record with the "Annie" series. "Work with Me Annie" was successfully covered by Georgia Gibbs as "Dance with Me Henry," and it contained many sexual double-entendres, so many that the Ballard sequel was "Annie Had a Baby." As a humorous answer to Gibbs's "Henry" cover, Ballard penned the great ditty "Henry Got Flat Feet."

B2.37*   **Chuck Berry. Golden Decade, v.1-3.** six discs. Chess 1514, 60023, and 60028.
Chuck Berry was one of two black innovators (the other was Little Richard) in the cross-over period from rhythm and blues to rock and roll. Berry developed his blues-based sound from country influences (around Memphis), the exact opposite of Elvis Presley and other rockabillies, who developed their country sounds from blues influences. If Presley led white singers in the fifties, then Berry showed the way for blacks. His sounds could be assimilated, and the upshot of this was the beginnings of the Rolling Stones and Beatles; he also figured in the development of the British blues and their subsequent transposition back into America for "hard rock" (with no roll). Berry possessed genius in his writings and in his guitar playing, emphasizing stops and warped notes with many arpeggios. While many copyists used his songs, few used his sound, so the music today sounds as fresh as it did when first issued.
His period was loosely 1955-1965, and these 6 discs (which include a complete discography) contain 71 items, ranging from hits to six items never before released. It seems incredible that Berry never had a million seller single until 1972, when he struck with "My Ding-A-Ling," a blatantly copied sexual euphemism from an earlier hit itself based on blues talk and the "dirty dozen." Important selections here include "Maybelline," "Johnny B. Goode," "Roll over Beethoven," "Memphis," "School Days," "Reelin' and Rockin'," "Sweet Little Sixteen," and "Jo Jo Gunne." His music was mostly fun-filled tales of teenage life styles, and it included "car" songs, humor, "personality" songs, romping instrumentals, plus some esoteric Spanish items.

B2.38*   **Roy Brown. Hard Luck Blues.** King KS 1130.
Brown was the first real r 'n' b act in New Orleans. Previously, he had played around various parts of southern Texas. But when he recorded in the Crescent City in the late forties (primarily for DeLuxe and King, as heard on this twelve track compilation), he brought with him his crying, pleading, swooping gospel-brand of stylish singing. His high pitched voice, coupled with his storyteller lyrics, makes him the first *soul* singer (before the term was actually coined). His biggest successes were "Boogie at Midnight" (1949) and the title selection (1950). Other equally impressive items include "Love Don't Love Nobody," "Long about Sundown," and "Big Town." His most oft-recorded tune was "Good Rockin' Tonight," covered by both Wynonie Harris (it was an even bigger hit for Harris in the *same* r 'n' b market) and Elvis Presley.

B2.39*   **Ray Charles. Greatest.** Atlantic 8054.

B2.40*   **Ray Charles. A Man and His Soul.** two discs. ABC 590X.

B2.41*   **Ray Charles. What'd I Say.** Atlantic 8029.
    These four discs contain the essence of the gospel-inspired Ray Charles, who employed a call-and-response pattern with his female chorus, the Raylettes. He established the funky piano with "What'd I Say"; his work with the saxophone electrified the Newport Jazz Festival, as well as a 1959 concert in Atlanta. The two disc ABC set contains photographs and text supplied by Charles, wherein he traces his history, development, and roots and influences. The material on this album comes from post-1959, his r 'n' b period of hits such as "Georgia on My Mind," "Ruby," "Hit the Road, Jack" (his biggest seller), "Unchain My Heart," "Busted," "Let's Go Get Stoned," and "Crying Time." The notes conclude with a complete discography up to 1965. His Atlantic material, from 1954, is more in the gospel and jazz bag. There are no slick productions here. His big hits album included "I Got a Woman," "Tell the Truth," "I'm Movin' On," and "Talkin' 'bout You." The "What'd I Say" album contains the standard definitive version of that hit, as well as such other gems "Tell Me How Do You Feel," "What Kind of Man Are You," "Rockhouse," and "My Bonnie." This was the record that carried Charles over to the white market, and established his superiority in r 'n' b tough epics.

B2.42*   **Sam Cooke. This Is Sam Cooke.** two discs. RCA VPS 6027.

B2.43   **Two Sides of Sam Cooke.** Specialty S 2119.
    Cooke was the lead singer of the gospel group the Soul Stirrers from 1951 to 1956. The Specialty disc has one side devoted to his gospel work, while the second side is all his pop material. When he switched to rhythm and blues, many people disowned both him and the Soul Stirrers, and he was forced to leave the group because nobody wanted an r 'n' b singer performing gospel. His attitude and vocals were casual, with spare phrasings. Often, though, he had a spine shivering voice that stayed with you, and it was very melodic at times. Perhaps his biggest gospel success was "Last Mile of the Way." The RCA material comes from 1960-1965, just before his tragic death. The material was a little more pop oriented, but includes such seminal items as "Chain Gang," "You Send Me," "Bring It on Home to Me," and "Let the Good Times Roll." In line with many other important rhythm 'n' blues artists, such as Percy Mayfield, Cooke also wrote his own material.

B2.44*   **Fats Domino.** two discs. United Artists UALA 233G.
    Domino developed out of New Orleans piano jump blues, which can be heard on "The Fat Man" (1949), by way of Louis Jordan. Dave Bartholomew, who plays trumpet on the early sides, looked after the superb arrangements and half of the writing, along with Fats. Here, we have his good Imperial records, from 1949 through "Let the Four Winds Blow" in 1961. This cross-section includes his big hits, good jazz and blues numbers, some novelties ("The Rooster Song"), and some remaking of Tin Pan Alley standards ("My Blue Heaven"), handled the way Fats Waller did his popular stuff. Domino provides the transition between whites and blacks in early r 'n' b, for he was acceptable to both. Most of his sidemen stayed with him over the years, but when he switched labels, he was given a new sound and fell from favour into blandness. The set features excellent sound, superior packaging, good notes, and a discography of Fats Domino's entire career (including post-Imperial material).

B2.45*   **Louis Jordan. Best.** two discs. MCA2-4079.

Jordan played alto saxophone for Chick Webb from 1936 to 1938. He struck out on his own at that time and from that time, he led a small group that concentrated on novelty items with a jump beat. These tunes sold exceptionally well, and certainly encouraged him and others to produce similar items. His version of "Caldonia" was on the market long before Woody Herman's, yet Herman is generally credited with both the hit and idea. Other big, big tunes from the forties included "Saturday Night Fish Fry" and "Choo Choo Boogie." The items on these two discs include the above-mentioned songs. They also furnish evidence of Jordan's singing plus a jumpy alto that was coarse-grained in sound. And his infectious style caught on with whomever worked for him, notably Wild Bill Davis, then a piano player, but soon an organist with the same r 'n' b style. Jordan's importance was twofold: first, he legitimatized r 'n' b jump blues in the forties by giving it a national exposure and ensuring fans that it was indeed available. Second, he was a steady influence on many other alto and tenor sax players, notably Albert Ayler, John Coltrane, Ornette Coleman, and Sonny Rollins—all of whom began life in an r 'n' b band.

B2.46*   **Little Richard. Greatest 17 Original Hits.** Specialty S 2113.

B2.47   **Little Richard. Well Alright!** Specialty S 2136.

Georgia-born Richard Penniman and Chuck Berry are the twin pillars of the conversion of r 'n' b to rock and roll and its gaining acceptability to the white public. Little Richard was possessed of demanding vocal chords that literally blew out the microphones in the studios, and his stage performance was the direct antecedent of that of James Brown and other such performers. On occasion, Little Richard would bash the piano, climb the drapery, writhe on the floor, and so forth—singing all the while. This was transposed to celluloid for millions of fans to see world-wide, and his antics on film, only slightly tamer, evoked much comment in the film press. But, along with Alan Freed's other boys (Fats Domino, Bill Haley and the Comets, and some minor stars), he created films that quite literally revolutionized rock music. He even performed title selections, such as "The Girl Can't Help It." His seven gold discs began with Specialty Records in 1955, and they are all here: "Tutti Fruiti" (covered by Pat Boone), "Long Tall Sally" (a good hit for the Beatles), "Rip It Up" (also covered by Elvis Presley), "Lucille," "Jenny Jenny," "Keep A-Knockin' " (covered weakly by Gale Storm), and "Good Golly Miss Molly" (revitalized by the Swingin' Blue Jeans and Creedence Clearwater Revival). Undoubtedly, all of these tunes were block-busters, heavily laden with sax riffs and raunchy lyrics that were more genteelly covered up by white performers ("Let's Ball Tonight" was translated as "Have a Ball Tonight" by Elvis Presley).

Male Standards

B2.48*   **Johnny Ace. Memorial Album.** Duke DLP 71.

This tragic figure, plagued all his life by mishappenings, finally did himself in by Russian roulette. The seriousness of his endeavours coupled with his personal failings, though, produced superb music from the early fifties. His two greatest hits were "Pledging My Love" and "Saving My Love for You." Ace has assumed the status of a cult figure; nevertheless, his interpretations of suffering are very good in a musical sense. Many current performers allude to his influences, although many had never met him. Similar songs on this set include "The Clock," "My Song," the dramatic "Still Love You So," and "Never Let Me Go."

B2.49*   **Bobby "Blue" Bland. Best.** two discs. Duke 84/86.

B2.50   **Bobby "Blue" Bland. Introspective of the Early Years.** two discs. Duke DLPD 92-2.
     Master of the delayed moment in singing and of a voice that characterized his name, Bland enveloped the then Memphis sound of 1950-1964. His long tenure with Duke records produced a continual stream of hits that preceded soul, with slick interpretations and instrumentations. His resigned way of singing, coupled with the songs he was given, led to his being pigeon-holed as a male "torch" singer. And, of course, all of this is revealed on "Ain't Nothing You Can Do," "Cry, Cry, Cry," "I Smell Trouble," and "I Can't Put You Down." His more notable successes included "That's the Way Love Is," "Call on Me," "Lead Me On," "Turn on Your Love Light," "Someday," and "Poverty."

B2.51   **Earl Bostic. Best.** King 500.
     Bostic was one of the originators of the heavy, funky instrumental sounds in early r 'n' b music. His alto sax, based largely on Louis Jordan's attack, greased the grooves on his big hits "Flamingo" and "Sleep." Along with Jordan, he was directly influential on such modern soul players as King Curtis and on the jazz saxists that worked through r 'n' b boogie bands. His main work and importance came from this 1951-1954 period.

B2.52   **Bo Diddley. Got My Own Bag of Tricks.** two discs. Chess 2CH 60005.
     Diddley only had two real hits—the fast "Bo Diddley" and the slow "I'm a Man." Every record since has been a variation on one or the other. Yet, the permutations are interesting because of the cross-rhythms that Diddley set up behind his vocals. The guitar riff on "Bo Diddley" (actually, the lyrics are just an updating of an English folksong) is worth the price of admission alone. His music was conceived as the logical development of gris-gris from New Orleans and voodoo music, both themes now successfully being employed by Dr. John. "I'm a Man," "Say Man," "Tell Me, Man"—all are slow blues with an incessant drone, and can be likened to the work of almost any run-of-the-mill bluesman today.

B2.53*   **Don and Dewey. Specialty/S2131.**
     Don "Sugarcane" Harris and Dewey Thomas now have separate careers; the former in the field of rock violin, the latter as a solo soul artist. Yet, when they were together in 1957-1960, they made great music that never seemed to get beyond the Los Angeles area. Even their regional hits were covered by black artists, rather than white performers. Some of their hits: "Leavin' It All up to You" (done by Dale and Grace, and number one on the charts for a while); "Big Boy Pete" (covered by the Olympics); "Farmer John" (which became a big hit for the Premiers); and "Koko Joe" (by Sonny Bono) and "Justine" (both covered by their biggest imitators, the Righteous Brothers). "Pink Champagne," never before

issued, features Don's searing violin. The other tracks have his guitar and bass. The supporting musicians were virtually the same as those that supported Little Richard on his epic-making sessions. Both Don and Dewey possessed vocalizing techniques that pre-dated soul by at least a decade, and one feature was the staggered phrasing between the two, and a distinct lack of harmony, often behind the beat.

B2.54   **Lee Dorsey. Best.** Sue ILP 925 (British import).
     The material on this disc comes from the early Fury sessions. Dorsey was one of New Orleans' best club performers. He had simple, catchy riffs that were exceptionally suitable for dancing, a blend of Carnival Mardi Gras sounds and early reggae. Some of the 1961 material, including his biggest successes "Ya-Ya" and "Do-Re-Mi," were nothing but well-hidden minor novelty masterpieces.

B2.55   **Cecil Gant. Rock Little Baby.** Flyright 4710 (British issue).
     Here are some rompin', stompin' blues from the late 1940s by a minor genius of the boogie jump blues piano. Gant presents rollicking versions of some old and some new material (at that time) through "Screwy Boogie," "Blues in L.A.," "Ninth Street Jive," "Owl Stew," and "Playing Myself the Blues."

B2.56   **Al Hibbler. Greatest Hits.** Decca DL 75068.
     Hibbler was once lead vocalist with Duke Ellington (and the Duke never did have much success with his vocalists). On this basis, the blind singer secured a major contract with Decca and began emulating Billy Eckstein and Billy Daniels in his emotional power with material given him by his producers. Thus, he had the eminently successful hit "Unchained Melody," and others such as "He," "11th Hour Melody," and "After the Lights Go Down Low."

B2.57   **Ernie K-Doe.** Minit 24002.
     Possessor of a very strong nasal voice, Ernie Kador made his name with New Orleans novelty records that were terrific to dance to. Most of them featured the rolling piano of Allen Toussaint, noted r 'n' b producer and composer. K-Doe's biggest success was the influential "Mother-In-Law Blues," which needs no further explanation. Other sob songs with a heavy background included "Hello My Lover" and "I Cried My Last Tear." The most effective period in his life was around 1960-1962, particularly with the warming novelty "Te-Ta-Te-Ta-Ta."

B2.58*   **Smiley Lewis. I Hear You Knocking.** Imperial LP 9141.
     Amos Overton Lemmon was vastly underrated, and it is only through discographic reference works (such as this one that attempts to trace roots and influences) that certain individuals get known beyond their cult following. Lewis was a loud shouter, just as rough as Joe Turner, and along with superb arrangements by Dave Bartholomew (who did similar work for Fats Domino), he brought shouting back into style in New Orleans. This disc covers the 1950s, his most important period. The title selection was covered by both Little Richard and Gale Storm after its release in 1955. Other important vocal stylings are revealed in the epic "Shame, Shame, Shame," the 1950 version of "Tee Nah Nah," the 1954 "Lost Weekend," and "The Bells Are Ringing," "Blue Monday," and "Real Gone Lover."

B2.59   **Little Milton. "Raise a Little Sound."** Red Lightnin' 0011.

B2.60*   **Little Milton. Sings Big Blues.** Checker 3002.
　　Many collectors do not know what to make of Little Milton. He can be a bluesman, and alternately, he can perform in a rhythm 'n' blues mode or even in soul stylings. Versatile, but whatever he does, he does it with gut emotion that many other singers do not have. His material is virtually all about ghetto existence, as on "Grits Ain't Groceries" or "Dark End of the Street." Other successful records, in an artistic if not sales sense, include "We're Gonna Make It," "Let Me Down Easy," and "Blind Man." He was Memphis born, and influenced by T-Bone Walker, Roy Brown, Joe Turner, and, later, B. B. King and Bobby Bland. The material on the Red Lightnin' reissue covers the four years from 1954 through 1958, and features Little Milton in his versatile mode. For Sun records, he was in the "Memphis blues" style. For Bobbin, he produced the jump sound, and for Chess, it was the smooth sophistication neatly illustrated by the standards on the Checker record above. From his early period, then, comes "Homesick for My Baby," "Begging My Baby," "Hold Me Tight," "Dead Love," and "Long Distance Operator."

B2.61*   **Little Willie John. Free at Last.** King KS 1081.
　　Willie John was a tragic figure; he died in a state prison from drugs and a complication with pneumonia. His first success was at the age of 17; he rose to prominence very fast, and his head was turned. His was the first version of "Fever," covered successfully later by Peggy Lee. He followed up with "Talk to Me, Talk to Me," a pleading "Leave My Kitten Alone," a dramatic "Sleep," and the tragic "Letter from My Darling" or "Need Your Love So Bad." As a native of Detroit, Willie John developed a slick, urbane style that was to set the lead for other such singers, particularly around the Motown area.

B2.62*   **Percy Mayfield. Best.** Specialty SPS 2126.
　　Mayfield was a master writer. Ray Charles recorded his "Hit the Road, Jack," and it turned out to be Charles' biggest hit in over 20 years. Aretha Franklin, Lou Rawls, and Peggy Lee tried "Please Send Me Someone to Love" and "The River's Invitation," but nobody can sing like Mayfield. He knows how to bring out the wistful melancholy of one line, the dark despair of another, the brightening optimism of a third. He can be subtle and emotional at the same time, reminding the listener of Billie Holiday. The items here come from the 1950s. Besides the last two above, Mayfield also recorded such minor gems as "What a Fool I Was," "Cry Baby," and "Lost Mind."

B2.63   **Mickey and Sylvia. Do It Again.** RCA ACM 1-0327.
　　This set nicely cumulates their fifties and sixties hits, largely in an r 'n' b mold. They began as a soft-singing duet, with "Love is Strange," and with other material, such as "A New Idea on Love" or "There'll Be No Backing Out," they had devised a new, fresh approach to love ballads: introspective searching in lyrics and melodies. Other interweaving melodies can be found on "No Good Lover" and "Say the Word." Sylvia had the notorious hit "Pillow Talk," one of the first of the very obviously sexual songs (no relation to the movie).

B2.64*   Johnny Otis. Pioneer of Rock. EMI Starline SRS 5129 (British issue).

Although these twelve recordings were made in 1957-1959 (past the important period in Otis' life when he had influence on the black r 'n' b scene), they are important for their impact on the white musicians of the day. White aspects of rock and roll were decidedly at least half a decade behind its black roots. The powerful Otis piano style hit a peak in the discovery of black roots during this period. Here are the extremely important and influential recordings of "Willie and the Hand Jive" (oft-recorded since), "All I Want Is Your Love," "Bye Bye Baby," and "Casting My Spell." Johnny Otis had, for years, led the Johnny Otis Show, a sort of touring platform that played anywhere and everywhere in the United States, and employed many black performers and encouraged their disparate styles.

B2.65   Lloyd Price. Original Hits. Specialty 2105.

B2.66   Lloyd Price. Mr. Personality. ABC S297.

Price became a recording star when still a teenager. His recording of "Lawdy Miss Clawdy" has never since been duplicated, but often imitated by both white and black singers. He was one of the followers of the New Orleans rhythm and blues sounds (two of the tracks on this first compilation of 14 items were composed by the legendary Huey Smith), and this resulted in such works as "I Wish Your Picture Was You," "Chee-Koo Baby," "Too Late for Tears," and "Mailman Blues." His later efforts, most notably "Stagger Lee" and "Personality" were to be released by ABC and the present disc also includes "Just Because" and "I'm Gonna Get Married." In the seventies, he moved into reggae music and Jamaican melodies with the Lloyd Price Group. Both of these albums present a careful documentation of his changing life and changing styles; both are important roots albums.

B2.67*   Professor Longhair. New Orleans Piano. Atlantic SD 7225.

Roy Byrd, to give his real name, was perhaps the key piano player and leader of the New Orleans version of jump music. Although his greatest influence was in the 1940s, when he went largely unrecorded or participated as a sideman, these tracks clearly show his continuing drive to sustain the power and thrust of his piano. They were largely recorded in 1949, but four tracks come from 1953: "On in the Night," the influential "Tipitina," "Ball the Wall," and "Who's Been Fooling You." Among his followers have been Fats Domino, Dr. John, Clarence Henry, and Allen Toussaint. To them, he is their guru. Byrd himself has described his style as a mixture of "rhumba, mambo, and Calypso." Of all the blues and r 'n' b artists in New Orleans, his sound was the most heavily influenced by non-North American roots. The "Blues Rhumba" and "Boogie Woogie" perfectly illustrate these sources.

B2.68   Snooky Pryor. Flyright LP 100 (British issue).

Little is known about Pryor, and the bulk of his recordings were done in the early fifties. The 14 tracks here cover 1948-1963, virtually his complete output under his own name. He has accompanied Leroy Foster, Sunnyland Slim, and Floyd Jones. His downhome flavor is enhanced by extended harmonica solos. Over the 15 years represented here, it is relatively easy to see his development from a

country-based singer to a powerful r 'n' b artist. His direct, economical approach
is best illustrated by "Cryin' Shame."

B2.69   **Frankie Lee Sims. Lucy Mae Blues.** Specialty/Sonet SNTF 5004
           (British issue).
      Influenced by Texas bluesman T-Bone Walker, Sims portrayed his own sweet
mixture of the blues. Material here can fall into the r 'n' b mode by virtue of its
accompaniment and jump tunes. Such tunes as "I'm So Glad" have taken on a
new meaning and derivation. His monster hit, of course, was the title selection.

B2.70*   **Chuck Willis. His Greatest Recordings.** Atco SD 33-373.
      Willis had been recording spotty discs since 1952, when he joined with
Atlantic. Their production teams (Ertegun and Wexler) gave him better material,
and he slowly regained the audience he had lost five years earlier. "Kansas City
Woman" and "It's Too Late" were two of his early classics that he had penned
himself. His greatest effort ever was, of course, the traditional "C.C. Rider,"
which coincided with a new dance that was breaking out all over the United States:
the Stroll. The pace of the song perfectly suited this new dancing craze. He cashed
in on the fad by calling himself "The King of the Stroll" and incorporating it into
his stage routines. With heavy blues inflections, as heard on "Thunder and
Lightning," "Betty and Dupree," "Love Me Cherry," and so forth, Willis ascended
the throne of the soft r 'n' b, swinging musical scene. His last song—"Hang up My
Rock and Roll Shoes"—served as his epitaph, for he died in 1958. For a short two
years, he dominated the r 'n' b world in the city.

Female Standards

B2.71*   **LaVern Baker. Her Greatest Recordings.** Atco SD 33-372.
      Originally known as "Little Miss Sharecropper," LaVern Baker brought her
rural sound (although she was born in Chicago) to the clubs as a jazz singer. When
spotted by Fletcher Henderson for Columbia records, she was reputedly giving
lessons to Johnny Ray in singing styles. This, of course, led to his renowned hit
"Cry" and other vocal mannerisms that surfaced later. Eventually she went to
Atlantic in 1953 and recorded "Soul on Fire." Atlantic played Ruth Brown (with
jazz phrasing) and Baker (from blues and gospel) against the white "thrushes" of
the time: Kay Starr, Teresa Brewer, Jo Stafford, Doris Day, Joni James, et al.
But losing the battle only gave Atlantic more adaptability. Thus, they were prepared
for the onslaught of rock and roll. Baker's blues produced the very catchy "Tweedlee
Dee" (covered by Georgia Gibbs). "Jim Dandy" was another r 'n' b tune that
quickly followed. Her career crested with the memorable "I Cried a Tear" in 1958.
Despite her gospel-type voice and the melismas that she used, her shadings were
light enough and sophisticated enough that she won ready acceptance from the
white market. Her discs sold equally well to both sectors.

B2.72   **Big Maybelle. Gabbin' Blues.** Epic EE 22011.
      Maybelle Smith recorded for the re-invigorated OKeh label, and these tracks
all come from 1952-1954. Her hard-driving sounds characterized her as a blues
shouter who straddled the ballad/blues/r 'n' b fence. Sexual imagery played a strong

role in her music, and had she recorded earlier, she might have been in the "classic blues" mould. Accompaniment is in the small band configuration, with Taft Jordan on trumpet, Sam "The Man" Taylor on sax, and Brownie McGhee and Mickey Baker on guitars. Her originals included "Just Want Your Love," "Way Back Home," "Maybelle's Blues," "Don't Leave Poor Me," and "My Big Mistake."

B2.73*   **Ruth Brown. Rock & Roll.** Atlantic 8004.

Despite the title, all of this music is pure rhythm 'n' blues. Ruth Brown had been recorded by Atlantic since the turn of the 1950 decade, and had been built into the best selling act on the Atlantic roster. Her long string of hits culminated in 1953 with "Mama, He Treats Your Daughter Mean." This was the biggest selling and most popular r 'n' b hit of the year. But Ruth Brown was a jazz singer. Her free phrasing was combined with solid band riffs to produce an exciting act unheard since Louis Jordan's heyday of a few short years before. Nicknamed "Miss Rhythm," Brown had other hits, including "5-10-15 Hours," and "Teardrops from My Eyes."

B2.74   **Lil Green. Romance in the Dark.** RCA LPV 574.

Lil Green was a remarkable women in that she was also a good composer of music. Her biggest success was undoubtedly the title track, recorded in 1940 with Big Bill Broonzy. Over the years, Broonzy contributed some songs, such as "Country Boy Blues" and "My Mellow Man," which became her favorites. Overall, she did not stick to the 12 bar blues format, and could be classed as an early performer in the r 'n' b mould. In a high-pitched voice, she sang material about male-female relationships, not all of it in the blues idiom. In 1940, she made "Just Rockin' " in the swing blues style. "Why Don't You Do Right?" was covered by Peggy Lee with Benny Goodman, and it became Lee's first success.

Gospel

GOSPEL

INTRODUCTION

"The fervor of gospel becomes the frenzy of soul."
—Arnold Shaw

As with blues music, gospel music is very difficult to describe accurately. Basically, it is traditional music (such as the jubilee, hymn, anthem, or spiritual) of varying moods and tempos, with Biblical or colloquial language, quite often meant in an evangelical tone (gospel = good news). The lyrics are simple, but they are always inspirational, devotional and, of course, sacred in intent. These lyrics—in a contradictory sense—are usually melded to secular instruments and techniques, such as jazz and blues.

Gospel is of comparatively recent origin, despite its traditional nature. Since the 1920s, it has been written by lyricists and composers with strong religious feelings. C. Albert Tindley, after the turn of the century, used spirituals and sacred motifs. Thomas A. Dorsey, once known as Georgia Tom, used the blues motif, whereas Lucie Campbell was more a traditionalist and wrote "churchy" music for Mahalia Jackson. During this period—and well into the Depression—"storefront" churches were formed: congregations that could not afford church property so they met in a store. But in addition to their spiritual function, their entertainment value was high, for they were the scene of a community's prime social functions as well. They had jumping and singing to the accompaniment of hand claps, drum beats, tambourines, and antiphonal shouting.

Through this development of strongly improvisational voices, resembling instruments in jazz, and the abandon and fervor in strong rhythms and crescendos, gospel music had three direct impacts on modern popular music. First, it was an influence on the singing styles of secular music, through Ray Charles, Della Reese, Aretha Franklin, Dionne Warwick, Roberta Flack, and so on, throughout modern soul. Second, it had dramatic impact on jazz from the late 1950s on through to the present day. And third, it had a pronounced influence on the freedom song movement of the civil rights period in the early 1960s and, thereby, also the folk music revivals.

Pre-World War II gospel music was of several types. There was the "sanctified" singing, such as that of Bessie Johnson and Blind Joe Taggart, that promoted traditional values of stern religious fervor. There were the gospel or religious songs of diverse blues singers, which were often merely toned-down versions of successful blues numbers. Nearly every blues singer had a few gospel numbers in his repertoire (the same is true of country music). A third type was the religious revival and sermon—this had the most emotional impact. Fourth was the normal singing of composed songs, either by a soloist or group who were known for singing gospel only. Post-World War II gospel singing changed in character, though. Four different styles can now be distinguished: male quartets, female groups, male and female groups, and choirs. Choirs primarily sing solemn, polished songs inspired by the Old Testament, such as black spirituals—as do many male quartets; on the other hand, female groups and soloists generally display exuberant, joyful direct songs inspired by the New Testament (these are literally "gospel" songs) but with frequent references to current life.

Modern gospel music can swing and rock like any other music. It is a collective vocal creation—any instrumental accompaniment is by piano or organ, rhythm section, guitar, drums, and even horns (as found on the music of Reverend Rice or Elder Charles Beck). The main characteristics of the music are its use of spontaneous antiphonal response, with a varying vocal tone and endless variation on the part of the lead singer. There is religious shouting and falsetto vocals, as well as repetition, improvisation, and such percussive techniques as hand claps (which is to "dance" a song) and striking of implements, and all of this communal participation leads to a sense of immediacy of communication. Virtually all of these characteristics have been carried over to soul music.

Literature

Heilbut's *Gospel Sound* (45) is the only book concerned with gospel music. Folk music survey books will mention early gospel and spirituals (see the bibliography in the *Grass Roots* volume). Cone (18) discusses the relationship of spirituals to blues; Lovell (61) deals with the history of spirituals from African roots.

Periodical literature simply does not exist for gospel. Occasional surveys occur in *Coda* (6) or *Blues Unlimited* (3), but not even the soul magazines deal with gospel except for an occasional record review. Look in *Annual Index to Popular Music Record Reviews* (1) under the religious section for reviews. Consult also *Popular Music Periodicals Index* (86) under the name of the artist or **Gospel** as a genre heading.

Discographic data on gospel artists can be located through Godrich and Dixon (40) for the 1902-1942 period (with corrections and additions in *Storyville* [21]), but there exists no other discographic venue for the post-1943 period of recording.

ANTHOLOGIES

B3.1*   **Ain't That Good News.** Specialty 2115.
A collection representative of the huge Specialty catalogue of gospel tunes, this includes songs from the Swan Silvertones, the Soul Stirrers, and the Pilgrim Travellers.

B3.2   **Black Diamond Express to Hell. v.1/2.** two discs. Saydisc Matchbox SDX 207/8 (British issue).
This set explores the motif of *trains* in gospel music. The same motif can be found in white sacred music, particularly with Roy Acuff. Volume one is largely from the pre-World War II period, while volume two is post-war. Typical tracks include "The Gospel Train Is Leaving," "Death's Black Train Is Coming," and the title selection.

B3.3   **Christ Was Born on a Christmas Morning.** Historical 34.

These tracks come from 1927 through 1936, and reflect both sacred and secular gospel music. There is no "Christmas" music here save for the title selection by the Cotton Top Mountain Sanctified Singers. Other performers include Blind Willie Johnson, Laura Henton (a marvelous "He's Coming Soon"), three tracks from Blind Willie McTell, the legendary Arizona Dranes, Edward W. Clayborn, Blind Mamie and A. C. Forehand, and Roosevelt Graves & Brothers.

B3.4   **Country Gospel Song.** RBF 19.

Sam Charters pulled together a few black and white performers to make some interesting comparisons between gospel and sacred music. Included here, then, are Ernest Phipps, Blind Willie Johnson, the Smith Brothers, Rev. J. M. Gates, and Uncle Dave Macon. Also included are the usually good Folkways notes.

B3.5*   **God Gave Me the Light, 1927-31.** Sanctified, v.2. Herwin 203.

This interesting anthology provides a good general overview of "sanctified" singing in the 1920s. In all songs can be found the customary characteristics of handclapping, answering phrases, "hallelujahs," and diverse accompaniment, including harmonica and jugs, with occasionally a mandolin. Edward Phipps is a white singer, but he does commendably on "If the Light Has Gone Out in Your Soul," with shrill syllables highlighting the performance. Other singers here include Elder Bryant (an exciting vocalist), the Holy Ghost Sanctified Singers, and the Louisville Sanctified Singers, who do the title selection and "Glad I'm Here."

B3.6*   **Golden Gems of Gospel.** Peacock PLP 140.

This is a good introduction to the Peacock catalogue of over 65 albums. During its time of the 1950s, Peacock was one of the most important of the gospel companies.

B3.7*   **Gospel Classics.** MCA Coral Cops 7453 (British issue).

Much of this anthology is gospel music sung in the jazz manner. Sister Rosetta Tharpe commands full attention with "Stand by Me" and "Rock Me," two selections from 1941, accompanied only by her guitar. The Ebony Four has marvelous jazz support from pianist Sammy Price, and clarinetist Buster Bailey. Their two spirituals—"Go Down Moses" and "Swing Low, Sweet Chariot"—are in the traditional spiritual sense, and this is highlighted even more by the jazz surroundings (there is even a scat vocal on "Chariot"). The Alphabetical Four group seem to have imitated the Mills Brothers in their vocal stylings, and one even goes so far as to make noises like a trumpet. The twelve items here are derived from Decca recordings of the 1937-1941 period and serve as a good representative example of what jazz-gospel could sound like.

B3.8   **Gospel Music. v.1.** Imperial 94007.

These 14 tracks are mostly from the Soul Stirrers' recordings for the Aladdin label in the early 1950s. The 14 tracks include "Pearl Harbor" (a report on that atrocity), "His Eye Is on the Sparrow," "Seek and Ye Shall Find." These were the group's biggest hits ever. Some other period songs include "Why I Like Roosevelt."

B3.9*   **The Gospel Sound, v.1/2.** four discs. Columbia G 31086 and KG 31595.

Columbia was not a major producer of gospel music. Thus, certain major figures are missing from this series, while some others turn in mediocre performances; however, some tracks were licensed from the Specialty collection. The discs were made to accompany Tony Heilbut's book *The Gospel Sound* (and naturally this set includes his liner notes). The arrangement is chronological, from the pre-war period to the present, on both sets. Thus volume one has the Angelic Gospel Singers, the Dixie Hummingbirds, Marion Williams, the Abyssinian Baptist Gospel Choir, Arizona Dranes, and the Rev. J. M. Gates (among others). In addition, with some returnees, volume two presents Blind Willie Johnson, R. H. Harris, Bessie Griffin, the Staple Singers, and the Golden Gate Jubilee Quartet.

B3.10   **The Gospel Stars in Concert.** Specialty 2153.

This set was recorded live in the early 1950s. The performers are Brother Joe May, the Pilgrim Travellers, the Soul Stirrers (with Sam Cooke), and Dorothy Love Coates and her Original Gospel Harmonettes.

B3.11*   **Great Golden Gospel Hits.** three discs. Savoy MG 14014, 14069, and 14165.

This is a judicious selection of tracks from the legendary Savoy collection of gospel music, including the Staple Singers, Sister Rosetta Tharpe, the Clara Ward Singers, and James Cleveland.

B3.12*   **Guitar Evangelists, v.1/2.** two discs. Truth 1002/3 (Austrian issue).

Emphasizing the street gospel singer and the street cry, this two-disc set is an important document that illustrates the story of the wandering minstrel in the American South. In this case, the message was the Word, and the street singers did their best to carry it out. Some important selections here include Rev. Moses Mason singing about "John the Baptist" and Rev. Edward W. Clayborn pleading that "Death Is Only a Dream" and "Your Enemy Cannot Harm You."

B3.13*   **In the Spirit, No.1/2.** two discs. Origin Jazz Library OJL-12/3.

These two records provide one of the finest introductions to black religious music of the 1920s and '30s. Indeed, because they covered the groundwork so thoroughly, it had been possible for even more specialized investigation of the genre by albums on such labels as Herwin and Blues Classics. Both anthologies successfully present musically compelling and historically significant items. As such, they can be treated as samplers of a vast trove of religious material, which sold very well to its audience on 78 rpms but has so far been relatively neglected on reissue LP. There is a good mixture of solo, duet, and group or congregational songs, and the artists (Sister Cathy Fancy, Elder Curry, Holy Ghost Gospel Singers), while not widely known to the general public, are considered by collectors to be among the best. These artists and performances are important to the history of black music and deserve a place on the shelves of general music libraries. As well, these issues are deserving on listening grounds, and are well recorded and annotated, with a sterling booklet by Bernie Klatzko.

B3.14   An Introduction to Gospel Song. RBF RF 5.
Another collection from the Folkways catalog, this contains relevant songs by the Rev. J. M. Gates and the Fisk University Jubilee Quartet.

B3.15   Nearer My God to Thee, 1926-1942. Roots RL 304 (Austrian issue).
This anthology collates many gospel items recorded by regular blues singers. Of note is the important recording concerning the Titanic disaster by Richard "Rabbit" Brown.

B3.16   Negro Church Music. Atlantic 1351.
Alan Lomax did a whole series of field recordings that were later released as a six-album set on Atlantic. The material encompassed blues, white folk music (old time music), and gospel. Material on the gospel album includes "Jesus Is Real to Me," "Jesus on the Mainline," and "Sail Like a Ship on the Ocean."

B3.17*   Negro Religious Music. v.1: The Sanctified Singers, Part One. Blues Classics BC 17. v.2: The Sanctified Singers, Part Two. Blues Classics BC 18. v.3: Singing Preachers and Their Congregations. Blues Classics BC 19.
As distinct from spirituals, "sanctified music" is a direct result of blacks embracing a form of Christianity that emphasized feeling and emotion as outward signs of inner conversion. The full range of traditional black sacred music in America, from antiquated country spirituals to the brisk jazz and r 'n' b-influenced gospel music, are contained on v.1 and 2. V.1 has 14 tracks of primarily pre-World War II material. Washington Phillips's "Denomination Blues [parts one and two]," recorded in Dallas in 1927, is profoundly religious and reverently set off by the delightful dulceola accompaniment. Guitar-accompanied country spirituals are represented by Blind Joe and Emma Taggart, Blind Willie Johnson, and Blind Roosevelt Graves—all sidewalk evangelists, which seems to have been a common occupation for blind black musicians in the Depression days. The post-war period is represented by Willie Mae Williams, Smokey Hogg, and Lightnin' Hopkins—the latter two being important bluesmen of the period. Other performers here include Blind Mamie Forehand, Brother George (really Blind Boy Fuller, a noted blues-man), the Two Gospel Keys, and blind Arizona Dranes. One of the most unusual pieces here is Elder Wilson's 1949 Detroit piece "Stand by Me," because of its three harmonicas used in accompaniment.
As Arhoolie does not "own" a catalogue, it has been quite fortunate in leasing the rights to as wide a variety of sources as possible, to present a perfectly balanced view of all kinds of gospel styles. This is even more important in volume 3. The reader must bear in mind that churches cater to a wide variety of cultural backgrounds; hence, there will be a wide variety of music available on many labels, and it is wise to select from many labels rather than restrict choices to one or two. Here, editor Strachwitz has chosen items that feature preachers who believe in physical communication with God, e.g., music, dancing, singing, shouting, testifying, etc. The period covered is 1930-1956, with locations ranging from Chicago to Los Angeles; Washington, D.C.; Detroit; New York; and other places. Superb notes are from Pete Welding.

B3.18   **Negro Religious Songs and Services.** Library of Congress AAFS L 10.
These are field recordings made by Harold Spivacke, John A. Lomax, Alan Lomax, and Lewis Jones. The period is 1936 to 1942, and the music is both accompanied and unaccompanied. The set has been edited with notes by B. A. Botkin. Some of the singers represented here, all non-commercial people, include Jimmie Strothers and Joe Lee, Bozie Sturdivant, the nom de plume of "Sin Killer," and Turner "Junior" Johnson.

B3.19*   **Precious Lord; Gospel Songs of Thomas A. Dorsey.** two discs. Columbia KG 32151.
This anthology of gospel pieces emphasizes the compositional skills of the great Reverend Thomas A. Dorsey, noted evangelist. Once known as Georgia Tom, Dorsey underwent a religious conversion when he lost his wife in childbirth and their baby son a day later. He wrote a song about the event in 1932, "Take My Hand, Precious Lord," and it is sung here by Marion Williams. Dorsey is said to have written about one out of every four "gospel standards" (as distinguished from hymns and spirituals). He was the son of a Baptist minister in Georgia and the nephew of a church organist. Sallie Martin, well on in years now, sings "Let Us Go Back to God," a very blues-oriented number. The Dixie Hummingbirds harmonize on three well-chosen songs. Bessie Griffen, the Obie Award winner Alex Bradford, R. H. Harris, and Delois Barrett Campbell also sing, and there is narration by Dorsey himself. Super liner notes are by Tony Heilbut, who also wrote the book *The Gospel Sound.*

B3.20   **The Rural Blues: The Sacred Tradition, 1927-1930.** Herwin 206.
As stated, this is rural religious music with guitar, banjo and tambourine. Artists represented here include Mother McCollum, Eddie Head and Family, and the Rev. Edward W. Clayborn.

B3.21   **Sorrow Come Pass Me Around; A Survey of Rural Black Religious Music.** Advent 2805.
This is non-commercial gospel, mainly from Southern church singers and musicians. Some of the material here is sung by bluesmen such as Babe Stovall ("The Ship Is at the Landing," "Will the Circle Be Unbroken") and Robert Nighthawk ("Can't No Grave Hold My Body Down," "Climbing High Mountains"); the title tune is performed by a fife and drum band and other selections are by obscure performers. The value of this set is as a 16 track compilation of the more serious, sombre (hence more "religious") renditions of rural gospel music as opposed to the more sophisticated urban music. A booklet accompanies the set, with pictures, bibliography, discography, and biographical notes.

B3.22   **Southern Sanctified Singers, 1926-1942.** Roots RL 328 (Austrian issue).
Another collection of rare gospel items, this includes the notorious Sam Butler from 1926 (he was also better known to blues enthusiasts as Bo Weavil Jackson).

B3.23   **Ten Years of Black Country Religion. 1926-1936.** Yazoo L 1022.
Despite an enormously rich blues catalog, Yazoo has only produced one gospel anthology (and some Rev. Gary Davis gospel albums). The fourteen items in this decade survey include Blind Lemon Jefferson's "Where Shall I Be?" and "All I Want Is That Pure Religion," and Charlie Patton singing "Prayer of Death" and "Lord I'm Discouraged." Other singers include Blind Willie Davis, Kid Prince Moore, and Jaybird Coleman.

B3.24   **To Mother.** Specialty SPS 2152.
Specialty has culled its immense catalog and has pulled out all the relevant (or some of the relevant) songs dealing with Mother—Momism, as it were. Thus, the key performers for this label are heard: the Pilgrim Travellers, the Five Blind Boys of Alabama, the Soul Stirrers, Bessie Griffen, the Swan Silvertones, Alex Bradford, and the Detroiters.

B3.25   **This Old World Is in a Hell of a Fix.** Biograph BLP 12017.
This is a cross-section of material ranging from an excerpt from a sermon by Rev. Dr. J. Gordan McPherson (who later styled himself as Black Billy Sunday) to the more familiar blues singers such as Blind Lemon Jefferson, Fred McDowell, Skip James, and so forth. There is an interesting mixture here of the sacred and secular blues and gospel. The album title is very unfortunate.

B3.26   **Traditional Jazz in Rural Churches, 1928-1930.** Truth 1001 (Austrian issue).
This is largely a good collection of preachers and their congregations, with diverse instrumental accompaniments. Here are the Rev. D. C. Rice and his congregation, the Rev. F. W. McGee, the Rev. Joe Lenley (with Arizona Dranes), the Southern Sanctified Singers, and the Texas Jubilee Singers.

B3.27   **Whole World in His Hand, 1927-1936 (Sanctified, v.3).** Herwin 207.
Herwin is the only company that concentrates on the more religious or church-related style that is a direct descendant from the spiritual period. "Secular" hymns have their equal place in old time or modern country music, but nothing can beat the passion or sincerity of Blind Roosevelt Graves in such Crown, Paramount, or ARC items as "Take Your Burdens to the Lord," "I'll Be Rested," or "Telephone to Glory." There are 26 separate items here, with 6 by Roosevelt Graves and others by obscure singers, such as Elder Curry, Elder Richard Bryant, Rev. E. D. Campbell, and the Brother Williams Memphis Sanctified Singers. The sermons here have been edited out to allow for more music. Klatzko states in his exemplary notes that the genuine article is hardly known today.

GROUPS AND INDIVIDUALS

B3.28   **Alex Bradford. One Step.** Vee Jay 5023.
Bradford has been nicknamed "the Singing Rage of the Gospel Age," and later, he went on to star in *Don't Bother Me, I Can't Cope* (the soundtrack of which is on Specialty S 2133).

B3.29*   **James Cleveland. With Angelic Choir, v.1/3.** three discs. Savoy 14076, 14131, 14252.

Cleveland (and his choir) have been hailed as the greatest all time male gospel stars. His call and response pattern is completely uncanny, and he has been used to good effect on various albums as a back-up choir, as with Aretha Franklin and Marion Williams.

B3.30   **Dorothy Love Coates. Best. v.1/2.** two discs. Specialty SPS 2134/2141.

On these two albums, Ms. Coates is with the original Gospel Harmonettes.

B3.31*   **Rev. Gary Davis. 1935-1949.** Yazoo L 1023.

The fourteen tracks on this set include "Angel's Message to Me," "The Great Change in Me," "You Got to Go Down," and "Twelve Gates to the City." Davis, dividing his music between blues and gospel, was undoubtedly the best and richest (in voice) of the country blues singers from the East Coast.

B3.32   **Rev. Gary Davis. When I Die, I'll Live Again.** two discs. Fantasy 24704.

These items were originally from a 1960 Bluesville 1015 and a 1961 Bluesville 1032. Davis, who passed on in 1972, was one of the greatest blues and gospel singers. He spent the greater part of his career as a street singer in Harlem. His inextinguishable guitar (six and twelve string) pulsated with moving rhythms, and he was especially good with syncopated ragtime melodies. Here is the definitive version of "Samson and Delilah," which he learned from Blind Willie Johnson. One of the best examples of his finger-picking style balanced against his voice can be found on "God I Feel Just Like Going On." Compared to other versions, such as that by Judy Collins, "Twelve Gates to the City" is noted here for its sparse simplicity. This was a troubled period in Davis's life, and consequently, at this juncture, he was singing only gospel tunes. Later, he would go back to the blues and ragtime. This set is an excellent performance by the South Carolina rural bluesman.

B3.33*   **Dixie Hummingbirds. Best.** Peacock PLP 138.

B3.34   **Dixie Hummingbirds. In the Morning.** Peacock PLP 108.

B3.35   **Dixie Hummingbirds. Prayer for Peace.** Peacock PLP 115.

One of the better known of the gospel quartets, the Dixie Hummingbirds perform inspirationally on such tunes as "Ye Shall Know," "Little Lambs," "Bedside of a Neighbor," "Will the Lord Be with Me," and "Have a Little Talk with Jesus."

B3.36   **Five Blind Boys of Mississippi. Best.** Peacock PLP 139.

B3.37   **Five Blind Boys of Mississippi. Father, I Will Stretch My Hand to Thee.** Peacock PLP 113.

B3.38   **Five Blind Boys of Mississippi. Precious Memories.** Peacock PLP 102.

There are other "Five Blind Boys" about, most notably "of Alabama" on Specialty 2123; but this quartet is the pre-eminent gospel group. This includes important recordings of "Don't Give Up," "Walk Together Children," "Save a Seat for Me," "Time Is Winding Up," "Waiting at the River," and "Jesus Rose." Peacock PLP 102 has some assistance from Archie Brownlee.

B3.39*   **Aretha Franklin. Amazing Grace.** two discs. Atlantic SD2-906.
   This album received mixed criticism when it was first issued. The gospel experts claimed that it was not emotional or inspirational enough; the followers of Ms. Franklin thought that she was out of her depth and went overboard (despite the fact that she has strong gospel roots through her family). On balance, she has been greatly assisted by James Cleveland and his choir, without whom she probably would not have had much impact. It is important to note that she helped to popularize gospel music even further among white audiences.

B3.40*   **Edwin Hawkins Singers. Oh Happy Day.** Buddah BDS 5070.
   The title selection here sold exceptionally well (over one million copies as a 45 rpm single). The lead singer at that time has now, unfortunately, turned to rock and soul music. This was a live recording, and two microphones were used: one for the lead singer and the rhythm section, and the second for the forty voice choir. Since they were a California-based group, it was not amazing to find that the Hawkins singers also perform pop soul and bossa nova music. But the impact of a swinging choir cannot be lessened once the listener has heard "To My Father's House," with the vocal by Elaine Kelly.

B3.41   **Institutional Church of God in Christ. Grace.** Cotillion 055.
   This recording won the title of "Best Gospel Choir" from the black National Association of Television and Radio Announcers. It is a prime example of church music in a largely non-gospel manner (with little shouting, but still much fervor).

B3.42*   **Mahalia Jackson. The Great Mahalia Jackson.** two discs. Columbia KG 31379.
   Ms. Jackson was perhaps the gospel singer most well-known to white audiences, through her many concerts, television and radio appearances. Here she performs exemplary material such as "I Believe," "Nobody Knows the Trouble I've Seen," "Rock of Ages," "Silent Night," "Abraham, Martin and John," "The Lord's Prayer," and "He's Got the Whole World in His Hands." Her appeal was universal, as she sang religious songs, hymns, gospel, contemporary inspiration, and even sacred music.

B3.43*   **Bessie Johnson Sanctified Singers, v.1: 1928-1929.** Herwin 202.
   Ms. Johnson, a resident of Memphis, sang with various groups in and around the Midwest. Her deep, rounded voice was mellow but slowly became more rasping and growling as her intensity reached fever pitch. She sang with McIntosh and Edwards ("Take a Stand," "The 1929 Flood," "Latter Rain Is Fall"), the Chicago Sanctified Singers ("What Kind of Man Jesus Is"), the Memphis Sanctified Singers ("He Got Better Things for You") and with her own group, Bessie Johnson's Sanctified Singers, a less successful effort.

B3.44   **Dr. C. J. Johnson. The Old Time Song Service.** Savoy MG 14126.
This is gospel music sung a cappella in the congregational style, from
Atlanta, Georgia.

B3.45*   **Blind Willie Johnson.** Folkways RBF 10.
Street singer Johnson had a good striking guitar style, using either finger
picking ("I Know His Blood Can Make Me Whole") or a slide with a knife. His
austere voice was commanding in tone. Sometimes he had antiphonal singing
in harmony duets with his wife, as on "Keep Your Lamp Trimmed and Burning"
(also done by Fred McDowell forty years later, with *his* wife), "God Don't
Change," and "Can't Nobody Hide from God." For blues and gospel scholars,
however, Johnson's best title was "Dark Was the Night, Cold Was the Ground,"
which contained no words. It was hummed and moaned, there was some gravelly
muttering, and a wildly archaic, even frightening, slide guitar. This music harkened
right back to Africa and the slave trade. His guitar was always a second voice (both
harmony *and* counterpoint). The good notes are by Sam Charters.

B3.46*   **Fred McDowell. Amazing Grace.** Testament T-2219.
Well-known slide blues guitarist and singer McDowell has always held strong
religious convictions, and many of his blues albums (see the section on **Blues**)
contain one or two "gospel" items. This set has McDowell with Hunter's Chapel
Singers, in McDowell's home town of Como, Mississippi. Present here is the
distinctly rural atmosphere of a religious service, especially in the cosmopolitan
"Amazing Grace." The set is enhanced by McDowell's excellent slide guitar work.
Included are well-known pieces such as "You Got to Move" (copied by the Rolling
Stones!!), "Tell the Angels," and "When You Get Out of the Wilderness."

B3.47   **Rev. F. W. McGhee. 1927-1930.** Roots RL-338 (Austrian issue).
Rev. McGhee died in 1971 at the age of 80. He was with the Church of God
in Christ, and gave them a lot of good gospel music. In his good communicative
voice, he ended spoken lines by singing them with a descending vocal slur. This
unique manner of phrasing soon became incorporated into gospel music in
general. There is much variety on this disc, including "Testifyin' Meetin'," the
sermonizing on "Holes in Your Pockets," the solo work on "Jesus the Lord Is
a Savior," and the finely crafted "I Looked Down the Line," which is a spoken
sermon with a rousing sing out.

B3.48*   **Mighty Clouds of Joy. Best.** Peacock PLP 136.

B3.49   **Mighty Clouds of Joy. The Family Circle.** Peacock PLP 114.
This group is another typical, well-thought-of gospel singing creation. On
these two albums will be found immaculate versions of "None but the Righteous,"
"I'll Go," "Glory Hallelujah," and "Nobody Can Turn Me Around."

B3.50   **Rev. Louis Overstreet.** Arhoolie F 1014.
The seven long items on this album come from the Reverend with his guitar,
four sons, and the congregation of St. Luke Powerhouse Church of God in Christ
(in Phoenix, Arizona).

B3.51   **Pilgrim Travellers. Best.** Specialty 2121.
Well-known for their regional hits, this group has sung and performed such items as "I Was There" and "Blessed Be His Name."

B3.52   **The Soul Stirrers. Going Back to the Lord Again.** Specialty 2150.

B3.53*   **The Soul Stirrers and Sam Cooke. Gospel Sound. v.1/2.** Specialty 2116/2128.
The Soul Stirrers are one of the longest lasting gospel groups; they have been in business for over 40 years. Of course, over the years, there have been many personnel changes. Perhaps their biggest drawing days was when Sam Cooke was the lead singer. When he went "pop," the group's popularity dropped, and Cooke was asked to leave. Specialty 2150 is a collection of recent recordings from the late sixties (without Sam Cooke), and includes "What Good Am I?," "We've Got to Have Love," "Set Me Free," and even "Let It Be." Changes wrought within the group have made it much more "pop" oriented today.

B3.54*   **The Staple Singers. Best.** Buddah 2009.

B3.55   **The Staple Singers. Hammer and Nails.** Riverside 3501.

B3.56   **The Staple Singers. Make You Happy.** two discs. Epic EG 30635.
The career of the Staple Singers has been a long and rich one. They are basically pop-oriented with soul-folk type music, especially on the Riverside album indicated above. The characteristics of the group—instantly recognizable—include Pop Roebuck's guitar and tough voice, plus Mavis's fluid voice. The Buddah collection is from their early Vee Jay days, and includes such seminal recordings as "Uncloudy Day." The Epic set is a reissue from the mid-fifties, and it includes "Why?," "King of Kings," "Pray On," and "Help Me Jesus."

B3.57   **The Staple Singers. The Twenty-Fifth Day of December.** Fantasy F 9442.
Of all Christmas holy day records, this one is perhaps the most endurable. It was originally released in 1962 on the Riverside label and features the Staples in their heyday of excellence. Roebuck ("Pop"), Mavis, Yvonne, and Pervis Staple form the gospel quartet, while Pop accompanies on guitar, assisted by the organ of Maceo Woods and the drums of Al Duncan. This collection of carols and other secular items referring to the religious aspects of Christmas clearly shows the rhythm and punch behind spirited singing of happiness. "The Last Month of the Year" has the Staple's funky guitar emphasizing the point of weariness. Traditional carols here include "The Virgin Mary Had One Son," "Joy to the World," "Oh Little Town of Bethlehem," and "Silent Night." The austere trappings of many of these carols have been set loose, and, indeed, the better efforts on this disc to non-gospel ears might possibly be "Go Tell It on the Mountain," "Sweet Little Jesus Boy," and "Wasn't That a Mighty Day."

B3.58   **Stars of Faith. Gospel Songs—Negro Spirituals.** Jewel LPS 0060.
The Stars of Faith are at the zenith of their career. The group has been together since 1958, but there have been some personnel changes. Some once sang

for the Clara Ward Singers and have been well-trained; versatile, they create good harmonies. Really, there are five lead singers in this quintet. This disc is an attempt to assimilate diverse material into some order by mixing of gospel items and spirituals from the past. It succeeds admirably. Much more, other, material from this group (which does not tend to stick with one company very long) is available on the Savoy, Vee Jay, Columbia, and Hob labels.

B3.59   **Swan Silvertones.** two discs. Upfront 139/141.

B3.60   **Swan Silvertones. Love Lifted Me.** Specialty 2122.
    This group's Vee Jay material is now available on the two Upfront discs. The Specialty item includes "Trouble in My Way" and "How I Got Over."

B3.61*   **Blind Joe Taggart.** Herwin 204.
    These 18 tracks represent his complete Paramount label output. Taggart was deep in the blues tradition, primarily a street gospel singer. The young Josh White even accompanied him around, and eventually stayed with him for many years. His most important songs include "Been Listening All Day Long," "Wonder Will My Trouble Then Be Over," and "There's Handwriting on the Wall." Good liner notes.

B3.62*   **Sister Rosetta Tharpe. Gospel Train.** Decca CL 8782.

B3.63   **Sister Rosetta Tharpe. Precious Memories.** Savoy MG 14214.
    Sister Rosetta never sang a secular note in her entire career, although many people tempted her with money and gifts. The Decca collection comes from the 1930s and early 1940s. Here she plays her own guitar as modest accompaniment, much in the style of black blues singers. And at this point in her career, she concentrated on the old songs, such as "Precious Lord" and "Peace in the Valley." The Savoy extends her career on records into the fifties. Her roots, as can be heard from listening to this disc, are deep in jazz and blues music. The material is still traditional, but she has some further plain backing in the form of an organ, piano, bass, and drums—all rather discreet.

B3.64*   **Clara Ward Singers. Lord Touch Me.** Savoy MG 14006.
    This female group was very popular in the clubs around the United States. It is one of the "boss" groups because so many gospel solo singers got their excellent training here.

B3.65   **Rev. Robert Wilkins.** Piedmont PLP 13162.
    This recording comes from 1964, after the conversion of this well-known bluesman. His greatest and most sensitive song was "The Prodigal Son."

B3.66*   **Marion Williams. Standing Here Wondering Which Way to Go.** Atlantic
         SD 8289.
    Ms. Williams used to sing with both the Clara Ward Singers and the Stars of Faith. She is now a soloist, with a pianist to accompany her. Since Mahalia Jackson's death, Ms. Williams has assumed the position of premiere female gospel singer.

Soul

SOUL

"That's what Soul is about—just living and having to get along."
—Aretha Franklin

INTRODUCTION

Modern soul music, dependent on an ethnic authenticity rather than a mastered art, involves rhythm, blues, gospel, and the syncopation of jazz back through to African music. The *polyrhythmic* nature of African music, where different rhythms are piled one on top of the other and played simultaneously in constantly shifting patterns, has found its way into modern soul through melody, harmony, and rhythm patterns where extra beats and accents are placed in all sections of the spaces between regular beats. The *antiphonal* nature of African music, best expressed in gospel music as an exchange between the leader and chorus or in blues as A-A-B pattern of observation and comment, is present through the jazz riff and the close integration of dance with song.

By adding "gospel" to "r 'n' b," then, soul resulted. This simplistic equation, of course, does not take into account the new and better compositional styles, the development of new instrumental arrangements (bass, keyboard), the advances in recording techniques, or the surprising dispersal of black styles. The fully urbanized black who may have broken out of the ghetto no longer demands his own music per se, but rather demands music that he likes—and it could be anything from a broad range. Some still like r 'n' b and blues; others derive pleasure from improvised jazz; the more socially mobile prefer sophisticated stylings of the Motown complex; the youngsters appreciate teeny bop music; the dancers want disco and sexual styles. In short, soul music is the black person's "popular music" in a development parallel to that of white people's diversified tastes.

There are, though, two main streams. One is called *authentic*, in the gospel-blues tradition, such as on Atlantic Records or the Memphis sound. The other is called *sophisticated*, where blacks sing as whites do in the popular music tradition, and can be found in Motown, West Coast Soul, or Philadelphia. This dichotomy harkens back to the doo wop vs. jump blues streams. Each is an equally valid form of music, although the sophisticated form is more palatable to the white public (= money).

Despite the social equalization of a black identity and musical expression (revolving around pride, disillusionment, resentment), much of soul music lies in the hands of the producer. It is he who decides the songs, their arrangements, and the groups or soloist. He has almost complete control, and he always works within the two hundred second format. There are no long extended soul songs, for if so then they wouldn't get played on radio, and many contain boring riffs and lyrics. It is awesome that a few certain people can control the market, but this is what happened with soul and r 'n' b music. Freedom does not exist as in the rock world (and that's also because there are not the large profits generated either). Different areas have their unique producers, but they generally fall into one of the two main

161

streams outlined above. New York—Harlem is still a leader through Atlantic Records; Detroit and the West Coast have a venue in Motown; Memphis has Hi and Stax records; New Orleans has Allen Toussaint producing for a variety of labels (Epic, Warner Brothers); Muscle Shoals and Memphis both have top flight white studio session men; Philadelphia has its "castrati" groups produced by Gamble and Huff, and Thom Bell does work there also; Chicago has had its ups and downs during the past decade.

The producer is heavily involved in the actual creation of each 45 rpm single, and this is where the soul market lies—in the three minute miniature rather than the album. Singles are important because they all sound the same, with no extended lengths to allow for improvisation. This guaranteed formula, which varies from producer to producer, seems to strike pay dirt each time, but artists and producers rarely play around with success. Many performers go into the studio to cut singles, with few ideas or plans for albums; consequently, their music is mainly a variation on a few hit themes at the same tempo. Such tempos and other technical devices (riffing horns, electric bass) render a whole album monotonous if one number follows another in the same manner and mode, so the best purchases in this category are anthologies, as they offer a selection of different stylings.

Technically, soul music retained the 12/8 pattern of r 'n' b and gospel, but tension has been added by replacing the second beat in each triplet by a rest, as for example, in 1-3, 1-3, 1-3, 1-3. The development of the Fender bass in the 1950s eliminated the rhythmic properties of the bass (plucking or walking the beat). It now had a different role: deep, throbbing notes to give bottom and drive to the rhythm. This bass riffing is the essence of the Memphis sound (indeed, Booker T. on "Green Onions" even had the bass do the top line). Musical advancement included the electric keyboard for decibels and dynamism through the organ and funky piano. Lyrically, soul music deals with much the same thematic material as white popular music: love, sex, heartbreak, jealousy, sadness. Soul lyrics can be informative and often revealing, reflecting economic conditions, sexual traditions and mores, and racial attitudes. Indeed, for the language student, soul lyrics are a valuable lexicon of street talk, slang and dialect. In content, as with much popular music, lyrics can be uninspired but remarkable for the *hook* that grabs the listener: a cadence, a phrase, an inflection. The vocal patterns of inflections and jargon make it difficult sometimes for the music to reach white listeners, and of course it is difficult to have white imitators. Thus, soul remains black music that cannot be reproduced. Many soul vocalists had their roots in gospel music and thus can use melismatic techniques with abandon. The late 1950s liberalization of gospel singers was important. Previous to this time, one sang either gospel or secular, but certainly not both! Indeed, Sam Cooke was fired from his gospel group the Soul Stirrers because of his secular singing. As a result of this change in attitude, then, more gospel singers were now available to join the pop music market.

The first song in authentic soul style is acknowledged as Ray Charles's "What'd I Say?" (1959). The tune was lifted directly from a gospel song; the antiphonal pattern was retained; the polyrhythmic structure developed in the instrumental passages; it was the first pop song to use an electric piano; the electric bass was prominent in drive; the song was about 6 minutes long—enough time to develop the theme; the new lyrics were raunchy; and there were dramatic crescendoes concluding in a call and response pattern.

In the 1970s, soul began to change. There was a broadening of appeal through the lyrics to capture the white market (that's where the money is). Superslick versions of *white* popular music were performed, from stage shows, ballads and standards, with a "soul" backing. "Blue-eyed Soul" has virtually lost its meaning, as there is much use now of white studio session men. But the main stresses remain: the bodily response of dancing; little emphasis on lyrics except to reinforce the dance mood or to proclaim blackness; vocal expressions of laughing, screaming, crying, moaning, grunting, etc. found in singers and their instruments, which try to imitate the human voice; and use of riff-like repetitions.

Literature

Soul music lacks the in-depth analysis that r 'n' b and blues have had. "Roots" are examined by Keil (53) and McCutcheon (63), and Millar (68) traces the rise of the black vocal group. There are five general surveys. Garland (36), Hoare (47), and Shaw (100) present all aspects. Redd (89) and Haralambos (44) give polemics based on past segregated music. Cummings (21) looks at the sound of Philadelphia, while Morse (70) discusses Motown. Stambler (101) gives some biographical detail in his encyclopedia of pop, rock and soul. Pleasants (85) looks at singing style, while Passman (83) makes some observances on the characteristics of disc jockeys. There are few discographic aids. Whitburn (111) gives a listing of top soul records through 1971 (based on *Billboard* surveys). Propes produced a guide to collecting singles records of the 1960s, *Golden Goodies* (Chilton, 1975). *Rolling Stone* (91) reissued over 1,000 pages of record reviews that contain notices of some soul albums. There are few American periodicals for soul. Most are the fanzine type of "biopix." England's *Black Music* (1) and *Blues and Soul* (2) present the entire spectrum of black music as an integrated whole (soul, blues, jazz, African, reggae, etc.)—and so does the weekly paper *Melody Maker* (15). *Downbeat* (9) and *Rolling Stone* (18) will have occasional articles. For coverage of these and other magazines, consult *Popular Music Periodicals Index* (86).

ANTHOLOGIES

B4.1 **Collection of 16 Original Big Hits, v.7.** Motown M 661.
Of all the Motown anthologies (and many are released each year), this is perhaps the best for variety: different styles, singers, instrumentation, tempi, material, etc. The Temptations lead off with their big gun "Ain't Too Proud to Beg," and there are contributions from the Elgins, Stevie Wonder, Tammi Terrell, Martha Reeves, and Marvin Gaye. Other anthology series from Motown, in a more discotheque-type vein, go under the title "Motown Chartbusters."

B4.2* **The Excello Story.** two discs. Excello DBL 28025.
Excello was one of the many independent r 'n' b labels that sprang up around the country during the post-war boom of the late forties. It developed out of Nashboro records, a gospel and sacred music label. Initial releases were poor, but, by 1955, owner Ernest Young found record producer Jay D. Miller, and thus began some of the best downhome blues found anywhere—Lightnin' Slim

("Goin' Home"), Lonesome Sundown ("My Home Is a Prison"), Lazy Lester ("Tell Me Pretty Baby"), Slim Harpo ("Rainin' in My Heart"), Silas Hogan ("Everybody Needs Somebody"), et al. The laid back feeling from these recordings, coupled with a frisky beat in the background, made them ideal "transfers" from the acoustic to the electric blues. They were largely made in Crawley, Louisiana, by Miller, who then shipped the tapes to Nashville to be pressed and released. The unique sound can be thought of as r 'n' b material from the early fifties, and it clearly shows the music's roots. Arthur Gunter recorded "Baby Let's Play House" (not found here), which was successfully covered by Elvis Presley. The first 16 selections here are in the blues mold; the other 16 are largely r 'n' b, and are by certain groups that broke through to the charts. Of note are the versions of "Little Darlin' " (by Maurice Williams and the Gladiolas, the original writers)— where the cover version by the Diamonds is exactly the same, note for note and word for word—and "Oh Julie" by the Crescendos, a good example of late doo wop music from 1958. Full discographical details and notes are by John Broven, an expert on southern r 'n' b music.

B4.3* **History of Rhythm 'n' Blues, v.5-8.** four discs. Atlantic SD 8193/4 and 8208/9.

This set covers the 1961-1967 period in the development of soul music. Each disc covers two years, with one reserved for 1967, perhaps the greatest year for the development of soul music as such. This set extends the earlier series of four albums, with the same titles, that covered 1947 to 1960 and dealt mainly with r 'n' b per se. The period 1961-1962 was characterized as the time when the beat retreated from soul—or late r 'n' b music. This was no doubt due to the quandary that rock and roll music had felt, a general slowing down and sophistication of sound on discs. Each song here covered a particular aspect of this movement. Here are "Early Morning" from Ray Charles, Ben E. King's "Stand by Me," the Mar-Keys' "Last Night," Rufus Thomas's "The Dog," and Otis Redding's first hit, "These Arms of Mine." 1963-1964 continued the trend. Atlantic developed new talent here: Carla Thomas, Wilson Pickett, and Barbara Lewis. The Drifters, Ben E. King, and the Coasters were at nadir at this time also. Their music was regarded as "too old," and the sounds here are their attempts to modernize themselves. The 1965-1966 period introduced Sam and Dave and Percy Sledge, but it was also a time of stagnation for Atlantic Records. The hits were not coming, and they had no girl singers. 1967 remedied that with Aretha Franklin's arrival and the teaming of Carla Thomas with Otis Redding.

B4.4* **Johnny Otis Show. Live at Monterey!** two discs. Epic EG 30473.

Subtitled "the historic rhythm & blues extravaganza that rocked the 1970 Monterey Jazz Festival," this double album pulls no punches. It is a complete definition of r 'n' b, featuring many of the originators of the sound and modified with the passing of time to fit into a soul context. Besides all this, it is one of the finest concert recordings to have ever been issued, with discreet audience reactions, a minimum of noise, and good microphone placement. Johnny Otis has been touring for a quarter of a century. During that time, he has developed many performers and has watched them become stars in their own right. His first real hit for himself was "Willie and the Hand Jive," covered of late by many rock groups (Creedence Clearwater Revival, Eric Clapton, New Riders of the Purple Sage, etc.). This was one of the first tunes to have a stunning funky riff—even back in the early fifties—that is still valid and unique today. This compelling theme (an immediate invocation to dance) can only be comparable to Booker T.'s "Green Onions" riff that dominated 1960s and 1970s soul music. Little Esther (Phillips) recreates her older works, such as "Cry Me a River Blues," "Jelly, Jelly," and "T Bone Blues." Pee Wee Crayton, a bluesman at heart, performs "The Things I Used to Do," Roy Brown attacks "Good Rockin' Tonight," and Ivory Joe Hunter plays his "Since I Met You Baby." Also present for their songs are Eddie "Cleanhead" Vinson, Joe Turner, Roy Milton, Gene Connors, Shuggie Otis, Margie Evans, and Delmar Evans. A stunning record for the point in time of 1970.

B4.5*   **The Motown Story; The First Decade.** five discs. Motown MS 5-726.
      Motown was instrumental in creating a certain sound that related to a specific geographic area. It began operations in 1959 in Detroit, first as "Anna" Records with Barrett Strong's important release "Money, That's What I Want." This song, with words and music by Berry Gordy Jr., became a sort of anthem for the British rock invasion. It was successfully covered by such groups as the Beatles. The Motown sound was simplicity in itself: four beats to the bar, with augmented drumming and cascading voices from behind a lead singer. This was a natural urban and sophisticated development from the earlier rhythm 'n' blues doo wop form of singing. And instrumentation was borrowed from white sources: violins and massed horns. The impact of Motown was to turn r 'n' b music into soul music. It also characterized soul music as coming from various places, almost as if the ghetto in these places was responsible for unique developments. Thus the Memphis sound arrived with Stax Records, the Philadelphia sound with Phillies and Gamble-Ruff, and, of course, the Detroit sound of Motown. This set illustrates through both songs and informal conversations the development of Motown, the impact of Holland-Dozier-Holland, and the importance of a few key groups (Motown does not support a full roster of artists). While key songs from singles-oriented performers may be missing (Edwin Starr's "War," R. Dean Taylor's "Indiana Wants Me," and some Isley Brothers material), there is the important "What Becomes of the Broken-Hearted?" by Jimmy Ruffin. The 58 songs here all have spoken introductions, and there is a booklet with notes and illustrations.

B4.6   **The Soul Years.** two discs. Atlantic SD2-504.
      As one of Atlantic's tributes to its own Silver Anniversary, this soul compilation is the best of the lot. Twenty-eight tracks cover 1949-1972, from the early days of r 'n' b to the full flowering of soul. Atlantic, as was indicated in Charlie Gillett's informative *Making Tracks; The Story of Atlantic Records*, produced many of the great nationally distributed r 'n' b classics, usually under the guidance of Jerry Wexler (who provided the exemplary notes on this release), the Ertegun Brothers, and later, Leiber and Stoller. The only competition that came close was the black Motown complex in Detroit. From Stick McGhee's "Drinkin' Wine Spo-Dee-O-Dee" to the Spinners' "I'll Be Around," the coverage includes Coasters, Drifters, Clovers, Ruth Brown, Joe Turner, LaVern Baker, Ray Charles, Wilson Pickett, Percy Sledge, Aretha Franklin, Otis Redding, et al. Most have been reissued before in some form, but outstanding selections include the Chords' 1954 "Sh-Boom" (covered more successfully by the Crewcuts), Ivory Joe Hunter's

"Since I Met You Baby," the Bobettes' novelty "Mr. Lee" (with a stunning and influential guitar riff), and the ultimate—Booker T. and the MGs' "Green Onions"— a real rocker. On this set are many, many seminal, important, and transitional r 'n' b-soul recordings.

B4.7   We're Leaving It up to You. Wand 1004 (British issue).

The soul material here is from New York City, in the early sixties, and it is in reality "uptown r 'n' b" as it was then called. Included are the Drifters' "Up on the Roof," the Chiffons' "He's So Fine," Chuck Jackson with "I Don't Want to Cry," and the important early Dionne Warwick "Anyone Who Had a Heart."

GROUPS

Innovators

Booker T. and the MGs added and extended the concept and capabilities of the bass electric guitar (Duck Dunn's), especially with "Green Onions." The Impressions created a weird and wonderful high harmony singing in the true doo wop style. The Supremes (with Diana Ross) fashioned the sophisticated style in soul music.

B4.8*   Booker T. and the MGs. Best. Atlantic 8202.

It is worthwhile to list the personnel here because this group, more than any other, was responsible for the drive of the Memphis Sound on Stax Records, and was a successful competitor to Motown. However, the two types of sound—from Detroit and Memphis—were entirely unlike one another. Yet, they attracted many singers to both places to reproduce their unique stylings. Booker T. Jones (organ), Steve Cropper (guitar), Duck Dunn (bass), and Al Jackson (drums) were the backbone of Memphis session men for the Stax funky sounds, characterized most by the instrumental "Green Onions," with a toppy drum and bass guitar overlay. They were the first really successful session men to record as a group, and thus paved the way for similar outings from Nashville and Los Angeles. Big hits here include "Jellybread," the inimitable "Hip Hug Her," the nostalgic "Red Beans and Rice," and "Slim Jenkins' Place."

B4.9*   The Impressions. Best. ABC 654.

B4.10   The Impressions. People Get Ready. ABC 505.

B4.11*   Curtis Mayfield. His Early Years with the Impressions. two discs. ABC 780.

This period of development for the Impressions, perhaps the premier soul group before soul was used as a musical genre term, was closely tied in with Curtis Mayfield. The double album above contains 20 tracks, with minimal duplication in comparison with the other two Impressions' albums. Mayfield always gave a special feeling to his songs, replete with silky backups and a high-pitched voice. Their biggest successes were with "I'm So Proud" and "People Get Ready." The *Best* album features Mayfield as lead singer, with songs such as "Keep on Pushing," the gospel "Amen," the proud "We're Rolling On" and "We're a Winner," "It's Alright," and "Gypsy Woman." ABC 505 contains all Mayfield-written songs, such as "We're in Love," "You Must Believe in Me," and "Sometimes I Wonder" (the latter featuring an excellent guitar break from Mayfield).

B4.12*　　**The Supremes. Greatest Hits.** two discs. Motown S 663.
　　Originally going by the name The Primettes, the Supremes and their rags-to-riches story are well known. In 1963, their first hit was created, "When the Lovelight Starts Shining," and their career as a girl trio really took off with "Where Did Our Love Go" in 1964. They were the most popular of all the Motown artists, and certainly the first of only a few groups to make a significant dent in white markets. They epitomized the Holland-Dozier-Holland approach to sophisticated music. They set an unparalleled record in the industry with five consecutive number one records in just one year: "Where Did Our Love Go?," "Baby Love," "Come See about Me," "Stop in the Name of Love," and "Back in My Arms Again." The appeal of the Supremes has been as much visual as musical. Diana Ross, lead singer on the hits of the sixties, does have a restricted range in her voicings, so much so that at times she sounds like she is whining. But then, this may be part of the appeal.

Standards

B4.13*　　**The Four Tops. Anthology.** three discs. Motown M9-809A3.
　　Originally known as the Four Aims, the group—Levi Stubbs, Duke Fakir, Obie Benson and Larry Payton—have retained the same personnel for over 20 years. Their first song for Motown was the 1964 "Baby I Need Your Loving," which was their first hit in over a decade. A continual stream of successes followed, and most are on this set of three records. Stubbs's dramatic vocal style is used against the lush orchestral backgrounds and the three background singers. Of all the groups at Motown, the Tops depended very heavily on the compositional skills and arrangements of the Holland-Dozier-Holland team. When the latter group left Motown, the Four Tops' music went into decline. Material here includes "Reach Out I'll Be There," the second best selling single for Motown of all time and all groups (from 1966), "Still Waters" (1970), "Walk Away Renee" (1967), "Standing in the Shadows of Love," "Simple Game" (1971), "It's All in the Game" (1970), "It's the Same Old Story," "I Can't Help Myself," "Baby I Need Your Loving," and the 1967 smash "Bernadette." A colorful 12 page booklet reviews their career.

B4.14　　**Jackson 5. Greatest Hits.** Motown S 741.
　　To crack the Top 40 AM radio stations, Motown developed a group that could affect pre-teens in the area of soul music. The Jackson 5 were the most commercially successful, and their achievements are quite spectacular. They have been playing as a group for eight years, and their initial success of four consecutive million-selling records ("I Want You Back," "ABC," "The Love You Save," and "I'll Be There") was unprecedented in the industry. And their material and style seem to be changing subtly with changing public taste. The youthful exuberance of the 1970 best selling single "I Want You Back" has been replaced in part by the ballad sounds of "Maybe Tomorrow." All in all, though, the Jackson 5 still remains a slick package, produced by The Corporation.

B4.15   Labelle. Nightbirds. Epic KE 33075.

The 1970s saw the resurgence of the raw power of New Orleans soul music, perhaps as a reaction to the lifeless castrato singing of the Philadelphia school. Allen Toussaint led the way with several of his own records, assisted by Dr. John (Mac Rebbenack) and the Meters. The punch here was developed by Toussaint in the 1950s, in the wake of Smiley Lewis, Fats Domino, and Dave Bartholomew. Patti LaBelle and the Bluebelles were a routine soul group that got turned around by Toussaint and a new recording contract. Prior to this, they offered the slick Motown version for Warner Brothers, RCA, and other labels. Surprisingly enough, LaBelle was born in Philadelphia (the other two—Nona Hendryx and Sarah Dash— came from New Jersey), but under the influence of producer Toussaint, the group jelled to present the diverse cultural impact of New Orleans. Cajun, Creole, Spanish, and other ethnic music origins all predominate at some time or another in LaBelle's current music. French is heavily employed, with uptempo riffing patterns. Nona Hendryx does most of the group's writing, a feat unique in soul music, where much material is fashioned by nameless writers in the back room. This is meaningful soul, as on "Lady Marmalade," a lady of the evening.

B4.16   The Marvelettes. Greatest Hits. Tamla S 253.

The Marvelettes were one of the earlier successes of Motown, and as such, they were very heavily into r 'n' b rather than soul productions. Their hit material was geared to and sold well in the black markets, but they were rarely heard outside of these areas. Their main impact appears to be on the Beatles, especially with the seminal recording of "Please Mr. Postman," an even bigger record for the lads from Liverpool. Other items by this trio include "Playboy," "Don't Mess with Bill," "Beachwood 4-5789," and the amusing "My Baby Must Be a Magician." All the tracks here come from the early sixties.

B4.17   The Meters. Fire on the Bayou. Reprise MS 2228.

The Meters appear to be the successors to Booker T. and the MGs. They are a New Orleans-based band, leading a positive resurgence of New Orleans style r 'n' b through the soul world, with definite roots in Toussaint, Professor Longhair, Dr. John, Fats Domino, and so forth. They have a sense of humor and inherent good taste in their material, which includes "Out in the Country," "Love Slip Upon Ya," "Talkin' 'Bout New Orleans," and "Can You Do Without."

B4.18*   The Temptations. Anthology. three discs. Motown M782 A3.*

Overall, this group has been the most successful of the Motown stable of male vocal groups. Among the original members were Otis Williams, Eddie Kendricks, and lead singer David Ruffin. They began slowly, scoring their first major hit with a Smokey Robinson song, "The Way You Do the Things You Do." The original group (there have been many personnel changes) worked with the Holland-Dozier-Holland writing team, Smokey Robinson, and producer Norman Whitfield. If the quintet always changed, at least the production or studio team achieved a certain measure of consistency. Indeed, this has been the one major criticism of the Motown sound: a certain sameness in the music, whether it is by one or several groups. The characteristics of the Temptations' singing has almost always been the same: a toppy drum sound for emphasis and punctuation, the falsetto of Eddie Kendricks, and the throaty lead of David Ruffin. The pattern of the songs, such as "My Girl" (a response to Mary Wells's "My Guy"), "Get Ready," "It's Growing," and "Since I Lost My Baby," has been a typical call-and-response harmony style. Ruffin's vocals were pointed against the weaving harmonies from the rest of the group, and the sum total of the music (including the drumming) resulted in a vast musical influence on other groups, most notably the so-called Philadelphia sound. In 1968, David Ruffin left; in 1970, Otis Williams left. By that time, the Temptations had shifted to the psychedelic sound pioneered by Sly and the Family Stone.

B4.19   **The Stylistics.** Avco AV 33023.

B4.20   **The Delphonics. Tell Me This Is a Dream.** Philly Groove PG 1154.

B4.21   **The Chi-Lites. For God's Sake Give More Power to the People.** Brunswick BL 754170.

B4.22   **The Main Ingredient. Spinning Around.** RCA LSP 4412.

B4.23   **The Persuaders. Thin Line between Love and Hate.** Atco SD 33-387.
    These five groups are discussed together because they exhibit very similar characteristics, songs, and tastes. If anything, they can be called "neo-classicists" because they have refined the traditional group sound—doo-wop—of the fifties, making it less rigid, more sophisticated, and also socially relevant. Yet, at the same time, they have not lost vitality or emotion. These are not innovations, or even progressions, but simply an updating of the sound that originally began with the Ravens, the Drifters, the Impressions, and the Miracles. Similar characteristics: silky smooth male groups, tenor and falsetto lead voices, simple melodies and emotions. Soft soul. The bright productions are replete with strings, punctuation (not percussions), and over-productions by highly stylized a & r men. But still, the five groups above are representative of the genre.

B4.23a   **War. Greatest Hits.** United Artists UALA 648-G.
    Eric Burdon, who split from the Animals (a British rock group), was so bound up with black blues and the meaning of soul music that he founded a rhythmic group originally known as Eric Burdon and War. Later, Burdon slipped away from this group as well. The hits here are very impressive ("All Day Music," "Slippin' into Darkness," "The World Is a Ghetto," "The Cisco Kid," "Gypsy Man," plus five others) as they mix soul with jazz, rock and pop drivel. It is very danceable music because this large (six to nine pieces) group with a reed section are brilliant inventors of the crisp style, saying only what they have to say.

INDIVIDUAL MALES

Innovators

James Brown continued on pretty much as before, augmenting his band, but, of course, he was involved in soul music long before the word was coined. Ray Charles was the man responsible for the gospel feel in soul at the time, and he took his stylings to prove that any musical form can be adaptive. Wilson Pickett best exemplified the Memphis sound. Otis Redding was one of the true composers in the field, and Smokey Robinson has been the most consistent stylist throughout the years. Sam and Dave were a dynamic duo from the Memphis sound. Sly and the Family Stone combined psychedelic rock with gospel, introducing a whole other dimension to white audiences. Jackie Wilson has influenced almost everybody and assisted many. Bill Withers is a singer-songwriter in the soul mold, and Stevie Wonder is the genius who took rock music and fused it with soul.

B4.24*   **James Brown. Live at the Apollo, v.1/2.** two discs. King 826/1022.

B4.25*   **James Brown. Unbeatable Sixteen Hits.** King 919.

When Brown signed on with King Records, nobody knew what to expect, least of all James Brown and his back-up group, the Flames. Throughout the years, the early blues (gutter type) and the heartbreak became smoothed out into a visual show, and it is for the show that Brown is well-known. The "best hits" album is largely pre-1963, and includes good items as "Please, Please, Please," "I Got You," "Shout and Shimmy," "I Feel Good," and the tearjerker, "You've Got to Cry." While working in this mode, Brown was just a few cuts above others of the same ilk. But live is something else again—the material from the Apollo is simply fantastic. I doubt whether we will ever see or hear anything like it again (Brown is now past 40 and slowing down). These two discs are perhaps the only pieces of vinyl (apart from B. B. King's *Live at the Regal* set) where the audience is on an equal level with the performer. There is much jive talk back and forth, and this actually enhances the situation. Brown is a good communicator, and this set amply shows why, as he recreates many of his studio recordings in live presentations (all long tracks): "I Want You So Bad," "Try Me," "Papa's Got a Grand New Baby," and others that duplicate *in title only* some of the tracks on the best hits collection. Unlike the Band, live and studio music are two different animals to James Brown.

B4.26*   **Ray Charles. Modern Sounds in Country and Western Music.** two discs. ABC 781/2.

Seven years before this set of records, Chuck Berry demonstrated that r 'n' b material could be written and played with a country music feel. Ray Charles took the opposite approach, and in doing so, he produced a masterpiece that clearly showed the transposition of musical styles that was possible; in no small measure, he was responsible for the resurgence of country-rock that bore fruit a few short years later, and even encouraged other soul singers to venture into country music (such as Joe Simon for Monument Records). Charles injected soul feel into country music. With Atlantic, he had produced a minor hit in Hank Snow's "I'm Movin' On." But this was a fast song, atypical of country music, and fit well with r 'n' b. In this present attempt, Charles added strings and orchestration to basically very sweet country music, and the end result was music that perhaps laid the foundations for present approaches to soul. Here are Eddie Arnold's "You Don't Know Me" and "Just a Little Lovin' "; Hank Williams's "Half as Much," "You Win Again," "Hey, Good Lookin' ," and "Your Cheatin' Heart" (thus showing where Hank Williams was; today Williams is acknowledged as a father of rock and roll); Don Gibson's "I Can't Stop Loving You," "Oh, Lonesome Me," and

"Don't Tell Me Your Troubles"; plus items written by Jimmy Davis ("You Are My Sunshine"), Fred Rose, Chet Atkins, and the Bryants.

B4.27*   **Wilson Pickett. Best.** two discs. Atco SD2-501.
     The powerful voice of Pickett, backed by an assortment of studio musicians from diverse places (and recorded in diverse places), exemplifies the Memphis sound. He was a gospel shouter who first recorded in 1964 with "In the Midnight Hour." Since that time he churned out "Land of 1000 Dances," "Mustang Sally," Solomon Burke's "Everybody Needs Someone to Love," "Funky Broadway," and a screaming "Found a Love."

B4.28*   **Otis Redding. Best.** two discs. Atco 2SA-301.
     The dynamic Otis Redding was stilled shortly after the 1967 Monterey Pop Festival, where he received his greatest acclaim outside of the black market. His best selling effort (and probably the greatest work he ever did) was "Sittin' on the Dock of the Bay." That this song should be a posthumous hit with references to his troubles and lack of a future is indicative of much *déjà vu* that occurs in the world of rock and r 'n' b. Redding's rough growl (with occasional tender nuances) was an ideal model for early soul music. He was also one of the few singers who actually wrote his own material. He recorded as well many items that had been written by Sam Cooke, his early mentor: "Shake," "A Change is Gonna Come," and "Chain Gang"—all here among 25 total selections. His own excellent material included the semi-tragic "These Arms Are Mine," "Just One More Day," the monster hit "Respect" and the vicious "I Can't Turn You Loose." Also here is the controversial recording of the Rolling Stones' "I Can't Get No Satisfaction." The recordings were done in Memphis, and besides featuring the Memphis Horns, demonstrate great support from Booker T. Jones and his group (the MGs).

B4.29*   **Smokey Robinson and the Miracles. Anthology.** three discs. Motown M793 R3.
     Robinson was perhaps Motown's most consistent artist. His literate and structural lyrics are perhaps unparalleled anywhere else in soul music. His manner of singing is in the sinuous mode, with the occasional lump-in-the-throat including falsetto. His best-selling song was "Tears of a Clown," from 1970. Other items here include "Shop Around," (their first hit, 1960), "Tracks of My Tears," "Baby, Baby, Don't Cry," plus others in a steady stream. Some clicked right away; others took over a year to climb into the charts of popularity. The simple sound of the group (vocal front, with chorus backing) is all dependent on Robinson's Sam Cooke-influenced voice. The swooping glissandi are sometimes suspenseful, in the pattern of Art Tatum's piano: is he going to make it? Robinson has been acknowledged by both Bob Dylan and the Beatles as the leading poet of the pop music world. (The Beatles had earlier recorded Robinson's hit, on this disc, "You've Really Got a Hold on Me".)

B4.30*   **Sam and Dave. Best.** Atlantic 8218.
     The Memphis sound on Stax records (released through Atlantic records) was definitely enhanced by the lyrical duo of Sam and Dave. They were the best of their kind for high voltage and energy, and even spawned a whole series of soul

duet imitators. Their smash hits here, in this largely singles market, included "Hold On, I'm Comin'," "Soul Man," "I Thank You," and "Soul Sister, Brown Sugar."

B4.31*   **Sly and the Family Stone. Greatest Hits.** Epic KE 30325.

B4.31a   **Sly and the Family Stone. Stand.** Epic BN 26456.

These two discs probe the mind of the musical genius Sylvester Stone. Beginning as a soul disc jockey in San Francisco, Sly took psychedelic rock and was most influential in blending soul and rock, when soul was still an oddity for white audiences. He experimented with vocal and instrumental sounds, sometimes playing aural games in the control room. His group even led the way for fashion in clothes. His progressions were an enormous influence on rock music, and thus it went: rock to soul, to rock, and back again—the phenomenon of imitation breeding imitation. Perhaps if one had to isolate the key to Sly's success then it would be bassist Larry Graham, who laid a great lowdown foundation that became the bedrock of Sly's music. His big hits included "Dance to the Music," "Everyday People," and "Hot Fun in the Summertime." The 1968 tune "Stand" is itself a monster instrumental jam based on the tune "Sex Machine" (not the James Brown version).

B4.32*   **Jackie Wilson. Greatest Hits.** Brunswick BL 754185.

Wilson has always been the sleeper of soul. Consistently brilliant, a master craftsman in his work, success has eluded him. He has attained the status of a cult, and his work has sold consistently well. He feels what he sings, in that soft, very urban style of his. He has been cited by many contemporary soul singers as being influential on their works, and, in many cases, he has even arranged for contracts and auditions for lesser-known singers. His material includes "Night," the sad "Lonely Teardrops," "Alone at Last," the unusually fast (for him) "Doggin' Around," "My Empty Arms." and the tender "I Get the Sweetest Feeling."

B4.33*   **Bill Withers. Best.** Sussex SBA 8037.

Withers has a rough, straightforward resonant voice—some may say down to earth. He writes most of his own material, and usually records with just a core quartet plus occasional backup services. He also plays acoustic guitar and does much of the production work himself (or with Booker T.). Relaxation is the keynote, yet to achieve this, he uses a tight sound with every note in place. Sometimes, he will duo with the piano, which often appears to have a hard flinty edge to it. Most of the material is reverent, almost gospel-like without the screaming, such as the slowly developing "Lean on Me," a source of much help. Songs also deal with stories from Harlem or his upbringing. If there is a soul-songwriter, then it is Bill Withers—"Grandma's Hands," "Everybody's Talkin'," "Who Is He?" and "Harlem," among the 10 tracks here.

B4.34*   **Stevie Wonder. Where I'm Coming From.** Tamla T 308.

B4.35   **Stevie Wonder. Music of My Mind.** Tamla T 314.

B4.36   **Stevie Wonder. Talking Book.** Tamla T 319.

B4.37*   **Stevie Wonder. Innervisions.** Tamla T 326.
    The musical development of Stevie Wonder came along with age and maturity. Throwing off the shackles of the tight Motown productions when he re-negotiated his contract, Wonder began to create all his albums from scratch. He wrote, produced, and often laid down all the instrumental tracks as a solo assault on the musical world; he created superb concept albums that were virtually unheard of in the soul music world, by borrowing a leaf from the rock world. *Where I'm Coming From* was released in 1972, and in the short two years since, he released the other three efforts. All of these soul-baring discs have placed him in the forefront of black musical progression.

Standards

B4.38   **Brook Benton. Golden Hits.** Mercury 60607.
    Dubbed "Mr. Casual," Benton appealed to a wide range of people, both white and black. He greatly assisted the cause of soul music, bringing it out of its rural roots in r 'n' b, by slick interpretations of such standards as "Boll Weevil Song" and "Kiddio." Working within 1958-1962, Benton's material included "Hotel Happiness," "So Many Ways," and the memorable "It's Just a Matter of Time." With Dinah Washington, he successfully developed the male-female duet, although in a largely popular sense.

B4.39*   **James Brown. Hot Pants.** Polydor PD 4054.
    For some strange reason, Sid Nathan of King Records was blackballed by the nation's disc jockeys, and this extended, of course, to James Brown as a King recording artist. In some measure, this prohibited his spread to the wider white markets. With a change of labels and more production money for studio work, Brown turned out some fine craftsmanlike items. It has been said that Brown's lyrics are secondary to his sound; thus, the meanings of words or his actions are surmounted by the highly evocative power of his singing and shouting. Mel Watkins says: "he is not singing *about* black life—he *is* black life." In substance (i.e., lyrics), there is not much here. But as a raw, vital life force, this is superb emotional dance music that harkens back to gospel sources. There is something mystifying about James Brown: the command that he has over people is phenomenal. Witness the impact he had in Boston a few years back when racial strife was threatening, and the mayor asked him (when in town for a concert) to speak publicly about staying indoors and not causing trouble. It worked. Such songs as the title track, "Blues and Pants," "Escape-Ism," and "Can't Stand It" are body songs in more ways than one. This is, of course, latter-day Brown in his song and dance period—the showman. For material detailing his heartbreak songs and soul-blues, the listener is asked to consult the King recordings.

B4.40*   **James Brown Band. Sho Is Funky Down Here.** King KS 1110.
    Brown does not appear vocally here, as these six extended items are all instrumentals. However, it is his band, and a well-disciplined one at that. Much soul music is vocal, with the usual instrumental breaks. There are very few instrumentals,

and a tune such as Ramsey Lewis's "The In Crowd" is the exception. Most such items come from the world of jazz, particularly soul-jazz as exemplified by Shirley Scott, Jimmy Smith, Groove Holmes, and others working on the organ-jazz trio format. The wailing sax influence was from King Curtis and earlier r 'n' b giants (in fact, Albert Ayler, Gene Ammons, Eric Dolphy, and John Coltrane began their careers playing their saxes in working rhythm and blues outfits). Brown's band (also known as the Flames) has here waxed a superb set of instrumentals. The cooking music has its jazz influence dominant against funky African rhythm patterns. Other bands that have been relatively successful with dancing music in this genre include Ike and Tina Turner's group, the Family Vibes.

B4.41 **Solomon Burke. Best.** Atlantic 8109.

Burke was yet again another Jerry Wexler-discovered pro with a tubby sound. His hits included "Tonight's the Night," "Just Out of Reach," "Take Me Just As I Am," and the masterful "Everybody Needs Somebody to Love." His importance in the early sixties transition into soul cannot be underestimated.

B4.42* **Jerry Butler. Best.** Polydor 2422 118.

B4.43 **Jerry Butler. Best.** Mercury 61281.

Butler was with Curtis Mayfield when they were both members of the Impressions. His r 'n' b material as a singer with that group was almost unsurpassed. The Polydor album includes his major efforts for the Vee Jay label, such items as "He Will Break Your Heart," "Moon River," "Make It Easy on Yourself," and "Need to Belong." He was instrumental in creating the softer sounds of soul music, and continued in the pop vein of a lively and colloquial manner under a contract with Mercury records in 1967. The resultant "greatest hits" album included "What's the Use of Breaking Up," "Mr. Dream Merchant," the big success "Hey, Western Union Man," and the emotional "Only the Strong Survive" (an important early protest song in the soul musical genre).

B4.44* **King Curtis. Best.** Atco 33-266.

Curtis was perhaps one of the most important r 'n' b and soul saxophone performers. Developing in the fifties, as did many jazz-inspired tenor saxists working in this musical mode, Curtis produced a very dirty sound on his instrument, raspy and nerve tingling. With funk background, there began a series of hits such as "I Was Made to Love Her," "Soul Serenade," and "Memphis Soul Stew." Later on in his career, in the two years before his tragic death, Curtis made many successful covers of rock music, such as "The Weight," "Hey Jude," and others.

B4.45 **Eddie Floyd. Knock on Wood.** Atlantic 7714.

Floyd was a soul singer who was very close to the blues mode. His bluesy-influenced voice and mannerisms come across very clear on such tracks as the title selection, "Don't Tell Your Mama Where You've Been," Sam Cooke's "Bring It On Home to Me," or even "I've Never Found a Girl." Of all such singers' voices, his was probably the most plaintive.

B4.46*   **Marvin Gaye. Greatest Hits. v. 1/2.** two discs. Tamla S 252/278.

B4.47   **Marvin Gaye. What's Going On?** Tamla S 310.
     Gaye was the son of a gospel minister. During the mid-fifties he sang with the Moonglows, who were then recording for Chess. An ex-Moonglow producing for Motown signed Gaye when he was available. His early recordings were very gospel inflected and rhythmic; by 1965, he had diversified into the Motown sound as did many other Motown performers: the same type of production and occasionally typecast lyrics and music. "How Sweet It Is To Be Loved by You" and "Can I Get a Witness?" are concrete examples of his earlier style. "I'll Be Doggone" and "Ain't That Peculiar" show off his changing style. By 1969, Gaye was turning out impeccable tunes such as "I Heard It through the Grapevine," "Too Busy Thinking about My Baby," and from 1970, everybody's favorite, "Abraham, Martin and John." He then retired to concentrate on his songwriting skills. Two years later, he was back with *What's Going On?*, an extremely polished effort that won both public and critical acclaim. This album changed his direction and for soul music in general, as it was the first concept or song-cycle album from the genre of soul music. It had a continuous, mellow, laid-back, spacey feel that was driven by congas over unorthodox changes in tempi. The lyrics were socially relevant and evev religious in tone. This whole attitude endeared him to rock audiences, and it opened up new avenues for other soul artists to follow.

B4.48*   **Al Green. Let's Stay Together.** Hi XSHL 32070.

B4.49   **Al Green. I'm Still in Love with You.** Hi XSHL 32074.
     Al Green is a phenomenon of the soul age. He came out of nowhere, aided and abetted by the Memphis sound and the knack of Hi records to contract important singers. His is a young, cool, intelligent, and dignified voice. He is perhaps worthy of attention at this time because his approach to music closely parallels changes occurring in the black music of the seventies. He is the first soul singer to take the approach of Frank Sinatra, Vic Damone, Dean Martin or any other Italian singer in the nightclub circuit; and of course, he is acceptable to both blacks and whites. He has a subtle, tension-building approach to his music, with a subsequent black feel to the music; but still, it is not really black music. He has done what Tommy Edwards and Brook Benton tried to do, and to a lesser extent Jerry Butler. But only Sam Cooke partially succeeded, and he may have gone further if he had not had gospel roots. Green's voice is very flexible: he can growl, scream, shout, croon, scat, and so forth with no apparent effort, including a rising falsetto. The title track "Let's Stay Together" sold as many copies as the Rolling Stones' version of "Satisfaction." Green can really manipulate an audience with his wavering voice and superb timing. These two albums contain his best work to date, and his last work for Hi records: "Old Time Lovin'," "It Ain't No Fun to Me," the tear-jerking "How Can You Mend a Broken Heart" (also covered by the Bee Gees), "Love and Happiness," and Roy Orbison's "Pretty Woman."

B4.50   **Donny Hathaway. Everything Is Everything.** Atlantic SD 33-332.
     Perhaps most widely known, at least among the white audience, as the singer-composer of "Maude's Theme" from the television show, Hathaway is a gifted and vastly underrated pianist and singer. But he suffers from excesses sometimes,

and this is most apparent when looking at his material for a total effect. He is a superb pianist, as on "Young, Gifted and Black." He projects an emotional prayer on "Thank You Master for My Soul," but this is countered by the very pretty "Je Vous Aime." The music in "The Ghetto" takes the form of an incessant and relentless dance. He also does quite well covering other people's successes, such as the Ray Charles's "I Believe to My Soul." Hathaway produces balanced albums, and he is one of the few soul singers to do so.

B4.51*   **Isaac Hayes. Hot Buttered Soul.** Enterprise 1001.

B4.52   **Isaac Hayes. Shaft.** two discs. Enterprise 5002.
     The theme and music from "Shaft" in 1969 was the start of a whole new thing in the soul world. Hayes found it necessary to pad out the number for Stax, with the consequence that he began long, elaborate readings of mostly well-known numbers; one of the selections here is over 18 minutes long! He worked a rich mine, with rock guitar and gospel opening monologue. Also, his soul was visually exemplified by his appearance in clubs—the most posh clubs, like Lake Tahoe— dressed in a chain mail shirt, with sunglasses and a gleaming bald head. In all of his appearances, he was surrounded by the chickie chorus on one side and the band on the other. The interplay between the chordal punctuations and the accompanying light show have had a devastating effect on Hayes's audiences.

B4.53*   **Ramsey Lewis. The "In" Crowd.** Cadet S-757.
     Lewis and his trio were, at the time of this recording in 1965, jazz performers. At this time, they discovered "funky," and developed a quick survey of music that was applicable to the driving, bluesy style of a nightclub performance (along with crowd noises). Thus, the title selection was a hands-down winner, and other recreations, lifted off as singles, began to move on the charts. Two were "Hang on Sloopy" and "A Hard Day's Night." Unfortunately, Lewis has been typecast for the past decade and has been unable to break the mold.

B4.54   **Lonnie Mack. For Collectors Only.** Elektra 74077.
     Mack's one big commercial hit was the instrumental on "Memphis." His funk organ, derived from Jimmy Smith and Shirley Scott, was set off to better material with the tracks he recorded for Fraternity (found on this present label): "Wham," "Susie-Q," "Bounce," "Chicken Picken," "Down in the Dumps," and "Satisfied." Such short titles to melodies indicate the crispness, and sometimes freshness, of the individual pieces that Mack played. Good, solid, dependable dance music.

B4.55   **(Curtis Mayfield). Superfly.** Curtom CRS 8014 ST.
     This soundtrack from the first really big "black" movie had enough impact to carry over into white markets. Curtis Mayfield is a unique individual, who came out of the Impressions and soloed for a few years before finding himself. His best songs have been the inspirational or truly heartbreaking ones. Both evidence pain and suffering, to some extent, and are nicely pointed off by his high voice, which often sounds like he is crying, whining, or pleading. *Super Fly* the movie dealt with a drug pusher on the way down; the album is a lot more convincing, and the drug message is stronger. Mayfield's music appears to follow rather closely the various

scenes that are represented, but the greatest quality of the music here is that it can stand alone. This is undoubtedly the best music that Mayfield produced since leaving the Impressions. One reviewer determined three distinct styles in this present song cycle: the established *Shaft* system of dramatic, heaving chords, combining guitar and synthesizer; the lyrical power and orchestration of Marvin Gaye; and the dramatic intensity of Mayfield's urgent whining voice. Important items here are "The Pusher" (*not* the same version as Hoyt Axton's), and "Freddie's Dead."

B4.56   **Johnny Nash. I Can See Clearly Now.** Epic KE 31607.
      For this album, Nash employed the Jamaican reggae beat. At the same time, he has contributed new instrumentation here, such as the moog and the accordion. In the fifties, Nash was one of many anonymous singers who flashed about on the Hit Parade every so often, later becoming a television actor. Following in the style of Sam Cooke, Nash produces almost perfect phrasing and vocal stylings, most eminent on "Stir It Up," the hit single from the record. The title track of the album and many of the other selections have individual philosophies that are applicable to ordinary day-to-day life yet they still manage to maintain a little spark of wishful thinking that the future will be rosier than at the present moment. The author of "Stir It Up" is Bob Marley, one of the giants of reggae music (he plays with the Wailers), and he has also written the problematic "Guava Jelly" and "Common Comma," both heard here. Nash has recorded a soul record based on reggae themes and philosophies (along with the insistent musical melodies, of course), and at one stroke, created a striking album, one new in terms of musical force and not monotonous. In other words, in American eyes, he legitimatized reggae.

B4.57   **Percy Sledge. Best.** Atlantic 8210.
      Sledge does *not* come on like a sledgehammer. He is the typical warm, tender ballad crooner, best exemplified, naturally, by "Warm and Tender Love." This album adequately covers his 1966 to 1969 career, and includes his biggest success, "When a Man Loves a Woman," in addition to "It Tears Me Up" and "Take Time to Know Her."

B4.58   **Johnnie Taylor. Greatest Hits.** Stax 2032.
      Neatly bridging the gaps between blues and soul, Taylor appeals to both audiences, albeit to the fringes of both. Yet, his significance lies in the mere fact that he does appeal to two distinct markets, as it can be said that largely influential singers are those who have appealed to two or more markets, thereby enhancing sales and gathering larger audiences. "Who's Making Love" is perhaps the most representative of his songs, and this album also includes "Next Time," "Mr. Nobody Is Somebody," and the long drawn out "I Am Somebody [pts. one and two]." A voice crying in the wilderness.

B4.59   **Rufus Thomas.** Atlantic 7704.
      Thomas found a theme and stuck with it during his early r 'n' b days. When soul arrived as a unique but progressive musical form, he simply transformed his themes to keep current. His first hit—"The Dog"—started it all, and over the years, it was followed by "Walking the Dog," "Jump Back," and "Can Your Monkey Do the Dog?" As the DOG was a type of shuffle dance, this last song was a reference to another dance craze—the MONKEY.

B4.60   **Joe Tex. Best.** Atlantic SD 8144.
These are from Tex's Dial sessions, as distributed by Atlantic Records. His biggest soul successes lay in the years between 1964 and 1967. Moderate popularity came with "I Gotcha" and "A Woman's Hands." In most of his songs, he introduced the business of talking to his listeners in the middle of the instrumental breaks. This was done effectively in "Hold What You've Got," "Skinny Legs and All" (displaying his marvelous sense of humor), and "Keep the One You've Got."

B4.61   **Junior Walker and the All Stars. Greatest Hits.** Soul S 718.
Walker is a lot of fun, and at times, it's difficult to determine whether he is serious or not. His good natured style and humorous touches are countered by a down home, almost rural style that harkens directly back to Louis Jordan. His limited tenor sax playing has almost never garnered him any big hits except for the instrumental "Shotgun." In this 1965-1968 period, he worked occasionally with a back-up female chorus that shouted or otherwise stated the main words of the song. Humor abounds on tracks like "Pucker Up Buttercup," "Hip City, [parts one and two]," and "Home Cookin'." In a more serious vein, there is the funky, danceable "What Does It Take?"

B4.62*   **Stevie Wonder. Greatest Hits. v.1/2.** two discs. Tamla S 282/313.
Blind since birth, Wonder was originally known as Little Stevie. He began as a harmonica player and scored with his first hit at the age of 13 in 1962 ("Fingertips"). This was his best-selling single ever, and, for some reason, he has never surpassed it. Other hits, with Wonder playing piano, developed: "Ma Cherie Amour," "I Was Made to Love Her," "Never Had a Dream Come True," "Yesterme, Yester-you, Yesterday," "Uptight (Everything's Alright)," and "Signed, Sealed and Delivered." He delivered his efforts with a workman-like approach, perhaps being sensitive due to his lack of eyesight. As he grew older, he developed into a regular producer of hits for Motown, and like most other artists recording for this company, he also suffered from over-production techniques. When he began his concept albums (see B4.35-37), he changed his approach very radically; this present two disc set forms a good summation of his pre-1972 material.

INDIVIDUAL FEMALES

Innovators

Roberta Flack, Aretha Franklin, and Nina Simone are the leaders in the gospel-soul world. Everything that they do relates to their suffering, pain, joys, and happiness. Gladys Knight is the entertainer of soul music; a veteran of over 20 years.

B4.63*   **Roberta Flack. Killing Me Softly.** Atlantic SD 7271.

B4.64*   **Roberta Flack. Quiet Fire.** Atlantic S1594.
A warm, gospel-inflected voice in distinctive stylings—Flack summarizes all to be said about soul music, with the possible exception of Nina Simone. Her voice is very easily the most persuasive around, entrapping the listener in her joys and sorrows. Although her later works tend to be over-produced (that is, concrete

music replacing the sparse emotionalism of persuasion), Ms. Flack still knows how to handle a song, such as "The First Time Ever I Saw Your Face" or the syrupy but provocative "Killing Me Softly (With Your Song)." All vocal styles are embraced, including the jazz-oriented "No Tears (In the End)"; but it is really on the slower ballads that Flack can get into a song and project her emotionalism.

B4.65* Aretha Franklin. **10 Years of Gold.** Atlantic SD 18204.

B4.66* Aretha Franklin. **Lady Soul.** Atlantic SD 8176.

B4.67* Aretha Franklin. **Young, Gifted and Black.** Atlantic SD 7213.
Ms. Franklin comes from a gospel family, and John Hammond tried to make her over into a pop singer along the lines of Billie Holiday when she was with Columbia. With the Memphis sound of Atlantic, she blossomed into the Queen of Soul Music, aided and abetted by Jerry Wexler. The compilation album comprises her top singles from 1967 through 1970, and includes important songs such as "I Never Loved a Man" (her first Atlantic Hit), Don Covay's "Chain of Fools," Otis Redding's "Respect," "Dr. Feelgood" (from blues roots), "Baby I Love You," "Natural Woman," and Sam Cooke's "You Send Me." All of the arrangements are fairly slick, and in later years, she employed many violins. *Lady Soul* shows Aretha at the peak of success, with her best band ever. This is a rock and roll, r 'n' b album more than a soul effort. "Ain't No Way" and "Baby, Baby Sweet Baby" are standouts. *Young, Gifted and Black* was her best concept album ever. Side one is autobiographical, stressing the blues and gospel. Side two contains cover versions of pop and soul r 'n' b. Here, she is at her most honest and emotional, full of restless energy. At the same time, her group speeds up certain sections of the music into double-time, and often adds a gospel chord progression to the bridges (especially on the first side). Right from her first hit "I Never Loved a Man," she was enveloped by the Atlantic recording environment. Here, the opening gospel piano chords as played by Franklin lead to antiphonal horns and a crescendo organ passage. The call and response pattern of gospel music, coupled with her innate sense of timing, meant that she could employ her melismatic moans, whoops and gasps to accentuate the sexual images that predominate in all of her material.

B4.68* **Gladys Knight and the Pips. Anthology.** two discs. Motown M702-52.
Gladys Knight and her brothers and cousins had been performing for almost a decade before being picked up by Motown. In retrospect, despite the good material here and her acceptance by the masses, she was ill-promoted by the company, and it is a wonder that she stayed with them as long as she did (until 1972). Since her departure, the group's status has increased, the material has gotten more "pop" for wider audience appeal, and Gladys Knight has been well-promoted by Bell Records. This collection of some of her Motown material is striking for the balance that it achieves. The group was not known as a one-hit-and-variation phenomenon; it covered all the bases that soul music is known to cover. Thus, there is Marvin Gaye's hit "I Heard It through the Grapevine," the slow burner "Didn't You Know?," the mid-tempo "Everybody Needs Love," and tearful songs like "Just Walk in My Shoes" and "The End of Our Road."

B4.69*   **Nina Simone. Best.** RCA LSP 4374.

B4.70*   **Nina Simone. Best.** Philips PHS 600.298

Ms. Simone is soul personified. Nothing more can be said about this very conscientious entertainer. Everything that soul is, she is; everything she is, soul is. The very guts of the music (the suffering, pain, joys, and happiness) come out in her vocal stylings and in her piano playing. Often, she has appeared in theatrical performances or in films, visually performing what she feels. The RCA material is latter-day Simone (from the mid-sixties to the present); it contains "Do What You Gotta Do," "Ain't Got No," and "I Got Life." Her biggest success ever was the seminal "To Be Young, Gifted and Black," which has been performed more times by other black singers than any other song in history.

Standards

B4.71   **Roberta Flack and Danny Hathaway.** Atlantic SD7216.

There have been some successful pairings of soul singers, but not as many as the era of rhythm 'n' blues might have led the observer to believe. Individual stardom among member of economically repressed groups is so rare that when it occurs it is likely to remain that way, with no shared billing. This is true of any musical genre, whether rock or country. (Parenthetically, country duos have a rich tradition because the performers are related or married to each other. Modern country duos even have the distinction of being developed rather late in life, when the two singers are virtually at middle age.) This present commercial venture was successful in terms of the "star" billing, for each singer saved the other from excesses that appeared on previous solo albums. All of the songs are of the familiar miniature variety (three minutes or so), with direct application to the potential of singles. Hathaway's dramatic voice has been softened by Flack's lightness, while Flack's solemnity in recording love songs has been balanced by the flair exhibited by Hathaway when he produces or acts as a sideman. Titles include "Ain't No Mountain High Enough" (a direct steal from another soul couple—Marvin Gaye and Tammi Terrell), "Baby I Love You," a pragmatic "Be Real Black for Me," and a defying conclusion of the old Phil Spector song "You've Lost That Loving Feeling."

B4.72   **Etta James. Golden Decade.** Chess 6318 126 (British issue).

Ms. James has had a chequered career as a shouting blues lady. With her original group "the Peaches," she had once made an answer to "Work with Me Annie" in the mid-fifties. The material on this disc comes from 1960-1970 and shows her in a superb soul mood. She appears to have made the transition quite easily, unlike some groups who fell by the wayside. From her Chess period, then, come heart-breakers such as "All I Could Do Was Cry," "My Dearest Darling," and "Stop the Wedding." Other numbers include "Trust in Me," "Push Over," and "Tell Mama."

B4.73   **Esther Phillips. Alone Again, Naturally.** Kudu 09.

B4.74*   **Esther Phillips. From a Whisper to a Scream.** Kudu 05.
More than a quarter of a century ago, Little Esther was touring with the
Johnny Otis Show as a 13-year-old wonder in the world of rhythm and blues. At
that time, she had improvised on a blues shouter scream and was always a favorite
with the audiences. As she grew up, a lot of bad things happened in her life, and
the sixties found her singing bland songs in order to make a living. Signing on
with Kudu in 1971 restored her confidence, and with superb material, she became
a tremendous interpreter of world-weary and bitter songs. A strong strident voice,
immaculate phrasing, and a good stage presence (she has to be seen to be believed)—
all are revealed on these two discs. The voice is up front, backed by the chorus
(occasionally) with the rhythm by their side, and strings and horns in the far back
of the studio. These Don Sebesky arrangements are a big help in projecting the
image of Esther Phillips as coming back, and coming back for the count. Songs
such as Marvin Gaye's "Baby, I'm for Real," Allen Toussaint's "Sweet Touch of
Love" and "From a Whisper to a Scream," Eddie Floyd's " 'Til My Back Ain't
Got No Bone," and Bill Withers's "Use Me" and "Let Me in Your Life" are the
types of grieving and painful melodies that really nobody wants to hear—but
the *feelings* must be expressed, the heart of "soul."

B4.75   **Martha Reeves and the Vandellas. Greatest Hits.** Gordy G 917.
Member of another burning girl trio from Motown, Reeves was particularly
effective in the earlier days of the corporation. In fact, this could be said about
many of Motown's artists; it was not until about 1965 that Motown decided to
concentrate very heavily on only a few groups, and let the rest fall where they
may. Reeves was one of the fallen, surfacing in 1969 with a hit that belies the
Motown attitude: "Dancing in the Streets." The other items here are derived
from the early sixties and include such fast-paced items as "Quicksand," "Heat
Wave," "Nowhere to Run," "I'm Ready for Love," and "Honey Chile." Most
of her epics dealt with the general nature of frustration.

B4.76   **Carla Thomas. Gee Whiz.** Atlantic 8057.
One of the mainstays of the Atlantic stable of female singers, Ms. Thomas
(daughter of Rufus) has been around for quite a while. Her biggest popularity was
in the sixties. In addition to the title selection, she also recorded "B-A-B-Y"
(written by Isaac Hayes), "Look at His Eyes," and "I'll Bring It on Home to You."

B4.77   **Ike and Tina Turner. Best.** Blue Thumb 49.

B4.78*   **Ike and Tina Turner. World of Ike and Tina.** two discs. United Artists
UA LA 064-G2.
Ike, at a very early age around the year 1950, was the pianist, arranger, and
talent scout for the Bihari brothers' West Coast record combine (Modern, RPM,
Flair, etc.). He did the bulk of his work in and around Memphis and quite often
arranged for the sale of masters to various companies. Thus, he is heard on many
records as the rock steady rhythm pianist. Around 1969, teaming with Tina, Ike
pushed on into soul music, and between the two of them (along with various
chickie choruses, sometimes called the "Ikettes," and the Family Vibes instrumental

group), they developed an electrifying stage show centered entirely around Tina's projection of raw, sensual sex. Songs that had been developed for them include the material on the Sue label ("A Fool in Love" and "It's Gonna Work Out Fine"), the important "River Deep, Mountain High" for the Phillies company, and a big 1969 smash hit—"I've Been Loving You Too Long." The Blue Thumb disc also includes "The Hunter" and "Bold Soul Sister." The United Artist collection includes some re-interpreted material, such as "Come Together" and "I Want to Take You Higher." But it also has the tragic "Nutbush City Limits." Ike and Tina Turner set the yardstick for other "revue"-type soul shows to follow.

B4.79*   **Dinah Washington. Unforgettable.** Mercury 60232.

The material that Ms. Washington was asked to handle from Mercury was largely pop-derived. "What a Difference a Day Makes" was probably her greatest hit, yet least deserved in terms of effort. Other tunes, like the title track, "This Bitter Earth," the seminal "September in the Rain," and "Love Walked In" served her far better. With Brook Benton, also under contract to Mercury, she created a series of good duets. Her blues material can be found on Roulette.

B4.80   **Mary Wells. Greatest Hits.** Motown MS 616.

Mary Wells was an early sensation for the Motown complex, and her strength is derived from the material she had and her singing style, very much in a pop vein. It is no wonder that what she produced was also accepted by the wider world that included white audiences. In fact, this material, from 1962-1964, is here, and that appeared to be the crest of her Motown career. It was also the start of a sequel song from the Temptations, entitled "My Girl." Other song titles of interest here include such singles action as "You Beat Me to the Punch," "The One Who Really Loves You," "Two Lovers," and "What's Easy for Two is So Hard for One." A tiny voice from a good singer.

Reggae

REGGAE

INTRODUCTION

Reggae (pronounced *ray*-gay) music has as many diverse roots as rock music. It is mainly the popular music of Jamaica and is always distinguished from the more folk-based rhythmic calypso music. Typical West African music is exhibited here (patterns of calls and responses, polyphony, improvisation, collective participation) plus the changes through the years by the addition of Cuban rhythms, French quadrilles, and Spanish tinges. The locally evolved "mento" styles, which performed the same functions as American blues at dances and social affairs, created the necessary instrumental formats of different percussions, violins, banjos, and even saxophones made of bamboo sticks.

During the 1950s, through the spread of high reception radios, American r 'n' b became assimilated into the style—and the label changed to "ska." Ska was more big band music, with horns and massive percussion used to create many levels of syncopation, unusual harmonies, and raw swinging rhythmic power. However, the rise of the electric bass (as in the United States), when coupled with the economic decline of the Caribbean, ousted the large formal structure of popular music. As was common in r 'n' b, British rock, Chicago blues, and many other emerging genres of music (though not at the same time), discontented street gangs took over and adopted the music as their own, grossly simplifying it to take into account the players' meagre musical knowledge. Itinerant disc jockeys became reggae's first producers and, to take advantage of the music quickly, they transformed the poetry of Jamaican music to political statements by simply having groups improvise songs on the spot (based on newspaper stories). Thus was born black Jamaican ghetto-type music.

As a Commonwealth country, Jamaica had close ties with Great Britain and exported music and musicians to her. British youth were extremely partial to ska music in the 1950s (not having any indigenous rhythmic music of their own; r 'n' b records were hard to come by at this time, and rock and roll never had the impact in Great Britain that it did in America at this time). Several recording companies opened offices in London, such companies as Island and Trojan soon establishing themselves as leaders. As ska evolved into reggae, then, record outlets were available for distribution. The music began to work its way into British popular music as second generation derivative sounds; it was re-exported to America several times (such as the 1964 single "My Boy Lollipop" sung by Millie Small, selling over 6 million copies); it was the sound track to a popular film, *The Harder They Come*; and it even showed up in American music, as in Three Dog Night's version of "Black and White," the 1972 "Coconut" by Harry Nilsson, Johnny Rivers's "Rockin' Pneumonia—Boogie Woogie Flu," Paul Simon's "Mother and Child Reunion," Johnny Nash's "Hold Me Tight" from 1968, and several others. The first true reggae singer's hit in America was Jimmy Cliff's "Wonderful World, Beautiful People" from 1969.

Economics continues to play a role in reggae music as it did in its origins. First, the music is encouraged so that political singers will and can leave the island,

and never return. Second, there is a strong market for exporting records. Third, it is cheaper for international pop stars to record in Jamaica (for studio time, session men, and tax purposes). And fourth, there is a distinctive style with Jamaican accompanying musicians plus, perhaps, a star's paying tribute to the music by including a selection or two on the album—and maybe seeing it take off as a hit single.

The basic rhythms of reggae are either a 1-3 or a 2-4 syncopation. It is essentially a dance beat, very easy and monotonous. What gives reggae its character is its lyrics, dealing with everyday misery, poverty, politics, protests, etc.—this pointed off against the stark instrumentation of (usually) a plucked lead electric guitar, syncopated drumming, and an electric bass underpinning the melody.

Literature

To our knowledge, neither a single lucid monograph nor parts of books dealing with black music cover reggae. *Sing Out!* (19) gives occasional coverage for folk roots (plus texts), but the major writings are to be found in three British periodicals: *Black Music* (1), *Blues and Soul* (2), and *Melody Maker* (15). To retrieve further information, consult *Popular Music Periodicals Index* (86) under the name of the performer or under **Reggae Music**. To check on the availability of discs, consult the *Annual Index to Popular Music Record Reviews* (1), either through the **Soul** section or the artist's name.

ANTHOLOGIES

B5.1*   **The Harder They Come.** Island ILPS 9202.

B5.2*   **This Is Reggae Music.** two discs. Island ICD 7.
Reggae as recorded by the Island label is a loose, wide-open commercial variant of the original sounds. Here, the sound is more polished and modern, reflecting most of the compositional changes of the 1970s (politics and penury). *The Harder They Come* is the soundtrack album from the movie of the same title, with Jimmy Cliff, the Maytals, the Slickers, Desmond Dekker, and the Melodians. It also has some good liner notes for an appreciation of the music. The twofer contains some of the finest "greatest" hits for Island, including the Wailers' "I Shot the Sheriff" and "Concrete Jungle," Jimmy Cliff performing his "Hey Mister Yesterday," Toots and the Maytals growling "Funky Kingston" and the American "Louie, Louie," Burning Spear's politically conscious "Old Marcus Garvey," and the Third World's "Freedom Song" amongst its twenty tracks.

B5.3   **The History of Ska, 1960-1965.** Bamboo BDLP 203 (British issue).

B5.4*   **Trojan's Greatest Hits, v.1/2.** two discs. Trojan TBL 170/180 (British issue).
No company in the United States bothered to release these albums domestically, despite the fact that they are the real thing in reggae music—the pure, honest

music of the Caribbean. Ska was the immediate predecessor of reggae, and it was
more a dance music than anything else: the application of American instruments
(electric guitar, etc.) to Caribbean rhythms. There are both vocal and instrumental
selections on the Bamboo program, with such performers as Don Drummond,
Lord Creator, Roland Alphonso, the Skatalites, the Wailers, etc.—all well-known
in Jamaica, where this music was recorded, and by extension, in the United Kingdom,
where most of it was released. Only the Wailers went on to real prominence in the
United States. There are superb liner notes by Roger St. Pierre. The 28 selections
on Trojan illustrate that company's emergence as the real innovator in reggae music,
borrowing many personnel and tunes from Jamaica (either as recorded there or
transformed in England). Here are some of the earliest examples of stylistic changes,
achieved by borrowing established hits and wrapping a reggae framework around
them: Delroy Williams's "Down in the Boondock," Nicky Thomas's "Tell It Like
It Is" and "If I Had a Hammer," Bob and Marcia's "But I Do," Byron Lee with
"My Sweet Lord" (the George Harrison tune), and even Marlene Webber's version
of the country epic "Stand by Your Man." Other titles are by Lee ("Birth Control"),
the Pioneers ("I Need Your Sweet Inspiration"), Desmond Dekker, the Maytals,
and Jimmy Cliff.

B5.5   **Reggae Chartbusters, v.1/2.** two discs. Trojan TBLS 105/147 (British
        issue).
        Reggae developed in the West Indies by way of New Orleans rhythm 'n' blues,
calypso and ska, and commercial influences (as often suggested by the Bahamian
Joseph Spence). Other tunes are subject to reinterpretation into reggae rhythms,
and indeed, this is how early r 'n' b was handled when it became commercialized
in, for instance, Jamaica. These two discs nicely illustrate the transfer of reggae
music to England, as well as the resultant changes in American Johnny Nash's
music and the impact of the sound on, for example, the Rolling Stones and Paul
Simon (both of whom recorded in Jamaica with backing by local reggae musicians).
Reggae is a novelty to us, but it is the people's music in the Caribbean. Tunes are
catchy, the lyrics (when comprehensible) are socially relevant, the bass is pounding,
and the cross-rhythms are simply 4/4—in short, excellent music for dancing (but
perhaps boring to just listen to, one track after another). Examples on these two
discs include Desmond Dekker's "The Israelites," Dandy's "Reggae in Your
Jeggae," and Tony Tribe's "Red, Red Wine," borrowed from an earlier Neil
Sedaka hit in America. All are infectious, and even suggestive, as are a lot of
reggae songs about sex. But to many people, the lyrics are too hard to hear, so
nobody minds, especially when dancing. Trojan Records in England has a hammer-
lock on this type of music, by releasing in Great Britain the tried and true hits
originally recorded in Jamaica. For example, two songs by the Pioneers, "Long
Shot Kick the Bucket" and "Poor Ramseses" were about racehorses in Jamaica.
By hitting the rhythms, many of the tunes harken back to Bill Black's Combo and
other such groups in the fifties. Jimmy Cliff, the most commercial of the
performers, tries for social comment in "Viet Nam," but with this chugging music
it is very difficult to get intellectually involved.

B5.6   **Soul of Jamaica.** Island HELP 15 (British issue).
        The name of the label comes from Jamaica, and it was with reggae material
that the recording company made its fame—long before signing contemporary

British rock giants. This anthology serves a useful purpose in summarizing the more commercial aspects of this danceable music. The only other two companies working well in this genre were Pioneer and Trojan, and the three had a firm hold on the market in Great Britain.

B5.6a*   Jimmy Cliff. Wonderful World, Beautiful People. A & M SP 4251.

As with many other reggae singers, Cliff learned from the records of the r 'n' b world (Fats Domino, Little Richard, and Dee Clark have been cited as his favorites). He moved to England in 1965 and began to play the appropriate clubs and recording dates. This eventually led to recordings, and the record here comes from 1969. One of the first to be offered to the United States with the reggae beat and music, it was also one of the first that had a distinctly non-commercial sound. It was Cliff's paean to freedom, with his feelings and experiences expressed through his high, strained voice. The 11 tracks include "Suffering in the Land," "Many Rivers to Cross," the deeply compassionate "Viet Nam" protest song, "Time Will Tell," and "Hard Road to Travel." Nine are originals.

GROUPS

B5.7*   Toots and the Maytals. Funky Kingston. Island ILPS 9330.

This group is an important reggae team at home in Jamaica. Their seminally important "Johnny Coolman" set off waves that ended up in England, and it was very important in beginning the craze for reggae rhythms. This album contains a number of their moderate successes ("Louie, Louie," "Time Tough," "In the Dark"), including the title selection, plus a few instrumentals. As a dance, reggae is unbeatable.

B5.8*   The Wailers. Catch a Fire. Island SW 9329.

This was the first Jamaican reggae record to make it across the ocean from Britain to the United States and be commercially successful. It includes "I Shot the Sheriff" (later covered by Eric Clapton and turned into a number one singles hit). The Wailers exhibit all of the characteristics of reggae dance forms (simple rhythms, simple beats, and simple, but often unintelligible, lyrics).

Citations,
Directories,
Index

BOOK CITATIONS

Most of the material in this book is based on a combination of readings from both book and periodical sources. In the listing that follows, the key books of concern to students of black music are numbered (after being alphabetized). Taken together, the books cited in the four volumes would constitute a library detailing popular music in America. We have excluded two categories of books. Generally, *biographies* have been omitted unless they deal substantially with an innovator, concentrate on his/her stylings, and show that artist's impact and influence on other performers in the same genre. Thus, for example, we list Gray's book on Bob Dylan rather than Scaduto's largely biographical offering. Second, we have omitted *songbooks* and instructional materials that look like songbooks, unless they deal substantially with the impact and influence of the music, such as Lomax's book.

It is very difficult to separate books about different musical genres, for there is much overlapping; thus, we discuss titles in the literature survey preceding each section by referring to a designated number, which then can be followed up here for source data and comment. At the same time, many books are called "reference works" (bibliographies, discographies) and "monographic surveys." To the student of music, these terms are interchangeable. In consideration of all of the above, a numerical reference listing seems the best way to handle the matter. At any rate, this is just a source list; please refer to the musical section for comments on the literature.

1 Annual Index to Popular Music Record Reviews, 1972– . Compiled by A. Armitage and D. Tudor. Metuchen, N.J.: Scarecrow, 1973– .
This annual provides location to about 15,000 record reviews in about 55 magazines, noting for each review the reviewer's evaluation of the record. It provides a synoptic report on the year's music, pre-selecting the "best of the year" and indicating the length of each review.

2 Backwoods Blues. Bexhill-on-Sea, Sussex, Eng.: Blues Unlimited, 1968. 55p. illus.
A collection of reprints from Blues Unlimited.

3 Bastin, Bruce. Crying for the Carolines. London: Studio Vista, 1971. 112p. illus. bibliog. discog.
East Coast blues, still a neglected area, are covered in this pioneering study. North Georgia and the legacy of Blind Boy Fuller are given good treatments.

4 Batcheller, John. Music in Recreation and Leisure. Dubuque, Iowa: W. C. Brown Co., 1972. 135p. paper.
A short treatise on the importance of music as a social function, with chapters on how to relax through music.

4a Beale Street, USA; Where the Blues Began. Bexhill-on-Sea, Sussex, Eng., Blues Unlimited, 196–?. unpaged. illus.
A photographic history of the Beale Street area in Memphis, Tennessee.

5   Belz, Carl. The Story of Rock. 2d ed. New York: Oxford University Press, 1972. 286p. discog. illus. bibliog.
This is a scholarly, chronological survey of a "sociological folk art," covering origins, style, influences, and the media. No musical analysis.

6   Bluestein, Gene. The Voice of the Folk; Folklore and American Literary Theory. Amherst: University of Massachusetts Pr., 1972. 170p. bibliog.
Half of this book is devoted to folk music, and includes a study of blues as a literary tradition, the black influence, and rock as poetry.

7   Boeckman, Charles. And the Beat Goes On; A Survey of Pop Music in America. Washington, D.C.; R. B. Luce, 1972. 224p. illus.

8   Bogaert, Karel. Blues Lexicon: Blues, Cajun, Boogie Woogie, and Gospel. Antwerp: Standard Uitg., 1972. 480p.

9   Borretti, Raffaele (comp.). Collectors' Catalog, v.2. Cosenza, Italy, 1972. 146p. discog.
This is a special issue of Collector magazine (July 1972); it is intended to be a guide to reissues in jazz and blues that were released 1969-1972. Information furnished includes original release number and recording date. All anthologies are analyzed.

10 Broven, John. Walking to New Orleans. Bexhill-on-Sea, Sussex, England: Blues Unlimited, 1974. 217p. illus. discog. bibliog.
A comprehensive history of the development of r 'n' b in New Orleans.

11 Burt, Jesse, and Bob Ferguson. So You Want to Be in Music! Nashville: Abingdon Pr., 1970. 175p.
This career-oriented handbook does a good job of explaining the mechanics behind breaking into the business—songwriting, studio techniques, and so forth. Glossary of recording terms.

12 Charters, Samuel B. The Bluesmen; The Story and the Music of the Men Who Made the Blues. New York: Oak, 1967. 223p. illus. bibliog. discog.
Brief descriptions of the singers and the styles from Mississippi, Alabama, and Texas to the time of the Second World War.

13 Charters, Samuel B. The Country Blues. New York: Holt, Rinehart, 1959. illus.
A well-illustrated mine of background information. There is much biographical detail on Blind Lemon Jefferson, Big Bill Broonzy, Leroy Carr, etc.

14 Charters, Samuel B. The Poetry of the Blues. New York: Oak, 1963. 174p. illus. bibliog.
This is an interpretative, explanatory study of the words of the blues, based on field recording activities.

15 Charters, Samuel. Robert Johnson. New York: Oak Publications, 1973. 87p. illus. discog. music.
"The story of Robert Johnson, his elusive life, and his music; Remembrances by great musicians who knew and played with him, along with music transcriptions of his entire recorded repertoire of blues classics." A full discography is appended.

16 Chasins, Abram. Music at the Crossroads. New York: Macmillan, 1972.
240p.
An appraisal of the current state of instrumental music, both classical and
popular, with consideration of the effects of jazz-rock-folk on "serious" music.

17 Chilton, John. Billie's Blues; Billie Holiday's Story, 1933-1959. New York:
Stein and Day, 1975. 264p. illus. discog.

18 Cone, James H. The Spirituals and the Blues; An Interpretation. New York:
seabury, 1972. 152p. bibliog.

19 Cook, Bruce. Listen to the Blues. New York: Charles Scribner's Sons, 1973.
263p. illus.
A good introduction to the blues and its relationship to white music, written
in a journalistic, synoptic style.

20 Courlander, Harold. Negro Folk Music, U.S.A. New York: Columbia Univ.
Pr., 1963. 324p. bibliog. discog. music.
A scholarly tracing of the development of black music in America, from
anthems and spirituals through arhoolies, work songs, and game songs to the
blues. While dances and instruments are mentioned, little is said about African
roots or urban extensions.

21 Cummings, Tony. The Sound of Philadelphia. London: Methuen, 1975.
157p. illus. paper only.
Traces the roots of rock and roll, r 'n' b, and modern soul that developed
in one city.

22 Delerma, Dominique-Rene. Reflections on Afro-American Music. Kent,
Ohio: Kent State University Pr., 1973. 271p. illus.
Proceedings of a conference that dealt with, to some extent, the history
of black music.

23 Denisoff, R. Serge. Solid Gold; The Record Industry, Its Friends, and
Enemies. New York: Transaction Books; distr. by Dutton, 1976. 350p.
Traces the steps through which a song goes to reach the public.

24 Denisoff, R. Serge., comp. The Sounds of Social Change; Studies in Popular
Culture. Chicago: Rand McNally, 1972. 332p.

25 Dixon, Robert M. W. and John Godrich. Recording the Blues. New York:
Stein and Day, 1970. 112p. illus. bibliog.
Traces blues records from the beginning in 1902 to 1945. In Britain, CBS
released an accompanying record.

26 Dundes, Alan, ed. Mother Wit from the Laughing Barrel. Englewood Cliffs,
N.J., Prentice-Hall, 1973. 673p.
Readings in the interpretation of Afro-American folklore.

27 Dutton, David, and Lenny Kaye. Rock 100. N.Y.: Grosset and Dunlap, 1977.
278p. illus.
About 100 influential rock and soul artists are discussed along with
commentaries on various styles and sounds (e.g., Motown Sound, disco).

28 Escott, Colin, and Martin Hawkins. Catalyst; The Story of Sun Records.
London: Aquarius, 1975. 173p. illus.

29 Evans, David. Tommy Johnson. London: Studio Vista, 1971. 112p. illus. bibliog. discog.

30 Ewen, David. History of Popular Music. New York: Barnes and Noble, 1961. 229p. bibliog. paper only.
    A brief introductory text to popular songs, the musical theater, and jazz
in America from Colonial times to 1960.

31 Fahey, John. Charley Patton. New York: Stein and Day, 1970. 112p. illus. bibliog. discog.
    Includes a discussion of his lyrics, tuning, music, and influence on the Delta
area.

31a Ferlingere, Robert D. A Discography of Rhythm and Blues and Rock and Roll Vocal Groups, 1945-1965. Pittsburg, Calif.: The Author (P.O. Box 1695), 1976. 600p.
    20,000 song titles are listed in chronological order by master number,
covering the output (78, 45, 33 1/3 RPM speeds, plus long-playing and extended
playing formats) of over 2,600 groups and single artists with groups. Unreleased
titles are also included, as well as recording dates.

32 Ferris, William R. Blues from the Delta. London: Studio Vista, 1970. 111p. bibliog. illus. discog.
    An overview of the blues tradition in Mississippi, with emphasis on the
people and the social context of their performances. There is an interesting
comparison of black and white blues songs. In Britain, CBS released an accompanying record.

33 Ferris, William R. Mississippi Black Folklore; A Research Bibliography and Discography. Hattiesburg: University and College Press of Mississippi, 1971. 61p.

34 Field, James J. American Popular Music, 1875-1950. Philadelphia: Musical Americana, 1956.

35 Fuld, James J. The Book of World Famous Music: Classical, Popular and Folk. Rev. and enl. ed. New York: Crown, 1971. 688p. bibliog.
    A discussion of 1,000 songs, primarily through tracing their roots.

36 Garland, Phyl. The Sound of Soul. Chicago: Henry Regnery, 1969. 246p. discog. bibliog.
    A very informal and emotional account of the history of soul music, having
also interviews with B. B. King, Nina Simone, and several jazz figures.

37 Garon, Paul. The Devil's Son-In-Law; The Story of Peetie Wheatstraw and His Songs. London: Studio Vista, 1971. 111p. illus. bibliog. discog.

38 Gillett, Charlie. Making Tracks; The Story of Atlantic Records. New York: Outerbridge and Lazard, 1973.
    This is probably the only book on the history of music recording, as it
is a corporate history of Atlantic Records. This company was the most influential
of the early r 'n' b labels—and still is.

38a Gillett, Charlie. The Sound of the City: The Rise of Rock 'n' Roll. New York: Dell Publishing, 1972. 343p. discog. bibliog.
Originally published in 1970, this "second" edition contains a general updating and revised discography. Of all the rock books, this is the most important and scholarly. Gillett knows what he is talking about, a trait often found among British writers. United Artists in England released an album to accompany the book, covering New Orleans from 1951 to 1962.

39 Glover, Tony. Blues Mouth Harp. New York: Oak, 1965. 72p. illus. paper only.
History and types of harmonicas, plus material on influences through illustrative examples.

40 Godrich, John, and Robert M. W. Dixon. Blues and Gospel Records, 1902-1942. Rev. ed. London: Storyville Publications, 1969. 912p.
A listing of all recordings of the period, with an appendix on microgroove reissues and small studies of rare labels. Alphabetical by performer. Updated by corrections and addenda in Storyville.

41 Groia, Philip. They All Sang on the Corner. Setauket, N.Y.: Edmond Pub. Co., 1973. 147p. illus. discog.
A pioneering work that details the rhythm 'n' blues vocal groups of New York City in the 1950s.

42 Groom, Bob. The Blues Revival. London: Studio Vista, 1971. 112p. illus. bibliog.
A summary of renewed interest in blues music by the editor of Blues World (now suspended).

43 Guralnick, Peter. Feel Like Goin' Home; Portraits in Blues and Rock 'n' Roll. New York: Outerbridge and Dienstfrey, 1971. 224p. illus. bibliog. discog.
Interviews with and perceptive comments on both black and white bluesmen.

44 Haralambos, Michael. Right On: From Blues to Soul in Black America. New York: 1975. 180p.
A clear description of the roots of soul as it passes through r 'n' b and gospel.

45 Heilbut, Tony. The Gospel Sound; Good News and Bad Times. New York: Simon and Schuster, 1971. 352p.
This is a series of profiles of the major leaders in gospel music. Columbia Records supplemented it by producing two two-disc sets (see text). Emphasis is on the 1945-1960 period.

46 Herdeg, Walter, ed. Graphics/Record Covers. New York: Hastings House, 1974. 192p. illus.
History and illustrations of record jacket designs.

47 Hoare, Ian, ed. The Soul Book. London: Methuen, 1975. 206p. illus. discog. paper only.
Traces the development of gospel, r 'n' b, Motown, Memphis, and New Orleans style, plus blue-eyed soul and modern funk.

48 Hoover, Cynthia. Music Machines—American Style; A Catalog of an Exhibition. Washington, D.C.: Smithsonian Institution Press; distr. by Govt. Print. Off., 1971. 139p. illus. bibliog.
The exhibition portrayed the development of music machines from cylinders and player pianos to Moog synthesizers, and the effect of technology on performers and audiences.

49 Horn, David. The Literature of American Music in Books and Folk Music Collections: A Fully Annotated Bibliography. Metuchen, N.J.: Scarecrow, 1977. 556p.
A detailed listing of 1,696 books considered essential for a library on all aspects of American music: folk, country, blues, rock, musical stage, soul, jazz, etc. Strong annotations.

50 Howard, John Tasker, and George Kent Bellows. A Short History of Music in America. New York: Crowell, 1967. 496p. illus. bibliog. notes.
A brief history that surveys folk, classical, spirituals, recorded music, and musical comedy.

51 Hughes, Langston, and Milton Meltzer. Black Magic; A Pictorial History of the Negro in American Entertainment. Englewood Cliffs, N.J.: Prentice-Hall, 1967. 375p.

51a Jepsen, Jorgen Grunnet. Jazz Records, 1942-1962. v.5-6, M-R. Copenhagen, Nordisk Tidsskrift Forlag. 1963; v.7-8, S-Z, Holte, Denmark, Knudsen, 1964-1965.

Jepsen, Jorgen Grunnet. Jazz Records, 1942-1965. v.1-3, A-El. Holte, Denmark, Knudsen, 1968.

Jepsen, Jorgen Grunnet. Jazz Records, 1942-1967. v.4b, Goo-Iwr. Copenhagen, Knudsen, 1969.

Jepsen, Jorgen Grunnet. Jazz Records, 1942-1968. v.4c, J-Ki. Copenhagen, Knudsen, 1970.

Jepsen, Jorgen Grunnet. Jazz Records, 1942-1969. v.4d, Kl-L. Copenhagen, Knudsen, 1970.
An indispensable series of discographies arranged alphabetically by artist. It continues Rust's 1897-1942 effort. It includes bluesmen, but no r 'n' b, nor some contemporary urban blues. Updated irregularly by reader contributions to Jazz Journal.

52 Jones, LeRoi. Blues People. New York, William Morrow, 1963. 244p.
The Negro experience in white America and the music that developed from it. Concentrates mostly on African origins, slave developments, and exploitation of the early jazz and bluesmen.

53 Keil, Charles. Urban Blues. Chicago: Univ. of Chicago Pr., 1966. 231p. illus. bibliog. discog.
Probably the most scholarly and authoritative work on urban blues. Gives a framework for understanding regional styles and influences.

54 Leadbitter, Mike. Crowley, Louisiana Blues. Bexhill-on-Sea, Sussex, Eng.: Blues Unlimited, 1968. 32p. illus.
The story of J. D. Miller and his blues artists, with a guide to their music.

55 Leadbitter, Mike. Delta Country Blues. Bexhill-on-Sea, Sussex, Eng.: Blues Unlimited, 1968. 48p. illus.
A series of articles on the changes in country blues and the evolution of jump singers from Memphis to Mississippi.

56 Leadbitter, Mike, ed. Nothing but the Blues. London: Hanover Books, 1971. 261p. illus.
Reprinted articles from Blues Unlimited. In Britain, CBS released an accompanying set of two long playing records.

57 Leadbitter, Mike, and Eddie Shuler. From the Bayou. Bexhill-on-Sea, Sussex, Eng.: Blues Unlimited, 1969. 64p. illus. discog.
The story of Goldband Records.

58 Leadbitter, Mike, and Neil Slaven. Blues Records, 1943-1966. New York: Oak, 1968. 381p.
Continues Godrich and Dixon's (#40) listings past 1942, but gospel music was eliminated because of its proliferation. Various addenda. Alphabetical arrangement by performer. Updated by reader corrections in Blues Unlimited.

59 Lee, George W. Beale Street; Where the Blues Began. Washington, D.C.: McGrath Publishing Co., 1969. 298p. illus.
Reprint of the classic 1934 edition.

60 Leiser, Willie. I'm a Road Runner Baby. Bexhill-on-Sea, Sussex, Eng.: Blues Unlimited, 1969. 40p. illus.
A Swiss blues fan reports on his 1968-1969 trip to the United States, in search of the real blues.

61 Lovell, John. Black Song; The Forge and the Flame: The Story of How the Afro-American Spiritual Was Hammered Out. New York: Macmillan, 1972. 588p. illus. bibliog.

62 Lydon, Michael. Boogie Lightnin'. New York, Dial, 1974. 229p. illus.
These reprints from his magazine articles stress the contribution of black music through rhythm 'n' blues and the blues to American culture. There are histories and profiles of John Lee Hooker, Bo Diddley, The Chiffons, Aretha Franklin, Ray Charles, and so forth, as well as a section on the development and use of the electric guitar.

62a Lydon, Michael. Rock Folk; Portraits from the Rock 'n' Roll Pantheon. New York, Dial, 1971. 200p.
Interviews, mostly from the New York Times magazine, with Janis Joplin, B. B. King, Chuck Berry, the Grateful Dead, the Rolling Stones, and others.

63 McCutcheon, Lynn Ellis. Rhythm and Blues; An Experience and Adventure in Its Origin and Development. Arlington, Virginia: Beatty, 1971. 306p. discog.
One of the best books written about rhythm and blues and soul music. Mr. McCutcheon has perhaps the finest collection of discs on this genre in North America.

64 Mahoney, Dan. The Columbia 13/1400 D Series. Stanhope, N.J.: Walter C. Allen, 1961. 80p.
A history and description of Columbia's "race records" with complete discographical information. Arranged in numerical order.

65   Mellers, Wilfrid. Music in a New Found Land. London: Barrie and Rockliff, 1964.
Here is wide coverage of the American musical tradition, relating classics to blues to jazz to pop.

66   Melly, George. Revolt into Style; The Pop Arts in Britain. London: Allen Lane, The Penguin Press, 1970. 245p.
Largely based on his periodical articles, this is an analytic history of popular culture in Britain in the 1960s. Its scope is wider than music, and includes television, films, stage, the press, and writings.

67   Merriam, Alan P. African Music on LP; An Annotated Discography. Evanston, Ill.: Northwestern University Press, 1970. 200p.

68   Millar, Bill. The Drifters; The Rise and Fall of the Black Vocal Group. New York: Macmillan, 1972. 180p. illus.
Coverage is extended to many other black vocal groups of the 1950s.

69   Mitchell, George. Blow My Blues Away. Baton Rouge: Louisiana State University Pr., 1971. 208p. illus.
These are contemporary portraits of then-living Mississippi Delta musicians. There is a two-record set available from Arhoolie that complements this book.

70   Morse, David. Motown and the Arrival of Black Music. New York: Macmillan, 1972. 144p. illus.
Examines the impact of the softer, urban sounds of black music.

71   The Music Yearbook: A Survey and Directory with Statistics and Reference Articles. 1972– . New York, St. Martin's Press, 1973– . 750p. average length.
This annual is the most up-to-date source of information on British music and musicians. Survey articles cover all aspects of classical and popular music, with lists of books and periodicals, addresses of relevant record companies, associations, halls, museums, etc. The American equivalent is the The Musician's Guide, from Music Information Service.

72   The Musician's Guide. 1954– . New York, Music Information Service, 1954– . (available every four years. Last edition: 1972).
The basic directory of music information for the United States. Sections include data on record collections, various recording awards such as the "Grammies," addresses of groups, books to read, and so forth. The British equivalent is The Music Yearbook.

73   National Portrait Gallery, Washington, D.C. "A Glimmer of Their Own Beauty; Black Sounds of the Twenties." Washington, D.C.: Govt. Print. Off., 1971. 32p., chiefly illus. bibliog.
A catalog of an exhibition of pictures of Negro musicians.

73a   Nite, Norm N. Rock On; The Illustrated Encyclopedia of Rock 'n' Roll for the Solid Gold Years. New York, Thomas Y. Crowell, 1974. 676p.
Includes all relevant pop material from the fifties.

74   New York Library Association. Children's and Young Adult Services Section. Records and Cassettes for Young Adults; A Selected List. New York, 1972. 52p. paper only. discog.
Categories include: rock, soul, blues, jazz, country and western, and various non-musical records and cassettes. Useful for the "now" sounds of 1972.

75 Oakley, Giles. The Devil's Music; A History of the Blues. London: British
   Broadcasting Corporation, 1976. 287p. illus. bibliog. discog. lyrics.
   "This book gives a background to the rise and development of the blues
both in relation to other forms of black music and in the context of American
social history as experienced by Black Americans"—cover blurb. Excellent
photographs, based on the television program in England.

76 Oliver, Paul. Aspects of the Blues Tradition. New York: Oak, 1970. 294p.
   illus. bibliog. discog.
   Oliver shows the relationship between blues and gospel music, and also
investigates gambling, protest songs, and sexual themes in the blues. In Britain,
where it was published under the title "Screening the Blues," CBS released an
accompanying record.

77 Oliver, Paul. Conversations with the Blues. New York: Horizon Pr., 1966.
   217p.
   Verbatim extracts from conversation the author has had with 68 singers
in 1960.

78 Oliver, Paul. Meaning of the Blues. New York: Collier-Macmillan, 1962.
   383p. paper only.
   Originally published in England as "Blues Fell This Morning," this well-
documented work (350 blues citations) shows the life of the rural Negro—work,
gambling, travel, love, crime, etc.

79 Oliver, Paul. Savannah Syncopators; African Retentions in the Blues. New
   York: Stein and Day, 1970. 172p. illus. bibliog. discog.
   A valid attempt to relate American blues to West African inland music.
In Britain, CBS released an accompanying record.

80 Oliver, Paul. Story of the Blues. Philadelphia: Chilton, 1969. illus. bibliog.
   discog.
   This oversized book presents a full survey with several hundred photographs.
In the United States, Columbia released a two-disc accompanying set of records;
in Britain, CBS released four discs.

81 Olsson, Bengt. Memphis Blues. New York: Stein and Day, 1970. 112p.
   illus. bibliog. discog.
   A general survey of the influence and structure of the music at the head
of the Delta area.

82 Oster, Harry. Living Country Blues. Detroit: Folklore Associates; distr.
   Gale, 1969. 464p. illus. bibliog. discog.
   Notes on poetry (texts to songs given) and life in the blues, with a good
section on Robert Pete Williams.

83 Passman, Arnold. The Dee Jays. New York: Macmillan, 1971. 320p.
   He traces the evolution of the "disc jockey" from 1909 to the underground
FM stations in San Francisco, with good detail on how songs are selected for
airplay.

84 Peel, David. The Peetie Wheatstraw Stomps. Burlington, Ontario, Canada:
   Belltower Books, 1972. 36p.
   A textual analysis of Wheatstraw's songs, their importance and influence.

85 Pleasants, Henry. The Great American Popular Singers. New York: Simon and Schuster, 1974. 384p. illus.

The author examines the vocal tradition in popular music, the phenomenon of imitation breeding imitation, the meaning of "art" as applied to popular music, and various evaluations of 22 innovators in the fields of jazz, musical stage, blues, gospel, country, soul, and so forth.

86 Popular Music Periodicals Index, 1973– . Comp. by Dean Tudor and Andrew Armitage. Metuchen, N.J.: Scarecrow Pr., 1974– .

An annual author-subject index to 60 or so periodicals utilizing a special thesaurus involving musical genres.

86a Propes, Steve. Those Oldies but Goodies; A Guide to 50's Record Collecting. New York, Macmillan, 1973. 192p. bibliog. discog.

A guide to current prices, sources and reading material devoted to collecting 78 and 45 RPM phonodiscs from the 1950-1960 period.

87 Ramsey, Frederic Jr. Been Here and Gone. New Brunswick, N.J.: Rutgers Univ. Pr., 1960. 177p. illus.

Text and photographs record the life and musical activity of black Americans in the Deep South. Their remembrances help to reveal the beginnings and development of Afro-American music in the United States.

88 Recording Industry Association of America. The White House Record Library. Washington, D.C.: White House Historical Association, 1973. 105p.

A catalog of 2,000 records presented to the White House in March, 1973. Categories include: popular, classical, jazz, folk, country, gospel, and spoken word.

89 Redd, Lawrence N. Rock is Rhythm and Blues; The Impact of Mass Media. East Lansing: Michigan State Univ. Pr., 1974. 167p. illus.

90 Roberts, John Storm. Black Music of Two Worlds. New York: Praeger, 1972. 296p. illus. bibliog. discog.

A detailed survey of black music in Africa and America.

91 Rolling Stone Magazine. The Rolling Stone Record Review. New York: Pocket Books, 1961. 556p. paper only.

Rolling Stone Magazine. The Rolling Stone Record Review. v.2. New York: Pocket Books, 1974. 599p. paper only.

92 Rooney, James. Bossmen; Bill Monroe and Muddy Waters. New York: Dial, 1971. 159p. illus. discog.

Espouses the belief that "bluegrass" and "urban blues" came from these two men and the various musicians they had employed over the past thirty years.

93 Rose, Al. Storyville, New Orleans. University of Alabama Press, 1974. 225p.

94 Rowe, Mike. Chicago Breakdown. New York: Drake, 1974. 228p. bibliog.

A very comprehensive study of the Chicago blues, with specific interest in the late 1940s and early 1950s. Many of the 150 illustrations have never been published before.

95   Rublowsky, John. Popular Music. New York: Basic Books, 1967. 164p.
      Emphasis is on country and western, rock and current popular materials.

96   Russell, Tony. Blacks, Whites and Blues. New York: Stein and Day, 1970.
      112p. illus. bibliog. discog.
      Examines the relationships of black blues musicians and white musicians,
emphasizing their traditions and differences. In Britain, CBS released an accompanying record.

97   Rust, Brian. The Complete Entertainment Discography: From the Mid-
      1890s to 1942. With Allen G. Debus. New Rochelle, N.Y.: Arlington
      House, 1973. 677p.
      This listing, in performer order by alphabetical arrangement, is similar to
other genre "discographies," except that its criteria for inclusion are based on
exceptions: anybody that does not fit into existing or contemplated listings.
Thus, most popular singers and all of vaudeville are here.

98   Sandberg, Larry, and Dick Weissman. The Folk Music Sourcebook. New
      York: Knopf, 1976. 260p. illus. bibliog. discog.
      A guide to North American folk music (blues, old time music, bluegrass,
ragtime, jazz, Canadian, ethnic): books, instruments, recordings, films, instructional materials, societies, etc. Essentially updates Lawless's Folksingers and
Folksongs in America (New York: Meredith, 1965).

99   Schicke, C. A. Revolution in Sound: A Biography of the Recording
      Industry. Boston: Little, Brown, 1974. 238p.
      A history of the recording industry, covering all forms of influences and
manipulation.

99a   Shaw, Arnold. The Street that Never Slept; New York's Fabled 52nd Street.
      New York: Coward, 1971. 378p. illus. discog.
      A remarkable book that concentrates on a very small geographic area,
and notes its decline.

100   Shaw, Arnold. The World of Soul: Black America's Contribution to the
      Pop Music Scene. New York: Cowles, 1970. 306p. discog.
      Building on the roots of the country blues and progressing through gospel
and black church music, Shaw comments on various personalities (e.g., Sister
Rosetta Tharpe, James Brown, Otis Redding, etc.). The last chapter comments
on white imitations.

101   Stambler, Irwin. Encyclopedia of Pop, Rock, and Soul. New York: St.
      Martin's Pr., 1975. 609p. illus.

101a Stearns, Marshall. The Story of Jazz. New York, New American Library,
      1958. 272p. illus. bibliog.
      On a more scholarly basis, this book is similar to Ulanov and Feather. The
above edition is different from the Oxford University Press publication by virtue
of an expanded bibliography and a syllabus of 15 lectures on the history of jazz.

102   Stewart-Baxter, Derrick. Ma Rainey and the Classic Blues Singers. New
      York: Stein and Day, 1970. 112p. illus. bibliog. discog.
      Includes Bessie Smith, Victoria Spivey, and other blues singers (female)
from the 1920s. In Britain, CBS released an accompanying record.

103 Strachwitz, Chris, ed. American Folk Music Occasional, No. 1 (from Arhoolie Records, 1964); No. 2 (from Oak Publications, 1970).
An irregular issue that lays stress on Strachwitz's interests: blues, Cajun music, Chicano music, Austrian folk music.

104 Taubman, Howard, editor. The New York Times Guide to Listening Pleasure. New York: Macmillan, 1968. 328p. discog.
This is mainly a how-to guide for the novice record collector. A good 2/3 of the book deals with classical music; the balance concentrates on folk, jazz, Latin America, and the musical theater.

105 Tudor, Dean, and Andrew Armitage. "Best of the Year." LJ/SLJ Previews, April and May issues, 1974-1976.
A round-up of the year's best records, as reflected by the reviewing media.

106 U.S. Library of Congress. Checklist of Recorded Songs in the English Language in the Archive of American Folk Song to July, 1940. Washington, D.C.: Govt. Print. Off., 1942. 3v.
This alphabetical list has a geographic index, and it is also available in one volume from Arno Press.

107 Vreede, Max E. Paramount 1200-/13000 Series. London: Storyville Publications, 1971. 260p. illus.
Numerical listing of the Paramount "race records" series of 1922/1933, with artists and title indexes. Illustrated with reproductions of labels.

108 Warren, Fred. The Music of Africa. Englewood Cliffs, N.J.: Prentice-Hall, 1970. 87p. illus. bibliog. discog.

109 Wells, Dicky. The Night People. Boston: Crescendo, 1971. 118p.
These are personal reminiscences of Harlem, Count Basie, Ray Charles, and so forth, particularly worthwhile because of the Wellsian use and misuse of words.

110 Whitburn, Joel. Top LP Records, 1945-1972. Menomenee Falls, WI: Record Research, 1974.
Artist arrangement and broad subject categories based on the Billboard charts of jazz, rock, pop, r 'n' b, etc.

111 Whitburn, Joel. Top R 'n' B Records, 1949-1971. Menomenee Falls, WI: Record Research, 1973.
Alphabetically arranged by artist, with all tunes having appeared on the Billboard charts.

112 Whitcomb, Ian. After the Ball. London: Allen Lane, The Penguin Press, 1972. 312p.
The author, a singer, explores the phenomenon of popular music, from "After the Ball" (written in 1892) through Tin Pan Alley to the Beatles. Concentration is mostly on British pop.

113 Zur Heide, Karl Gert. Deep South Piano; The Story of Little Brother Montgomery. London: Studio Vista, 1970. 67p. illus. discog.

PERIODICAL CITATIONS

For many of the same reasons as in the Book Citations section, periodical titles here are listed alphabetically, sequentially numbered, and keyed to references in the section discussing musical genres. Periodicals come and go in the popular music world, depending on interests, finances, and subscriptions sold, and much valuable information is thereby lost. The following 21 periodicals show some stability and should at least be around when this book is two years old; consequently, prices are not noted, nor are street addresses given for foreign publications that tend to move around. The annotations give a physical description of their contents, but please refer to the music genre for more complete details on specific articles or discussions. In addition to periodicals listed, about 40 more are printed in the English language (all are indexed in *Popular Music Periodicals Index*, 1973; Scarecrow Press), about 75 more in non-English languages, and countless scores of fanzine and very specialized publications.

1   Black Music. 1974— . Monthly. London, England.
A glossy but expertly edited magazine concerned with blues, rhythm 'n' blues, soul, gospel, reggae, jazz, African music—all musical fields of interest to blacks. Good reviews of records and various current awareness services.

2   Blues and Soul. 1971— . Weekly. London, England.
Much the same as Black Music, with concentration on blues, jazz, soul, and reggae music.

3   Blues Unlimited. 1963— . Bimonthly. London, England.
The leading blues magazine, oldest in the world, with exceptional photographs and good record reviews. Many interviews and obscure personages. Music also covers gospel and r 'n' b.

4   Cadence. 1976— . Monthly. Rt. 1, Box 345, Redwood, N.Y. 13679.
An excellent source for interviews with both jazz and blues performers, this also has superb record reviews and notations. Tries to cover every single jazz album released in the world.

5   Circus. 1966— . Semi-monthly. 866 United Nations Plaza, New York, N.Y. 10017.
A rock fan magazine, with lots of color pictures and interviews/biographies; intended for the younger audience.

6   Coda. 1958— . 6x/yr. Toronto, Canada.
International coverage of largely modern jazz. In-depth articles and interviews, good design, and superb (and critical) jazz and blues record reviews.

7   Contemporary Keyboard. 1975— . Bimonthly. P.O. Box 907, Saratoga, Calif. 95070.
Emphasizes all aspects of keyboards (piano, organ, electronic music synthesizers, etc.) with reviews, articles on personalities in both popular and classical modes of music, plus performance tips and instructions.

8   Creem. 1969– . Monthly. Birmingham, Michigan.
       Calls itself "America's only rock 'n' roll magazine." Articles deal with
music exclusively. Good reviews.

9   Downbeat. 1934– . Biweekly. 222 W. Adams St., Chicago, Ill. 60606.
       The oldest continuing jazz magazine, now spreading its coverage to progres-
sive rock music and the new jazz personalities. Good record reviews, transcriptions
of improvised jazz solos.

10   Guitar Player. 1967– . Monthly. 348 North Santa Cruz, Los Gatos, Calif.
       95030.
       Emphasizes all aspects of guitars (bass, pedal, acoustic, electric, etc.) with
reviews, articles on personalities in both popular and classical modes of music,
plus performance instructional guidance.

11   High Fidelity. 1951– . Monthly. P. O. Box 14156, Cincinnati, Ohio 45214.
       A general magazine with slight coverage of popular music.

12   Jazz Journal International. 1948– . Monthly. London, England.
       Detailed articles about mainstream jazz and some few modern performers
as well. Good record reviews with added discographic descriptions.

13   Journal of American Folklore. 1888– . Quarterly. University of Texas Press,
       Box 7819, University Station, Austin, Texas 78712.
       Scholarly articles and lengthy, comparative record and book reviews. Not
limited to music.

14   Living Blues. 1970– . Bimonthly. P.O. Box 11303, Chicago, Ill. 60611.
       Good coverage of modern blues and living bluesmen, especially in Chicago.
In-depth interviews.

15   Melody Maker. 1931– . Weekly. London, England.
       The best of the five British weeklies devoted to popular music. News, views,
and articles on rock, jazz, folk, blues, soul, reggae, country, etc. Unusually good
record reviews.

16   Micrography. 1968– . Quarterly. Alphen aan den Rijn, Holland.
       A new format in 1976 led to articles and discographic details concerning
the issuance of 78 rpms and air shots in the elpee format. A good service for tracking
down rare albums and duplications of tracks on reissued albums.

17   Popular Music and Society. 1971– . Quarterly. 318 South Grove Street,
       Bowling Green, Ohio 43402.
       An interdisciplinary journal "concerned with music in the broadest sense
of the term." Scholarly articles.

18   Rolling Stone. 1968– . Biweekly. 625 Third Street, San Francisco, Calif.
       94107.
       America's strongest youth culture magazine, describing music as a way of
life. Very opinionated, but only about 1/3 of it is now solely music.

19   Sing Out! 1950– . Bimonthly. 595 Broadway, New York, New York 10012.
       News and articles on folk, blues and bluegrass, plus some ethnic articles.
Very influential in the first 15 years of its existence, with songs, some commentaries,
transcriptions, etc.

20 Stereo Review. 1958– . Monthly. P. O. Box 2771, Boulder, Colo. 80302.
    A general magazine favoring audio equipment, classical music, and popular
music about equally.

21 Storyville. 1965– . Bimonthly. Chigwell, Essex, England.
    Specializes in traditional and New Orleans jazz, with some blues and subsequent
re-interpretations or revivals. Articles are devoted to exploring minor performers or
minor facts about famous jazzmen. Good research, copious discographies.

DIRECTORY OF LABELS AND STARRED RECORDS

This directory presents, in alphabetical order, the names and addresses of all the American manufacturers of long-playing records cited in this set of books. Similarly, the starred records from all four volumes are listed here, not simply those for the present volume. British, Japanese, Swedish, French, Danish, etc., records can be obtained from specialist stores or importers. Other information here includes some indication of the types of popular music that each firm is engaged in and a listing in label numerical order of all the starred (special importance) records as indicated in the text, along with the entry number for quick reference. For this reason, starred foreign discs are also included in this directory/listing. This directory notes the latest **issuance** of a disc. Some albums may have been reissued from other labels, and they will be found under the label of the latest release. **In all cases, please refer to the main text.** Cross-references are made here where-appropriate, especially for "family" names within a label's corporate ownership. To expedite filing and ease of retrieval, this listing of records follows the **numerical order of each label's issues**, ignoring the alphabetical initialisms.

A & M, 1416 North LaBrea Avenue, Hollywood, CA 90028
specialty: general rock and pop

SP 4245—Herb Alpert. Greatest Hits. P3.1
SP 4251—Jimmy Cliff. Wonderful World, Beautiful People. B5.7a
SP 4257—Fairport Convention. Liege and Lief. F2.49
SP 4519—Cat Stevens. Greatest Hits. F10.90

ABC, 8255 Beverly Blvd., Los Angeles, CA 90048
specialty: general

S 371—Paul Anka. R2.15
490X—Ray Charles. A Man and His Soul. two discs. B2.40
654—Impressions. Best. B4.9
724—B. B. King. Live at the Regal. B1.296
780—Curtis Mayfield. His Early Years with the Impressions. two discs. B4.11
781/2—Ray Charles. Modern Sounds in Country and Western Music.
2 discs. B4.26
ABCX 1955-1963—Rock 'n' Soul; The History of the Pre-Beatle Decade of Rock, 1953-1963. 9 discs. R2.12

Ace of Clubs (English issue)
specialty: older popular music, jazz

ACL 1153—Spike Hughes and His All-American Orchestra. J4.47
ACL 1158—Django Reinhardt and Stephane Grappelli. J6.113

Ace of Hearts (English issue). recently deleted
specialty: MCA reissues (all forms of popular music)

AH 21—Andrews Sisters. P2.145
AH 28—Jack Teagarden. Big T's Jazz. J3.91

Ace of Hearts (cont'd)
 AH 58—Carter Family. A Collection of Favourites. F5.108
 AH 112—Carter Family. More Favourites. F5.111
 AH 119—Jimmy Rushing. Blues I Love to Sing. B1.426
 AH 135—Uncle Dave Macon. F5.31
 AH 168—Jack Teagarden. "J.T." J3.92

Adelphi, P. O. Box 288, Silver Spring, MD 20907
 specialty: blues, folk

Advent, P. O. Box 635, Manhattan Beach, CA 90266
 specialty: blues music
 2803—Johnny Shines. B1.359

Ahura Mazda (c/o Southern Record Sales)
 specialty: blues
 AMS 2002—Robert Pete Williams. B1.130

All Platinum, 96 West Street, Englewood, NJ 07631
 specialty: blues and soul, mainly from the Chess catalog which it
  purchased; see also CHESS records
 2ACMB 201—Howlin' Wolf. A.K.A. Chester Burnett. two discs. B1.284
 2ACMB 202—Little Walter. Boss Blues Harmonica. two discs. B1.297
 2ACMB 203—Muddy Waters. A.K.A. McKinley Morganfield. two discs.
  B1.303

Alligator, P.O. Box 11741, Fort Dearborn Station, Chicago, IL 60611
 specialty: blues
 AL 4706—Koko Taylor. I Got What It Takes. B1.407

Angel, 1750 N. Vine Street, Hollywood, CA 90028
 specialty: classical and classical interpretations of popular music
 S 36060—New England Conservatory Ragtime Ensemble. Scott Joplin:
  The Red Back Book. J2.28

Antilles, 7720 Sunset Blvd., Los Angeles, CA 90046
 specialty: folk and pop
 AN 7017—Shirley Collins and the Albion Country Band. No Roses. F2.47

Apple, 1750 N. Vine Street, Hollywood, CA 90028
 specialty: rock
 SKBO 3403/4—The Beatles. 1962-1970. four discs. R4.3/4.

Argo (English issue)
 specialty: folk (British), classical, spoken word
 ZDA 66-75—Ewan MacColl and Peggy Seeger. The Long Harvest. ten discs.
  F2.23

Arhoolie, 10341 San Pablo Avenue, El Cerrito, CA 94530
    specialty: blues, old time music, ethnic music

    1001—Mance Lipscomb, Texas Sharecropper and Songster. B1.213
    1007—Mercy Dee Walton. B1.369
    1008—Alex Moore. B1.228
    1021—Fred McDowell. Delta Blues. B1.120
    1027—Fred McDowell. volume 2. B1.119
    1028—Big Mama Thornton. In Europe. B1.408
    1036—Juke Boy Bonner. I'm Going Back to the Country Where They Don't
      Burn the Buildings Down. B1.146
    1038—Clifton Chenier. Black Snake Blues. B1.324
    1066—Earl Hooker. His First and Last Recordings. B1.279
    2003—Lowell Fulson. B1.332
    2004—Joe Turner. Jumpin' the Blues. B1.431
    2007—Lightnin' Hopkins. Early Recordings, v.1. B1.182
    2010—Lightnin' Hopkins. Early Recordings, v.2. B1.182
    2011—Robert Pete Williams. Angola Prisoner's Blues. B1.131
    2012—Prison Worksongs. B1.55
    2015—Robert Pete Williams. Those Prison Blues. B1.134
    5011—Snuffy Jenkins. Carolina Bluegrass. F6.82

Arista, 6 West 57th St., New York, NY 10019
    specialty: rock, jazz, pop

    B 6081—The Monkees. Re-Focus R3.20

Asch *See* Folkways

Asylum, 962 N. LaCienega, Los Angeles, CA 90069

    SD 5068—Eagles. Desperado. R7.12
    7E-1017—Jackson Browne. Late for the Sky. F10.3

Atco, 75 Rockefeller Plaza, New York, NY 10019
    specialty: blues, rock, soul, rhythm 'n' blues

    SD 33-226—Buffalo Springfield. Again. R7.6
    SD33-259—Jerry Jeff Walker. Mr. Bojangles. F10.92
    SD33-266—King Curtis. Best. B4.44
    SD33-291—Cream. Best. R8.1
    SD33-292—Bee Gees. Best, v.1. R4.22
    SD33-371—The Coasters. Their Greatest Recordings: The Early Years. B2.27
    SD33-372—LaVern Baker. Her Greatest Recordings. B2.71
    SD33-373—Chuck Willis. His Greatest Recordings. B2.70
    SD33-374—The Clovers. Their Greatest Recordings. B2.26
    SD33-375—The Drifters. Their Greatest Recordings: The Early Years. B2.31
    SD33-376—Joe Turner. His Greatest Recordings. B1.430
    2SA-301—Otis Redding. Best. two discs. B4.28
    SD2-501—Wilson Pickett. Best. two discs. B4.27
    SD2-803—Eric Clapton. History. two discs. R5.16

Atlantic, 75 Rockefeller Plaza, New York, NY 10019
   specialty: jazz, blues, rock, soul, rhythm 'n' blues
      1224—Lennie Tristano. Line Up. J5.87
      1234—Joe Turner. The Boss of the Blues. B1.428
      1237—Charles Mingus. Pithecanthropus Erectus. J5.128
      1238—Jimmy Giuffre. Clarinet. J5.90
      1305—Charles Mingus. Blues and Roots. J5.125
      1317—Ornette Coleman. The Shape of Jazz to Come. J5.112
      1327—Ornette Coleman. Change of the Century. J5.108
      1353—Ornette Coleman. This Is Our Music. J5.113
      1357—Lennie Tristano. New. J5.88
      1364—Ornette Coleman. Free Jazz. J5.109
      1378—Ornette Coleman. Ornette. J5.110
      SD 1429—Modern Jazz Quartet and Laurindo Almeida. Collaboration. P3.15
      SD 1588—Ornette Coleman. Twins. J5.150
      S 1594—Roberta Flack. Quiet Fire. B4.64
      SD 1598—Gary Burton. Alone at Last. J5.143
      SD 1613—Turk Murphy. The Many Faces of Ragtime. J2.26
      SD 1614—Billie Holiday. Strange Fruit. J6.123
      SD 1639—Art Ensemble of Chicago. J5.136
      SD 1652—Modern Jazz Quartet. Blues on Bach. P3.14
      SD 7200—Crosby, Stills, Nash and Young. Déjà Vu. R7.10
      SD 7213—Aretha Franklin. Young, Gifted and Black. B4.67
      SD 7224—Blind Willie McTell. Atlanta Twelve String. B1.125
      SD 7225—Professor Longhair. New Orleans Piano. B2.67
      SD 7262—Willie Nelson. Shotgun Willie. F8.119
      SD 7271—Roberta Flack. Killing Me Softly. B4.63
      SD 7291—Willie Nelson. Phases and Stages. F8.118
      SD 8004—Ruth Brown. Rock & Roll. B2.73
      SD 8020—T-Bone Walker. T-Bone Blues. B1.315
      SD 8029—Ray Charles. What'd I Say. B2.41
      SD 8054—Ray Charles. Greatest. B2.39
      SD 8153—The Drifters. Golden Hits. B2.30
      SD 8161/4—History of Rhythm 'n' Blues, v.1-4. four discs. B2.13
      SD 8176—Aretha Franklin. Lady Soul. B4.66
      SD 8193/4—History of Rhythm 'n' Blues, v. 5-6. two discs. B4.3
      SD 8202—Booker T. and the MGs. Best. B4.8
      SD 8208/9—History of Rhythm 'n' Blues. v. 7-8. two discs. B4.3
      SD 8218—Sam and Dave. Best. B4.30
      SD 8236—Led Zeppelin. II. R8.8
      SD 8255—Champion Jack Dupree. Blues from the Gutter. B1.329
      SD 8289—Marion Williams. Standing Here Wondering Which Way to Go. B3.66
      SD 8296—John Prine. F10.82
      SD 18204—Aretha Franklin. 10 Years of Gold. B4.65
      SD2-305—Chick Corea. Inner Space. two discs. J6.128
      SD2-306/7—The Tenor Sax: The Commodore Years. four discs. J6.8
      SD2-316—Jazz Years; 25th Anniversary. two discs. J5.101

Atlantic (cont'd)
    SD2-700—Cream. Wheels of Fire. two discs. R8.3
    SD2-904—Carmen McRae. The Great American Songbook. two discs. P2.77
    SD2-906—Aretha Franklin. Amazing Grace. two discs. B3.39
    MM4-100—Mabel Mercer. A Tribute to Mabel Mercer on the Occasion of Her
        75th Birthday. four discs. P2.78

Atteiram, P.O. Box 418, 2871 Janquil Drive, Smyrna, GA 30080
    specialty: bluegrass

Audiofidelity, 221 W. 57th Street, New York, NY 10019
    specialty: folk, jazz

Basf, 221 W. 57th Street, New York, NY 10019
    specialty: jazz

Bandstand (c/o Southern Record Sales)
    specialty: big bands

    7106—Screwballs of Swingtime. P4.3

Barclay (France)
    specialty: general

    920067—Stuff Smith and Stephane Grappelli. Stuff and Steff. J4.148

Barnaby, 816 N. LaCienega Blvd., Los Angeles, CA 90069
    specialty: rock and roll

    BR 4000/1—Cadence Classics, v. 1-2. two discs. R2.3
    BR 6006—Everly Brothers. Greatest Hits. two discs. R2.18

Barnaby/Candid (recently deleted from CBS)
    specialty: jazz, blues

    Z 30246—Otis Spann. Is the Blues. B1.310
    Z 30247—Lightnin' Hopkins. In New York. B1.183
    Z 30562—Cecil Taylor. Air. J5.132
    KZ 31034—Charles Mingus. The Candid Recordings. J5.126
    KZ 31290—Otis Spann. Walking the Blues. B1.311

Bear Family (West Germany)
    specialty: old time music

    FV 12.502—Jules Allen. The Texas Cowboy. F7.19
    FV 15.507—Dock Walsh. F5.79

Bearsville, 3300 Warner Blvd., Burbank, CA 91505
    specialty: rock

Bell, 6 West 57th Street, New York, NY 10019
    specialty: general pop

    1106—The Fifth Dimension. Greatest Hits on Earth. P2.137

Biograph, 16 River Street, Chatham, NY 12037
    specialty: jazz, blues, popular

    BLP C3—Boswell Sisters. 1932-1935. P2.135
    BLP C4—Mississippi John Hurt. 1928: His First Recordings. B1.190
    BLP C7/8—Ted Lewis. 1926-1933, v. 1-2. two discs. P5.13
    BLP 1008Q—Scott Jopkin. Ragtime, v. 2. J2.10
    BLP 12003—Blind Blake. v.1. B1.145
    BLP 12005—Chicago Jazz, 1923-1929, v. 1. J3.63
    BLP 12022—Ethel Waters. Jazzin' Babies Blues, v. 1. B1.411
    BLP 12023—Blind Blake. v.2. B1.145
    BLP 12026—Ethel Waters. v.2. B1.411
    BLP 12029—Skip James, Early Recordings. B1.198
    BLP 12031—Blind Blake. v.3. B1.145
    BLP 12037—Blind Blake. v.4. B1.145
    BLP 12043—Chicago Jazz, 1923-1929, v.2. J3.63
    BLP 12050—Blind Blake. v.5. B1.145

Birchmount (Canada)
    specialty: country and popular

    BM 705—Hank Williams. In the Beginning. F8.41

Black Lion, 221 West 57th Street, New York, NY 10019
    specialty: jazz and blues

    BL 173—Barney Kessel and Stephane Grappelli. Limehouse Blues. J6.106

Black Lion (England)
    specialty: jazz and blues

    BLP 30147—Jimmy Witherspoon. Ain't Nobody's Business! B1.433

Blue Goose, 245 Waverly Place, New York, NY 10014
    specialty: blues, jazz

Blue Horizon (England) recently deleted
    specialty: blues

    7-63222—Otis Rush. This One's a Good 'Un. B1.357
    7-63223—Magic Sam. 1937-1969. B1.346

Blue Note, 6920 Sunset Blvd., Hollywood, CA 90028
    specialty: jazz and blues

    BST 81201/2—Sidney Bechet. Jazz Classics, v.1-2. two discs. J3.20
    BST 81503/4—Bud Powell. Amazing, v.1-2. two discs. J5.31
    BST 81505/6—J. J. Johnson. The Eminent, v.1-2. two discs. J5.64

Blue Note (cont'd)

    BST 81518—Horace Silver with the Jazz Messengers. J5.36

    BST 81521/2—Art Blakey. A Night at Birdland. two discs. J5.9

    BST 84003—Art Blakey. Moanin'. J5.8

    BST 84008—Horace Silver. Finger Poppin'. J5.35

    BST 84067—Jackie McLean. Bluesnik. J5.66

    BST 84077—Dexter Gordon. Doin' All Right. J5.56

    BST 84163—Eric Dolphy. Out to Lunch. J5.155

    BST 84194—Wayne Shorter. Speak No Evil. J5.161

    BST 84237—Cecil Taylor. Unit Structures. J5.135

    BST 84260—Cecil Taylor. Conquistador. J5.133

    BST 84346—Thad Jones—Mel Lewis Orchestra. Consummation. J4.171

    BNLA 158/160—Blue Note's Three Decades of Jazz, v.1-3. six discs. J1.6

    BNLA 401-H—Sonny Rollins. 2 discs. J5.76

    BNLA 456—H2—Lester Young. Aladdin Sessions. two discs. J4.124

    BNLA 507—H2—Fats Navarro. Prime Source. two discs. J5.26

    BNLA 533—H2—T-Bone Walker. Classics of Modern Blues. two discs. B1.313

    BNLA 579—H2—Thelonious Monk. Complete Genius. two discs. J5.24

Blues Classics, 10341 San Pablo Ave., El Cerrito, CA 94530

    specialty: blues, gospel

    BC 1—Memphis Minnie, v.1. B1.388

    BC 2—The Jug, Jook and Washboard Bands. B1.414

    BC 3—Sonny Boy Williamson, No. 1., v.1. B1.136

    BC 4—Peetie Wheatstraw. B1.253

    BC 5/7—Country Blues Classics, v.1-3. B1.14

    BC 9—Sonny Boy Williamson, No. 2. The Original. B1.318

    BC 11—Blind Boy Fuller. B1.168a

    BC 12—Detroit Blues: The Early 1950s. B1.58

    BC 13—Memphis Minnie, v.2. B1.388

    BC 14—Country Blues Classics, v.4. B1.14

    BC 16—Texas Blues: The Early 50s. B1.101

    BC 17/19—Negro Religious Music, v.1-3. three discs. B3.17

    BC 20—Sonny Boy Williamson, No. 1., v.2. B1.136

    BC 24—Sonny Boy Williamson, No. 1., v.3. B1.136

Blues on Blues (c/o Southern Records Sales) recently deleted

    specialty: blues

Bluesville (recently deleted)

    specialty: blues

    BV 1044—Lonnie Johnson and Victoria Spivey. Idle Hours. B1.208

Bluesway *See* ABC

Boogie Disease, Box 10925, St. Louis, MO 63135

    specialty: blues

Boogie Woogie (c/o Southern Records Sales)
  specialty: jazz and blues

  BW 1002—Meade Lux Lewis. J6.94

Brunswick (recently deleted); see also MCA
  specialty: jazz and soul

  BL 754185—Jackie Wilson. Greatest Hits. B4.32

Buddah, 810 Seventh Ave., New York, NY 10019
  specialty: pop, soul, gospel

  2009—Staple Singers. Best. B3.54
  BDS 5070—Edwin Hawkins Singers. Oh Happy Day. B3.40
  BDS 5665-2—Steve Goodman. Essential. two discs. F10.58

CBS, 51 West 52nd Street, New York, NY 10019
  specialty: general; formerly known as Columbia

  CL 997—Count Basie. One O'Clock Jump. J4.17
  CL 1098—The Sound of Jazz. J1.22
  CL 1228—Jo Stafford. Greatest Hits. P2.79
  CL 1230—Rosemary Clooney. Rosie's Greatest Hits. P2.96
  CL 1780—James P. Johnson. Father of the Stride Piano. J6.30
  CL 2604—Sophie Tucker. The Last of the Red Hot Mamas. P2.130.
  CL 2639—Chick Webb. Stompin' at the Savoy. J4.52
  CL 2830—Paul Whiteman. P5.19
  CS 1065—Bill Monroe. 16 All Time Greatest Hits. F6.41
  CS 1034—Roy Acuff. Greatest Hits. F8.17
  CS 8004—Mitch Miller. Sing Along with Mitch. P2.139
  CS 8158—Marty Robbins. Gunfighter Ballads and Trail Songs. F7.30
  PC 8163—Miles Davis. Kind of Blue. J5.151
  PC 8271—Miles Davis. Sketches of Spain. J5.85
  CS 8638—Mitch Miller. Mitch's Greatest Hits. P2.138
  CS 8639—Marty Robbins. Greatest Hits. R1.17
  CS 8807—Barbra Streisand. P2.126
  CS 8845—Lester Flatt and Earl Scruggs. Carnegie Hall. F6.28
  KCS 8905—Bob Dylan. The Times They Are A-Changin'. F10.19
  PC 9106—Miles Davis. My Funny Valentine. J5.153
  KCS 9128—Bob Dylan. Bringing It Back Home. F10.14
  PC 9428—Miles Davis. Milestones. J5.152
  KCS 9463—Bob Dylan. Greatest Hits, v.1. F10.16
  CS 9468—18 King Size Country Hits. F8.11
  CS 9478—Johnny Cash. Greatest Hits, v.1. F8.19
  G 31224—Count Basie. Super Chief. two discs. J4.18
  KG 31345—Johnny Mathis. All Time Greatest Hits. two discs. P2.13
  PC 31350—Simon and Garfunkel. Greatest Hits. F10.46
  KC 31352—Weather Report. I Sing the Body Electric. J6.138
  KG 31361—Marty Robbins. All Time Greatest Hits. two discs. F8.78
  KG 31364—Ray Price. All Time Greatest Hits. two discs. F8.76

CBS (cont'd)

KG 31379—Mahalia Jackson. Great. two discs. B3.42

KG 31547—Benny Goodman. All Time Hits. two discs. J4.58

KG 31564—Eddie Condon's World of Jazz. two discs. J3.66

KG 31571—Ethel Waters. Greatest Years. two discs. P2.86

KG 31588—Percy Faith. All Time Greatest Hits. two discs. P5.79

KG 31595—The Gospel Sound, v.2. two discs. B3.9

G 31617—Teddy Wilson All Stars. two discs. J4.122

KC 31758—Earl Scruggs. Live at Kansas State. F6.124

KG 32064—Duke Ellington. Presents Ivie Anderson. two discs. P5.10

KG 32151—Precious Lord; Gospel Songs of Thomas A. Dorsey. two discs. B3.19

KC 32284—Clifford Brown. The Beginning and the End. J5.38

KG 32338—Luis Russell. His Louisiana Swing Orchestra. two discs. J4.85

KG 32355—A Jazz Piano Anthology. two discs. J6.12

KG 32416—Bob Wills. Anthology. two discs. F7.48

G 32593—Cab Calloway. Hi De Ho Man. two discs. P5.23

KG 32663—Gene Krupa. His Orchestra and Anita O'Day. two discs. P5.36

KC 32708—The Original Boogie Woogie Piano Giants. J6.91

KG 32822—Benny Goodman and Helen Forrest. two discs. P5.11

KG 32945—The World of Swing. two discs. J4.11

CG 33639—Johnny Cash. At Folsom Prison and San Quentin. two discs. F8.18

C2-33682—Bob Dylan. Basement Tapes. two discs. F10.12

C 33882—Lefty Frizzell. Remembering the Greatest Hits. F8.57

CS 9533—Leonard Cohen. Songs. F10.6

CS 9576—The Byrds. Greatest Hits. R7.7

KCS 9604—Bob Dylan. John Wesley Harding. F10.18

PC 9633—Miles Davis. Miles Ahead. J5.83

CS 9655—Art Tatum. Piano Starts Here. J6.38

CS 9660—Ballads and Breakdowns of the Golden Era. F5.1

CS 9670—The Byrds. Sweetheart of the Rodeo. R7.8

KCS 9737—Laura Nyro. New York Tendaberry. F10.80

LE 10043—Lester Flatt and Earl Scruggs. Foggy Mountain Banjo. F6.29

LE 10106—Little Jimmie Dickens. Greatest Hits. F8.53

G 30008—The Story of the Blues, v.1. two discs. B1.17

G 30009—Big Bands Greatest Hits, v.1. two discs. P5.2

C 30036—Bukka White. Parchman Farm. B1.257

G 30126—Bessie Smith. Any Woman's Blues. two discs. B1.394

KC 30130—Santana. Abraxas. R4.42

KC 30322—Janis Joplin. Pearl. R5.20

G 30450—Bessie Smith. Empty Bed Blues. two discs. B1.395

C 30466—Maynard Ferguson. M. F. Horn. J4.168

C 30496—Leroy Carr. Blues Before Sunrise. B1.107

G 30503—Great Hits of R & B. two discs. B2.12

C 30584—Earl Scruggs. Family and Friends. F6.122

G 30592—The Fifties Greatest Hits. two discs. P1.5

G 30628—Charles Mingus. Better Get It in Your Soul. two discs. J5.124

G 30818—Bessie Smith. The Empress. two discs. B1.396

CBS (cont'd)

KC 30887—Johnny Cash. Greatest Hits, v.2. F8.19

KC 31067—John McLaughlin. The Inner Mounting Flame. J6.137

G 31086—The Gospel Sound, v.1. two discs. B3.9

G 31093—Bessie Smith. Nobody's Blues But Mine. two discs. B1.397

KC 31170—Blood, Sweat, and Tears. Hits. R4.9

KG 31213—Big Bands Greatest Hits, v.2. two discs. P5.2

KC 33894—George Morgan. Remembering. F8.103

PC 34077—Leonard Cohen. Best. F10.5

KG ———Robert Johnson. Complete. three discs. B1.110 (to be released).

C4L 18—Thesaurus of Classic Jazz. four discs. J3.86

C4L 19—Fletcher Henderson. A Study in Frustration, 1923-1938. four discs. J4.41

C3L 21—Billie Holiday. Golden Years, v.1. three discs. J6.121

C3L 22—Mildred Bailey. Her Greatest Performances, 1929-1946. three discs. P2.87

C2L 24—Joe Venuti and Eddie Lang. Stringing the Blues. two discs. J3.98

C3L 25—Woody Herman. The Thundering Herds. three discs. J4.46

C2L 29—Gene Krupa. Drummin' Man. two discs. J4.71

C3L 32—Jazz Odyssey: The Sound of Chicago. three discs. J3.67

C3L 33—Jazz Odyssey: The Sound of Harlem. three discs. J3.83

C3L 35—Original Sounds of the 20s. three discs. P1.9

C3L 40—Billie Holiday. Golden Years, v.2. three discs. J6.121

GP 26—Miles Davis. Bitches Brew. two discs. J6.131

GP 33—Bessie Smith. The World's Greatest Blues Singer. two discs. B1.393

O2L 160—Benny Goodman. Carnegie Hall Concert. two discs. J4.38

C2S 823—Tony Bennett. At Carnegie Hall. two discs. P2.2

C2S 841—Bob Dylan. Blonde on Blonde. two discs. F10.13

C2S 847—Eubie Blake. The Eighty-Six Years of Eubie Blake. two discs. J2.9

CBS Canada

specialty: general; formerly known as Columbia

CBS (England)

specialty: general

52538—Charlie Christian, v.1. J5.10

52648—Big Bill Broonzy. Big Bill's Blues. B1.152

52796—Blacks, Whites and Blues. F3.32

52797—Recording the Blues. B1.20

52798—Ma Rainey and the Classic Blues Singers. B1.375

63288—Screening the Blues. B1.36

66232—The Story of the Blues, v.2. two discs. B1.17

CBS (France)

specialty: general

62581—Charlie Christian, v.2. J5.10

62853—Benny Goodman. Trio and Quartet, v.1. J4.96

CBS (France) (cont'd)
    62876—Teddy Wilson. Piano Solos. J6.41
    63052—Django Reinhardt. Paris, 1945. J6.116
    63086—Benny Goodman. Trio and Quartet, v.2. J4.96
    63092—Clarence Williams Blue Five, with Louis Armstrong and Sidney Bechet. J3.50
    64218—Rare Recordings of the Twenties, v.1. B1.381
    65379/80—Rare Recordings of the Twenties, v.2-3. B1.381
    65421—Rare Recordings of the Twenties, v.4. B1.381
    66310—Miles Davis. Essential. three discs. J5.122
    67264—Duke Ellington. Complete, v.1. two discs. J4.27
    68275—Duke Ellington. Complete, v.2. two discs. J4.27
    80089—Roy Eldridge. Little Jazz. J4.25
    88000—Duke Ellington. Complete, v.3. J4.27
    88001/4—Louis Armstrong. Very Special Old Phonography. eight discs. J3.17
    88031—Buck Clayton. 1953-1955. two discs. J4.157
    88035—Duke Ellington. Complete, v.4. two discs. J4.27
    88082—Duke Ellington. Complete, v.5. two discs. J4.27
    88129—Erroll Garner. Play It Again, Erroll. two discs. P3.8
    88137—Duke Ellington. Complete, v.6. two discs. J4.27
    88140—Duke Ellington. Complete, v.7. two discs. J4.27
    J 27—New York Scene in the 1940s. J3.85

CBS (Japan)
    specialty: general
    20 AP 13/4—Stanley Brothers, v.1-2. F6.54 and F9.73

Cadence (recently deleted); most available on *Barnaby* label.
    specialty: pop
    3061—Andy Williams. Million Seller Songs. P2.67

Cadet (recently deleted); see All Platinum
    specialty: rhythm 'n' blues and soul
    S 757—Ramsey Lewis. The "In" Crowd. B4.53

Caedmon, 505 Eighth Avenue, New York, NY 10018
    specialty: spoken word, educational, folk music
    TC 1142/6—Folksongs of Britain, v.1-5. five discs. F2.9
    TC 1162/4—Folksongs of Britain, v.6-8. three discs. F2.9
    TC 1224/5—Folksongs of Britain, v.9-10. two discs. F2.9

Camden *See* RCA

Cameo (recently deleted)
    specialty: pop, rock and roll
    P 7001—Chubby Checker. Twist. R2.16

Canaan, 4800 W. Waco Drive, Waco, TX 76703
    specialty: sacred

Capitol, 1750 N. Vine Street, Hollywood, CA 90028
    specialty: general (country, rock, mood)

    SKAO 143—Ferlin Husky. Best. F8.64
    SKAO 145—Buck Owens. Best, v.3. F8.75
    ST 294—Fred Neil. Everybody's Talkin'. F10.36
    DTBB 264—Jim and Jesse. 20 Great Songs. two discs. F6.33
    DKAO 377—Peggy Lee. Greatest. three discs. P2.75
    SW 425—The Band. Stage Fright. R7.5
    SM 650—Merle Travis. The Merle Travis Guitar. F8.37
    SM 756—Tennessee Ernie Ford. Hymns. F9.39
    ST 884/6—Country Hits of the 40s, 50s, and 60s. three discs. F8.9
    SM 1061—Louvin Brothers. The Family Who Prays. F9.49
    ST 1253—Jean Shepard. This Is F8.146
    ST 1312—Rose Maddox. The One Rose. F8.140
    ST 1380—Tennessee Ernie Ford. Sixteen Tons. F8.56
    ST 1388—Les Baxter. Best. P5.78
    T 1477—Ray Anthony. Hits. P5.77
    SWBO 1569—Judy Garland. At Carnegie Hall. two discs. P2.69
    SWCL 1613—Nat "King" Cole. Story. three discs. P2.5
    ST 2089—Hank Thompson. Golden Hits. F7.47
    ST 2105—Buck Owens. Best, v.1. F8.75
    ST 2180—Kingston Trio. Folk Era. three discs. F4.11
    ST 2373—Merle Haggard. Strangers. F8.111
    ST 2422—Beatles. Rubber Soul. R4.7
    ST 2576—Beatles. Revolver. R4.6
    ST 2585—Merle Haggard. Swinging Doors. F8.112
    DT 2601—Dean Martin. Best. P2.54
    SM 2662—Merle Travis. Best. F8.36
    STFL 2814—Frank Sinatra. Deluxe Set. six discs. P2.16
    ST 2897—Buck Owens. Best, v.2. F8.75
    SKAO 2939—Cannonball Adderley. Best. J6.126
    SKAO 2946—Al Martino. Best. P2.58
    DTCL 2953—Edith Piaf. Deluxe Set. P2.113
    SKAO 2955—The Band. Music from Big Pink. R7.3
    STCL 2988—Judy Garland. Deluxe Set. three discs. P2.70
    T 10457—Django Reinhardt. Best. J6.110
    M 11026—Miles Davis. Birth of the Cool. J5.82
    M 11029—Gerry Mulligan. Tentette. Walking Shoes. J5.97
    M 11058—Duke Ellington. Piano Reflections. J6.17a.
    M 11059—Tadd Dameron. Strictly Bebop. J5.14
    M 11060—Lennie Tristano. Crosscurrents. J5.86
    ST 11082—Merle Haggard. Best of the Best. F8.110
    ST 11177—Supersax Plays Bird. J5.5
    ST 11193—Louvin Brothers. The Great Gospel Singing of the Louvin
       Brothers. F9.50
    SKC 11241—Tex Ritter. An American Legend. three discs. F7.13

Capitol (cont'd)
    ST 11287—Gene Vincent. The Bop That Just Won't Stop (1956). R1.18
    ST 11308—Les Paul and Mary Ford. The World Is Still Waiting for the Sun-
        rise. P2.112
    SVBO 11384—Beach Boys. Spirit of America. two discs. R3.3
    ST 11440—The Band. Northern Lights. R7.4
    SKBO 11537—The Beatles. Rock 'n' Roll Music. two discs. R3.4
    ST 11577—Glen Campbell. Best. F8.98

Capitol (Japan)
    ECR 8178—Rose Maddox. Sings Bluegrass. F6.87

Capricorn, 3300 Warner Blvd., Burbank, CA 91505
    specialty: rock

    2CP 0108—Duane Allman. An Anthology, v.1. two discs. R4.20
    2CP 0139—Duane Allman. An Anthology, v.2. two discs. R4.20
    2CP 0164—Allman Brothers Band. The Road Goes On Forever. two discs.
        R5.12a

Charisma (England)
    specialty: folk, rock

    CS 5—Steeleye Span. Individually and Collectively. F2.58

Charly (England)
    CR 300-012—Yardbirds, Featuring Eric Clapton. R5.12
    CR 300-013—Yardbirds, Featuring Jeff Bech. R5.12
    CR 300-014—Yardbirds, Featuring Jimmy Page. R5.12

Checker (recently deleted); see All Platinum
    specialty: rhythm 'n' blues, soul

    3002—Little Milton. Sings Big Blues. B2.60

Chess (recently deleted, but many copies still available); see All Platinum and
    Phonogram
    specialty: blues

    1483—Muddy Waters. Folk Singer. B1.302
    1514—Chuck Berry. Golden Decade, v.1. two discs. B2.37
    1553—Muddy Waters. They Call Me Muddy Waters. B1.304
    2CH 50027—Sonny Boy Williamson, No. 2. This Is My Story. two discs.
        B1.319
    2CH 50030—The Golden Age of Rhythm 'n' Blues. two discs. B2.10
    60023—Chuck Berry. Golden Decade, v.2. two discs. B2.37
    60028—Chuck Berry. Golden Decade, v.3. two discs. B2.37

Chiaroscuro, 221 W. 57th Street, New York, NY 10019
    specialty: jazz

    CR 101—Earl Hines. Quintessential Recording Sessions. J6.26

Chiaroscuro (cont'd)
  CR 106—Don Ewell. A Jazz Portrait of the Artist. J6.53
  CR 108—Eddie Condon. Town Hall Concerts, 1944/5. J3.71
  CR 113—Eddie Condon. Town Hall Concerts, 1944/5. J3.71
  CR 120—Earl Hines. Quintessential Continued. J6.25

Chrysalis, 1750 N. Vine Street, Hollywood, CA 90028
  specialty: folk, rock

  CHR 1008—Steeleye Span. Below the Salt. F2.57
  CHR 1119—Steeleye Span. Please to See the King. F2.59

Classic Jazz, 43 W. 61st Street, New York, NY 10023
  specialty: jazz

Classic Jazz Masters (Denmark)
  specialty: jazz

  CJM 2/10—Jelly Roll Morton. Library of Congress Recordings. nine discs.
    J3.27

Collectors Classics (c/o Southern Record Sales)
  specialty: bluegrass

  CC 1/2—Stanley Brothers, v.1-2. two discs. F6.55
  CC 3—Lonesome Pine Fiddlers. F6.85
  CC 6—Banjo Classics. F6.2

Columbia *See* CBS

Columbia (England)
  specialty: pop, mood

  SCX 6529—Shirley Bassey. Very Best. P2.90

Concert Hall (France)
  specialty: jazz, pop

  SJS 1268—Tribute to Fletcher Henderson. J4.12

Concord Jazz, P.O. Box 845, Concord, CA 94522
  specialty: jazz

Contact (recently deleted)
  specialty: jazz

  LP 2—Earl Hines. Spontaneous Explorations. J6.27

Contemporary, 8481 Melrose Place, Los Angeles, CA 90069
  specialty: jazz

Contour (England)
    specialty: pop, rock
    2870.388—Dell-Vikings. Come and Go With Me. R2.31

Coral, 100 Universal City Plaza, Universal City, CA 91608
    specialty: reissues of MCA material; general
    CXB 6—McGuire Sisters. Best. P2.151

Coral (England)
    specialty: reissues of MCA material; general
    COPS 7453—Gospel Classics. B3.7
    CDMSP 801—Bing Crosby. Musical Autobiography. five discs. P2.11

Coral (West Germany)
    specialty: reissues of MCA material; general
    COPS 6855—Roy Eldridge. Swing Along with Little Jazz. two discs. J4.26
    COPS 7360—The Bands Within the Bands. two discs. J4.91

Cotillion, 75 Rockefeller Plaza, New York, NY 10019
    specialty: rock, contemporary folk
    SD2-400—Woodstock Two. two discs. R4.2
    SD3-500—Woodstock Three. three discs. R4.2

Country Music History (West Germany)
    specialty: old time music
    CMH 211—Jenks "Tex" Carman. The Dixie Cowboy. F7.24

County, Box 191, Floyd, VA 24091
    specialty: old time music, bluegrass
    402—Delmore Brothers. Brown's Ferry Blues, 1933-1941. F8.21
    404—Wade Mainer. F5.90
    405—The Hillbillies. F5.85
    505—Charlie Poole, v.1. F5.69
    506—Gid Tanner, v.1. F5.76
    509—Charlie Poole, v.2. F5.69
    511—Mountain Blues, 1927-1934. F5.15
    515—Mountain Banjo Songs and Tunes. F5.19
    516—Charlie Poole, v.3. F5.69
    518/20—Echoes of the Ozarks, v.1-3. three discs. F5.21
    521—Uncle Dave Macon. Early Recordings, 1925-1935. F5.35
    524—DaCosta Woltz's Southern Broadcasters. F5.61
    526—Gid Tanner, v.2. F5.76
    536—Kessinger Brothers. 1928-1930. F5.114
    540—Charlie Poole, v.4. F5.69
    541/2—Grand Ole Opry Stars. two discs. F8.13
    714—Kenny Baker and Joe Greene. High Country. F6.67
    729—Lilly Brothers. Early Recordings. F6.35

County (cont'd)
    733—Clark Kessinger. Legend. F5.62
    738—Stanley Brothers. That Little Old Country Church House. F9.76
    742—Lilly Brothers. What Will I Leave Behind. F9.48
    749—Springtime in the Mountains. F6.18

Creative World, 1012 S. Robertson Blvd., Los Angeles, CA 90035
    specialty: progressive jazz, Stan Kenton

    ST 1030—Stan Kenton. The Kenton Era. four discs. J4.173

Davis Unlimited, Route 11, 16 Bond Street, Clarksville, TN 37040
    specialty: country, bluegrass, old time music

    DU 33015—Fiddlin' Doc Roberts. Classic Fiddle Tunes Recorded during the
        Golden Age. F5.99
    DU 33030—Vernon Dalhart. Old Time Songs, 1925-1930, v.1. F5.29a

Dawn Club (c/o Southern Record Sales)
    specialty: jazz reissues

    DC 12009—Bud Freeman. Chicagoans in New York. J3.72

Debut (Denmark)
    specialty: modern jazz

    DEB 144—Albert Ayler. Ghosts. J5.140

Decca *See* MCA

Delmark, 4243 N. Lincoln, Chicago, IL 60618
    specialty: jazz, blues

    201—George Lewis. On Parade. J3.15
    202—George Lewis. Doctor Jazz. J3.12
    203—George Lewis. Memorial Album. J3.14
    212—Earl Hines. At Home. J6.23
    DS 420/1—Anthony Braxton. For Alto. two discs. J5.105
    DS 605—Curtis Jones. Lonesome Bedroom Blues. B1.338
    DS 612—Junior Wells. Hoodoo Man Blues. B1.370

Deram (England)
    specialty: rock, folk, pop

    SMK 1117—Shirley Collins. A Favourite Garland. F2.14

Dot, 8255 Beverly Blvd., Los Angeles, CA 90048
    specialty: country, pop

    ABDP 4009—Mac Wiseman. 16 Great Performances. F6.112
    25071—Pat Boone. Pat's Greatest Hits. R2.26
    25201—Billy Vaughan. Golden Hits. P5.91
    25820—Original Hits—Golden Instrumentals. R2.10

Duke, 8255 Beverly Blvd., Los Angeles, CA 90048
specialty: blues, soul

DLP 71—Johnny Ace. Memorial Album. B2.48
DLP 83—Junior Parker. Best. B1.352
DLP 84—Bobby "Blue" Bland. Best, v.1. B2.49
DLP 86—Bobby "Blue" Bland. Best, v.2. B2.49

Dunhill, 8255 Beverly Blvd., Los Angeles, CA 90048
specialty: rock, folk

DSD 50132—Jimmy Buffett. A White Sport Coat and a Pink Crustacean.
F10.54
DXS 50145—Mamas and Papas. 20 Golden Hits. two discs. R3.19

ECM, 810 Seventh Avenue, New Yorkl NY 10019
specialty: modern jazz
1014/6—Chick Corea. Piano Improvisations, v.1-3. three discs. J6.130
1018/9—Circle. Paris Concert. two discs. J5.149
1035/7—Keith Jarrett. Solo Concerts: Bremen and Lausanne. J6.64

EMI (Denmark)
specialty: general

EO 52-81004—Session at Riverside: New York. J4.164
EO 52-81005—Bobby Hackett and Jack Teagarden. Jazz Ultimate. J4.142
EO 52-81006—Session at Midnight: Los Angeles. J4.163

EMI (England)
specialty: general

Odeon CLP 1817—Django Reinhardt. Legendary. J6.111
One Up OU 2046—Big 'Uns from the 50s and 60s. R2.2
Starline SRS 5120—Wanda Jackson. R2.20
Starline SRS 5129—Johnny Otis. Pioneer of Rock. B2.64

EMI (France)
specialty: French music, general

Pathe CO 54-16021/30—Swing Sessions, 1937-1950. ten discs. J1.5
Pathe SPAM 67.092—Edith Piaf. Recital, 1962. P2.115
CO 62-80813—Jay McShann's Piano. J6.67

ESP, 5 Riverside Drive, Krumville, NY 12447
specialty: jazz

1014—Sun Ra. Heliocentric Worlds, v.1. J5.130
1017—Sun Ra. Heliocentric Worlds, v.2. J5.130

Eclipse (England)
specialty: reissues of jazz and nostalgia

ECM 2051—Django Reinhardt. Swing '35-'39. J6.112

Elektra, 962 N. LaCienega, Los Angeles, CA 90069
    specialty: folk, rock

    EKS 7217—Folk Banjo Styles. F3.30
    EKS 7239—Bob Gibson. Where I'm Bound. F4.9
    EKS 7277—Tom Paxton. Ramblin' Boy. F10.44
    EKS 7280—Judy Collins. Concert. F4.6
    EKS 7287—Phil Ochs. I Ain't Marching Anymore. F10.41
    EKS 7310—Phil Ochs. In Concert. F10.42
    EKS 74007—The Doors. R6.1
    EKS 74014—The Doors. Strange Days. R6.2
    EKS 75032—David Ackles. American Gothic. F10.48
    EKS 75035—Judy Collins. Colors of the Day: Best. R4.27
    EKL-BOX—The Folk Box. four discs. F3.7
    ELK 271/2—Woody Guthrie. Library of Congress Recordings. three discs.
        F10.20
    EKL 301/2—Leadbelly. Library of Congress Recordings. three discs. B1.209
    7E-2005—Paul Butterfield. Golden Butter. two discs. R5.8

Elektra (England)
    specialty: folk, rock

    K 52035—Dillards. Country Tracks: Best. F6.120

Enterprise, 2693 Union Avenue, Memphis, TN 38112
    specialty: soul, gospel

    1001—Isaac Hayes. Hot Buttered Soul. B4.51

Epic, 51 W. 52nd Street, New York, NY 10019
    specialty: general

    EE 22001—Johnny Hodges. Hodge Podge. J4.109
    EE 22003—Bobby Hackett. The Hackett Horn. J4.140
    EE 22005—The Duke's Men. J4.133
    EE 22007—Chuck Berry and His Stomping Stevedores. J4.131
    EE 22027—Gene Krupa. That Drummer's Band. J4.75
    BN 26246e—The Yardbirds. Greatest Hits. R5.12
    BN 26486—Tammy Wynette. Greatest Hits, v.1. F8.133
    KE 30325—Sly and the Family Stone. Greatest Hits. B4.31
    EG 30473—Johnny Otis Show Live at Monterey. two discs. B4.4
    E 30733—Tammy Wynette. Greatest Hits, v.2. F8.133
    KE 31607—Johnny Nash. I Can See Clearly Now. B4.56
    KE 33396—Tammy Wynette. Greatest Hits, v.3. F8.133
    PE 33409—Jeff Beck. Blow by Blow. R4.8
    BG 33752—George Jones and Tammy Wynette. Me and the First Lady/We
        Go Together. two discs. F8.151
    BG 33779—Jeff Beck. Truth/Beck-Ola. two discs. P5.14.
    BS 33782—Bob Wills/Asleep at the Wheel. Fathers and Sons. two discs.
        F7.49
    B2N 159—Those Wonderful Girls of Stage, Screen and Radio. two discs. P6.86

Epic (cont'd)
    B2N 164—Those Wonderful Guys of Stage, Screen and Radio. two discs.
        P6.87
    CE2E-201/2—Bing Crosby. Story. four discs. P2.8
    SN 6042—Swing Street. four discs. J4.10
    SN 6044—Jack Teagarden. King of the Blues Trombone. three discs. J3.93
    L2N 6072—Encores from the 30s, v.1 (1930-1935). two discs. P1.4 [v.2
        never released]

Epic (France)
    specialty: general

    LN 24269—Johnny Dodds and Kid Ory. J3.24
    66212—Count Basie with Lester Young. two discs. J4.19

Eubie Blake Music, 284A Stuyvesant Ave., Brooklyn, NY 11221
    specialty: ragtime and reissues

Euphonic, P.O. Box 476, Ventura, CA 93001
    specialty: piano jazz, blues

Everest, 10920 Wilshire Blvd. West, Los Angeles, CA 90024
    specialty: reissues in folk, blues, and jazz

    FS 214—Charlie Parker. v.1. J5.71
    FS 216—Otis Spann. B1.305
    FS 217—Champion Jack Dupree. B1.327
    FS 219—Charlie Christian. At Minton's. J5.11
    FS 232—Charlie Parker. v.2. J5.71
    FS 253—Fred McDowell. B1.118
    FS 254—Charlie Parker. v.3. J5.71
    FS 293—Al Haig. Jazz Will O' the Wisp. J6.56

Excello, 1011 Woodland St., Nashville, TN 37206
    specialty: blues

    DBL 28025—Excello Story. two discs. B4.2

Extreme Rarities, c/o Ken Crawford, 215 Steuben Ave., Pittsburgh, PA 15205
    specialty: jazz and soundtrack reissues

Fantasy, 10th and Parker Sts., Berkeley, CA 94710
    specialty: blues, jazz

    9432—Woody Herman. Giant Step. J4.170
    9442—Staple Singers. The Twenty-Fifth Day of December. B3.57
    CCR-2—Creedence Clearwater Revival. Chronicle. two discs. R3.6
    F 24720—Jack Elliott. Hard Travellin': Songs by Woody Guthrie and Others.
        two discs. F4.30

Fat Cat's Jazz, Box 458, Manassas, VA 22110
    specialty: jazz

Flying Dutchman, 1133 Avenue of the Americas, New York, NY 10036
    specialty: jazz

    FD 10146—Coleman Hawkins. Classic Tenors. J4.99

Flying Fish, 3320 N. Halstead, Chicago, IL 60657
    specialty: bluegrass and Western swing, blues

    101—Hillbilly Jazz. two discs. F7.38

Flyright (England)
    specialty: blues, r'n'b

    LP 108/9—Memphis Minnie. 1934-1949. two discs. B1.389

Folk Legacy, Sharon Mt. Rd., Sharon, CT 06069
    specialty: folk

    FSB 20—Harry Cox. Traditional English Love Songs. F2.18
    FSA 26—Sarah Ogan Gunning. A Girl of Constant Sorrow. F3.66
    FSA 32—Hedy West. Old Times and Hard Times. F3.93
    FSI 35—Michael Cooney. The Cheese Stands Alone. F3.62

Folklyric, 10341 San Pablo Avenue, El Cerrito, CA 94530
    specialty: blues and folk reissues

    9001—Son House. Legendary, 1941/42 Recordings. B1.189

Folkways, 43 W. 61st Street, New Yorkl NY 10023
    specialty: folk, blues, jazz

    2301/2—Jean Ritchie. Child Ballads in America. two discs. F3.84
    2314—American Banjo Tunes and Songs in Scruggs Style. F6.1
    2315—Stoneman Family. Banjo Tunes and Songs. F5.74
    2316—Ritchie Family. F3.85
    2318—Mountain Music Bluegrass Style. F6.17
    2320/3—Pete Seeger. American Favorite Ballads. four discs. F4.65
    2351—Dock Boggs. v.1. F5.45
    2356—Old Harp Singing. F9.11
    2392—Dock Boggs. v.2. F5.45
    2395/9—New Lost City Ramblers. v.1-5. five discs. F5.66
    2409—Country Songs—Old and New. F6.25
    2426—Doc Watson and Jean Ritchie. F4.20
    2431/2—Newport Folk Festival, 1959/60. v.1-2. two discs. F3.15
    2433—Lilly Brothers. Folksongs from the Southern Mountains. F6.36
    2445—Pete Seeger. American Favorite Ballads. F4.65

Folkways (cont'd)
    2456—Pete Seeger. Broadsides. F3.89
    2480—Cisco Houston. Sings Songs of the Open Road. F10.67
    2492—New Lost City Ramblers. Play Instrumentals. F5.67
    2501/2—Pete Seeger. Gazette, v.1-2. two discs. F3.89
    2641/5—New Orleans, v.1-5. five discs. J3.2
    2801/11—Jazz, v.1-11. eleven discs. J1.9
    2941/2—Leadbelly. Last Sessions, v.1-2. four discs. B1.115
    2951/3—Anthology of American Folk Music. six discs. F3.4
    3527—Little Brother Montgomery. Blues. B1.223
    3562—Joseph Lamb. A Study in Classic Ragtime. J2.11
    3575—Irish Music in London Pubs. F2.35
    3810—Buell Kazee. His Songs and Music. F3.71
    3903—Dock Boggs. v.3. F5.45
    5212—Woody Guthrie. Dust Bowl Ballads. F10.61
    5264—New Lost City Ramblers. Songs of the Depression. F5.95
    5272—Harry K. McClintock. Haywire Mac. F10.70
    5285—Almanac Singers. Talking Union. F4.1
    5801/2—American History in Ballads and Songs. six discs. F3.21
    FTS 31001—Woody Guthrie. This Land Is Your Land. F10.22
    FTS 31021—Watson Family. F4.19

Fontana, 1 IBM Plaza, Chicago, IL 60611
    specialty: general

    27560—New Vaudeville Band. P2.153

Fontana (England)
    specialty: general

    STL 5269—Martin Carthy. F2.13

Fountain (England)
    specialty: jazz and blues reissues

    FB 301—Ida Cox, v.1. B1.401
    FB 304—Ida Cox, v.2. B1.401

Freedom (England)
    specialty: modern jazz

    FLP 40106—Cecil Taylor. D Trad That's What. J5.134

GHP (West Germany)
    specialty: old time music

    902—Riley Puckett. Old Time Greats. F5.39
    1001—Dock Walsh. F5.81

GNP Crescendo, 9165 Sunset Blvd., Hollywood, CA 90069
    specialty: jazz

GNP Crescendo (cont'd)
S18—Max Roach-Clifford Brown. In Concert. J5.33
9003—Coleman Hawkins. The Hawk in Holland. J4.101

Gannet (Denmark)
specialty: jazz

GEN 5136/7—Jimmy Yancey, v.1-2. two discs. J6.96

Good Time Jazz, 8481 Melrose Place, Los Angeles, CA 90069
specialty: dixieland jazz, piano jazz

10035—Luckey Roberts/Willie "The Lion" Smith. Harlem Piano. J6.34
10043—Don Ewell. Man Here Plays Fine Piano. J6.50
10046—Don Ewell. Free 'n' Easy. J6.49
12001/3—Lu Watters. San Francisco Style, v.1-3. three discs. J3.59
12004—Kid Ory. 1954. J3.42
12022—Kid Ory. Tailgate! J3.46
12048—Bunk Johnson. Superior Jazz Band. J3.10

Gordy, 6464 Sunset Blvd., Hollywood, CA 90028
specialty: soul, blues

Greene Bottle (c/o Southern Record Sales)
specialty: blues

Groove Merchant, Suite 3701, 515 Madison Avenue, New York, NY 10022
specialty: jazz, blues

Gusto, 220 Boscobel Street, Nashville, TN 37213
specialty: reissues of Starday and King records

Halcyon, Box 4255, Grand Central Station, New York, NY 10017
specialty: jazz

Halcyon (England)
specialty: reissues of jazz and nostalgia items

HAL 5—Annette Hanshaw. Sweetheart of the Thirties. P2.104

Harmony (recently deleted); see also CBS
specialty: budget line reissues of Columbia and Brunswick items

HL 7191—Harry James. Songs That Sold a Million. P5.83
HL 7233—Wilma Lee and Stoney Cooper. Sacred Songs. F9.30
HL 7290—Bill Monroe. Great. F6.39
HL 7299—Molly O'Day. Unforgettable. F8.131
HL 7308—Johnny Bond..Best. F7.6
HL 7313—Bob Atcher. Best Early American Folksongs. F7.22
HL 7317—Sons of the Pioneers. Best. F7.16
HL 7340—Lester Flatt and Earl Scruggs. Great Original Recordings. F6.30
HL 7382—Gene Autry. Great Hits. F7.4

Harmony (cont'd)
 HL 7396—Carter Family. Great Sacred Songs. F9.26
 HL 7402—Lester Flatt and Earl Scruggs. Sacred Songs. F9.37
 HS 11178—Wilma Lee and Stoney Cooper. Sunny Side of the Mountain.
  F6.73
 HS 11334—Roy Acuff. Waiting for My Call to Glory. F9.15
 H 30609—Johnny Ray. Best. R2.22

Harmony (Canada)
 HEL 6004—Jazzmen in Uniform, 1945, Paris. J1.4

Herwin, 45 First Street, Glen Cove, NY 11542
 specialty: jazz and blues reissues

 101—Freddie Keppard. J3.6
 106—King Oliver. The Great 1923 Gennetts. J3.7
 202—Bessie Johnson. 1928-29. B3.43
 203—Sanctified, v.2: God Gave Me the Light, 1927-1931. B3.5
 204—Blind Joe Taggart. B3.61
 207—Sanctified, v.3: Whole World in His Hands, 1927-1936. B3.27
 208—Cannon's Jug Stompers. two discs. B1.419
 401—They All Played the Maple Leaf Rag. J2.8

Hi, 539 W. 25th Street, New York, NY 10001
 specialty: soul

 XSHL 32070—Al Green. Let's Stay Together. B4.48

Hilltop (recently deleted)
 specialty: Mercury budget reissues of country material through Pickwick
  records

 JS 6036—Louvin Brothers. F8.29
 JS 6093—Lester Flatt and Earl Scruggs. F6.27

Historical, P.O. Box 4204, Bergen Station, Jersey City, NJ 07304
 specialty: reissued jazz, blues, and country materials

 HLP 9—Benny Moten. Kansas City Orchestra, 1923-29. J4.83
 HLP 10—Chicago Southside, 1926-1932, v.1. J3.64
 HLP 24—The Territory Bands, 1926-1931, v.1. J3.103
 HLP 26—The Territory Bands, 1926-1931, v.2. J3.103
 HLP 30—Chicago Southside, 1926-1932, v.2. J3.64
 HLP 8001—Fields Ward. Buck Mountain Band. F5.101
 HLP 8004—Stoneman Family. 1927-1928. F5.73

Imperial (recently deleted); see United Artists
 specialty: blues and soul

 LP 9141—Smiley Lewis. I Hear You Knocking. B2.58

Impulse, 8255 Beverly Blvd., Los Angeles, CA 90048
    specialty: jazz (modern and mainstream)

      AS 6—John Coltrane. Africa Brass. J5.115
      AS 10—John Coltrane. Live at the Village Vanguard. J5.120
      AS 12—Benny Carter. Further Definitions. J4.24
      AS 77—John Coltrane. A Love Supreme. J5.121
      AS 95—John Coltrane. Ascension. J5.116
      AS 9108—Earl Hines. Once Upon a Time. J4.69
      AS 9148—John Coltrane. Cosmic Music. J5.117
      AS 9183—Charlie Haden. Liberation Suite. J5.156
      AS 9229-2—Pharoah Sanders. Nest. two discs. J5.158
      ASH 9253-3—The Saxophone. three discs. J6.5
      ASY 9272-3—The Drum. three discs. J6.2
      ASY 9284-3—The Bass. three discs. J6.1

Increase (recently deleted); see All Platinum
    specialty: rock and roll and rhythm 'n' blues in a disc jockey simulation

    2000/12—Cruisin', 1955-1967. thirteen discs. R2.4

Island, 7720 Sunset Blvd., Los Angeles, CA 90046
    specialty: folk and reggae music

      SW 9329—The Wailers. Catch a Fire. B5.9
      ILPS 9330—Toots and the Maytals. Funky Kingston. B5.8
      ILPS 9334—The Chieftains. 5. F2.39

Island (England)
    specialty: folk and reggae music

      FOLK 1001—The Electric Muse. four discs. F2.45
      HELP 25—Albion Country Band. F2.46a

Jamie (recently deleted)
    specialty: rock and roll

      S 3026—Duane Eddy. 16 Greatest Hits. R2.17

Jazum, 5808 Northumberland St., Pittsburgh, PA 15217
    specialty: jazz and nostalgia reissues

      21—Boswell Sisters. P2.136
      30/1—Boswell Sisters. two discs. P2.136
      43/4—Boswell Sisters. two discs. P2.136

Jazz Archives, P.O. Box 194, Plainview, NY 11805
    specialty: jazz

      JA 6—Charlie Christian. Together with Lester Young, 1940. J5.12
      JA 18—Lester Young. Jammin' with Lester. J4.127
      JA 23—Charlie Christian, with Benny Goodman's Sextet, 1939/41. J5.13

Jazz Composers' Orchestral Association, 6 West 96th Street, New York, NY 10024
specialty: modern jazz

JCOA 1001/2—Jazz Composers' Orchestra. two discs. J5.123

Jazzology, 3008 Wadsworth Mill Place, Decatur, GA 30032
specialty: jazz

Jazz Piano (Denmark)
specialty: piano jazz reissues

JP 5003—Library of Congress Sessions. J6.84

Jim Taylor Presents, 12311 Gratiot Ave., Detroit, MI 48205
specialty: mainstream jazz and blues

JTP 103—Olive Brown and Her Blues Chasers. B1.398

John Edwards Memorial Foundation, c/o Center for Study of Folklore &
Mythology, UCLA, Los Angeles, CA 90024
specialty: reissues of blues, and country and western material

Kama Sutra, 810 Seventh Ave., New York, NY 10019
specialty: rock and roll

KSBS 2010—Sha Na Na. Rock & Roll Is Here to Stay! R2.51
KSBS 2013—Lovin' Spoonful. Very Best. R3.18

Kapp (recently deleted); see also MCA
specialty: mood

3530—Roger Williams. Gold Hits. P3.24
3559—Jack Jones. Best. P2.48

Kent, 96 West Street, Englewood, NJ 07631
specialty: blues

KST 533—B. B. King. From the Beginning. two discs. B1.294
KST 534—Johnny Otis. Cold Shot. B1.351
KST 537—Jimmy Reed. Roots of the Blues. two discs. B1.232
KST 9001—Elmore James. Legend, v.1. B1.286
KST 9010—Elmore James. Legend, v.2. B1.286
KST 9011—B. B. King. 1949-1950. B1.291

Kicking Mule, P.O. Box 3233, Berkeley, CA 94703
specialty: blues, folk, and guitar albums

106—Rev. Gary Davis. Ragtime Guitar. J2.25

King, 220 Boscobel St., Nashville, TN 37213
specialty: blues, bluegrass and country music, soul

541—Hank Ballard. Greatest Jukebox Hits. B2.36
552—Don Reno and Red Smiley. F6.47

King (cont'd)

    553—Cowboy Copas. All Time Hits. F8.49
    615—Stanley Brothers. F6.58
    826—James Brown. Live at the Apollo, v.1. B4.24
    848—Don Reno and Red Smiley. F6.47
    872—Stanley Brothers. America's Finest Five String Banjo Hootenanny.
       F6.59
    919—James Brown. Unbeatable Sixteen Hits. B4.25
    1022—James Brown. Live at the Apollo, v.2. B4.24
    1059—Freddy King. Hideaway. B1.340
    1065—Don Reno. Fastest Five Strings Alive. F6.99
    1081—Little Willie John. Free At Last. B2.61
    1086—Wynonie Harris. Good Rockin' Blues. B1.423
    1110—James Brown Band. Sho Is Funky Down Here. B4.40
    1130—Roy Brown. Hard Luck Blues. B2.38

King Bluegrass, 6609 Main Street, Cincinnati, OH 45244
    specialty: bluegrass

Kudu, 6464 Sunset Blvd., Hollywood, CA 90028
    specialty: soul

    05—Esther Phillips. From a Whisper to a Scream. B4.74

Leader (England)
    specialty: folk

    LEAB 404—Copper Family. A Song for Every Season. four discs. F2.16

Lemco, 6609 Main Street, Cincinnati, OH 45244
    specialty: bluegrass

    611—J. D. Crowe. The Model Church. F9.31
    612—Red Allen and the Allen Brothers. Allengrass. F6.113

Library of Congress, Washington, D.C.
    specialty: folk and ethnic music, blues; see also Flyright

    LBC 1/15—Folk Music in America, v.1-15. fifteen discs. F3.9 [in progress]
    AAFS L 26/7—American Sea Songs and Shanties, v.1-2. two discs. F3.25
    AAFS L 62—American Fiddle Tunes. F3.16

London, 539 W. 25th Street, New York, NY 10001
    specialty: general

    NPS 4—Rolling Stones. Let It Bleed. R4.16
    PS 114—Edmundo Ros. Rhythms of the South. P5.112
    PS 483—Mantovani. Golden Hits. P5.100
    PS 492—John Mayall. Blues Breakers. R5.10
    PS 493—Rolling Stones. Got Live (If You Want It). R4.14
    PS 534—John Mayall. Alone. R5.9
    PS 539—Rolling Stones. Beggar's Banquet. R4.13

London (cont'd)
   NPS 606/7—Rolling Stones. Hot Rocks, v.1. two discs. R4.15
   XPS 610—Mantovani. 25th Anniversary Album. P5.101
   NPS 626/7—Rolling Stones. Hot Rocks, v.2. two discs. R4.15
   XPS 906—Mantovani. All Time Greatest. P5.99

MCA, 100 Universal City Plaza, Universal City, CA 91608
   specialty: general; formerly known as Decca, and consequently many older
      records were renumbered

   DL 8044—Kansas City Jazz. J3.101
   DL 8671—Gateway Singers. At the Hungry i. F4.8
   DL 8731—Bill Monroe. Knee Deep in Bluegrass. F6.45
   DL 8782—Sister Rosetta Tharpe. Gospel Train. B3.62
   DL 9034/8—Al Jolson. Story. five discs. P2.12
   DL 75326—Conway Twitty and Loretta Lynn. Lead Me On. F8.153
   DS 79175—The Who. Live at Leeds. R4.17
   DL 9221—Earl Hines. Southside Swing, 1934/5. J4.68
   DL 9222/3—Chick Webb, v.1-2. two discs. J4.51
   DL 9224—Duke Ellington, v.1: In the Beginning (1926/8). J4.28
   DL 9227/8—Fletcher Henderson, v.1-2. two discs. J4.40
   DL 9236—Jay McShann. New York—1208 Miles (1941-1943). J4.80
   DL 79237/40—Jimmie Lunceford, v.1-4. four discs. J4.77
   DL 9241—Duke Ellington, v.2: Hot in Harlem (1928/9). J4.28
   DL 9242—Big Bands Uptown, 1931-1943, v.1. J3.78
   DL 9243—Jan Savitt. The Top Hatters, 1939-1941. P5.44
   DL 9247—Duke Ellington, v.3: Rockin' in Rhythm (1929/31). J4.28
   1—Loretta Lynn. Greatest Hits, v.1. F8.130
   81—Jimmy Martin. Good 'n' Country. F6.38
   86—Red Foley. Songs of Devotion. F9.38
   104—Bill Monroe. Bluegrass Instrumentals. F6.43
   110—Bill Monroe. The High, Lonesome Sound. F6.44
   115—Jimmy Martin. Big 'n' Country Instrumentals. F6.37
   131—Bill Monroe. A Voice from On High. F9.61
   420—Loretta Lynn. Greatest Hits, v.2. F8.130
   527—Bill Monroe. I Saw the Light. F9.60
   2106—Neil Diamond. His 12 Greatest Hits. P2.33
   2128—Elton John. Greatest Hits. R4.10
   DEA 7-2—Those Wonderful Thirties. two discs. P1.14
   DXS 7181—Webb Pierce. Story. two discs. F8.30
   2-4001—Bill Anderson. Story. two discs. F8.44
   2-4005—Inkspots. Best. two discs. B2.22
   2-4006—Billie Holiday. Story. two discs. J6.122
   2-4008—Fred Waring. Best. two discs. P2.141
   2-4009—Buddy Holly. two discs. R1.8
   2-4010—Bill Haley and His Comets. Best. two discs. R1.7
   2-4018—A Jazz Holiday. two discs. J3.82
   2-4019—Art Tatum. Masterpieces. two discs. J6.36
   2-4031—Kitty Wells. Story. two discs. F8.132
   2-4033—Four Aces. Best. two discs. P2.149

MCA (cont'd)

    2-4038—Patsy Cline. Story. two discs. F8.129
    2-4039—Mills Brothers. Best. two discs. P2.140
    2-4040—Ernest Tubb. Story. two discs. F8.38
    2-4041—Guy Lombardo. Sweetest Music This Side of Heaven. two discs. P5.37
    2-4043—Bert Kaempfert. Best. two discs. P5.85
    2-4047—Ella Fitzgerald. Best. two discs. P2.68
    2-4050—Count Basie. Best. two discs. J4.13
    2-4052—The Weavers. Best. F4.21
    2-4053—Red Foley. Story. two discs. F8.101
    2-4056—Carmen Cavallaro. Best. two discs. P5.106
    2-4067—The Who. A Quick One (Happy Jack). two discs. R4.19
    2-4068—The Who. Magic Bus. two discs. R4.18
    2-4071—Eddie Condon. Best. two discs. J3.68
    2-4072—Xavier Cugat. Best. two discs. P5.107
    2-4073—Jimmy Dorsey. Best. two discs. P5.26
    2-4076—Glen Gray and the Casa Loma Orchestra. Best. two discs. P5.32
    2-4077—Woody Herman. Best. two discs. J4.43
    2-4079—Louis Jordan. Best. B2.45
    2-4083—Bob Crosby. Best. two discs. J3.54
    2-4090—Bill Monroe. Best. two discs. F6.42
    2-8001—American Graffiti. two discs. R2.1
    2-11002—That's Entertainment! two discs. P6.85

MCA (England)
    specialty: general; formerly Decca American

    MCFM 2720—Dick Haymes. Best. P2.45
    MCFM 2739—Connie Boswell. Sand in My Shoes. P2.68a

MCA (France)
    specialty: general; jazz reissues from American Decca

    510.065—Lucky Millinder. Lucky Days, 1941-1945. B2.22a
    510.071—The Swinging Small Bands, v.1. J4.93
    510.085—James P. Johnson. J6.29
    510.088—The Swinging Small Bands, v.2. J4.93
    510.090—Kings and Queens of Ivory, v.1. J6.15 (set in progress)
    510.111—The Swinging Small Bands, v.3. J4.93
    510.123—The Swinging Small Bands, v.4. J4.03

MCA (West Germany)
    specialty: general; reissued Decca material

    628.334—Tex Ritter. The Singing Cowboy. two discs. F7.14

MGM, 810 Seventh Ave., New York, NY 10019
    specialty: general

    GAS 140—Osborne Brothers. F6.93
    SE 3331—Hank Williams. I Saw the Light. F9.85

MGM (cont'd)
> SE 4946—Tompall and the Glaser Brothers. Greatest Hits. F8.128

MGM (England)
> specialty: general; reissues of American MGM product

> 2353.053—Hank Williams. Greatest Hits, v.1. F8.40
> 2353.071—Billy Eckstine. Greatest Hits. P2.34
> 2353.073—Hank Williams. Greatest Hits, v.2. F8.40
> 2353.118—Hank Williams. Collector's, v.1. F8.39
> 2683.016—Hank Williams. Memorial Album. two discs. F8.42
> 2683.046—Hank Williams. On Stage! two discs. F8.43

MPS (West Germany)
> specialty: jazz

> 20668—Oscar Peterson. Exclusively for My Friends, v.1. J6.69
> 20693—Oscar Peterson. Exclusively for My Friends, v.6. J6.69
> 206696—Oscar Peterson. Exclusively for My Friends, v.2. J6.69
> 206701—Oscar Peterson. Exclusively for My Friends, v.3. J6.69
> 206718—Oscar Peterson. Exclusively for My Friends, v.4. J6.69

Magpie (England)
> specialty: blues

> PY 18000—Robert Wilkins. Before the Reverence, 1928-1935. B1.129a

Mainstream, 1700 Broadway, New York, NY 10019
> specialty: jazz and blues

> MRL 311—Lightnin' Hopkins. The Blues. B1.181
> MRL 316—Maynard Ferguson. Screamin' Blues. J4.169
> MRL 399—Andy Kirk. March, 1936. J4.70

Mamlish, Box 417, Cathedral Station, New York, NY 10025
> specialty: blues

> S3804—Mississippi Sheiks. Stop and Listen Blues. B1.220

Master Jazz Recordings, 955 Lexington Avenue, New York, NY 10024
> specialty: jazz

> MJR 8116—Billy Strayhorn. Cue for Saxophone. J4.150

Matchbox (England)
> specialty: blues

> SDR 213—Little Brother Montgomery. 1930-1969. B1.222

Melodeon, 16 River Street, Chatham, NY 12037
> specialty: blues, jazz, bluegrass reissues

> MLP 7321—Skip James. Greatest of the Delta Blues Singers. B1.199
> MLP 7322—Stanley Brothers. Their Original Recordings. F6.57

Melodeon (cont'd)

MLP 7323—Blind Willie McTell. The Legendary Library of Congress Session, 1940. B1.127
MLP 7324—Part Blues. B1.34
MLP 7325—Red Allen. Solid Bluegrass Sound of the Kentuckians. F6.21

Mercury, 1 IBM Plaza, Chicago, IL 60611
specialty: general

MG 20323—Carl Story. Gosepl Quartet Favorites. F9.81
60232—Dinah Washington. Unforgettable. B4.79
60587—Frankie Laine. Golden Hits. P2.50
60621—George Jones. Greatest Hits. F8.26
60645—Sarah Vaughan. Golden Hits. P2.83
SR 61268—Dave Dudley. Best. F8.121
SR 61369—Tom T. Hall. Greatest Hits, v.1. F8.113
SRM 1-1044—Tom T. Hall. Greatest Hits, v.2. F8.113
SRM 1-1078—Johnny Rodriguez. Greatest Hits. F8.105
SRM 1-1101—Bachman-Turner Overdrive. Best. R8.11
SRM 20803—Jerry Lee Lewis. The Session. two discs. R2.49
SRM 2-7507—Rod Stewart. Best. R4.44

Milestone, 10th and Parker Streets, Berkeley, CA 94710
specialty: jazz and blues; reissues from the Riverside catalog

M 2012—Earl Hines. A Monday Date, 1928. J6.21
47002—Bill Evans. Village Vanguard Session. two discs. J6.55
47003—Wes Montgomery. While We're Young. two discs. J6.108
47004—Thelonious Monk. Pure Monk. two discs. J6.32
47007—Sonny Rollins. Freedom Suite, Plus. two discs. J5.77
47018—Jelly Roll Morton. 1923-1924. two discs. J6.33
47019—Bix Beiderbecke and the Chicago Cornets. two discs. J3.53
47020—New Orleans Rhythm Kings. two discs. J3.57
47021—Ma Rainey. two discs. B1.392

Monmouth/Evergreen, 1697 Broadway, Suite 1201, New York, NY 10019
specialty: jazz, reissued stage and show soundtracks, reissued nostalgia-pop music

MES 6816—Ray Noble and Al Bowlly, v.1. P5.102
MES 6917—Maxine Sullivan and Bob Wilber. The Music of Hoagy Carmichael. P2.82
MES 7021—Ray Noble and Al Bowlly, v.2. P5.102
MES 7024/5—Claude Thornhill. two discs. P5.89 and P5.90
MES 7027—Ray Noble and Al Bowlly, v.3. P5.102
MES 7033—Jack Hylton, v.1. P5.98
MES 7039/40—Ray Noble and Al Bowlly, v.4-5. two discs. P5.102
MES 7055—Jack Hylton, v.2. P5.98
MES 5056—Ray Noble and Al Bowlly, v.6. P5.102

Monument, 51 W. 52nd Street, New York, NY 10019
  specialty: country music

  18045—Roy Orbison. Very Best. R2.21
  Z 30817—Kris Kristofferson. Me and Bobby McGee. F10.24
  Z 32259—Arthur Smith. Battling Banjos. F6.105

Motown, 6255 Sunset Blvd., Hollywood, CA 90028
  specialty: soul

  663—The Supremes. Greatest Hits. two discs. B4.12
  702-S2—Gladys Knight and the Pips. Anthology. two discs. B4.68
  MS5-726—Motown Story; The First Decade. five discs. B4.5
  782-A3—The Temptations. Anthology. three discs. B4.18
  793-R3—Smokey Robinson and the Miracles. Anthology. three discs. B4.29

Muse, Blanchris, Inc., 160 W. 71st Street, New York, NY 10023
  specialty: jazz and blues

  MR 5087—Elmore James/Eddie Taylor. Street Talkin'. B1.368

Muskadine, Box 635, Manhattan Beach, CA 90266
  specialty: blues reissues

Nonesuch, 962 N. LaCienega, Los Angeles, CA 90069
  specialty: mainly classical, but here includes ragtime music

  H 71305—Joshua Rifkin. Joplin Piano Rags, v.3. J2.23
  HB 73026—Joshua Rifkin. Joplin Piano Rags, v.1/2. J2.23

Ode, 1416 North LaBrea, Hollywood, CA 90028
  specialty: popular

  SP 77009—Carole King. Tapestry. R3.15

Odeon *See* EMI Odeon (England)

Old Homestead, P.O. Box 100, Brighton, MI 48116
  specialty: bluegrass, old time music, sacred music, and reissues

  OH 90001—Wade Mainer. Sacred Songs of Mother and Home. F9.54
  OHCS 101—Molly O'Day. A Sacred Collection. F9.63

Old Masters, Max Abrams, Box 76082, Los Angeles, CA 90076
  specialty: jazz and pop reissues

  TOM 23—Ted Weems. 1928-1930. P5.46a

Old Timey, 10341 San Pablo Ave., El Cerrito, CA 94530.
  specialty: reissues of old time music and western swing

  OT 100/1—The String Bands, v.1-2. two discs. F5.24
  OT 102—Ballads and Songs. F5.3

Old Timey (cont'd)
>OT 103/4—Cliff Carlisle, v.1-2. two discs. F8.48
>OT 105—Western Swing, v.1. F7.36
>OT 106/7—J. E. Mainer's Mountaineers, v.1-2. two discs. F5.65
>OT 112—Tom Darby and Jimmy Tarlton. F5.113
>OT 115—Allen Brothers. The Chattanooga Boys. F5.117
>OT 116/7—Western Swing, v.2-3. two discs. F7.36

Oldie Blues (Holland)
>specialty: blues reissues

>OL 2801—Pete Johnson, v.1. J6.93
>OL 2806—Pete Johnson, v.2. J6.93

Onyx, Blanchris, Inc., 160 W. 71st Street, New York, NY 10023
>specialty: jazz reissues

>ORI 204—Red Rodney. The Red Arrow. J5.75
>ORI 205—Art Tatum. God Is in the House. J6.35
>ORI 207—Hot Lips Page. After Hours in Harlem. J5.67
>ORI 208—Don Byas. Midnight at Minton's. J5.42
>ORI 221—Charlie Parker. First Recordings! J5.28

Origin Jazz Library, Box 863, Berkeley, CA 94701
>specialty: blues and gospel reissues

>OJL 12/3—In the Spirit, No. 1-2. two discs. B3.13

Pablo, 1133 Avenue of the Americas, New York, NY 10036
>specialty: mainstream jazz

>2625.703—Art Tatum. Solo Masterpieces. thirteen discs. J6.39
>2625.706—Art Tatum. Group Masterpieces. eight discs. J4.155

Paltram (Austria)
>specialty: blues and gospel

>PL 102—Texas Blues. B1.97

Paramount, 8255 Beverly Blvd., Los Angeles, CA 90048
>specialty: popular, rock

>PAS 6031—Commander Cody and His Lost Planet Airmen. Hot Licks, Cold Steel, and Truckers' Favorites. F8.108

Parlophone (England)
>specialty: general, jazz reissues

>PMC 7019—Lonnie Johnson and Eddie Lang. Blue Guitars, v.1. B1.207
>PMC 7038—The Chocolate Dandies. 1928-1933. J4.55
>PMC 7082—The Territory Bands, 1926-1929. J3.104
>PMC 7106—Lonnie Johnson and Eddie Lang. Blue Guitars, v.2. B1.207

Parrot, 539 W. 25th Street, New York, NY 10001
  specialty: general
  XPAS 71028—Tom Jones. This Is P2.49

Peacock, 8255 Beverly Blvd., Los Angeles, CA 90048
  specialty: gospel
  136—Mighty Clouds of Joy. Best. B3.48
  138—Dixie Hummingbirds. Best. B3.33
  139—Five Blind Boys of Mississippi. Best. B3.36
  140—Golden Gems of Gospel. B3.6

Philadelphia International, 51 W. 52nd Street, New York, NY 10019
  specialty: soul

Philips, 1 IBM Plaza, Chicago, IL 60611
  specialty: general; see also Phonogram
  PHS 600.298—Nina Simone. Best. B4.70

Philo, The Barn, North Ferrisburg, VT 05473
  specialty: folk music

Phoenix, 7808 Bergen Line Ave., Bergenfield, NJ 07047
  specialty: jazz and blues reissues
  LP 7—Wynonie Harris. Mister Blues Meets the Master Saxes. B1.424

Phonogram (England)
  specialty: general, reissues of Philips and Chess materials
  6414.406—Alan Stivell. Renaissance of the Celtic Harp. F2.61
  6467.013—Memphis Country. F8.12
  6467.025/7—Sun Rockabillies, v.1-3. three discs. R1.5
  6467.306—Muddy Waters. At Newport. B1.300
  6641.047—Genesis, v.1. four discs. B1.275
  6641.125—Genesis, v.2. four discs. B1.276
  6641.174—Genesis, v.3. four discs. B1.277
  6641.180—The Sun Story, 1952-1968. two discs. R1.6

Pickwick, 135 Crossways Park Drive, Woodbury, Long Island, NY 11797
  specialty: reissues of Mercury and Capitol material, all fields

Piedmont (c/o Southern Record Sales)
  specialty: blues
  PLP 13157—Mississippi John Hurt. Folksongs and Blues, v.1. B1.191
  PLP 13161—Mississippi John Hurt. Folk Songs and Blues, v.2. B1.191

Pine Mountain, Box 584, Barbourville, KY 40906
  specialty: reissues of old time material
  PM 269—The Blue Sky Boys. Precious Moments. F9.22

Polydor, 810 Seventh Avenue, New York, NY 10019
 specialty: general pop and soul

 PD 4054—James Brown. Hot Pants. B4.39
 104.678—James Last. This Is P5.86

Polydor (England)
 specialty: pop and soul

 2310.293—Charlie Feathers/Mac Curtis. Rockabilly Kings. R1.14
 2384.007—Oscar Peterson. Exclusively for My Friends, v.5. J6.69
 2424.118—Jerry Butler. Best. B4.42

Prestige, 10th and Parker Streets, Berkeley, CA 94710
 specialty: jazz, blues and folk music

 7159—Thelonious Monk. Monk's Mood. J5.25
 7326—Sonny Rollins. Saxophone Colossus. J5.79
 7337—Stan Getz. Greatest Hits. J5.89c
 7593—Dickie Wells. In Paris, 1937. J4.156
 7643—Benny Carter. 1933. J4.20
 7827—Lee Konitz. Ezz-thetic. J5.92
 PR 24001—Miles Davis. two discs. J5.16
 PR 24020—Clifford Brown. In Paris. two discs. J5.40
 PR 24024—The Greatest Jazz Concert Ever. two discs. J5.6
 P 24030—Dizzy Gillespie. In the Beginning. two discs. J5.22
 PR 24034—Miles Davis. Workin' and Steamin'. two discs. J5.21
 P 24039—Eddie "Lockjaw" Davis. The Cookbook. two discs. P3.6
 P 24040—Buck Clayton and Buddy Tate. Kansas City Nights. two discs.
  J4.161
 P 24044—Sonny Stitt. Genesis. two discs. J5.80
 PR 24045—25 Years of Prestige. two discs. J5.104
 P 34001—Charles Mingus. The Great Concert. three discs. J5.127

Puritan, P.O. Box 946, Evanston, IL 60204
 specialty: bluegrass

Pye (England)
 specialty: general

 502—Donovan. History. F10.8

RBF, 43 W. 61st Street, New York, NY 10023
 specialty: jazz, blues and old time music reissues

 RF 3—A History of Jazz: The New York Scene, 1914-1945. J3.80
 RBF 8/9—The Country Blues, v.1-2. two discs. B1.11
 RBF 10—Blind Willie Johnson. B3.45
 RBF 11—Blues Rediscoveries. B1.10
 RBF 15—Blues Roots: The Atlanta Blues. B1.63
 RBF 19—Country Gospel Song. F9.5
 RBF 51—Uncle Dave Macon. F5.32

RBF (cont'd)
>   RBF 202—The Rural Blues. two discs. B1.22
>   RBF 203—New Orleans Jazz: The Twenties. two discs. J3.5

RCA, 1133 Avenue of the Americas, New York, NY 10036
>   specialty: general; formerly known as Victor

>   LSPX 1004—Guess Who. Best. R3.10
>   LPM 1121—Rosalie Allen. Queen of the Yodellers. F8.134
>   LPM 1183—Eartha Kitt. That Bad Eartha. P2.109
>   LPE 1192—Glenn Miller. Plays Selections from "The Glenn Miller Story."
>   P5.15
>   LPM 1223—Eddy Arnold. All Time Favorites. F8.88
>   LPM 1241—Artie Shaw's Gramercy Five. J4.146
>   LPM 1246—Fats Waller. Ain't Misbehavin'. J4.117, P2.65
>   LPM 1295—Muggsy Spanier. The Great Sixteen. J3.58
>   LPM 1364—Duke Ellington. In a Mellotone. J4.32
>   LPM 1649—Jelly Roll Morton. King of New Orleans Jazz. J3.26
>   LPM 2078—Bunny Berigan. P5.5
>   LPM 2323—Bix Beiderbecke. Legend. J3.88
>   LPM 2398—Dizzy Gillespie. The Greatest. J5.53
>   LSP 2587—Lena Horne. Lovely and Alive. P2.72
>   LSP 2669—Elton Britt, v.1. F8.47
>   LSP 2887—Chet Atkins. Best. F8.90
>   LSP 2890—Jim Reeves. Best, v.1. F8.92
>   LSC 3235—Spike Jones. Is Murdering the Classics. P4.8
>   LSP 3377—Glenn Miller. Best. P5.14
>   LSP 3476—Sons of the Pioneers. Best. F7.17
>   LSP 3478—Hank Snow. Best, v.1. F8.32
>   LSP 3482—Jim Reeves. Best, v.2. F8.92
>   LSP 3766—Jefferson Airplane. Surrealistic Pillow. R6.7
>   LSP 3956—Nilsson. Aerial Ballet. F10.75
>   LSP 3957—Jose Feliciano. P2.40
>   LSP 3988—Gary Burton. A Genuine Tong Funeral. J5.144
>   LSP 4187—Jim Reeves. Best, v.3. F8.92
>   LSP 4223—Charley Pride. Best, v.1. F8.104
>   LSP 4289—Harry Nilsson. Nilsson Sings Newman. F10.77
>   LSP 4321—Porter Wagoner. Best, v.2. F8.83
>   LSP 4374—Nina Simone. Best. B4.69
>   LSP 4459—Jefferson Airplane. Worst. R6.9
>   LSP 4682—Charley Pride. Best, v.1. F8.104
>   LSP 4751—Waylon Jennings. Ladies Love Outlaws. F8.11
>   LSP 4798—Hank Snow. Best, v.2. F8.32
>   LSP 4822—Elton Britt, v.2. F8.47
>   LSP 4854—Waylon Jennings. Lonesome, On'ry, and Mean. F8.115
>   ARL1-0035—Arthur Fiedler and the Boston Pops. Greatest Hits of the 20s.
>   P5.81
>   ARL1-0041/5—Arthur Fiedler and the Boston Pops. Greatest Hits of the
>   30s, 40s, 50s, 60s, and 70s. five discs. P5.81

RCA (cont'd)
    KPM1-0153—Elvis Presley. The Sun Sessions. R1.11
    APL1-0240—Waylon Jennings. Honky Tonk Heroes. F8.116
    CPL1-0374—John Denver. Greatest Hits. F10.56
    APL1-0455—George Hamilton IV. Greatest Hits. F8.61
    APL1-0928—Neil Sedaka. His Greatest Hits. R2.42
    ANL1-1035—Spike Jones. Best. P4.7
    ANL1-1071—Carter Family. 'Mid the Green Fields. F5.110
    ANL1-1083e—The Browns. Best. F8.97
    APL1-1117—Dolly Parton. Best. F8.143
    ANL1-1137—Perry Como. I Believe. F9.28
    ANL1-1140—Vaughan Monroe, Best. P2.59
    ANL1-1213—Porter Wagoner. Best, v.1. F8.83
    CPL1-1756e—Russ Columbo. A Legendary Performer. P2.29
    CPL1-2099—Woody Guthrie. Dust Bowl Ballads. F10.62
    CPL1-5015—Cleo Laine. Live!! At Carnegie Hall. P2.74
    CPL2-0466—Stars of the Grand Ole Opry, 1926-1974. two discs. F8.8
    ADL2-0694—Wilf Carter. Montana Slim's Greatest Hits. two discs. F7.10
    VPS 6014—Hank Snow. This Is My Story. two discs. F8.33
    LSP 6016—Willie "The Lion" Smith. Memoirs. two discs. J6.74
    VPS 6027—Sam Cooke. This Is. . . . two discs. B2.42
    VPS 6032—Eddy Arnold. This Is. . . . two discs. F8.89
    VPM 6040—Benny Goodman. This Is. . . . , v.1. two discs. J4.62
    VPM 6042—Duke Ellington. This Is. . . . two discs. J4.33
    VPM 6043—This Is the Big Band Era. two discs. P5.4
    VPM 6056—Gene Austin. This Is. . . . two discs. P2.1
    VPM 6063—Benny Goodman. This Is. . . . , v.2. J4.62
    VPSX 6079—Chet Atkins. Now and . . . Then. two discs. F8.91
    VPM 6087—Tommy Dorsey. Clambake Seven. two discs. P5.9

RCA Bluebird (series devoted to reissues)
    AXM2-5501—Tampa Red. two discs. B1.242
    AXM2-5503—Bill Boyd. Country Ramblers, 1934-1950. two discs. F7.39
    AXM2-5506—Big Maceo. Chicago Breakdown. two discs. B1.283
    AXM2-5507—Fletcher Henderson. Complete, 1923-1936. two discs. J4.39
    AXM2-5508—Earl Hines. The Father Jumps. two discs. J4.65
    AXM2-5510—Monroe Brothers. Feats Here Tonight. F5.115
    AXM2-5512—Glenn Miller. Complete, v.1. two discs. P5.39 (in progress,
        about 20 discs)
    AXM2-5517—Artie Shaw. Complete, v.1. two discs. P5.45 (in progress, about
        12 discs)
    AXM2-5518—Fats Waller. Piano Solos, 1929-1941. two discs. J6.40a
    AXM2-5521—Tommy Dorsey. Complete, v.1. two discs. P5.8 (in progress,
        about 12 discs)
    AXM2-5525—Blue Sky Boys. two discs. F5.105
    AXM2-5531—The Cats and the Fiddle. I Miss You So. two discs. B2.24
    AXM2-55??—Grand Ole Opry Stars. two discs. F8.14 (forthcoming)
    AXM2-55??—Patsy Montana. two discs. F7.11 (forthcoming)
    AXM6-5536—Lionel Hampton. Complete, 1937-1941. six discs. J4.97

RCA Camden (reissues)

>2460—Pee Wee King. Biggest Hits. F7.44

RCA Vintage (jazz and blues and folk reissues; series recently deleted)

>LPV 501—Coleman Hawkins. Body and Soul. J4.98
>LPV 504—Isham Jones. P5.12
>LPV 507—Smoky Mountain Ballads. F5.7
>LPV 513—John Jacob Niles. Folk Balladeer. F3.79
>LPV 519—The Bebop Era. J5.2
>LPV 521—Benny Goodman. Small Groups. J4.95
>LPV 522—Authentic Cowboys and Their Western Folksongs. F7.1
>LPV 532—The Railroad in Folksong. F3.40
>LPV 533—Johnny Hodges. Things Ain't What They Used to Be. J4.112
>LPV 548—Native American Ballads. F5.5
>LPV 551—Charlie Barnet, v.1. P5.21
>LPV 552—Early Rural String Bands. F5.22
>LPV 554—Fred Waring. P2.143
>LPV 555—Paul Whiteman, v.1. P5.18
>LPV 558—Johnny Dodds. J3.22
>LPV 565—Leo Reisman, v.1. P5.17
>LPV 566—Barney Bigard/Albert Nicholas. J4.132
>LPV 567—Charlie Barnet, v.2. P5.21
>LPV 569—Early Bluegrass. F6.15
>LPV 570—Paul Whiteman, v.2. P5.18
>LPV 581—Bunny Berigan. His Trumpet and Orchestra, v.1. P5.7
>LPV 582—Artie Shaw. J4.86

RCA (England)
>specialty: general

>SD 1000—Frank Sinatra, with Tommy Dorsey. six discs. P2.14
>INTS 1072—Gene Krupa. Swingin' with Krupa. J4.74
>INTS 1343—Rudy Vallee Croons the Songs He Made Famous. P2.22
>DPS 2022—Jimmy Driftwood. Famous Country Music Makers. two discs.
>   F10.9
>LSA 3180—Hoagy Carmichael. Stardust. P2.26
>LPL1-5000—Cleo Laine. I Am a Song. P2.73
>LFL4-7522—Perry Como. The First Thirty Years. four discs. P2.6

RCA (France)
>specialty: jazz and blues reissues

>730.549—Jelly Roll Morton, v.1. J3.25
>730.561—Boogie Woogie Man. J6.82
>730.581—Memphis Slim. B1.349
>730.605—Jelly Roll Morton, v.2. J3.25
>730.703/4—Original Dixieland Jazz Band. two discs. J3.51
>730.708—Erskine Hawkins, v.1. J4.64
>730.710—Barney Kessel. J6.101

RCA (France) (cont'd)

    731.051/2—Louis Armstrong. Town Hall Concert, 1947. two discs. J3.38
    731.059—Jelly Roll Morton, v.3. J3.25
    741.007—Ethel Waters. 1938/1939. P2.85
    741.040—Jelly Roll Morton, v.4. J3.25
    741.044—Benny Goodman. The Fletcher Henderson Arrangements, v.1.
        J4.37
    741.054—Jelly Roll Morton, v.5. J3.25
    741.059—Benny Goodman. The Fletcher Henderson Arrangements, v.2.
        J4.37
    741.061—Don Redman. 1938/1940. J4.50
    741.070—Jelly Roll Morton, v.6. J3.25
    741.073—Benny Carter. 1940/1941. J4.21
    741.080—McKinney's Cotton Pickers. Complete, v.1. J4.48
    741.081—Jelly Roll Morton, v.7. J3.25
    741.087—Jelly Roll Morton, v.8. J3.25
    741.088—McKinney's Cotton Pickers. Complete, v.2. J4.48
    741.089—The Greatest of the Small Bands, v.1. J4.92
    741.103—The Greatest of the Small Bands, v.2. J4.92
    741.106—The Greatest of the Small Bands, v.3. J4.92
    741.107—New Orleans, v.1. J3.3
    741.109—McKinney's Cotton Pickers. Complete, v.3. J4.48
    741.116—Erskine Hawkins, v.2. J4.64
    741.117—The Greatest of the Small Bands, v.4. J4.92
    DUKE 1/4—Duke Ellington. Integrale. J4.31
    FPM1-7003—New Orleans, v.2. J3.3
    FPM1-7059—McKinney's Cotton Pickers. Complete, v.4. J4.48
    FPM1-7014—The Greatest of the Small Bands, v.5. J4.92
    FPM1-7024—Erskine Hawkins, v.3. J4.64
    FPM1-7059—McKinney's Cotton Pickers. Complete, v.5. J4.48
    FXM1-7060—Henry "Red" Allen, v.1. J3.33
    FXM1-7090—Henry "Red" Allen, v.2. J3.33
    FXM1-7124—The Greatest of the Small Bands, v.6. J4.92
    FXM1-7136—Jean Goldkette. 1928-1929. P5.28
    FXM1-7323—Big Joe Williams. B1.259
    FXM3-7143—History of Jazz Piano. three discs. J6.10
    FXM1-7192—Henry "Red" Allen, v.3. J3.33

RCA (Japan)
    specialty: jazz, blues, and country

    RA 5459/66—Jimmie Rodgers. 110 Collection. eight discs. F8.31
    RA 5641/50—Carter Family. The Legendary Collection, 1927-1934, 1941.
        ten discs. F5.109

RSO, 75 Rockefeller Plaza, New York, NY 10019
    specialty: rock music

    RSO 3016—Blind Faith. R8.12

Radiola Records

> 2MR 5051—The First Esquire All-American Jazz Concert, January 18, 1944. two discs. J1.19

Ranwood, 9034 Sunset Blvd., Los Angeles, CA 90069
> specialty: mood music

Rebel, Rt. 2, Asbury, WV 24916
> specialty: bluegrass

> 1497—Country Gentlemen. Gospel Album. F9.29
> 1506—Country Gentlemen. Award Winning. F6.23
> 1511—Seldom Scene. Act One. F6.126
> 1514—Ralph Stanley. Plays Requests. F6.52
> 1520—Seldom Scene. Act Two. F6.126
> 1528—Seldom Scene. Act Three. F6.126
> 1530—Ralph Stanley. A Man and His Music. F6.51
> 1547/8—Seldom Scene. Recorded Live at the Cellar Door. two discs. F6.128

Red Lightnin' (England)
> specialty: blues reissues

> RL 001—Buddy Guy. In the Beginning. B1.337
> RL 006—When Girls Do It. two discs. B1.274
> RL 007—Junior Wells. In My Younger Days. B1.371
> RL 009—Earl Hooker. There's a Fungus Amung Us. B1.281
> RL 0010—Clarence "Gatemouth" Brown. San Antonio Ballbuster. B1.322

Reprise, 3300 Warner Blvd., Burbank, CA 91505
> specialty: general, troubador music

> FS 1016—Frank Sinatra. A Man and His Music. two discs. P2.17
> 6199—Tom Lehrer. An Evening Wasted. P4.10
> 6216—Tom Lehrer. Songs. P4.11
> 6217—The Kinks. Greatest Hits. R4.11
> 6261—Jimi Hendrix. Are You Experienced? R8.4
> 6267—Arlo Guthrie. Alice's Restaurant. F10.60
> 6286—Randy Newman. F10.38
> 6341—Joni Mitchell. Clouds. F10.30
> 6383—Neil Young. After the Gold Rush. R7.19
> 6430—Pentangle. Cruel Sister. F2.53
> 2RS 6307—Jimi Hendrix. Electric Ladyland. two discs. R8.5
> MS 2025—Jimi Hendrix. Greatest Hits. R8.6
> MS 2038—Joni Mitchell. Blue. F10.29
> MS 2064—Randy Newman. Sail Away. F10.39
> MS 2148—Maria Muldaur. R4.35

Rimrock, Concord, AR 72523
> specialty: sacred, bluegrass

> 1002—The Family Gospel Album. F9.2

Rome, 1414 E. Broad St., Columbus, OH 43205
  specialty: bluegrass

  1011—Don Reno and Red Smiley. Together Again. F6.49

Roots (Austria)
  specialty: blues and gospel reissues; old time music reissues

  RL 301—Blind Lemon Jefferson, v.1. B1.112
  RL 306—Blind Lemon Jefferson, v.2. B1.112
  RL 317—Lucille Bogan and Walter Roland. Alabama Blues, 1930-1935.
    B1.386
  RL 322—Memphis Jug Band, v.1. B1.421
  RL 330—Tommy Johnson/Ishman Bracey. Famous 1928 Sessions. B1.113
  RL 331—Blind Lemon Jefferson, v.3. B1.112
  RL 337-Memphis Jug Band, v.2. B1.421
  RL 701—Riley Pickett. Story, 1924-1941. F5.40

Roulette, 17 W. 60th Street, New York, NY 10023
  specialty: general and jazz

  RE 124—Count Basie. Echoes of an Era: Kansas City Suite/Easin' It. two
    discs. J4.166

Roulette (England)
  specialty: general and jazz

  SRCP 3000—Count Basie. The Atomic Mr. Basie. J4.165

Rounder, 186 Willow Avenue, Somerville, MA 02143
  specialty: blues, old time music, bluegrass

  001—George Pegram. F5.96
  0011—Tut Taylor. Friar Tut. F5.44
  0014—Don Stover. Things in Life. F6.109
  0017—Almeda Riddle. Ballads and Hymns from the Ozarks. F3.83
  1001—Blind Alfred Reed. How Can a Poor Man Stand Such Times and Live?
    F5.41
  1002—Aunt Molly Jackson. Library of Congress Recordings. F3.68
  1003—Fiddlin' John Carson. The Old Hen Cackled and the Rooster's Gonna
    Crow. F5.29
  1004—Burnett and Rutherford. A Rambling Reckless Hobo. F5.118
  1005—Gid Tanner. "Hear These New Southern Fiddle and Guitar Music."
    F5.78
  1006—Blue Sky Boys. The Sunny Side of Life. F5.106
  1007—Frank Hutchison. The Train That Carried My Girl from Town. F5.30
  1008—Stoneman Family. 1926-1928. F5.72
  1013/20—Early Days of Bluegrass, v.1-8. eight discs. F6.16
  2003—Martin, Bogan and Armstrong. Barnyard Dance. B1.218
  3006—Boys of the Lough. Second Album. F2.10

Rural Rhythm, Box A, Arcadia, CA 91006
 specialty: bluegrass

Sackville (Canada)
 specialty: jazz

 2004–Willie "The Lion" Smith and Don Ewell. Grand Piano Duets. J6.76

Savoy, 6 West 57th Street, New York, NY 10019
 specialty: jazz; in the process of being reissued by Arista

 MG 12020–Dizzy Gillespie. Groovin' High. J5.54
 MG 12106–J. J. Johnson. Boneology. J5.63
 MG 14006–Clara Ward Singers. Lord Touch Me. B3.64
 MG 14014–Great Golden Gospel Hits, v.1. B3.11
 MG 14019–Sonny Terry and Brownie McGhee. Back Country Blues. B1.248
 MG 14069–Great Golden Gospel Hits, v.2. B3.11
 MG 14076–James Cleveland, v.1. B3.29
 MG 14131–James Cleveland, v.2. B3.29
 MG 14165–Great Golden Gospel Hits, v.3. B3.11
 MG 14252–James Cleveland, v.3. B3.29
 SJL 2201–Charlie Parker. Bird: The Savoy Recordings. two discs. J5.30
  [in progress]
 SJL 2202–Lester Young. Pres. two discs. J4.126
 SJL 2211–Dexter Gordon. Long Tall Dexter. two discs. J5.55
 SJL 2214–Billy Eckstine. Mr. B and the Band. two discs. P2.35
 SJL 2216–Fats Navarro. Savoy Sessions: Fat Girl. two discs. J5.27

Scepter, 254 W. 54th Street, New York, NY 10019
 specialty: pop

Shandar (France)
 specialty: modern jazz

 SR 10000–Albert Ayler, v.1. J5.139
 SR 10004–Albert Ayler, v.2. J5.139

Shelter, 100 Universal City Plaza, Universal City, CA 91608
 specialty: rock

 SW 8901–Leon Russell. R4.41

Sire, 8255 Beverly Blvd., Los Angeles, CA 90048
 specialty: rock

 SAS 3702–The History of British Rock, v.1. two discs. R4.1
 SAS 3705–The History of British Rock, v.2. two discs. R4.1
 SAS 3712–The History of British Rock, v.3. two discs. R4.1
 SASH 3715–Fleetwood Mac. In Chicago. two discs. R5.18

Solid State, 6920 Sunset Blvd., Hollywood, CA 90028
 specialty: jazz
 18048–Thad Jones-Mel Lewis Orchestra. Monday Night. J4.172

Sonet (Sweden)
specialty: jazz and blues

SLP 2547—Barney Kessel and Red Mitchell. Two Way Conversation. J6.107

Sonyatone Records (c/o Southern Record Sales)

STR 201—Eck Robertson. Master Fiddler, 1929-1941. F5.41a

Smithsonian Classic Jazz, P.O. Box 14196, Washington, D.C. 20044
specialty: jazz reissues

Speciality, 8300 Santa Monica Blvd., Hollywood, CA 90069
specialty: rhythm 'n' blues, blues, soul, gospel music

2113—Little Richard. Greatest 17 Original Hits. B2.46
2115—Ain't That Good News. B3.1
2116—Soul Stirrers and Sam Cooke, v.1. B3.53
2126—Percy Mayfield. Best. B2.62
2128—Soul Stirrers and Sam Cooke, v.2. B3.53
2131—Don and Dewey. B2.53
2177/8—This Is How It All Began, v.1-2. two discs. B2.4

Spivey, 65 Grand Ave., Brooklyn, NY 11205
specialty: blues

2001—Victoria Spivey. Recorded Legacy of the Blues. B1.405

Spotlite (England)
specialty: reissues of bop jazz

100—Billy Eckstine. Together. J5.49
101/6—Charlie Parker. On Dial. six discs. J5.29
119—Coleman Hawkins and Lester Young. J4.106
131—Howard McGhee. Trumpet at Tempo. J5.23

Springboard, 947 U.S. Highway 1, Rahway, NJ 07601
specialty: reissues of jazz and rock 'n' roll

Stanyan, 8440 Santa Monica Blvd., Hollywood, CA 90069
specialty: mood

SR 10032—Vera Lynn. When the Lights Go On Again. P2.76

Starday, 220 Boscobel St., Nashville, TN 37213
specialty: country and western, bluegrass and sacred materials

SLP 122—Stanley Brothers. Sacred Songs from the Hills. F9.75
SLP 146—Bill Clifton. Carter Family Memorial Album. F6.71
SLP 150—George Jones. Greatest Hits. F8.28
SLP 161—Lewis Family. Anniversary Celebration. F9.46
SLP 174—Country Gentlemen. Bluegrass at Carnegie Hall. F6.24
SLP 250—Diesel Smoke, Dangerous Curves, and Other Truck Driver
    Favorites. F8.10

Starday (cont'd)
   SLP 303—Preachin', Prayin', Singin'. F9.14
   SLP 398—Moon Mullican. Unforgettable Great Hits. F8.72
   SLP 482—New Grass Revival. F6.121
   SLP 772—Stanley Brothers. Sing the Songs They Like Best. F6.61
   SLP 953—Stanley Brothers. Best. F6.60
   SLP 956—Carl Story. Best. F9.80
   SLP 961—Don Reno and Red Smiley. Best. F6.48

Starline *See* EMI Starline (England)

Stash, Record People, 66 Greene Street, New York, NY 10012
   specialty: jazz and blues reissues [thematic: drugs and alcohol]
   100—Reefer Songs. P4.4

Stax, 2693 Union Ave., Memphis, TN 38112
   specialty: soul

Storyville (Denmark)
   specialty: jazz and blues
   670.184—Boogie Woogie Trio. J6.83
   671.162—Lonnie Johnson. B1.203

Strata East, 156 Fifth Avenue, Suite 612, New York, NY 10010
   specialty: modern jazz

String (England)
   specialty: old time music, western swing
   801—Beer Parlor Jive. F7.33

Sun, 3106 Belmont Blvd., Nashville, TN 37212
   specialty: rock 'n' roll, rhythm 'n' blues, blues, country; see also Phonogram
      and Charly for English reissues
   100/1—Johnny Cash. Original Golden Hits, v.1-2. two discs. R1.13
   102/3—Jerry Lee Lewis. Original Golden Hits, v.1-2. two discs. R1.9
   106—Original Memphis Rock & Roll. R1.4
   128—Jerry Lee Lewis. Original Golden Hits, v.3. R1.9

Sunbeam, 13821 Calvert St., Van Nuys, CA 91401
   specialty: big band reissues, Benny Goodman
   SB 101/3—Benny Goodman. Thesaurus, June 6, 1935. three discs. J4.61

Sussex, 6255 Sunset Blvd., Suite 1902, Hollywood, CA 90028
   specialty: soul

Swaggie (Australia)
   specialty: jazz and blues reissues

Swaggie (cont'd)

    S 1219/20—Sleepy John Estes, v.1-2. two discs. B1.164
    S 1225—Lonnie Johnson. B1.204
    S 1235—Cripple Clarence Lofton/Jimmy Yancey. B1.216, J6.98
    S 1242—Bix Beiderbecke. Bix and Tram, 1927/8, v.1. J3.87
    S 1245—Bob Crosby's Bob Cats. 1937-1942, v.1. J3.56
    S 1251/2—Django Reinhardt. two discs. J6.114/5
    S 1269—Bix Beiderbecke. Bix and Tram, 1927/8, v.2. J3.87
    S 1275—Count Basie. Swinging the Blues, 1937/39. J4.14
    S 1288—Bob Crosby's Bob Cats. 1937-1942, v.2. J3.56

Swing Era (c/o Southern Record Sales)
    specialty: reissues of big band material

    LP 1001—Themes of the Big Bands. P5.3

Takoma, P.O. Box 5369, Santa Monica, CA 90405
    specialty: folk guitar and blues

    B 1001—Bukka White. Mississippi Blues. B1.256
    C 1002—John Fahey, v.1: Blind Joe Death. F4.32
    C 1024—Leo Kottke. 6 and 12 String Guitar. F4.37

Tamla, 6464 Sunset Blvd., Hollywood, CA 90028
    specialty: soul

    S 252—Marvin Gaye. Greatest Hits, v.1. B4.46
    S 278—Marvin Gaye. Greatest Hits, v.2. B4.46
    S 282—Stevie Wonder. Greatest Hits, v.1. B4.62
    T 308—Stevie Wonder. Where I'm Coming From. B4.34
    T 313—Stevie Wonder. Greatest Hits, v.2. B4.62
    T 326—Stevie Wonder. Innervisions. B4.37

Tangerine, 8255 Beverly Blvd., Los Angeles, CA 90048
    specialty: soul

Tax (Sweden)
    specialty: jazz reissues

    m8000—Lester Young. The Alternative Lester. J4.125
    m8005—Cootie Williams. The Boys from Harlem. J4.87
    m8009—The Territory Bands. J3.107
    m8011—Cootie Williams. The Rugcutters, 1937-1940. J4.88

Testament, 577 Lavering Avenue, Los Angeles, CA 90024
    specialty: blues

    T 2207—Chicago Blues: The Beginning. B1.270
    T 2210—Muddy Waters. Down on Stovall's Plantation. B1.301
    T 2211—Otis Spann. Chicago Blues. B1.307
    T 2217—Johnny Shines and Big Walter Horton. B1.361
    T 2219—Fred McDowell. Amazing Grace. B3.46
    T 2221—Johnny Shines. Standing at the Crossroads. B1.235

The Old Masters *See* Old Masters

Tishomingo (c/o Southern Record Sales)
    specialty: western swing

    2220—Rollin' Along. F7.34

Topic (England)
    specialty: folk music

    12 T 118—Bert Lloyd. First Person. F2.21
    12 T 136—The Watersons. Frost and Fire. F2.31

Tradition, 10920 Wilshire Blvd., Los Angeles, CA 90024
    specialty: folk

    2050—The Clancy Brothers and Tommy Makem. Best. F2.40
    2053—Oscar Brand. Best. F4.5

Trip, 947 U.S. Highway 1, Rahway, NJ 07065
    specialty: reissues of Emarcy jazz catalog (Mercury)

    TLP 5501—Sarah Vaughan. 1955. P2.84

Truth (Austria)
    specialty: gospel music

    1002/3—Guitar Evangelists, v.1-2. two discs. B3.12

Twentieth Century, 8255 Sunset Blvd., Los Angeles, CA 90046
    specialty: general

Union Grove (c/o Southern Record Sales)
    specialty: material from the Union Grove Fiddlers' Convention

United Artists, 6920 Sunset Blvd., Hollywood, CA 90028
    specialty: general

    UAS 5596—Country Gazette. A Traitor in Our Midst. F6.117
    UAS 5632—Duke Ellington. Money Jungle. J6.18
    UA 6291—George Jones. Best. F8.23
    UAS 9801—Will the Circle Be Unbroken? three discs. F8.16
    UAS 9952—Miles Davis. two discs. J5.15
    UALA 089-F2—Vicki Carr. The Golden Songbook. two discs. P2.93
    UALA 127-J3—John Lee Hooker. Detroit. three discs. B1.175
    UALA 233G—Fats Domino. two discs. B2.44
    UALA 243-G—Gordon Lightfoot. The Very Best. F10.27

United Artists (England)
    specialty: general

    UAS 29215—Sound of the City: New Orleans. B2.19
    UAS 29898—Slim Whitman, Very Best. 2 discs. F8.94

United Artists (England) (cont'd)
    UAD 60025/6—The Many Sides of Rock 'n' Roll, v.1. two discs. R2.8
    UAD 60035/6—The Many Sides of Rock 'n' Roll, v.2. two discs. R2.8
    UAD 60091/2—Lena Horne. Collection. two discs. P2.71
    UAD 60093/4—The Many Sides of Rock 'n' Roll, v.3. two discs. R2.8

Vanguard, 71 W. 23rd Street, New York, NY 10010
    specialty: folk music and blues

    2053/5—Newport Folk Festival. three discs. F3.15
    2087/8—Newport Folk Festival. two discs. F3.15
    6544—Bert Jansch and John Renbourn. Jack Orion. F2.50
    VSD 79144/9—Newport Folk Festival. six discs. F3.15
    VSD 79180/6—Newport Folk Festival. seven discs. F3.15
    VSD 79216/8—Chicago/The Blues/Today! three discs. B1.266
    VSD 79219/25—Newport Folk Festival. seven discs. F3.15
    VSD 79306/7—Joan Baez. Any Day Now. two discs. F10.1
    VSD 79317—Greenbriar Boys. Best. F6.80
    VSD 5/6—Ian and Sylvia. Greatest Hits, v.1. two discs. F4.35
    VSD 9/10—Doc Watson. On Stage. two discs. F4.18
    VSD 15/16—The Weavers. Greatest Hits. two discs. F4.22
    VSD 23/24—Ian and Sylvia. Greatest Hits, v.2. two discs. F4.35
    VSD 35/36—The Greatest Songs of Woody Guthrie. two discs. F3.37
    VSD 39/40—Max Morath. The Best of Scott Joplin and Other Rag Classics.
        two discs. J2.17
    VSD 41/42—Joan Baez. Ballad Book. two discs. F4.3
    VSD 43/44—Odetta. Essential. two discs. F4.45
    VSD 47/48—From Spirituals to Swing, 1938/39. two discs. J4.2
    VSD 49/50—Joan Baez. Contemporary Ballad Book. two discs. F10.2
    VSD 65/66—Jimmy Rushing. Best. two discs. B1.425
    VSD 79/80—Joan Baez. Lovesong Album. two discs. F4.4
    VSD 99/100—Vic Dickenson. Essential. two discs. J4.137
    VSDB 103/4—Buck Clayton. Essential. two discs. J4.158

Vanguard (England)
    specialty: jazz, blues and folk

    VRS 8502—Mel Powell. Thingamagig. J4.114
    VRS 8528—Mel Powell. Out on a Limb. J4.113

Verve, 810 Seventh Ave., New York, NY 10019
    specialty: jazz

    FTS 3008—Blues Project. Projections. R5.6
    VC 3509—Charlie Parker. J5.69
    V6-8412—Stan Getz. Focus. J5.89b
    V6-8420—Oscar Peterson. Trio Live from Chicago. F6.71
    V6-8526—Bill Evans. Conversations with Myself. J6.54
    V6-8538—Oscar Peterson. Night Train. J6.72
    V6-8808—Billie Holiday. Best. J6.120

Verve (England)
    specialty: jazz, reissues of American Verve

    2304.074—Stan Getz. Greatest Hits. P3.9
    2304.169—Coleman Hawkins and Ben Webster. Blue Saxophones. J4.105,
        J4.119
    2317.031—Woody Herman. At Carnegie Hall, March 25, 1946. J4.42
    2610.020—Jazz at the Philharmonic, 1944-1946. two discs. J1.12
    2682.005—Johnny Hodges. Back to Back/Side by Side. two discs. J4.107
    2683.023—Ben Webster and Oscar Peterson. Soulville. two discs. J4.120
    2683.025—Teddy Wilson and Lester Young. Prez and Teddy. two discs.
        J4.123, J4.128
    2683.049—Ben Webster. Ballads. two discs. P3.21

Vetco, 5828 Vine Street, Cincinnati, OH 45216
    specialty: old time music reissues

    101—Uncle Dave Macon. The Dixie Dewdrop, v.1. F5.33
    105—Uncle Dave Macon. The Dixie Dewdrop, v.2. F5.33

Vocalion, 100 Universal City Plaza, Universal City, CA 91608
    specialty: reissues of MC material

    VL 3715—Sons of the Pioneers. Tumbleweed Trails. F7.18
    VL 73866—Jo Stafford. Sweet Singer of Songs. P2.80

Virgin, 75 Rockefeller Plaza, New York, NY 10019
    specialty: rock

Viva, 6922 Hollywood Blvd., Hollywood, CA 90028
    specialty: reissues of nostalgia materials

Vogue (France)
    specialty: reissues of jazz and blues

    SB 1—Sidney Bechet. Concert à l'Exposition Universelle de Bruxelles, 1958.
        J3.19
    LAE 12050—Gerry Mulligan. J5.95

Volt, 2693 Union Ave., Memphis, TN 38112
    specialty: soul

Voyager, 424 35th Avenue, Seattle, WA 98122
    specialty: old time music

    VRLP 303—Gid Tanner. A Corn Licker Still in Georgia. F5.77

Wand (recently deleted)
    specialty: rhythm 'n' blues

    653—Isley Brothers. Twist and Shout. B2.34

Warner Brothers, 3300 Warner Blvd., Burbank, CA 91505
    specialty: general

    2WS 1555—Peter, Paul and Mary. In Concert. two discs. F4.13
    WS 1749—Grateful Dead. Anthem of the Sun. R6.5
    WS 1765—Petula Clark. Greatest Hits. P2.95
    WS 1835—Van Morrison. Moondance. F10.33
    WS 1843—James Taylor. Sweet Baby James. F10.47
    WS 1869—Grateful Dead. Workingman's Dead. R6.6
    BS 2607—Deep Purple. Machine Head. R8.17
    BS 2643—Bonnie Raitt. Give It Up. R4.39
    2LS 2644—Deep Purple. Purple Passages. two discs. R8.15
    BS 2683—Eric Weissberg. Dueling Banjos. F6.63
    3XX 2736—Fifty Years of Film Music. three discs. P6.79
    2SP 9104—Phil Spector's Greatest Hits. two discs. R2.11a

World Jazz, 221 West 57th Street, New York, NY 10019
    specialty: jazz

World Pacific Jazz (recently deleted)
    specialty: jazz

    1211—Cy Touff and Richie Kamuca. Having a Ball. J4.115

World Records (England)
    specialty: nostalgia, jazz, British dance bands; formerly World Record Club

    F 526—The Anatomy of Improvisation. J5.1
    SH 118/9—Golden Age of British Dance Bands. two discs. P5.93
    SH 146—Al Bowlly. P2.4
    SH 220—Original Dixieland Jazz Band. London Recordings, 1919-1920.
        J3.52
    SHB 21—Ambrose. two discs. P5.94

Xanadu, 3242 Irwin Ave., Knightsbridge, NY 10463
    specialty: reissues of jazz

Yazoo, 245 Waverly Place, New York, NY 10014
    specialty: blues

    L 1001—Mississippi Blues, 1927-1941. B1.84
    L 1002—Ten Years in Memphis, 1927-1937. B1.76
    L 1003—St. Louis Town, 1927-1932. B1.94
    L 1005—Blind Willie McTell. The Early Years, 1927-1933. B1.126
    L 1011—Big Bill Broonzy. Young. B1.155
    L 1013—East Coast Blues, 1926-1935. B1.65
    L 1016—Guitar Wizards, 1926-1935. B1.41
    L 1017—Bessie Jackson and Walter Roland. 1927-1935. B1.387
    L 1020—Charley Patton. Founder of the Delta Blues. two discs. B1.129
    L 1022—Ten Years of Black Country Religion, 1926-1936. B3.23
    L 1023—Rev. Gary Davis. 1935-1949. B3.31

Yazoo (cont'd)
    L 1024—Mister Charlie's Blues. F5.14
    L 1025—Cripple Clarence Lofton/Walter Davis. B1.215
    L 1033—Roosevelt Sykes. The Country Blues Piano Ace. B1.238
    L 1036—Leroy Carr. Naptown Blues, 1929-1934. B1.108
    L 1037—Blind Willie McTell. 1927-1935. B1.124
    L 1041—Georgia Tom Dorsey. Come on Mama, Do That Dance. B1.162
    L 1050—Furry Lewis. In His Prime, 1927-1929. B1.211

DIRECTORY OF SPECIALIST RECORD STORES

The record stores listed here handle orders for hard-to-find and rare items (primarily covering blues, country, ethnic, folk, and jazz). In fact, where many labels are concerned, record stores will be the only means of distribution. The following stores are highly recommended because of the superior service they give in obtaining issues from small, independent labels. Request a current catalog. (Note: These stores *may* offer library discounts, but since they are *not* library suppliers per se, this should be clarified at the outset of any transaction.)

UNITED STATES

County Sales
Box 191
Floyd, VA 24091

Rare Record Distributing Co.
417 East Broadway
P.O. Box 10518
Glendale, CA 91205

Roundhouse Record Sales
P.O. Box 474
Somerville, MA 02144

Southern Record Sales
5101 Tasman Drive
Huntington Beach, CA 92649

CANADA

Coda Jazz and Blues Record Centre
893 Yonge Street
Toronto M4W 2H2

GREAT BRITAIN (INCLUDING EUROPE)

Dave Carey—The Swing Shop
18 Mitcham Lane
Streatham, London SW16

Collet's Record Centre
180 Shaftesbury Ave.
London WC2H 8JS

Dobell's Record Shop
75 Charing Cross Road
London WC 2

Flyright Records
18 Endwell Rd.
Bexhill-on-Sea
East Sussex

Peter Russell Record Store
24 Market Avenue
Plymouth PL1 1PJ

Every performing artist in this book is listed alphabetically, and immediately following the name is a series of alphanumeric codes referring the reader to the appropriate annotation in the main text. Included are references to those annotations in which the artist is noted as having been influential or influenced but does not necessarily appear on the relevant phonodisc. Also, in the case of annotations covering several offerings by one performer or group, the alphanumeric code here listed refers only to the *first* code of a series in which that first code is obviously the first entry of a combined review. The code numbers in boldface type refer to an artist or group's major main entry phonodiscs (those items starred in text).

Ace, Johnny, **B2-48**
Alexander, Dave, B1.356
Alexander, Texas, B1.16, B1.53, B1.195, B1.99, B1.201, B1.332
Allison, Luther, B1.266, **B1.320**
Allman, Duane, B1.312
Ammons, Albert, B2.2
Arnold, Billy Boy, B1.266
Arnold, Kokomo, B1.18, B1.22, B1.65, B1.90, B1.110, **B1.140-42**, B1.253
Armstrong, Louis, **B1.381**
Ayler, Albert, B2.45

Bailey, Buster, B2.22a, B3.7
Bailey, Pearl, B2.3
Baker, LaVern, B2.13, **B2.71**
Baker, Mickey, B2.72
See also Mickey and Sylvia
Ballard, Hank, B2.12, **B2.36**
Barbecue, Bob, B1.53, B1.62
Bartholomew, Dave, B2.14
Basie, Count, B1.426, B2.3
Beale Street Jug Band, B1.42, B1.416
Bechet, Sidney, B1.33
Beck, Jeff, B1.312
Belvin, Jesse, B2.5
Benton, Brook, B4.38
Berry, Chuck, **B2.37**
Big Maceo, B1.56, B1.242, **B1.283**, B1.305
Big Maybelle, B1.16, B2.3, **B2.72**
Birmingham Jug Band, B1.59, B1.416
Black Ace, B1.8, B1.95, B1.143
Black Bob, B1.242
Blackwell, Scrapper, B1.49, B1.107-109, **B1.144**, B1.312
Blake, Blind, B1.33, B1.49, B1.65, **B1.145**, B1.193, B1.230, B1.263
Bland, Bobby, B1.77, B2.8, **B2.49-50**, B2.59
Bloomfield, Mike, B1.312
Bluejays, B2.10

Bobettes, B4.6
Bogan, Lucille, B1.33, B1.242, **B1.386-87**
See also Jackson, Bessie
Boines, Houston, B1.81
Bonner, Juke Boy, B1.102, **B1.146-47**
Booker T. and the MGs, B4.6, **B4.8**, B4.28
Bostic, Earl, **B2.51**
Boyd, Eddie, B2.6, B1.283
Bracey, Ishman, B1.81, **B1.113**
Bradford, Alex, B2.4, B3.19, B3.24, **B3.28**
Brenston, Jackie, B2.6
Brian, Grace, B1.56, B1.278
Brian, John, B1.16, B1.269, B1.275
Broonzy, Big Bill, B1.11, B1.15, **B1.148-55**, B1.171, B1.251, B1.275, B1.363, B2.74
Brown, Charles, **B1.321**
Brown, Clarence "Gatemouth", **B1.322**
Brown, "Hi" Henry, B1.90
Brown, James, B2.12, B2.46, **B4.25-26**, B4.39
Brown, Lloyd, B2.14
Brown, Olive, **B1.398**
Brown, Pete, B2.1
Brown, Roy, B1.33, B219, B2.38, B2.59, B4.4
Brown, Ruth, B2.15, **B2.73**
Bumble Bee Slim, B1.16, B1.33
Burke, Solomon, **B4.41**
Burnby, Spear, B5.1
Butler, Jerry, B2.9, **B4.42-43**
Butterbeans and Susie, B1.33, B1.37, B1.374, B2.3

Cadillacs, **B2.23**
Calicott, Joe, B1.81
Calloway, Cab, B2.3
Cannon's Jug Stompers, B1.11, B1.69, B1.412, **B1.419**
Capris, B2.16
Cardinals, B2.13

Carr, Leroy, B1.49, **B1.107-109**, B1.110,
B1.144, B1.253, B1.312
Carter, Bo, B1.37, B1.49, B1.81, **B1.156-
57**
Cats and the Fiddle, **B2.24**
Channels, B2.16
Chantels, **B2.25**
Charles, Bobby, B2.6
Charles, Ray, B1.283, B2.13, **B2.39-41**,
B4.3, B4.26
Chatmon, Lonnie, B1.220
Chatmon, Mississippi Sam, B1.218
Chenier, Clifton, B1.21, **B1.323-24**
Chiffons, B4.7
Chi-Lites, **B4.21**
Chimes, B2.7
Chords, B2.13, B4.6
Clapton, Eric, B1.110, B1.291, B1.312
Clarke, Dee, B2.9
Clearwater, Eddie, B1.269
Cleveland, James, B3.11, **B3.29**, B3.39
Cliff, Jimmy, B5.1, B5.4, B5.5,
B5.6a
Clovers, B2.13, **B2.26**
Coasters, B2.13, **B2.27**, B4.3
Coates, Dorothy Love, B3.10, **B3.30**
Coleman, Lonnie, B1.4, B1.62
Coleman, Ornette, B2.45
Collins, Cryin' Sam, B1.81
Coltrane, John, B2.45
Cooder, Ry, B1.45, B1.23a
Cooke, Sam, **B2.42-43**, **B3.53**, B4.56
Coronets, B2.10
Cotton, Elizabeth, B1.5, **B1.399-400**
Cotton, James, B1.15, B1.77, B1.266,
B1.325
Cox, Ida, B1.15, B1.374, **B1.401**,
B2.3
Crayton, Pee Wee, B1.102, B4.4
Crescendos, B4.2
Crows, B2.28
Crudup, Arthur, B1.22, B1.275, **B1.158-
59**
Curtis, King, B2.51, **B4.44**

Dallas String Band, B1.95
Daniels, Billy, B2.56
Darin, Bobby, B2.13
Davenport, Cow Cow, B1.8, B1.43
Davis, Blind John, B1.152, B1.171,
B1.363
Davis, Rev. Gary, B1.5, B1.10, B1.15,
B3.31-32
Davis, Jesse, B1.239
Davis, Walter, B1.8, B1.43, B1.49, B1.90,
B1.136, **B1.160-61**
Day, Will, B1.95
Dekker, Desmond, B5.1, B5.4, B5.5
Delegates, B2.20

Dells, B2.9, B2.16, B2.20
Delphonics, **B4.20**
Dickson, Tom, B1.69
Diddley, Bo, **B2.52**
Dixie Hummingbirds, B3.9, **B3.33-35**
Dixon, Willie, B1.316
Dr. John, B2.14, B2.52, B2.67
Dodds, Baby, B1.1
Dodds, Johnny, B1.145, B1.413
Doggett, Bill, B2.12, B2.22a
Domino, Fats, B2.19, B2.21, **B2.44**
Don and Dewey, B2.4, **B2.53**
Dorsey, Georgia Tom, **B1.162**
  See also Dorsey, Thomas A.
Dorsey, Lee, **B2.54**
Dorsey, Thomas A., **B3.19**
  See also Dorsey, Georgia Tom
Douglas, K. C., B1.102
Dranes, Arizona, B3.3, B3.9, B3.17
Drifters, B2.13, **B2.30-31**, B4.3
Dupree, Champion Jack, B1.33, B1.43, B1.163,
B1.326-30, B2.2

Eaglin, Snooks, B1.21, **B1.35, B1.163**
Ebony Four, B3.7
Eckstine, Billy, B2.56
El Dorados, B2.11, B2.32
Estes, Sleepy John, B1.5, B1.11, B1.15, B1.22,
B1.69, B1.80, **B1.164-66**, B1.239
Everett, Betty, B2.9

Fitzgerald, Ella, B2.3
Five Blind Boys of Alabama, B3.24
Five Blind Boys of Mississippi, **B3.36-38**
Five Royales, B2.12
Flack, Roberta, **B4.63-64, B4.71**
Flamingos, B2.10, B2.16, **B2.33-33a**
Floyd, Eddie, **B4.45**
Foster, Leroy, B1.275
Four Tops, **B4.13**
Franklin, Aretha, **B3.39**, B4.3, **B4.65-67**
Fuller, Jesse, B1.15, **B1.169**
Fuller, Blind Boy, B1.8, B1.14, B1.22, B1.65,
B1.167-68a, B1.245, B3.17
Fuller, Johnny, B1.102, B1.331
Fulson, Lowell, B1.21, **B1.332-35**

Gant, Cecil, B2.55
Gates, Rev. J. M., B1.20, B3.4, B3.9, B3.14
Gaye, Marvin, B4.1, **B4.46-47**
George, Barbara, B2.19
Gibson, Clifford, B1.49, B1.59, **B1.170**
Gillespie, Dizzy, B2.22a
Gillum, Jazz, **B1.177**
Golden Gate Jubilee Quartet, B3.9
Graves, Roosevelt, B3.3, B3.17, B3.27
Green, Al, **B4.48-49**

Green, Lee, B1.90
Green, Lil, B1.163, **B2.74**
Griffen, Bessie, B3.24
Grimes, Tiny, B2.1
Guitar Slim, B1.172
Gunter, Arthur, B4.2
Guy, Buddy, B1.15, B1.266, B1.291,
  B1.316, B1.320, **B1.336-37**, B1.349,
  B1.370

Harmonica, Frank, B1.77
Harpo, Slim, B1.21
Harptones, **B2.28**
Harris, Wynonie, B1.33, **B1.423-24**,
  B2.21, B2.22a, B2.38
Harrison, Wilbert, B2.18
Hathaway, Donny, **B4.50, B4.71**
Hawkins, Buddy Boy, B1.95
Hawkins, Dale, B2.6
Hawkins, Edwin, B3.40
Hawkins, Roy, B1.102
Hayes, Isaac, **B4.51-52**
Heartbeats, **B2.29**
Hegamin, Lucille, B1.374, B1.384
Henderson, Rosa, B1.374
Hendrix, Jimi, B1.312
Henry, Clarence "Frogman," B2.6
Henton, Laura, B3.3
Hibbler, Al, **B2.56**
Hill, Bertha, B1.374, B1.381, B1.382
Hines, Earl, B1.145
Hogan, Silas, B4.2
Hogg, Smokey, B1.53, B1.95, B1.99,
  B1.173, B1.173a
Hokum Boys, B1.37
  See also Tampa Red, Georgia Tom
  Dorsey
Holiday, Billie, B2.3
Holts, Roosevelt, B1.113
Homesick James, B1.15, B1.266
Hooker, Earl, **B1.279-82**, B1.370
Hooker, John Lee, B1.5, B1.15, B1.31,
  B1.56, **B1.174-79**
Hopkins, Claude, B2.3
Hopkins, Lightnin', B1.5, B1.21, B1.31,
  B1.99, B1.111, B1.146, **B1.180-87**,
  B3.17
Horton, Walter, B1.77, B1.244, B1.266,
  B1.361
House, Son, B1.5, B1.81, B1.110,
  B1.129, **B1.188-89**
Howard, Rosetta, B1.18
Howell, Peg Leg, B1.11, B1.62
Howlin' Wolf, B1.77, B1.276, **B1.284-85**
Hunter, Alberta, B1.374, B1.384
Hunter, Ivory Joe, B2.13, B2.15, B4.4
Hurt, Mississippi John, B1.5, B1.10,
  B1.15-16, B1.22, B1.81, **B1.190-92**
Hulto, J. B., B1.266, B1.269

Impressions, **B4.9-4.11**
Ink Spots, B2.22
Isley Brothers, **B2.34**

Jackson, Bessie, B1.33
  See also Bogan, Lucille
Jackson, Chuck, B4.7
Jackson, Jim, B1.69
Jackson, John, **B1.193-94**, B1.213
Jackson, Li'l Son, B1.99
Jackson, Mahalia, **B3.42**
Jackson, Papa Charlie, B1.37, **B1.195-96**
Jackson Five, **B4.14**
James, Elmore, B1.14, B1.43, B1.77, B1.110,
  B1.275, **B1.286-90**, B1.368
James, Etta, B2.5, B4.72
James, Skip, B1.5, B1.11, B1.15, B1.22, B1.81,
  B1.197-99, B3.25
Jefferson, Blind Lemon, B1.11, B1.20, B1.33,
  B1.95, B1.99, **B1.111-12**, B1.209, B1.230,
  B1.312, B3.23, B3.25
Jelly Belly, **B1.172**
Jenkins, Bobo, B1.56
John, Little Willie, B2.12, **B2.61**
Johnson, Bessie, **B3.43**
Johnson, Blind Willie, B1.95, B3.3, B3.4,
  B3.9, B3.17, **B3.45**
Johnson, Herman E., B1.200
Johnson, Lil, B1.33
Johnson, Lonnie, B1.8, B1.11, B1.18, B1.53,
  B1.90, B1.152, B1.170, **B1.201-208**, B1.253,
  B1.312, B2.12
Johnson, Margaret, B1.374
Johnson, Pete, B1.15, B1.427, B2.2
Johnson, Robert, B1.4, B1.11, B1.22, B1.33,
  B1.81, **B1.110**, B1.234, B1.239, B1.286,
  B1.300, B1.359
Johnson, Tommy, B1.11, **B1.113**, B1.284
Jones, Curtis, B1.43, **B1.338-39**
Jones, Floyd, B1.266, B1.269, B1.275,
  B1.278, B1.367
Jones, Jonah, B1.18
Jordan, Charlies, B1.90, B1.253
Jordan, Louis, B1.423, B2.15, **B2.45**

K-Doe, Ernie, **B2.57**
Kessel, Barney, B1.312
King, Albert, B1.358
King, B. B., B1.279, **B1.291-96**, B1.312,
  B1.320, B1.336, B1.340, B1.345, B1.358,
  B2.59
King, Ben E., B4.3
King, Freddy, **B1.340**
Kirkland, Eddie, B1.56
Knight, Gladys, B2.9, B2.18, **B4.68**

Labelle, **B4.15**
Lang, Eddie, B1.95, **B1.207**
Lazy Lester, B1.342, B4.2
Leadbelly, B1.111, **B1.115-17**, **B1.209-210**, B1.213
Leake, Lafayette, B1.336
Lee, Peggy, B2.61
Lenoir, J. B., B1.16, B1.31, **B1.341**
Lewis, Barbara, B4.3
Lewis, Furry, B1.10, B1.22, B1.69, B1.80-81, **B1.211-12**
Lewis, Meade Lux, B1.43, B2.2
Lewis, Ramsey, **B4.53**
Lewis, Smiley, B2.14, B2.21, **B2.58**
Liggins, Joe, B2.4, B2.15
Lightnin' Slim, **B1.342**, B4.2
Lincoln, Charlie, B1.62
Lipscomb, Marie, B1.5, B1.99, B1.193, **B1.213-14**
Little Anthony and the Imperials, **B2.35**
Little Milton, **B2.59-60**
Little Richard, **B2.46-47**
Little Walter, B1.269, **B1.297-99**, B1.300, B1.370
Lockwood, Robert Junior, B1.81
Lofton, Cripple Clarence, B1.43, B1.49, B1.160, **B1.215-16**
Lonesome Sundown, **B1.343**, B4.2
Louis, Joe Hill, B1.77, B1.275, **B1.344**
Louisiana Red, **B1.345**
Love, Willie, B1.77

Mabon, Willie, B2.6
McAuliffe, Leon, B1.356
McClennan, Tommy, B1.81, **B1.217**
McCoy, Kansas Joe, B1.388
McCracklin, Jimmy, **B1.321**, B2.6
McDowell, Fred, B1.5, B1.80-81, **B1.118-23**, B3.25, **B3.46**
McGhee, Brownie, B1.5, B1.15, B1.65, B1.167, **B1.247-48**
McGhee, Sticks, B4.6
McGriff, Jimmy, B1.355
Mack, Lonnie, **B4.54**
Macon, Uncle Dave, B3.4
McPhatter, Clyde, B2.13, B2.15
McTell, Blind Willie, B1.8, B1.11, B1.16, B1.22, B1.62, B1.111, **B1.124-28**, B1.239, B3.3
Magic Sam, B1.266, B1.340, **B1.346-48**
Magnificents, B2.20
Main Ingredient, **B4.22**
Mar-Kays, B4.3
Marley, Bob, B4.56
Martin, Bogan, and Armstrong, **B1.218**
Martin, Carl, B1.65
Marvelettes, **B4.16**
Marvin and Johnny, B2.5

Mayall, John, B1.110
Mayfield, Curtis, **B4.9-4.11**, **B4.55**
Mayfield, Percy, B2.4, **B2.62**
Maytals, B5.1, B5.4, **B5.7**
Memphis Jug Band, B1.11, B1.412, **B1.420-21**
Memphis Minnie, B1.18, B1.33, B1.37, B1.69, **B1.128**, B1.129a, B1.275, B1.278, **B1.388-91**
Memphis Slim, B1.32, B1.43, B1.152, **B1.349-50**
Mercy Dee, B1.99, **B1.369**
Meters, **B4.17**
Mickey and Sylvia, **B2.63**
Mighty Clouds of Joy, **B3.48**
Milburn, Amos, B1.163, B2.21
Miles, Lizzie, B1.374
Miller, Punch, B1.152
Millindor, Lucky, **B2.22a**
Mills Brothers, B2.3
Milton, Roy, B2.4, B4.4
Miracles, **B4.29**
Mississippi Sheiks, B1.20, B1.81, B1.156, **B1.219-20**
Montgomery, Little Brother, B1.31, B1.43, **B1.221-27**
Moonglows, B2.6, B2.10, **B2.33**
Moore, Alex, B1.16, B1.20, B1.95, B1.99, **B1.228-29**
Moore, Monette, B1.374
Morton, Jelly Roll, B1.33
Moss, Buddy, B1.62, B1.65, **B1.230**
Muddy Waters, B1.110, B1.269, B1.275, B1.297, **B1.300-304**, B1.305, B1.316

Nash, Johnny, **B4.56**
Nighthawk, Robert, B1.275, B1.278, B3.21
Nixon, Hammie, B1.164
Nutmegs, B2.11

Odetta, **B1.402**
Old Southern Jug Band, B1.42
One String Sam, B1.56
Orchids, B2.20
Orioles, B2.13
Otis, Johnny, **B1.351**, **B2.64**, **B4.4**
Otis, Shuggie, B1.351

Page, Hot Lips, B1.163
Page, Jimmy, B1.312
Parham, Tiny, B1.413
Parker, Junior, B1.77, **B1.352-55**
Patton, Charley, B1.81, **B1.129**, B1.284, B3.23
Pelicans, B2.17
Persuaders, **B4.23**
Phillips, Esther, B4.4, **B4.73-74**
Phillips, Washington, B3.17

Phipps, Ernest, B3.4
Piano Red, B1.80
Pickett, Wilson, B4.3, **B4.27**
Pilgrim Travellers, B3.1, B3.10, B3.24, **B3.51**
Pioneers, B5.4, B5.5
Platters, B2.12
Presley, Elvis, B1.158, B2.38, B2.46
Price, Lloyd, B2.4, **B2.65-66**
Price, Sammy, B1.18, B3.7
Professor Longhair, B2.14, **B2.67**
Pryor, Snooky, B1.269, **B2.68**

Rachell, Yank, B1.69, B1.136, B1.373
Rainey, Ma, B1.312, B1.374, **B1.392**
Raitt, Bonnie, B1.118
Ramblin' Thomas, B1.95, **B1.250**
Ravens, B2.13
Ray, Johnny, B2.71
Redding, Otis, B2.12, B4.3, **B4.28**
Reed, Jimmy, B1.146, **B1.231-32**
Reeves, Martha, B4.1, **B4.75**
Robins, B2.2a, B2.17
Robinson, Bill "Bojangles," B2.3
Robinson, L. C., B1.102, **B1.356**
Robinson, Smokey, **B4.29**
Rogers, Jimmy, B1.193, B1.269, B1.300, B1.316
Roland, Walter, B1.43, **B1.386-87**
Rolling Stones, B1.110, B1.118
Rollins, Sonny, B2.45
Rosie and the Originals, B2.11
Ross, Diana, **B4.12**
Ross, Dr., B1.56, B1.275
Ruffin, Jimmy, B4.5
Rush, Otis, B1.15, B1.266, B1.336, B1.340, **B1.357-58**
Rushing, Jimmy, B1.15, B1.291, **B1.425-26**

Sahm, Doug, B1.312
Sam and Dave, B4.3, **B4.30**
Seeger, Pete, B1.148
Shade, Will, B1.69, B1.420
Shaw, Robert, B1.99, B1.233
Shep and the Limelites, **B2.28-29**
Shines, Johnny, B1.14, B1.16, B1.110, **B1.234-35**, B1.266, B1.269, **B1.359-61**
Short, J. D., B1.90
Simone, Nina, **B4.69-70**
Sims, Frankie Lee, B2.4, **B2.69**
Skatalites, B5.3
Sledge, Percy, B4.3, **B4.57**
Slickers, B5.1
Slim Harpo, **B1.362**, B4.2
Sly and the Family Stone, **B4.31-31a**
Smith, Bessie, B1.374, B1.392, **B1.393-97**, B2.3

Smith, Clara, B1.33, B1.381, **B1.404**
Smith, "Funny Paper," B1.95, **B1.236**
Smith, Huey "Piano," B2.14
Smith, Mamie, B1.374, B2.3
Smith, Pinetop, B1.53
Smith, Thunder, B1.99
Smith, Trixie, B1.18
Soul Stirrers, B2.4, B2.42, B3.1, B3.8, B3.10, B3.24, **B3.52-53**
Spand, Charlie, B1.49, B1.107
Spaniels, B2.11, B2.16, B2.20
Spann, Otis, B1.15-16, B1.31, B1.43, B1.53, B1.110, B1.201, B1.266, B1.275, B1.300, **B1.305-311**, B1.316, B1.336, B1.359, B1.370, B1.373
Speckled Red, B1.43
Spinners, B4.6
Spires, Big Boy, B1.275
Spivey, Sweet Peas, B1.374
Spivey, Victoria, **B1.208**, B1.374, B1.381, B1.384, **B1.405-406**
Stackhouse, Houston, B1.81, B1.113
Staple Singers, B3.9, B3.11, **B3.54-57**
Stars of Faith, **B3.58**
Stokes, Frank, B1.69, B1.129a
Stovall, Babe, B1.113, B3.21
Strong, Barrett, B4.5
Stylistics, **B4.19**
Sumlin, Hubert, B1.284
Sunnyland Slim, B1.43, B1.77, B1.269, B1.275, **B1.363-65**, B1.388
Supremes, **B4.12**
Swan Silvertones, B2.4, B3.1, B3.24, **B3.59-60**
Sykes, Roosevelt, B1.21, B1.31, B1.43, B1.49, B1.77, B1.160, **B1.237-38**, B1.349

Taggart, Blind Joe, B3.17, **B3.61**
Taj Mahal, **B1.239-41**
Tampa Red, B1.33, **B1.242-44**, B1.283, B1.382
Tate, Buddy, B1.425
Taylor, Eddie, B1.266, B1.278-79, **B1.366-68**
Taylor, Eva, B1.381
Taylor, Johnnie, **B4.58**
Taylor, KoKo, **B1.407**
Taylor, Montana, B1.43
Taylor, Sam "The Man," B2.72
Teen Queens, B2.5
Temptations, B4.1, **B4.18**
Terrell, Tammi, B4.1
Terry, Sonny, B1.5, B1.15, B1.23, B1.51, B1.167, **B1.245-47**
Tex, Joe, **B4.60**
Tharpe, Sister Rosetta, B1.163, B2.22a, B3.7, B3.10, B3.11, **B3.62-63**
Thomas, Carla, B4.3, **B4.76**
Thomas, Henry, B1.95, **B1.249**
Thomas, Nicky, B5.4
Thomas, Rufus, B2.6, B4.3, **B4.59**

Thornton, Big Mama, **B1.408-409**, B2.8
Thunder 'n' Lightnin', B1.99
Toots and the Maytals, B5.1, **B5.8**
Toussaint, Allen, B2.57, B2.14, B4.15
Townsend, Henry, B1.90
Tribe, Tony, B5.5
Turner, Ike and Tina, B2.18, **B4.77-78**
Turner, Joe, B1.15, B1.18, B1.291,
  B1.427-32, B2.2, B2.13, B2.59, B4.4

Vinson, Eddie, B2.15, B4.4
Vinson, Walter, B1.81, B1.219-20

Wailers, B5.1, B5.3, **B5.8**
Walker, Junior, **B4.61**
Walker, T-Bone, B1.291, **B1.312-15**,
  B1.340, B2.59
Wallace, Sippi, B1.374, B1.381, **B1.410**
War, **B4.23a**
Ward, Clara, B3.11, **B3.64**
Warwick, Dionne, B4.7
Washboard Sam, B1.152, B1.171,
  B1.251-52
Washington, Dinah, B4.79
Waters, Ethel, **B1.411**
Watson, Johnny "Guitar," B1.102
Weaver, Curley, B1.65
Weaver, Sylvester, B1.65
Webster, Ben, B2.1
Weldon, Casey Bill, B1.69
Wells, Junior, B1.15, B1.266, B1.269,
  B1.279, B1.336, B1.349, **B1.370-72**

Wells, Mary, **B4.80**
Wells, Viola, B2.1
Wheatstraw, Peetie, B1.4, B1.16, B1.18, B1.90,
  B1.253-54
White, Bukka, B1.10, B1.22, B1.80-81, B1.129,
  B1.255-57
White, Josh, B1.65, B2.15
Wilkins, Robert, B1.5, B1.69, B1.81, **B1.129a**,
  B3.65
Williams, Big Joe, B1.10, B1.14, B1.53, B1.81,
  B1.138, B1.258-62
Williams, Bill, **B1.263-64**
Williams, Delroy, B5.4
Williams, Marion, B3.9, B3.19, B3.66
Williams, Otis, B2.12
Williams, Robert Pete, B1.5, B1.15, **B1.130-35**
Williamson, Sonny Boy, No. 1, B1.32, B1.51,
  B1.136-39, B1.258
Williamson, Sonny Boy, No. 2, B1.239, B1.275,
  B1.286, **B1.316-19**, B1.370
Willis, Chuck, B2.13, B2.70
Wilson, Edith, B1.374
Wilson, Jackie, **B4.32**
Wilson, Jimmy, B1.102
Winter, Johnny, B1.312
Withers, Bill, **B4.33**
Witherspoon, Jimmy, **B1.433-34**
Wonder, Stevie, B4.1, **B4.34-37**, **B4.62**
Woods, Oscar, B1.8, B1.95

Yancey, Jimmy, B2.2
Young Jessie, B2.5
Young, Johnny, B1.266, B1.269, **B1.373**